ISBN 978-1-330-62593-4
PIBN 10084185

1 MONTH OF
FREE
READING

at

www.ForgottenBooks.com

By purchasing this book you are
eligible for one month membership to
ForgottenBooks.com, giving you
unlimited access to our entire
collection of over 1,000,000 titles via
our web site and mobile apps.

To claim your free month visit:

www.forgottenbooks.com/free84185

English
Français
Deutsche
Italiano
Español
Português

www.forgottenbooks.com

Mythology Photography **Fiction**
Fishing Christianity **Art** Cooking
Essays Buddhism Freemasonry
Medicine **Biology** Music **Ancient
Egypt** Evolution Carpentry Physics
Dance Geology **Mathematics** Fitness
Shakespeare **Folklore** Yoga Marketing
Confidence Immortality Biographies
Poetry **Psychology** Witchcraft
Electronics Chemistry History **Law**
Accounting **Philosophy** Anthropology
Alchemy Drama Quantum Mechanics
Atheism Sexual Health **Ancient History**
Entrepreneurship Languages Sport
Paleontology Needlework Islam
Metaphysics Investment Archaeology
Parenting Statistics Criminology
Motivational

MEN OF LETTERS AND SCIENCE

OF THE

TIME OF GEORGE III.

L I V E S

OF

[EN OF LETTERS AND SCIENCE,

WHO FLOURISHED IN

THE TIME OF GEORGE III.

BY

HENRY, LORD BROUGHAM, F.R.S.,

MEMBER OF THE NATIONAL INSTITUTE OF FRANCE, AND OF THE
ROYAL ACADEMY OF NAPLES.

WITH PORTRAITS, ENGRAVED ON STEEL.

LONDON:
CHARLES KNIGHT AND CO., 22, LUDGATE STREET.

1845.

London; Printed by WILLIAM CLOWES and Sons, Stamford Street.

TO

SIR JOHN WILLIAMS,

&c.   *&c.*   *&c.*

ONE OF THE JUDGES OF THE COURT OF KING'S BENCH,

THIS WORK IS INSCRIBED,

AS A SMALL MEMORIAL OF ANCIENT FRIENDSHIP.

PREFACE.

THE reign of George III. may in some important respects be justly regarded as the Augustan age of modern history. The greatest statesmen, the most consummate captains, the most finished orators, the first historians, all flourished during this period. For excellence in these departments it was unsurpassed in former times, nor had it even any rivals, if we except the warriors of Louis XIV.'s day, one or two statesmen, and Bolingbroke and Massillon as orators. But its glories were not confined to those great departments of human genius. Though it could show no poet like Dante, Milton, Tasso, or Dryden; no dramatist like Shakspeare or Corneille; no philosopher to equal Bacon, Newton, or Locke,—it nevertheless in some branches, and these not the least important of natural science, very far surpassed the achievements of former days, while of political science, the most important of all, it first laid the foundations, and then reared the superstructure. The science of chemistry almost entirely, of political economy entirely, were the growth

of this remarkable era; while even in the pure mathematics a progress was made which almost changed
its aspect since the days of Leibnitz and Newton. The
names of Black, Watt, Cavendish, Priestley, Lavoisier,
Davy, may justly be placed far above the Boyles, the
Stahls, the Hales, the Hookes of former times; while
Euler, Clairault, Lagrange, La Place, must be ranked
as analysts close after Newton himself, and above Descartes, Leibnitz, or the Bernouillis; and in economical
science, Hume, Smith, and Quesnai really had no parallel, hardly any forerunner. It would also be vain to
deny great poetical and dramatic genius to Goldsmith,
Voltaire, Alfieri, Monti, and the German school, how
inferior soever to the older masters of song.

But, above all, it must not be forgotten, that in our
times the mighty revolution which has been effected in
public affairs, and has placed the rights of the people
throughout the civilized world upon a new and a
firm foundation, was brought about, immediately indeed by the efforts of statesmen, but prepared, and
remotely caused, by the labours of philosophers and
men of letters. The diffusion of knowledge among the
community at large is the work of our own age, and
it has made all the conquests of science both in recent
and in older times of incalculably greater value, of incomparably higher importance to the interests of mankind, than they were while scientific study was confined within the narrow circles of the wealthy and
the learned.

Having, therefore, on retiring from office, more time left for literary pursuits than professional and judicial duties had before allowed me, I was not minded to waste, indolent and inactive, or enslaved by lower occupations, that excellent leisure :—"Non fuit consilium socordiâ atque desidiâ bonum otium conterere; neque vero agrum colendo, aut venando, servilibus officiis intentum, ætatem agere. Statutum res gestas populi nostri carptim, ut quæque memoriâ digna videbantur, perscribere; eo magis quod mihi a spe, metû, partibus reipublicæ, animus liber erat."* For I conceived that as portrait-painting is true historical painting in one sense, so the lives of eminent men, freely written, are truly the history of their times; and that no more authentic account of any age, its transactions, the springs which impelled men's conduct, and the merits which different actors in its scenes possessed, can be obtained than by studying the biography of the personages who mainly guided affairs, and examining their characters, which by their influence they impressed upon the times they flourished in. Such a work had moreover this advantage, that beside preserving the memory of past events, and the likeness of men who had passed from the stage, it afforded frequent opportunities of inculcating the sound principles of an enlightened and virtuous policy, of illustrating their tendency to promote human happiness, of exhi-

---

* Sall., Cat., cap. iv.

biting their power to raise the genuine glory as well of individuals as of nations.

Though I could entertain no doubt that this plan was expedient, no one could more doubt than I did the capacity brought to its execution, or feel more distrustful of the pen held by a hand which had so long been lifted up only in the contentions of the Senate and the Forum. My only confidence was in the spirit of fairness and of truth with which I entered on the performance of the task ; and I now acknowledge with respectful gratitude the favour which the work has hitherto, so far above its deserts, experienced from the public, both at home, in spite of party opposition, and abroad, where no such unworthy influence could have place. It is fit that I also express my equal satisfaction at the testimony which has been borne to its strict impartiality by those whose opinions, and the opinions of whose political associates, differed the most widely from my own. That in composing the work I never made any sacrifice of those principles which have ever guided my public conduct, is certain ; that I never concealed them in the course of the book is equally true ; nay, this has been made a charge against it, as if I was at liberty to write the history of my own times, nay, of transactions in many of which I had borne a forward part, and not show what my own sentiments had been on those very affairs. But if my opinions were not sacrificed to the fear that I might offend the living by speaking plainly of the dead, so neither were truth and justice ever sacrificed to those opinions.

The Statesmen of George the Third's age having thus formed the subject of the volumes already published, I now offer to the attention of the reader a more full and elaborate view of the Learned Men who flourished in the same period. In my opinion, these, the great teachers of the age, covered it with still greater glory than it drew from the Statesmen and the Warriors who ruled its affairs. It was necessary to enter much more into detail here than in the former branch of this work, because a mere general description of scientific or of literary merit is of exceedingly little value, conveying no distinct or precise idea of the subject sought to be explained. It appeared the more necessary to discuss these matters minutely, because upon some of them much prejudice prevailed, and no attempt had hitherto been made to examine them completely, or even impartially. Of this a remarkable example is afforded by the want of any thing that deserves the name of a Life of Voltaire, and by the great prejudices, both favourable and unfavourable to him, which, among different classes, exist on the subject. But it must also be observed that Dr. Black's discoveries have been far from attaining the reputation which they so well deserve as the foundation of modern chemistry; and justice to this illustrious philosopher required that the consequences arising from his modesty and his great

indifference to fame should be counteracted by a full
history of his scientific labours, comparing the state of
the science as he found it with that in which he left
it.   My own personal acquaintance with some of the
great men whose history I have ventured to write,
enabled me to throw additional light upon it; and respecting one, whom of course I could not have known,
Mr. Hume, I have obtained information from good
sources through the kindness of friends.   The materials of his life are, however, chiefly to be sought in
his writings, and especially in his letters.   The same
remark is applicable to the life of Voltaire.   Those
who have written it, like the Marquis de Condorcet,
without ever referring to the fourteen large volumes
(containing nine thousand closely-printed pages) of his
Correspondence, might just as well have undertaken to
give a life of Rousseau without consulting his 'Confessions,' or of Hume without reading his 'Autobiography.'—I have, besides, had access to valuable original documents both of Voltaire, Robertson, and
Cavendish; to some respecting Watt and Simson.

The course of this work has kept me, for the most
part, at a distance from questions touching political
affairs, or the constitution and progress of society, but
not always.   The reader will find that no opportunity
has been left unimproved, as far as I was capable of
seizing it with any effect, for inculcating or illustrating the great doctrines of peace, freedom, and religious
liberty.   The observations on historical composition in

the life of Robertson, I especially consider as pointing to an improvement in that department of letters, highly important to the best interests of mankind, as well as to the character of historians.

But although I have no political animosities to encounter, I fear my historical statements and my commentaries on some lives, as those of Voltaire, Rousseau, and Hume, may find enemies among the two great parties whose principles come in question. The Free-thinkers will object to the blame which I have ventured to pronounce upon their favourite authors; the friends of the Church may take exception to the praises which I have occasionally bestowed. It may, however, be expected from the justice of both these conflicting bodies, that they will read with attention and with calmness before they condemn. From the former class I can expect no favour beyond what every one has a right to claim from avowed adversaries; a fair hearing is all I desire. To the latter I would address a few words in the spirit of respectful kindness, as to those with whom I generally agree.

Whoever feels disposed to treat as impious any writer that has the misfortune not to be among the great body of believers, like the celebrated men above named, should bear in mind that the author of these pages, while he does justice to their great literary merits, has himself published, whether anonymously or under his own name, nearly as much in defence of religion as they did against it; and if, with powers so infinitely below theirs, he may hope to have obtained some little success, and done some small service to the good cause, he can only ascribe this fortune to the intrinsic merits of that cause which he has ever supported.*   He ventures thus to hope that no one will suspect him of being the less a friend to religion, merely because he has not permitted his sincere belief to make him blind regarding the literary merit of men whose opinions are opposed to his own.   His censures of all indecorous, all unfair, all ribald or declamatory attacks, however set off by wit or graced by eloquence, he has never, on any occasion, been slow to pronounce.

Château Eleanor-Louise (Provence), Jan. 8, 1845.

---

* It has given me a most heartfelt satisfaction to receive many communications from persons both at home and abroad, which intimated their having been converted from irreligious opinions by the ' Commentaries and Illustrations of Paley,' published in 1835 and 1838.—It must be noted that the passage of the present work in which Dr. Lardner is mentioned as an orthodox writer, refers to the great question between Christians and Infidels.   He was an Unitarian, undoubtedly ; but his defence of Revelation forms really the groundwork of Dr. Paley's ' Evidences.'

CONTENTS.

,, 9, ,, 7 from foot, *for* guidés *read* arrondis.

,, 17, ,, 7, *for* 1769, *read* 1762.

,, 18, ,, 9 from foot, *for* sixty *read* a hundred.

,, 23, ,, 11 from foot, *for* règne dans l' *read* commande en.

,, 39, ,, 3 from foot, *for* ses *read* son.

,, 46, ,, 13 from foot, *for* pardonnez *read* pardonne.

,, 50, ,, 9, *for* of the, *read* of this.

,, 60, ,, 19, *after* consequence *insert* and one.

,, 128, ,, 9, *for* avons tort *read* nous trompons.

,, 163, ,, 3 from foot, *for* fonder *read* fondre.

,, 172, ,, 4 from foot, *for* ont *read* sont.

,, 290, ,, 18, *for* Henry VIII. *read* Henry VII.

,, 296, lines 1, 27, and 34, *for* Irvine *read* Irving.

,, 316, line 21, *for* him *read* to him.

,, 355, ,, 18, *for* settled *read* living.

,, 360, ,, 11, *after* and *insert* he.

,, 378, ,, 15, *for* 1834 *read* 1829.

,, 381, ,, 17, *before* a little *insert* which were.

,, 383, ,, 1, *after* he *insert* has.

,, —, ,, 4, *for* he *read* Mr. Watt.

I have been favoured with the following Memorandum from the Foreign Office. The correspondence of 1763 and 1765 I examined, and have alluded to at p. 225.

" A search has been made in the offices of the Secretaries of State and in the State Paper Office for the correspondence of Mr. David Hume when Under-Secretary of State with Marshal Conway ; but although letters have been found addressed to Mr. Hume in 1767-8, no letter signed by Mr. Hume can be found in any of the entry books of the period during which Mr. Hume was Under-Secretary of State ; nor can any such letter be found in the books of the same period in the State Paper Office.

" It would appear from the postscript of a letter from Mr. Carroll, dated at Dresden, April 13, 1768, that Mr. Hume's retirement had then been spoken of.

" There are some letters in the State Paper Office in Mr. Hume's handwriting while Secretary to the Earl of Hertford, at Paris in 1763 ; and also his own letters when left as Chargé d'Affaires in France, from the 28th of July to the 13th of November, 1765.

" FOREIGN OFFICE, *April* 8, 1845.'

MEN OF LETTERS

TIME OF GEORGE III.

VOLTAIRE.

THIS name is so intimately connected in the minds of all men with infidelity, in the minds of most men with irreligion, and, in the minds of all who are not well-informed, with these qualities alone, that whoever undertakes to write his life and examine his claims to the vast reputation which all the hostile feelings excited by him against himself have never been able to destroy, or even materially to impair, has to labour under a great load of prejudice, and can hardly expect, by any detail of particulars, to obtain for his subject even common justice at the hands of the general reader. It becomes, therefore, necessary, in the outset, to remove a good deal of misunderstanding which, from the popular abuse of language, creates great confusion, in considering the history and weighing the merits of this extraordinary person.

The mention of Voltaire at once presents to every one the idea, not so much of a philosopher whose early inquiries have led him to doubt upon the foundations of religion, or even to disbelieve its truths, as of a bitter enemy to all belief in the evidence of things

B

unseen—an enemy whose assaults were directed by
malignant passions, aided by unscrupulous contrivances,
and, above all, pressed by the unlawful weapon of
ridicule, not the fair armoury of argument; in a
word, he is regarded as a scoffer, not a reasoner. Akin
to this is the other charge which makes us shudder
by the imputation of blasphemy. Now, upon this
manner of viewing Voltaire some things are to be
explained, and some to be recalled, that they may be
borne in mind during the discussion of his character.

Let us begin with the last charge, because, until it
is removed, no attention is likely to be gained by anything that can be urged in defence or in extenuation.
It is evident that, strictly speaking, blasphemy can
only be committed by a person who believes in the
existence and in the attributes of the Deity whom he
impugns, either by ridicule or by reasoning. An atheist
is wholly incapable of the crime. When he heaps
epithets of abuse on the Creator, or turns His attributes
into ridicule, he is assailing or scoffing at an empty
name—at a being whom he believes to have no
existence. In like manner if a deist, one who dis-
believes in our Saviour being either the Son of God
or sent by God as his prophet upon earth, shall argue
against his miracles, or ridicule his mission or his
person, he commits no blasphemy; for he firmly
believes that Christ was a man like himself, and that
he derived no authority from the Deity. Both the
atheist and the deist are free from all guilt of blasphemy, that is, of all guilt towards the Deity or
towards Christ. It is wholly another question
whether or not they are guilty towards men. They

plainly are so if they use topics calculated to wound the feelings of their neighbour who believes what they disbelieve; because religion, unlike other subjects of controversy, is one that mixes itself with the strongest feelings of the heart, and these must not be rudely outraged; because no man can be so perfectly certain that he is himself right and others are wrong, as to justify him in thus making their opinions the subject of insolent laughter or scurrilous abuse; because it is our duty, even when fully convinced that we are dealing with error, and with dangerous error, to adopt such a course as will rather conciliate those we would gain over to the truth than make them shut their eyes to it by revolting their strongest feelings. Hence all law-givers have regarded such scoffing and insolent attacks on the religion professed by the great majority of their subjects as an offence justly punishable; although it may fairly be doubted whether the interposition of the law has ever had a tendency to protect religious belief itself, and may even be suspected of having favoured the designs of those who impugn it, both by the reaction which such proceedings always occasion, and by the more cautious and successful methods of attack to which they usually drive the opponents of the national faith. But the offence, whether punished by the laws or not, is very incorrectly, though very generally, termed blasphemy, which is the offence of scoffing at the Deity, and assumes that the scoffer believes in him. Now it is barely possible that this offence may be committed; but it is the act of a mad rather than a bad man. If, indeed, any one really believing pretends to unbelief in order to indulge in scoffing, no language is too strong to express the reprobation he deserves, if he be in his senses; for he adds falsehood to a crime so horrible as almost to pass the bounds of belief—the frightful act of wilfully rebelling against the Almighty Creator of heaven and earth.—This is the *first* and worst form of the offence.

Secondly: The like guilt will, to a certain extent, be incurred by him who vents his ribaldry, upon the mere ground of his scepticism. On such a subject doubting is not enough. Unless there is an entire conviction in the mind that the popular belief is utterly groundless in the one case (that of attacking the Deity) that there is a God, in the other (attacking Christianity) that there is a foundation for revelation, the guilt of blasphemy is incurred. He must be convinced, not merely doubt, or see reason for doubting; because no one has a right to speculate and take the chances of being innocent; guiltless if his doubts are well founded, guilty if they are not. The virtuous course here is the safe one. This is the moral of the fable in which the hermit answers the question of the rake, "Where are you, father, if there be not another world?" with the other question, "And you, my son, if there be?" We need not go so far as some have done, who on this ground contend that it is safer always to believe than to doubt, because belief must ever, to be of any value, depend on conviction. But we may assuredly hold that the better conduct is that which abstains from attack and offence where the reasons hang in suspense—abstains because of the great guilt incurred if the doubts should prove groundless.

It is a *third* and lesser degree of this offence if a

person carelessly gives way to a prevailing unbelief, and does not apply his faculties to the inquiry with that sober attention, that conscientious diligence, which its immense importance demands of all rational creatures. No man is accountable for the opinion he may form, the conclusion at which he may arrive, provided that he has taken due pains to inform his mind and fix his judgment. But for the conduct of his understanding he certainly is responsible. He does more than err if he negligently proceeds in the inquiry; he does more than err if he allows any motive to sway his mind save the constant and single desire of finding the truth; he does more than err if he suffers the least influence of temper or of weak feeling to warp his judgment; he does more than err if he listens rather to ridicule than reason, unless it be that ridicule which springs from the contemplation of gross and manifest absurdity, and which is in truth argument and not ribaldry.

Now by these plain rules we must try Voltaire; and it is impossible to deny that he possessed such sufficient information, and applied his mind with such sufficient anxiety to the discovery of truth, as gave him a right to say that he had formed his opinions, how erroneous soever they might be, after inquiring, and not lightly. The story which is related of the Master in the Jesuits' Seminary of Louis le Grand, where he was educated, having foretold that he would be the Corypheus of deists, if true, only proves that he had very early begun to think for himself; and whoever doubted the real presence, or questioned the power of absolution, was at once set down for an infidel in

those countries and in those times. It would be the
fate of any young scholar in the Roman colleges at
this day, especially were he to maintain his doubts
with a show of cleverness; and were he to mingle
the least wit with his argument, he would straightway be charged with blasphemy. But it must be
added that an impression unfavourable to the truths of
religion, and its uses, was made upon Voltaire's mind
by the sight of its abuses, and by a consideration of the
manifest errors inculcated in the Romish system. It is
not enough to bring him within the blame above stated
under the third head, that he was prejudiced in conducting his inquiries, if that prejudice proceeded from the
errors of others which he had unjustly been summoned
to believe. He is not to be blamed for having begun
to doubt of the truths of Christianity in consequence
of his attention having originally been directed to the
foundations of the system by a view of the falsehoods
which had been built upon those truths. Even if the
bigotry of priests, the persecutions of sovereigns, the
absurdities of a false faith, the grovelling superstitions
of its votaries, their sufferings, bodily as well as mental,
under false guides and sordid pastors, roused his
indignation and his pity, and these alternating emotions
first excited the spirit of inquiry, afterwards too much
guided its course, we are not on that account to condemn him as severely as we should one who, from
some personal spleen or individual interest, had
suffered his judgment to be warped, and thus, as it
were, lashed himself into disbelief of a system altogether pure, administered by a simple, a disinterested,
a venerable hierarchy.

Let us for a moment, independent of what may be termed the political view of the question—independent of all that regards the priesthood—consider the position of a person endowed with strong natural faculties, and not under the absolute dominion of his spiritual guides, nor prevented by their authority from exercising his reason; but, on the contrary, living at a moment when a spirit of free inquiry was beginning generally to prevail. He is told that the mystery of transubstantiation must be believed by him as a fact; he is told that there has been transmitted through a succession of ages from the apostles one of the Divine attributes, the power of pardoning sin, and that the laying a priest's hands on a layman gives him this miraculous power, to be exercised by him how guilty soever may be his own life, how absolutely null his own belief in the Divine being—nay, that this power has come through certain persons notorious atheists themselves, and whose lives were more scandalously profligate than anything that a modest tongue can describe. Presented to a vigorous mind, and not enforced by an authority which suffers no reasoning, or if enforced yet vainly so enforced, these dogmas and these claims became the subject of discussion, and were rejected almost as soon as they were understood. But in company with them were found many other doctrines and pretensions of a very different complexion, yet all of them were pronounced to have the same Divine original; and no greater sanctity, no higher authority, no deeper veneration was claimed for them than for the real presence of the Creator at the summons of the priest, or the participation of that priest in the attributes of the God-head. Let us be just towards the youth who was placed in these circumstances, and let us not condemn him for hastily rejecting the wheat with the chaff, before we endeavour to place ourselves in the same situation, asking what effect would be produced on our minds by severe denunciations against us should we doubt the priest's power, or refuse an explicit assent to his dogmas, which our reason, nay our senses rejected, while he refused all access to the inspired volumes which contained, or were said to contain, their only warrant. Rejecting the false doctrines, the chances are many that our faith would be shaken in the true. How many Protestants were made in the sixteenth century by the sale of indulgences! But how many unbelievers in Christianity have been made in all ages of the Church by the grosser errors of Rome, the exorbitant usurpations of her bishops, and the preposterous claims of her clergy!

It is also to be observed that Voltaire was, through his whole life, a sincere believer in the existence and attributes of the Deity. He was a firm and decided, and an openly declared unbeliever in Christianity, but he was, without any hesitation or any intermission, a theist. Then in examining the justice of the charge of blasphemy it is to be borne in mind that not one irreverent expression is to be found in all his number-less writings towards the Deity in whom he believed. He has more ably than most writers stated and illus-trated the arguments in favour of that belief. He has consecrated some of his noblest poetry to celebrate the powers of the Godhead.* Whatever exception to this assertion may seem to be found in those writings will, on consideration, prove to be only apparent. It will be found that he is speaking only of the Deity as represented in systems of religion which he disbelieved; consequently he is there ridiculing only the idols, the work of men's hands, and the objects of superstitious worship, not the great Being in whom he believed and whom he adored. Even his 'Candide,' one of his greatest, perhaps his most perfect work, is only intended to expose the extravagance of the optimist doctrine; and however we may lament its tone in some sort, it is certainly not chargeable with ridiculing anything which a philosophic theist must necessarily believe.

But no one can exempt Voltaire from blame for the manner in which he attacked religious opinions, and outraged the feelings of believers. There he is without defence. Had all men been prepared to make the step

---

* His dramatic compositions abound in such religious sentiments, clothed in the noblest language of poetical abstraction; but his celebrated verses, said to have been written extempore in a company that were admiring the firmament one summer's evening, may be placed by the side of the finest compositions in that kind—

> " Tous ces vastes pays d'azur et de lumière,
> Tirés du sein du vide, formés sans matière,
> Guidés sans compas, tournans sans pivot,
> N'ont à peine coûté la dépense d'un mot."

When I once cited these to my illustrious friend Monti, who never would allow any poetical merit to the French, he objected to the last phrase, which he called the *pivot*, as low and prosaic, and as affording a proof of his constant position that the French have no poetical language.

which he had himself taken, the wound would have
been inconsiderable.   But he must have written with
the absolute certainty that their religious belief would
long survive his assaults, and that consequently, to the
vast majority of readers, they could only give pain.
Indeed he must, in the moments of calm reflection,
have been aware that reasoning, and not ridicule, is the
proper remedy for religious error, and that no one can
heartily embrace the infidel side of the great question
merely because he has been made to join in a laugh at
the expense of absurdities mixed up with the doctrines
of believers ; nay, even if he has been drawn into a
laugh at the expense of some portion of those doctrines
themselves   It is no vindication for Voltaire against
this heavy charge, but it may afford some palliation of
his offence, if we reflect on the very great difference
between the ecclesiastical regimen under which he
lived, and that with which we are acquainted in our
Protestant community.   Let no man severely condemn
the untiring zeal of Voltaire, and the various forms of
attack which he employed without measure, against
the religious institutions of his country, who is not
prepared to say that he could have kept entire possession
of his own temper, and never cast an eye of suspicion
upon the substance of a religion thus abused, nor ever
have employed against its perversions the weapons of
declamation and of mockery ; had he lived under the
system which regarded Alexander Borgia as one of its
spiritual guides, which bred up and maintained in all
the riot of criminal excess an aristocracy having for
one branch of its resources the spoils of the altar, which
practised persecution as a favourite means of conviction,

and cast into the flames a lad of eighteen, charged with laughing as its priests passed by. Such dreadful abuses were present to Voltaire's mind when he attacked the Romish superstitions, and exposed the profligacy, as well as the intolerance, of clerical usurpation. He unhappily suffered them to poison his mind upon the whole of that religion of which these were the abuse; and, when his zeal waxed hot against the whole system, it blinded him to the unfairness of the weapons with which he attacked both its evidences and its teachers.

The doctrine upon toleration, upon prosecutions for infidelity, even for blasphemy, which I have now ventured to propound, is supported by the very highest authority among persons of the most acknowledged piety, and of the warmest zeal for the interests of religion. It was the constant maxim of my revered friend, Mr. Wilberforce, that no man should be prosecuted for his attacks upon religion. He gave this opinion in Parliament; and he was wont to say, that the ground of it was his belief in the truths of religion. "If religion be, as I believe it, true, it has nothing to fear from any such assaults. It may be injured by the secular arm interfering." Just so the well-known Duke of Queensberry, when conversing upon the writings of Paine, and other assailants of the constitution, made answer to a sycophant, who said of those attacks, "And so false too,"—"No," said his Grace, "not at all: they are true, and that is their danger, and the reason I desire to see them put down by the law; were they false, I should not mind them at all."

In the like spirit we have the unsuspected testimony of men like Dr. Lardner and Bishop Jeremy Taylor,

Christians whose piety and virtue, and whose orthodoxy, are beyond all suspicion :—"The proper punishment," says Lardner, "of a low, mean, indecent, scurrilous way of writing, seems to be neglect, contempt, scorn, and final indignation" (*Letter to the Bishop of Chester on the Prosecution of Woolston,* 1729).—"Blasphemy" (says Taylor) "is *in aliena republica,* a matter of another world. You may as well cure the colic by brushing a man's clothes, or fill a man's belly with a syllogism, as prosecute for blasphemy. Some men have believed it the more as being provoked into a confidence and vexed into a resolution. Force in matters of opinion can do no good, but is very apt to do hurt ; for no man can change his opinion when he will. But if a man cannot change his opinion when he list, nor ever does heartily or resolutely but when he cannot do otherwise, then to use force may make him a hypocrite, but never to be a right believer ; and so, instead of erecting a trophy to God and true religion, we build a monument for the devil" (*Liberty of Prophesying,* s. xiii. 19.)—Bishop Warburton says plainly, "he should have been ashamed of even projecting to write in defence of Moses had he not thought that all infidels had equal liberty to attack him." (*Dedication to the Divine Legation.*)

These things being premised, we may now proceed with more ease and less interruption from controversial topics, to examine the extraordinary history of this eminent person.

He was the son of the Sieur Arouet, a person of respectable family, filling the place of treasurer in the Chamber of Accounts, an exchequer office of considerable emolument. His mother was of a noble family, that of d'Aumart. A small estate possessed by the father was called Voltaire; and the custom in those days being for the younger children of wealthy commoners to take the name of their estate, leaving the family name to the eldest, François Marie, as the younger of two sons, took the name of Voltaire, which on his brother's death many years after he did not change. He was born the 20th of February, 1694; and being so feeble that his life was not expected, he was baptised immediately, the christening being deferred till the 22d of November following. This has given rise to doubts at which of the two periods his birth took place. It has frequently been remarked as a singular circumstance, that two eminent authors who have lived to extreme old age, Fontenelle and Voltaire, were both thus unlikely at their birth to live at all, both being born almost in a dying condition ; yet not only did they enjoy unusually long life, but they retained their great faculties entire to the last, although the one died in his eighty-fifth year, and the other lived to within a few weeks of a hundred.

When only twelve years of age, he distinguished himself by the excellence of some begging verses to the Dauphin from an invalid who had served under the prince, and who applied for this help to the Master of the College of Louis le Grand, where Voltaire then was. The master being busy, handed him over to his promising scholar, as being quite able to do what was desired. The lines are very good, and the idea sufficiently happy. The old soldier is made to say that the different heathen gods having given

Monseigneur various gifts at his birth, a more benefi-
cent Deity had provided the petitioner's Christmas-
box by bestowing on their favourite the boon of generosity. It is known that this incident procured for
him the favour of the famous Ninon de l'Enclos, then
in her ninetieth year, and to whom he was presented
by his godfather, the Abbé de Châteauneuf. She died
soon after, and left him a legacy of 2,000 francs, to
buy books with.* When his father found that he was
introduced by the Abbé into this and other fashionable society, and that he was cultivating his taste for
poetry, he became alarmed for his success in life,
having destined him for the profession of the law.
He placed him, therefore, in a school of jurisprudence,
intending to purchase for him a President's place, according to the practice of the French bar in those days.
Voltaire, however, had already begun to taste the sweets

---

* He has, in a letter which remains (Mélanges Lit., ii. 294), recorded
many particulars of her extraordinary life and great qualities. Her
portrait by St. Evremond is well known ; it is happily drawn :—

> " L'indulgente et sage Nature
> A formé l'ame de Ninon
> De la volupté d'Epicure,
> Et de la vertu de Caton."

In consequence of a quarrel between two of her lovers there was a
proposition of sending her to a convent of " *Filles repenties :*" she
said that would not suit her, as she was " *ni fille, ni repentie.*"
The provident parents in good society used to place their sons
under her patronage to form them for polite company. Of one
Renaud, a coxcomb whom she was said to have formed, she observed,
" Qu'elle faisait comme Dieu, qui s'était repenti d'avoir fait l'homme."
When her old and intimate friend, Madame de Maintenon, became *dévote,* and offered to provide handsomely for her would
she but follow her example, her answer was, " Je n'ai nul besoin
ni de fortune, ni de masque."

of classical study, and he had lived in a society frequented by the Abbé his godfather, who appears to have been a person of loose morals and of sceptical opinions. The extreme bigotry which Madame de Maintenon had introduced into the Court of Versailles when the declining faculties and health of Louis XIV. had rendered him the victim of superstitious terrors, and, through these, the tool of priestly intolerance, gave rise to a reaction in the gay circles of Paris ; and in resisting the inroads of that gloom by which the asceticism of the ancient mistress had signalised her late repentance, the Contis, the Chaulieus, the Sullys, the La Fères, carried their opposition further than they perhaps at first intended, or even afterwards were aware of : they patronised universal discussion, even of the most sacred subjects, and best received opinions, until a fashion of free thinking was set; and from being at first revolted at the intolerance which destroyed Catinat at Court, notwithstanding his genius and his probity, on account of his supposed infidelity, and ascribed the defeats of Vendôme to his occasional absence from mass, without reflecting that Marlborough was a heretic and Eugene a deist; the frequenters of the most polished society in the world became accustomed to believe more sparingly than Catinat, and see less of the Host than Vendôme.

It was in this association that Voltaire, then a boy, became inured to the oblivion both of his law books and of his religious principles, when his parent made a last effort to save him, and restore him to the learned profession, and to the bosom of the church, by sending him as page or attaché to the French ambassador at the Hague, a near kinsman of the Abbé Châteauneuf. He there fell in love with the daughter of a profligate woman, Madame Dunoyer, who considering the match a bad one, had him sent home by the ambassador, and published his love letters, which are admitted to have no merit. His father would only receive him on condition of his consenting to serve in a notary's office. A friend of the family, M. de Caumartin, had compassion on the sufferings which this arrangement occasioned, and obtained permission to have him pass some months in his country residence at St. Ange. The Bishop Caumartin, then an elderly man, and who had lived with all the more learned persons of the past age, excited him, by his conversation upon the Sullys and the Henrys, to meditate two of the greatest of his works, his epic poem and his history.

The death of Louis, which happened on Voltaire's return to Paris, gave rise to a very indecent expression of public joy, and to many libels upon his memory. One of these being without any foundation ascribed to him, his confinement in the Bastille was the consequence. Here, however, his spirit continued unbroken. He sketched the poem of the 'League,' afterwards called the 'Henriade;' and he corrected a tragedy, 'Œdipe,' which he had written several years before, when only eighteen years old. The imprisonment being in the course of a few weeks found to be entirely illegal and vexatious, the Regent ordered his immediate liberation, with a sum of money by way of compensation. The tragedy was not acted till two years after, in 1718; and it is a singular fact, that when, in 1713, it had been in its original imperfect state submitted to Dacier, with the pedantry of his nature he strongly recommended the introduction of choruses, to be sung after the manner of the Greek tragedy. A letter of his is still extant, giving this sage and practical counsel ; but the Greek critic was not the only pedant. When in 1769, Voltaire had gained the famous cause of Sirven, through the exertions of M. Merville, a leading advocate of Toulouse, he refused all pecuniary remuneration, but desired as his reward, that his client would now consent to add choruses to the ' Œdipe.'

How powerful was the sentiment of ambition in his nature appears not merely from his bold attempt at a tragedy—audaxque juventâ—in his eighteenth year, but from his adventurous competition for the prize of poetry proposed by the Académie Française a year or two before ; the king having, in the superstition of his declining age, at length resolved to fulfil the promise of his predecessor by decorating the altar of Notre Dame. This formed the subject of the ode, which was rejected in favour of a ridiculous piece by the Abbé Dujarri ; so that it is a singular fact in Voltaire's history that his first published work was a devotional poem.

The tragedy of ' Œdipe' was successful ; and Lamotte, then of established reputation, but which with ordinary poets is by no means a security against jealousy, had the noble candour to declare that this tragedy gave sure promise of a successor to Corneille and Racine. But the prejudices of the stage forced Voltaire to introduce a love scene against his better judgment, which had decided against the incongruous mixture of

C

tenderness with the horrors of the subject. It is
related of him, and he has himself countenanced the
anecdote, that in the giddiness of youth, and plunged
in dissipation, he was insensible to the dangers of
failure, and felt so little of the nervous agitation
belonging to a dramatic author's first night, as to
be seen carrying in mockery the train of the High
Priest. Madame la Maréchale de Villars, then at the
head of Parisian society, asked who that young man
was, who appeared as if trying to have the play
damned ; and upon being told that it was neither
more nor less than the author himself, she was so
struck with the originality, that she desired to have
him presented to her. Becoming one of her circle, he
conceived for her the first and probably the only
passion which he ever seriously felt. His love was
unsuccessful ; but it interrupted his studies, nor did
he ever after allude to it but with a feeling of
regret bordering upon remorse.

The merits of 'Œdipe' no longer form a debateable
question. If the continued representation for forty-
five nights had left any doubt upon this subject, the
concurrent voices of so many different audiences during
the sixty years and upwards that it has kept possession
of the stage pronounce a sentence from which there
is no appeal.* For an author of any age it is a fine

---

* The judgments pronounced by the audience on a first representation are a very different test, being necessarily much more subject
to accident, to caprice, and to party manœvures. The striking
example of the ' Britannicus,' nay, even of the ' Phèdre' and the
' Athalie ' themselves (these two now admitted on all hands to be
Racine's masterpieces), may well guard us against yielding to the

performance; for a young man of eighteen or nineteen, a truly wonderful one; promising, perhaps, considerably greater dramatic success than even the author of 'Zaire' ever attained. But he unfortunately preferred writing *multa* than *multum*; and this remark is more peculiarly applicable to his dramatic compositions than to any of his other important efforts.

The distinguishing beauty of the 'Œdipe' is its fervid, correct, and powerful declamation; and though the most magnificent passage be taken from Sophocles, there are numberless others of undoubted originality. Into some of the inconsistencies, and even absurdities, of the Greek plot he has fallen, and the most of whatever is good in that plot certainly is not his own. But no one who has either seen the representation or read the poem, can easily forget the powerful impression which its diction leaves on the mind. Some of the passages are marked by their supposed allusion to the priesthood of his own times; and one especially is generally given as his first declaration of war against the sacred order:—

> " Nos prêtres ne sont point ce qu'un vain peuple pense—
> Notre crédulité fait toute leur science."—(Act iv. sc. 4.)

But surely, when we observe that this is only the

---

first expressions of the vox populi. Perhaps even the great union of opinion in France, placing Corneille so far above Racine, is another instance of erroneous judgment produced by accidental circumstances. Had Racine preceded Corneille, would the decision have been the same? There may, however, be some ground for giving the same precedence to the latter that we yield to Massillon and Bourdaloue over Bossuet.

summing up of an invective satirical, but perfectly just, against the Pagan superstitions which are specified, we may well suppose, that had not his future writings supplied the commentary, no one could have deemed the allusion in these fine lines irreverent to the hierarchy of Rome. Now, it is true, they are sufficiently marked ; and in consequence of that commentary they never fail to be applied. I recollect the thunder of applause which they called forth in 1814, when I saw this play during the first restoration. The court of Louis XVIII. was supposed to favour the Church in an especial manner, and this pointed the public attention more peculiarly to such allusions. Two other lines were productive of nearly equal applause :—

"Un prêtre, quel qu'il soit, quelque Dieu qui l'inspire,
Doit prier pour ses rois, et non pas les maudire."
(Act iii. sc. 3.)

The reason of this excitement was, that the lines contain a reproof of the High Priest's insolence, and that was sufficient. On another occasion, the same season, I heard much louder applause in that theatre. It was of the lines,

"Le premier qui fût roi, fût un soldat heureux :
Qui sert bien son pays n'a pas besoin d'aïeux."

The reference was instantly made to Napoleon, and the piece could hardly proceed for the boisterous plaudits.

It is certain that the tragedies of Voltaire are the works of an extraordinary genius, and that only a great poet could have produced them ; but it is equally certain that they are deficient for the most

part in that which makes the drama powerful over
the feelings,—real pathos, real passion, whether of
tenderness, of terror, or of horror. The plots of
some are admirably contrived; the diction of all is
pure and animated; in most passages it is pointed,
and in many it is striking, grand, impressive; the characters are frequently well imagined and portrayed,
though without sufficient discrimination; and thus
often running one into another, from the uniformity
of the language, terse, epigrammatic, powerful, which
all alike speak. Nor are there wanting situations of
great effect, and single passages of thrilling force;
but, after all, the heart is not there; the deep feeling,
which is the parent of all true eloquence as well as
all true poetry, didactic and satirical excepted, is
rarely perceived; it is rather rhetoric than eloquence,
or, at least, rather eloquence than poetry. It is declamation of a high order in rhyme; no blank
verse, indeed, can be borne on the French stage, or
even in the French tongue; it is not fine dramatic
composition : the periods roll from the mouth, they
do not spring from the breast; there is more light
than heat; the head rather than the heart is at work.

It seems that if there be any exception to this
remark, we must look for it in the 'Zaire,' his most
perfect piece, although, marvellous to tell, it was
written in two and twenty days. In my humble
opinion, it is certainly obnoxious to the same general
objection, though less than any of his other pieces;
yet it is truly a noble performance, and it unites many
of the great requisites of dramatic excellence. The
plot, which he tells us was the work of a single day,

is one of the most admirable ever contrived for the
stage, and it is a pure creation of fancy. Nothing
can be conceived more full of interest and life and
spirit —nothing more striking than the combinations
and the positions to which it gives rise, while at the
same time it is quite natural, quite easy to conceive,
in no particular violating probability. Nor can anything be more happy or more judicious than the
manner in which we are, at the very first, brought
into the middle of the story, and yet soon find it
unravelled and presented before our eyes without
long and loaded narrative retrospects. Then the
characters are truly drawn with a master's hand, and
sustained perfectly and throughout both in word and
in deed. Orosman, uniting the humanized feelings
of an amiable European with the unavoidable remains
of the Oriental nature, ambitious, and breathing war,
more than becomes our character, yet generous and
simple-minded; to men imperious, but as it were by
starts, when the Tartar predominates; to women delicate and tender, as if the Goth or the Celt prevailed
in the harem; unable to eradicate the jealousy of the
East, yet, like a European, too proud not to be
ashamed of it as a degradation, and thus subduing it
in all instances but one, when he is hurried away by
the Asiatic temperament and strikes the fatal blow,
which cannot lessen our admiration, nor even wholly
destroy our esteem. The generous nature of Nourestan and Lusignan excites our regard, and, perhaps,
alone of all the perfect characters in epic or in dramatic
poetry, they are no way tiresome or flat. But Zaire
herself, unlike other heroines, is, if not the first, at

least equal to the first, of the personages in touching
the reader and engaging his affections.   Nothing can
be conceived more tender; and the conflict between
her passion for the Sultan and her affection for her
family, between her acquired duty to the crescent and
her hereditary inclination to the cross, is most beautifully managed.   Of detailed passages it would be
endless to make an enumeration, but some may be
shortly marked.   Few things in poetry are finer than
Lusignan's simple answer to Chatillon, who tells
him that he was impotent to save his children :

> " *C.* Mon bras chargé de fers ne les pût pas secourir.
> *L.* Hélas ! et j'étais père, et je ne pûs mourir."

Nourestan's indignation, the boiling over of a fanatical crusader's enthusiasm against his sister for falling
in love with an infidel prince (Act iii. sc. 4), is a truly
noble piece of declamation.   Orosman's proud feeling
towards the sex, for the first time following the Asiatic
course (Act iii. sc. 7), is not less finely expressed :

> " Mais il est trop honteux de craindre une maitresse—
> Aux mœurs de l'Occident laissons cette bassesse !
> Ce sexe dangereux, qui veut tout asservir,
> S'il règne dans l'Europe, ici doit obéir."

The famous passage " Zaire, vous pleurez ?" which
electrified the audience in France, and never fails
still to produce this effect, needs not be specified, except for the purpose of noting, that the exclamation
" Zaire, vous m'aimez !" is hardly less touching, or less
powerful to paint the Sultan's character.

Next to ' Zaire ' the ' Mérope ' certainly is Voltaire's
finest drama ; and its success at first was even greater
than that of ' Zaire.'   At one part the audience were so
intoxicated with admiration, that they called out for

Voltaire, and forced him to show himself—the first time that the honour was ever bestowed, which has now become worthless, because lavished on the author of every successful piece. But the multitude went a step further in his case, and insisted upon the beautiful daughter-in-law of the Maréchale de Villars publicly saluting him; a requisition savouring much more of indecorum than enthusiasm.

It is impossible to deny either the great merits of the 'Mérope,' or to doubt its marked inferiority to 'Zaire.' The composition, and, in general, the execution, must be confessed to be in the best manner of that eloquence, or rather rhetoric, which I have ventured to describe as the character of Voltaire's tragedies; but it is not, like 'Zaire,' at least many portions of 'Zaire,' a successful incursion into the adjoining, though far loftier domain of feeling: in a word, the high region of fine verse is here under the author's power; the higher region of poetry does not submit to his control. The fable is excellently pursued; while there is little original or very happy in the characters, of which the principal one is so possessed by a feeling of love and anxiety for a son whom she had barely seen, that it is difficult to sympathise with the leading sentiment of the piece. Fine passages no doubt abound, and bursts (*mouvemens*) of an impressive, and of a surprising and even elevating kind, are occasionally introduced, though by far the finest is imitated professedly from the 'Merope' of Maffei—it is when Egisthe mentions his mother; and Merope then believing that he had murdered her son, that is himself, exclaims—

" Barbare ! il te reste une mere !
Je serois mère encore sans toi," &c.—(Act iii. sc. 4.)

The verses on a military usurper have been already cited. Lines such as the concluding couplet of the second act are not rarely scattered through the piece, and never fail to produce a great effect in the delivery. They have, like the former, been not rarely applied to Napoleon.

" Quand on a tout perdu, quand on n'a plus d'espoir,
La vie est un opprobre, et la mort un devoir."

These, the ' Zaire' and 'Mérope,' seem, beyond all comparison, and without any doubt, to be the finest of Voltaire's dramatic works. His own favourite, however, appears to have been the 'Catiline,' or 'Rome Sauvée.' He dwells with great complacency on its having been more applauded than ' Zaire' on its first representation, and accounts for its not having, like ' Zaire,' kept possession of the stage, by observing that nobody now-a-days conspires, but every one has loved. The superiority of this to its rival, the ' Catiline' of Crebillon, is also admitted ; nor can we deny it a considerable degree of that which constituted Voltaire's dramatic merit, his eloquence far more remarkable than his poetry. It may also be admitted that if this criticism can ever lose its force, it must be in a composition of which the hero is Cicero ;—nor, if the eloquence were of a higher order,—if it were fervid and impassioned,—if it were warm from the heart, and addressed and moved the feelings,—would the decision of which the author appears to complain ever have gone forth against it. But the tragedy has, beside many other faults, that of frigid declamation, in pure diction, often happy, generally pointed, even to epigram, but still cold and artificial. There is also to

be remarked in the piece a singular want of judgment.
The history of Catiline is not professed to be followed,
yet all the departures from it are in diminution of the
dramatic interest; and nothing can be less correct
than the assertion which accompanies the confession
that the facts of the story are changed—it is not true,
or anything like the truth, that the " genius and the
character of Cicero, Catiline, Cato, and Cæsar, are
faithfully painted." Can anything be less excusable,
whether we regard dramatic interest or the truth of
history, than representing Catiline as uxorious, and
all but won over to abandon his enterprise by his
wife's remonstrances and tears? The absurdity of
making Cæsar put down the conspiracy, and supersede
C. Antonius and Petreius in the command at the
battle in which Catiline fell, requires no comment.
This, and Cæsar's rhodomontade before setting out, his
embracing Cicero, and vowing that he goes either to
die, or to justify the Consul's good opinion of him, and
his being overpersuaded by a speech of Cicero, not
merely to abandon Catiline but to destroy him, is as
utterly unlike that great man's character as anything
that can well be imagined. For Cato, it is surely as
little in his manner as can be, to tell Cicero that
Rome calls him her father and her avenger; and that
Envy at his feet trembles and adores him

> " Et l'Envie à tes pieds l'admire avec terreur."

But the grand defect of this piece is the absurd and
hopeless attempt of bringing Cicero upon the stage.
Brutus and Antony had been successfully so dealt
with by Shakspeare; but they were men of action;

Cicero, a mere orator, never could be endured as the
hero of a piece; eloquence, the triumphs of the tongue,
are wholly unfitted to form the subject of a drama.
Voltaire has endeavoured to supply the defect by making Catiline murder not his step-son, which he was
supposed to have done, but his father-in-law, a certain
Nonnius, which no one ever dreamt of but the poet;
and his wife, in her grief and rage, puts herself to
death by stabbing herself on the stage.

But if we desire to perceive how great is Voltaire's
failure, we must not only consider what he has done to
make his drama cold and uninteresting, but what materials he had within his reach, and avoided using.
Few narratives present so lively, nay, so dramatic a
picture as that of Sallust. The diction is fine; but
had Livy written it, his exquisite and dignified style
would have placed the Catiline conspiracy at the
head of historical works. The character of Catiline,
better given in some parts of Cicero, particularly the
Pro Sulla, Pro Cœlio, and Pro Muræna; his dark,
designing, and unscrupulous nature; his utter profligacy of life and manners; his fierce temper; his un-
tameable ambition; his powers, as well of body as of
mind; his invincible courage—all form a personage
made for stage effect, and only prevented from producing it in the highest degree by such preposterous
conceits as making him tender-hearted to his wife,
a thing to have been carefully avoided by the dramatist, even if his letter, given by Sallust, shows some
care for that very profligate woman and his child.
But then what can be finer than the meeting holden
in a remote recess of his house, and his address under

cloud of night to his associates—to say nothing of the
dark suspicion thrown out by the historian, that he
made them drink human blood mixed with their wine
when he swore them to the enterprise!* But the
speech is very fine—bold, abrupt, simple, concise, eminently calculated for the occasion:—" Quin igitur,
expergiscemini ? En illa, illa quam sæpe optastis
libertas ! Fortuna omnia victoribus præmia posuit: res,
tempus, pericula, egestas, belli spolia magnifica, magis
quam oratio mea vos hortentur. Vel imperatore, vel
milite me utimine. Neque animus, neque corpus a
vobis aberit." The other speech which he makes on
the eve of the fight is also very noble and characteristic :—" Quod si virtuti vestræ fortuna inviderit,
cavete inulte animam amittatis; neu capti potius sicuti
pecora trucidemini, quam virorum more pugnantes, cruen-
tam atque luctuosam victoriam hostibus relinquatis."†
With such noble materials, Voltaire makes as poor a
speech as it was possible to manufacture—as wordy
and unimpressive. He calls his conspirators " an
assemblage of the greatest of human kind ;" and that
being not enough, they are " conquerors of kings—
avengers of their countrymen—his true friends, his
equals, his supports." He tells them that " they had
subdued Tigranes and Mithridates, and made the
Euphrates red with their blood, only to make worthless senators proud, who, as a recompence, allowed the
conspirators to adore their persons at a distance."
How much finer is the simple description in Sallust !—
" The Patricians squander away their wealth in

---

* Fuere eâ tempestate qui dicerent.—(Cap. xxii.)
† Cap. lviii.

building out the sea, and levelling mountains, while we are without the necessaries of life!" But the whole comparison is to the same effect.

Then, can anything be finer than the scene in the Senate where Cicero made his first famous speech? First the historian paints Catiline as full of dissimulation, and acting the part of a suppliant, with downcast look and submissive voice, appealing to the senators whether it was likely a man of his rank and former services should be guilty of the things laid to his charge, while the state was defended by " M. Tullius Cicero, inquilinus civis urbis Romæ" (one living in a hired lodging). Thereupon a loud cry was raised against him, and he was saluted with the name of rebel and parricide. "Tum ille furibundus—' Quoniam quidem circumventus, inquit, ab inimicis, præceps agor, incendium meum ruinâ extinguam.' "*

Thus the Catiline of Sallust; but he of Voltaire, after saying his part is taken, and calling his followers to come away, departs quietly enough—not the *furibundus proripuit* of Sallust, or even the *triumphans gaudio erupit* of Tully—but

> " Vous, sénat, incertain, qui venez de m'entendre,
> Choisissez à loisir le parti qu'il faut prendre."

And so it is throughout; the same contrast between the tame, feeble, vague verses of the modern poet, and

---

* Cap. xxxi. Cicero (pro Muræna, c. xxv.) gives a different account, but less picturesque : " erupit senatû triumphans gaudio ;" and adds, that he had some days before used the famous words in answer to a threat of prosecution from Cato ; but Voltaire was at perfect liberty to choose either version of the fact, and he preferred his own mean and most tame design.

the spirited, the picturesque of the ancient historian,
really a finer poet than he who would needs drama-
tise the story into prose. The battle so exquisitely
painted by Sallust could not indeed be rendered on
the stage, but something of the noble speech that
preceded might have been given. Then how tamely
does Cæsar, in recounting the fight, render the "Memor
generis atque pristinæ dignitatis, in confertissimos
hostes incurrit," and the sad and striking scene displayed after the battle, when "quisque quem pugnando
locum ceperat eum amissâ animâ corpore tegebat;"
but Catiline, on the contrary, was found " longe a suis
inter hostium cadavera, paululum etiam spirans, fero-
ciamque animi quam habuerat vivus in voltu retinens."* This is far from the greatest failure of
Voltaire, but it is a failure, and a failure by de-
parting from the admirable simplicity of the original.

> " Catiline terrible au milieu du carnage,
>   Entouré d'ennemis immolés à sa rage,
>   Sanglant, couvert de traits, et combattant toujours,
>   Dans nos rangs éclairés a terminé ses jours.
>   Sur des morts entassés l'effroi de Rome expire :
>   Romain, je le condamne ; et soldat, je l'admire."

It may here be observed that the admirable trait of
each soldier falling where he fought, but the terrible
chief far apart from all his men, because in advance of
them all, being first left out, the extraordinary effect of
paululum etiam spirans where he had fallen, and the
ferociam animi voltu retinens, are equally abandoned.

---

* One never can read this great masterpiece of narrative without
recollecting Quinctilian's phrase, " Salustii immortalem velocitatem."

One is really tempted to question (as some have questioned) Voltaire's thorough acquaintance with the force of the Latin tongue. Assuredly he very differently judges the eloquence of Massillon, in a language of which, like him, he was so accomplished a master.

It would be unjust to close the ' Rome Sauvée' without awarding just praise to many of its detached parts, and especially of the lines, worthy of Cicero himself, which he is made to pronounce—

> " Romains, j'aime la gloire, et ne veux point m'en taire !
> Des travaux des humains, c'est le digne salaire :
> Sénat ! en vous servant, il la faut acheter ;
> Qui n'ose la vouloir, n'ose la mériter !"

All accounts agree that when Voltaire, at the first representation of the piece in a private theatre, acted this part, his enthusiastic delivery of these words conveying a sentiment so intimately mixed with his whole soul produced such an effect that the audience could hardly tell if it was the poet or the great orator they heard.

The conspiracy of Catiline has afforded not only to Crebillon but to our Ben Jonson. the subject of a tragedy. He copies, by translating, Sallust and Cicero ; but he does not preserve the fire of the one, or the picturesque effect of the other. The speech to the conspirators is but poorly rendered. Thus the *Quin expergiscemini?* by being made an exhortation instead of a reproach, sinks into

> " Wake, wake, brave friends,
> And meet the liberty you oft have wished for."

How much finer the literal version, " Why wake ye

not? See! see! that liberty you so often have wished for." Nothing can be more poor than the version in blank verse of the first Catilinarian, unless perhaps it be Catiline's exclamation on rushing forth from the Senate—

> " I will not burn without my funeral pile :
> It shall be in the common fire rather than mine own,
> For fall I will with all, ere fall alone."

Nor is the speech before the battle better rendered; thus—

> " And if our destiny envy our virtue
> The honour of the day, yet let us vow
> To sell ourselves at such a price as may
> Undo the world to buy us, and make Fate,
> While she tempts ours, fear her own estate."

A piece of rant and fustian which the poet probably thought Sallust had not the genius to think of. The description of Catiline's body after the battle is not perhaps quite so bad, nor the idea lent to the historian so feeble—

> " Yet did his look retain
> Some of its fierceness, and his hands still moved,
> As if he laboured yet to grasp the state
> With these rebellious parts."

Altogether the piece is incomparably inferior to Voltaire's in every part on which a comparison can be made. In learning, it is true, the Frenchman is far surpassed, who might have written his ' Catiline ' without ever having read a line either of the orator or of the historian ; but the Englishman's far greater failure is not excused by his attempt being the more learned.

Of the inferior dramas, 'Alzire' and 'Mahomet' or 'Le Fanatisme' are certainly the best; but they are far from being equal to the 'Zaire' and 'Mérope,' though far superior to the 'Catiline.' The object of both is to present fanaticism in its most dangerous shape—in the union which it not unfrequently forms with great and even with good qualities. This object is well attained, and there is also a mixture of softness in the characters of Alzire and Palmire which forms a pleasing relief to the harsher features of Mahomet, Gusman, and Zamore. Both tragedies contain fine passages of declamation; and the picture of the revolting and hateful character of the Spaniards (in the New World, at least)—that execrable and yet despicable mixture of cruelty and fanaticism, fraud and avarice—with which 'Alzire' opens, is not surpassed in moral descriptive poetry. 'Alzire' was perfectly successful from the first; but the favour which it then enjoyed has worn out. 'Mahomet' was at first only performed at Lile, and during its first representation the news of Frederick's victory at Molwitz having been received by Voltaire, he interrupted the performance to make it known, saying to those around him, "You'll see, that piece of Molwitz will make mine pass." At Paris it was forbidden by the timidity of Cardinal Fleury, alarmed by some passages. Voltaire presented it to the Pope Benedict XIV. (Lambertini), accompanying it with two very indifferent Latin verses as an inscription for his Holiness's portrait. He received an answer full of kindness and liberality from that eminent priest, who also mentioned that an ignorant Frenchman had objected to the quantity of *Hic* in the Latin lines,

and that he had put him down with two lines of
Virgil, showing it to be either long or short, though
he had not read' Virgil for fifty years. Voltaire
replied that a third verse should have been given, and
inscribed on the Pope's picture by all his subjects—

" Hic vir, hic est tibi quem promitti sæpius audis ;"

adding very inaccurately, if not ignorantly, that the
word is both long and short in this line, whereas it is
only long by position.

The late Lord Grantley told me that when he was
a young man fresh from Eton, he passed a few days at
Ferney, and found Voltaire much puzzled to restore,
consistently with the metre, a Latin couplet which a
stranger had made upon him, of which a word or two
had been displaced. The Etonian pleased him exceedingly by at once performing the easy operation—

" Ecce domus qualem Augusti non protulit ætas
    Hic sunt Mæcenas, Virgiliusque simul."

The author of ' Catiline ' had confounded himself by
beginning with *domus*. It must be added, however,
that he wrote an excellent motto for a dissertation
upon heat, which he preferred in the competition for
an academy prize—

" Ignis ubique latet, naturam amplectitur omnem
    Cuncta parit, renovat, dividit, unit, alit."

Crebillon, then director of the Parisian stage, was
far less tolerant towards the ' Mahomet ' than the
Roman pontiff had been, and prohibited the representation of the play for ten years, when D'Alembert
(in 1751), named by D'Argenson to examine it,

reported in its favour with a courage wholly to be expected from him. The success of the piece was great, but, like 'Alzire,' it has not retained its place on the stage.

Many of his other pieces were damned from the first. This was the fate of 'Artemire,' the second which he produced ; but he changed it in some particulars, and it had a great success under the name of 'Mariamne,' as indeed 'Zaire' itself had been the substitute for 'Eryphyle,' which failed. 'Adelaide,' in like manner, failed, and ' Gaston de Foix,' its substitute, had some success. The failure was owing to a jest passed on one of the passages much admired by critics. When Vendôme exclaims, " Es tu content, Couci ?" a wag in the pit cried—" Couci-couci," the French for so-so, or indifferent. A similar practical joke had for a while endangered the performance of ' Mariamne'—some one, on the Queen drinking, cried out "*La Reine boit.*" The panegyrists of Voltaire dwell on these and similar anecdotes, to account for the loss of many of his pieces, but no play of real merit was ever thus destroyed. Many, also, praise the construction of some of them, and dwell especially upon the excellence of the plots. But the theatrical hell is paved with good designs ill executed, as well as the other.

As for the comedies of Voltaire, they are wholly to be rejected : the utmost praise to which they can aspire is as *pièces de société*. They were indeed very little played at any time, except in private parties. The best is the ' Ecossaise,' which never was played at all. It is a bitter satire on Freron, under the name of Frelon (hornet), a profligate, mercenary, libeller,

who, like some of his vile tribe in our own day, earned
a miserable subsistence by selling the venom of his pen
to the cowardly malice of some, and his forbearance to
the less malignant but as despicable timidity of others.
The ' Enfant Prodigue' had considerable success, being
played, it is said, nearly thirty times ; but it was never
known to be Voltaire's till he claimed it some years
after. It is his most elaborate attempt in comedy,
being a piece in five acts. Its verse, in five feet (or ten
syllables), was an innovation, and apparently was not
relished.

Thus, if the distance were less which separates Voltaire's tragedies from the rude and awful grandeur of
the ' Cid,' and the exquisite pathos and perfect harmony
of the ' Phèdre' and ' Athalie,' he would still be, on the
comparison, left far behind Corneille, whose ' Menteur,'
and Racine, whose ' Plaideurs,' continue to keep their
place in the line with the comedies of Molière himself, though the former is partially imitated from the
Spanish, and the latter from the Attic stage.*

The ' Œdipe,' which was first performed in 1718, was
followed in 1722 and 1724 by the ' Artemire' and ' Mariamne,' of which mention has been made, and the poem
of the ' Ligue ' was finished and published in the latter
year, and afterwards given under the name of the ' Henriade.' To this work may be applied the same observation
which the dramatic poetry of the author gives rise to,
—it is beautifully written—it abounds in fine description, in brilliant passages of a noble diction, in senti-

---

* The ' Wasps' of Aristophanes, a satire on the Athenian special
jurymen.

ments admirable for their truth, their liberality, their
humanity,—its tendency is to make fanaticism hateful,
oppression despicable, injustice unbearable; but it is
the grand work of a philosopher and a rhetorician,
more than the inspiration of a poet. No one ever
ventured upon a comparison of this epic with the
' Iliad ' or the ' Odyssey ;' the 'Æneid' has been reckoned
to present more facilities of approach, but at how great
a distance does it leave the ' Henriade !' Even Lucan,
if less tender, is far more majestic ; Tasso has, in every
one essential quality, immeasurably surpassed Voltaire ; with Milton he will not bear to be named,
far less compared ; and Dante, little epic as he is, has
more touches of the poetic fire, more inimitable pictures drawn with a single stroke, more appeals to our
feelings of horror, wonder, and even pity, in a single
canto, than can be found in the whole ten of the ' Henriade.' There abounds in the poem fine writing,
smooth versification, noble ideas, admirable sentiments
—but poetry is wanting. The objection made by
all, or nearly all critics, that the plot is so clumsily
framed as to make the hero a subordinate person for
nearly the first half, and to place over his head as his
sovereign and master one of the most despicable and
even disgusting voluptuaries that ever reigned in modern times, is perhaps not altogether well grounded,
though it has some foundation. Although the
first in rank, Valois (Henry III.) is a cipher, while
his successor is the person actively employed in the
conduct of affairs ; and were the last a sort of mayor of
the palace, the objection would lose its whole force :
but Valois is not at all a *roi fainéant;* we are called

upon to recognise his existence and his acts; we are
even required to feel for him when he falls by the
hands of an assassin;· to accomplish his destruction
the spirits Discord and Fanaticism are evoked from
hell; the form of Guise, whom Valois had murdered,
is assumed, and the King expires uttering a speech
calculated to excite great interest in his fate.

This, however, must be reckoned as the least of the
objections to which the poem is exposed; nor is the
want of scenes surrounded with peril to try the hero's
courage, nor even the feeble and unskilful manner in
which the great event of the piece, Henry's conversion
to obtain the crown, the most fatal defect. The piece
is without dramatic interest; the characters are not
sustained in action, still less in speech—indeed there is
hardly any speaking in the poem. It is truly singular to find a writer, whose forte as a poet lay in
dramatic composition, almost entirely abandon his
stronghold when he comes to compose his epic. The
action proceeds, but it proceeds by way of narrative.
The characters are unfolded, but it is by the descriptions of the author, not by their own words. Indeed
there are very few characters brought forward, and
scarcely any but the hero himself bear their parts in
the action. Want of fine metaphors, and penury of
figurative expression, have been always imputed to it;
and though there is no lack of similes, these are not
very happy. But the cardinal defect is that the author
appears perpetually before us; it is a history rather than
a poem—a history in numerous verse, and beautifully
composed, but not more dramatic, and certainly less
beautifully composed, than many passages of Livy, and

some of Sallust. The objection made to the introduction of philosophy, as having no warrant from the
ancients, is hypercritical, beside being incorrect; Virgil's cosmogony in the sixth Æneid afforded a prece-
dent, if, in a modern poem, any were wanting. The
same answer may be given to the cavil against his
giving characters of persons introduced. Even Virgil
has a few touches of this kind, and Lucan largely
uses his moral pencil. But however admirable these
passages of the 'Henriade,' and how easily soever we
may be disposed to admit them as legitimate, they are
exceptionable, as the only means on which the poet
relies for bodying forth his conceptions. Again and
again the remark occurs; we take the whole of the
portraits and of the action from the artist, and not
from the actors.

If the failures are signal in great passages, such as
called for the full exertion of the poet's power—for
example, the St. Bartholomew, and the famine; the
death of Coligny in the former being altogether tame,
with the exception of the lines which represent him
as a king adored by his people, while his assassins,
awe-struck by his presence, kneel before him;* the
latter being described by words conveying general ideas
of suffering or of disgust, not by things; and the picture of the infernal Catherine de' Medicis receiving
Coligny's head,†—if the failure be still more signal in

---

* " Et de ces assassins ce grand homme entouré,
    Semblant un roi puissant par ses peuple adoré."—(ii. 219.)

† " Medicis le reçut avec indifférence,
    Sans paraître jouir du fruit de sa vengeance,

Sans

the dénouement, Henry's conversion operated by an address of St. Louis to the Almighty, in which, forgetting Massillon's celebrated exordium to Louis XIV.'s funeral sermon, the Saint is actually made to call the hero "*Le Grand Henri*,"—nay, if the details of that conversion are so described as to make it almost appear that Voltaire is laughing in his sleeve,* we must allow the very great beauty of other passages. The description of the Temple of Love, with which the ninth canto opens, is rich and splendid; the picture of St. Louis descending to stay the conqueror's hand in the sixth; the characters drawn so finely and forcibly in the seventh, especially those of Richelieu and Mazarin; the more concise traits by which he paints Guise in the third—

> " Connaissant ses périls, et ne redoutant rien,
> Heureux guerrier, grand prince, et mauvais citoyen ;"

and Morney in the sixth—

> " Il marche en philosophe, où l'honneur le conduit,
> Condamne les combats, plaint son maitre, et le suit ;"—

these are all of the very highest excellence in their kind, though that kind is not epic, hardly poetical. So are such passages of profound sense as the strains of the immortal choir in the seventh canto,—strains " which each star repeated in its course,"—

> Sans remords, sans plaisir, maitresse de ses sens,
> Et comme accoutumée à de pareil encens."—(ii. 242.)

* See particularly x. 480, et seq.—This passage contains the line on transubstantiation which Marmontel admires so much as to pronounce that curse of Fenelon against those who are not moved by

> " A ta faible raison garde-toi de te rendre,
> Dieu t'a fait pour l'aimer, et non pour le comprendre ;
> Invisible à tes yeux, qu'il règne dans ton cœur,
> Il confonde l'injustice, il pardonne à l'erreur ;
> Mais il punit aussi toute erreur volontaire,
> Mortel ouvre les yeux quand son soleil t'éclaire !"

But the finest of all these extraordinary passages are such as in the same Canto, by far the finest of the poem, paint not merely by abstract ideas and by verbose descriptions, but by strokes of genuine poetry, the fiend of Envy :—

> " Là git la sombre Envie, à l'œil timide et louche,
> Versant sur des lauriers les poisons de sa bouche ;
> Le jour blesse ses yeux, dans l'ombre étincelans,
> Triste amante des morts, elle hait les vivans."

> " Pale Envy see, with faltering step advance,
> With look suspicious, indirect, askance,
> With eyes that quiver and abhor the light,
> But flash with fire and sparkle in the night :
> She pours her venom o'er each laureled head,
> Hates all that live, sad lover of the dead."

Of Pride :—

> " Auprès d'elle est l'Orgueil, qui se plait et s'admire."

Of Weakness :—

> " La Faiblesse au teint pale, aux regards abattus :
> Tyran qui cède au crime et détruit les vertus."

> " Weakness, with paly hue and downcast eyes,
> Under whose iron rule vice thrives and virtue dies."

---

the famous couplet in the first Eclogue, "Fortunate senex," &c., " Malheur à qui n'est pas émû en le lisant." I fear many a reader lies under this anathema. The verse is—
> " Et lui découvre un Dieu dans un pain qui n'est plus."
> " And in a loaf that is no more reveals a God."

Of Ambition :—

> " Sanglante, inquiète, égareé,
> De trônes, de tombeaux, d'esclaves entourée."

> " Restless, bloodstain'd, all perils wildly braves,
> Stalks among thrones, and sepulchres, and slaves."

Of Hypocrisy :—

> " La tendre Hypocrisie aux yeux pleins de douceur :
> Le ciel est dans ses yeux, l'enfer est dans son cœur."

> " The tender creature's eyes with sweetness swell :
> Heaven 's in those eyes, and in her heart is hell."

Nor is the song of these furies, on seeing Henry approach their impious troop, without the highest merit :—

> " Quel mortel, disent-ils, par ce juste conduite,
> Vient nous persécuter dans l'éternelle nuit ?"

These are passages of true poetry ; they even approach the seventh Canto to the sixth book of the ' Æneid.' It may be questioned if the ideas of making Envy " triste amante des morts"—Feebleness " tyran qui cède aux crimes et détruit les vertus"—and Hypocrisy " tendre," are equalled by any of Virgil's moral pictures. Certainly to all in the eleventh book of the ' Odyssey ' it is beyond doubt immeasurably superior, as indeed is the sixth Æneid. Nor can we hesitate to affirm that, had the rest of the ' Henriade' been composed in the same poetic spirit, we should not have been suffered with impunity to consider it an elegant history.

In the year 1730 Voltaire wrote part of another poem, which he finished at intervals during the seven or eight years following—his too famous mock-heroic, the ' Pucelle d'Orléans.' It is painful and humiliating to human genius to confess, what yet is without any

doubt true, that this is, of all his poetical works, the
most perfect, showing most wit, most spirit, most of
the resources of a great poet, though of course the
nature of the subject forbids all attempts at either the
pathetic or the sublime ; but in brilliant imagery—in
picturesque description—in point and epigram—in
boundless fertility of fancy—in variety of striking and
vigorous satire—all clothed in verse as natural as
Swift's, and far more varied as well as harmonious—
no prejudice, however naturally raised by the moral
faults of the work, can prevent us from regarding it as
the great masterpiece of his poetical genius. Here of
course the panegyric must close, and it must give way
to indignation at such a perversion of such divine
talents. The indecency, often amounting to absolute
obscenity, which pervades nearly the whole composition, cannot be excused on the plea that it is only a
witty licentiousness, instead of one which excites the
passions ; still less can it be palliated by citing bad precedents, least of all by referring to such writers as
Ariosto, who more rarely violates the laws of decorum ;*

---

* In some of the author's correspondence he is fond of referring
to indelicate passages of other writers in his justification ; nay, even
to the plain language used in some parts of the Old Testament. This
flimsy reason is at once put to flight by Sir Joshua Reynolds's illustration of the nakedness of the Indian and the prostitute. But it is worth
while to observe how carefully the first and greatest of poets avoids
all cause of blame in the passages where he is brought towards the
verge of indecency. The Song of the Bard, in the 8th Odyssey,
where Vulcan's discovery of Mars and Venus is related, is the most
remarkable of these ; and the jocose talk of Apollo and Mars on the
subject savours somewhat of ribaldry. But see the short and simple
expressions used, and mark that nothing is liquorishly dwelt on :—

Ὡς τα πρωτα μιγησαν εν Ἡφαιστοιο δομοισιν.—(viii. 269.)

And—

whereas Voltaire is ready to commit this offence at every moment, and seems ever to take the view of each subject that most easily lends itself to licentious allusions. But this is not all. The 'Pucelle' is one continued sneer at all that men do hold, and all that they ought to hold, sacred, from the highest to the least important subjects, in a moral view—from the greatest to the most indifferent, even in a critical view. Religion and its ministers and its professors—virtue, especially the virtues of a prudential cast—the feelings of humanity —the sense of beauty—the rules of poetical composition—the very walks of literature in which Voltaire had most striven to excel—are all made the constant subjects of sneering contempt, or of ribald laughter; sometimes by wit, sometimes by humour, not rarely by the broad grins of mere gross buffoonery. It is a sad thing to reflect that the three masterpieces of three such men as Voltaire, Rousseau, Byron, should all be the most immoral of their compositions. It seems as if their prurient nature had been affected by a bad but criminal excitement to make them exceed themselves.—Assuredly if such was not Voltaire's case, he well merits the blame; for he scrupled not to read his 'Pucelle' to his niece, then a young woman.*

And—

Αυταρ εγων ευδοιμι παρα χρυσιη Αφροδιτη.—(viii. 342.)

So when describing in the 11th Odyssey Neptune's rape of Pyro, the old bard only says—

Αυσε δε παρθενιην ζωνην, κατα δ'υπνον εχευεν.—(xi. 244.)

* Correspondance Générale, iii. 454.

But here it would be unjust to forget that the same genius which underwent this unworthy prostitution, was also enlisted by its versatile possessor in the service of virtue and of moral truth. There may be some doubt if his moral essays, the 'Discours sur l'Homme,' may not be placed at the head of his serious poetry—none whatever that it is a performance of the highest merit. As the subject is didactic, his talents, turned towards grave reasoning and moral painting, adapted rather to satisfy the understanding than to touch the heart, and addressing themselves more to the learned and polite than to the bulk of mankind, occupied here their appointed province, and had their full scope. Pope's moral essays gave the first hint of these beautiful compositions; but there is nothing borrowed in them from that great moral poet, and there is no inferiority in the execution of the plan. A strict regard to modesty, with the exception of a line or two, reigns throughout, and the object is to inculcate the purest principles of humanity, of tolerance, and of virtue. None but a Romanist bigot could ever have discovered the lurking attack upon religion in the noble verses against substituting vain ceremonies for good works, and attempting to honour the Deity by ascetic abstinence from the enjoyments which he has kindly provided for our happiness. Nay, the finest panegyric on the ministry of Christ is to be found mingled with the same just reprehensions of those who pervert and degrade his doctrines (Disc. vii.), and even the optimism of which in his other works he has ridiculed the extravagant doctrines, is here preached with a pious approval of its moderate and rational faith, (Disc. iii. v.)

His ridicule of saints is confined to the fanatical
devotees or hypocritical pretenders who degrade and
desecrate the name. If he mentions any miracles with
disrespect, it is their false ones, as in that fine passage,
which yet gave offence, in the seventh Discourse—

> " Les miracles sont bons ; mais soulager son frère,
>   Mais tirer son ami du sein de la misère,
>   Mais à ses ennemis pardonner leur vertus,
>   C'est un plus grand miracle, et qui ne se fait plus."

To judge of the admirable tendency of this noble
poem, we need only cite such lines as give the subject
of the first discourse—omitted strangely with some of
the very finest of the whole, as those on Timante,
Cyrus, and De Thou, in the seventh :

> " Mortel, en quelque état que le ciel t'ait fait naitre,
>   Sois soumis, sois content, et rend grace à ton maitre :"

and those on tolerance in the second—

> " Ferme en tes sentimens et simple dans ton cœur,
>   Aime la vérité, mais pardonnez à l'erreur ;
>   Fuis les importuner d'un zèle atrabilaire.
>   Ce mortel qui s'égare est un homme, et ton frère ;
>   Sois sage pour toi seule, compatissant pour lui,
>   Fais ton bonheur enfin par le bonheur d'autrui."

The panegyric on friendship in the fourth is perhaps
unequalled on that trite subject. That point and
satire should be found in this poem was to be expected,
but they are by no means overdone ; nay, they are kept
in subjection to the great and good design of the
work ; and if we have a dark picture strongly but
admirably drawn, it is that of the despicable Des
Fontaines —:

> " Ce vil fripier d'écrits que l'intérèt dévore,
>   Qui vend au plus offrant son encre et ses fureurs,
>   Méprisable en son goût, détestable en ses mœurs.
>   Médisant, qui se plaint des brocards qu'il essuye,
>   Satirique, ennuyeux, disant que tout l'ennuye,
>   Criant que le bon goût s'est perdu dans Paris,
>   Et le prouvant très bien, du moins, par ses écrits."
>
> (Disc. iii.)

> " Huckster of printed wares, who barters still
>   The oil or venom of his hireling quill ;
>   Whose taste and morals are alike impure,
>   And none his writings, none his life endure ;
>   A general slanderer, touch him and he roars,
>   Dully, the dulness of the age deplores,
>   Cries that at Paris taste in books there's none,
>   And proves it if he can but sell his own."

We have also such wholesome morality as the couplet against asceticism in the tenth :

> " Malgré la sainteté de son auguste emploi,
>   C'est n'être bon à rien de n'être bon qu'à toi."

And the noble one in the third against envy—

> " La gloire d'un rival s'obstine à t'outrager,
>   C'est en le surpassant que tu dois t'en venger !"

But some passages have high merit of a more purely poetical cast. There is nothing finer, if anything so fine, in Pope, as the close of the fifth, where he compares his own prosecution of his literary labours, while arrested at Francfort, to Pan's continuing to play while Cacus seized his flocks ; and then breaks out in a strain not surpassed by Virgil—

> " Heureux qui jusqu'au temps du terme de sa vie,
>   Des beaux arts amoureux, peut cultiver les fruits !
>   Il brave l'injustice, ii calme les ennuis,
>   Il pardonne aux humains, il rit de leur délire,
>   Et de sa main mourant il touche encore la lyre."

" Ah, happy he who to life's latest hour
  Of the arts enamour'd, plucks their fruit and flower;
  He braves injustice, snail-pac'd time beguiles,
  Forgives his foes, at human folly smiles.
  Life's glimmering lamp feeds with poetic fire,
  And with his dying fingers sweeps the lyre."

There is, perhaps, one yet greater passage, the conclusion of the third canto:

" Qu'il est grand, qu'il est doux, de se dire à soi-même,
  Je n'ai point d'ennemis, j'ai des rivaux que j'aime,
  Je prends part à leur gloire, a leur maux, à leur biens,
  Les arts nous ont unis, leurs beaux jours sont les miens :
  C'est ainsi que la terre avec plaisir rassemble,
  Ces chênes, ces sapins, qui s'élèvent ensemble,
  Un suc tojuours égal est préparé pour eux ;
  Leur pieds touchent aux enfers, leur cime est dans les cieux ;
  Leur trônc inébranlable, et leur pompeuse tête,
  Résiste, en se touchant, aux coups de la tempête ;
  Ils vivent l'un par l'autre, ils triomphent du temps,
  Tandis que sous leur ombre on voit de vil serpens,
  Se livrer, en sifflant, des guerres intestines,
  Et de leur sang impure arroser leur racines."

The following translation is most imperfect, and has only the merit of being very literal :—

" How grand, how sweet, the heavenly strains ascend,
  Foes I have none, my rival is my friend ;
  The arts unite us, common are our cares,
  And each the other's griefs and glories shares :
  So Earth, our common parent, loves to rear
  Yon oak, yon pine, and make them flourish near ;
  On one green spot the sylvan giants stand,
  Cast one broad shadow o'er the grateful land ;
  Feel the same juice through all their veins arise ;
  Deep pierce their roots entwined, their tops approach the skies.
  Their trunks unshaken, of majestic form,
  Embracing each the other, mock the storm ;
  O'er time they triumph, strong in mutual aid,
  While envious snakes, obscure, frequent their shade,

> And hiss, and sting, and with each other's blood
> Impure, profane the monarchs of the wood."

The ' Loi Naturelle,' though not without considerable beauties, and altogether free from exceptionable
passages, is every way inferior to this fine poem. The
' Désastre de Lisbonne' is of the same merit; and
though the object is to cry down those who deny the
existence of evil, it conducts the argument with perfect
decency—nay, the turn given to it at the close is of a
purely religious character.

> " Le passé n'est pour nous qu'un triste souvenir.
> Le présent est affreux s'il n'est point d'avenir ;
> Si la nuit du tombeau détruit l'être qui pense,
> Un jour tout sera bien—' voilà notre espérance !'
> Tout est bien aujourd'hui—voilà l'illusion !"

> " Sad the remembrance of the moments past,
> And sad the present, if they be the last !
> O'er all our landscape evil sheds a gloom,
> If all our prospect 's bounded by the tomb;
> When we say, ' all is well,' from truth we stray,
> Our comfort is, ' all will be well one day.' "

It is melancholy to reflect on the use which was
sometimes made of such a rich genius, and to think of
the benefits which might have been showered down
upon mankind by the wise and temperate employment
of those treasures. Great as were the services undeniably rendered in spite of the evil mixture, they sink
into nothing compared with what might have been
hoped from their pure and diligent devotion to the
best interests of mankind.

There needs no comment upon the numerous class
of the lighter and shorter productions, the *vers de
société*, the epigrams, the *jeux d'esprit*, in which he

was by common consent admitted to have excelled all
his contemporaries—probably all the wits that ever
lived and wrote. Their great inequality is no doubt
as certain, and it was an inevitable consequence of such
a facility as he possessed, and such an active spirit as
moved him. Their peculiar adaptation to the circumstances that gave them birth is also a necessary concomitant of this kind of composition. But it is singular that the most elaborate of the whole class of his
writings, and the one which he probably most valued,
the ' Guerres civiles de Genève,' is without exception
the worst of all his productions, and can hardly be
matched for dulness and flatness by any undoubted
production in verse of any other eminent poet.

It seemed convenient to discuss the question, or
rather the kind and the degree of what is unquestionable—Voltaire's poetical excellence—on the occasion
of his first success, the ' Œdipe,' in order to take the
whole subject at once, and not to break the continuity
of our narrative each time that a new drama or a new
poem was produced by his fertile genius. We must
now return to the history of his life.

The success of ' Œdipe' placed him, though young,
on the lists of fame, and of dramatic fame, the most
quick of all others, especially at Paris, in its returns
both of profit and social enjoyment. He became the
friend, even the confidant, of the Duc de Richelieu,
and shared in his disgrace under the Regent, being
obliged for a while to quit Paris. But on the representation of the ' Mariamne,' he was permitted to

return, and he soon after accompanied Madame de
Rupelmonde to the Low Countries. To her he addressed in that year, 1722, the 'Epître à Uranie,' a
sceptical rather than a plainly deistical ode, which
possessed some poetical merit, but was forgotten
among his subsequent successes. At Brussels he made
the acquaintance of J. B. Rousseau, and laid the
foundation of the unrelenting animosity with which
that middling writer and irritable personage pursued
him ever after. This he owed to a jest; having told
him, on reading his 'Ode to Posterity,' "that it would
never reach its destination." Rousseau, himself the
author of many licentious epigrams against the clergy,
hypocritically affected to take offence at the 'Epître à
Uranie,' and at Voltaire's irreverent demeanour during
mass. Had he but spared the truth which he spoke
in jest on the bad ode, he might have scoffed with
Lucian and blasphemed with Borgia.

He now endeavoured in vain to regain the enjoyment he most loved—the society of Paris. An
unfortunate quarrel with the Chevalier de Rohan
exposed him to the resentment of the Court, and the
risk of again inhabiting the Bastille. Some epigram
or jest at the Chevalier's expense had been reported
to him, and he basely set his servants on the wit,
whom they severely beat. A challenge was the consequence; but as the poet's rank did not authorize this
liberty, he was on the point of being handed over to
the police, or secured by a *lettre de cachet*, and he
resolved to fly. His plan was to visit England, attracted by her liberty, and above all, by that which he
seems ever to have valued most—the spirit of toler-

ance and the security against ecclesiastical oppression. He lived above two years in London and its neighbourhood, chiefly at Wandsworth, in the house of a friend, Mr. Falconer, then a respectable Turkey merchant, afterwards Ambassador to the Porte and Secretary to the Duke of Cumberland. During this residence he corrected the 'Henriade:' it was now published under that name, by a subscription, which Queen Caroline, then Princess of Wales, warmly patronized, and which produced a large sum of money. He likewise devoted himself with his wonted zeal and success to the study of the Newtonian philosophy. He lived in the society of our literary men; though the great age of Sir Isaac Newton prevented him from forming any acquaintance with him whose system he was destined first to make known in Europe. With Pope and with Congreve he had many interviews: for the former he acquired a respect and esteem which the similarity of their poetical genius naturally cemented, and which no envy or jealousy ever interrupted; of the latter, he is said to have formed a less favourable judgment. The silly affectation of telling him, when he came to admire the Molière of England, that he valued himself, not on his authorship, but would be regarded as a man of the world, received a just rebuke: "I should never have come so far to see a gentleman," said Voltaire.

This journey to England had two important consequences. The money which he obtained, and which he afterwards increased by a lucky chance in the lottery, and by engaging in one or two successful mercantile speculations, yielded him an ample income for the rest of his life; so that he cared little for the profits of his works, and indeed gave many of them to the booksellers and the actors for nothing. Not only was he thus secured in the state of independence which is an author's best protection against crude and hasty composition, but he was able to follow the bent of his taste in choosing his subjects, and of his disposition both to encourage young authors of merit, and to relieve the distresses of deserving persons. Proofs also remain which place beyond all doubt his kindness to several worthless men, who repaid it with the black ingratitude so commonly used as their current coin by the base and spiteful, who salve their own wounded pride by pouring venom on the hand that saved or served them.

But his residence in England had a still more important result—the importation he made from thence of the Newtonian system, or rather, of all Sir Isaac Newton's wonderful discoveries. So deeply rooted were the prejudices of our Continental neighbours in favour of the Cartesian philosophy, that when Fontenelle pronounced his éloge of Newton, at the Académie des Sciences, he gave the preference to Des Cartes; and even ten years later, the Chancellor D'Aguesseau refused the licence to print Voltaire's work because it denied and disproved the *Vortices*— an act of narrow-minded bigotry in science scarcely to be matched in all its annals. Voltaire, soon after his return from England, published his ' Lettres sur les Anglais'—a candid and intelligent work; and in three of these he gives a very correct though extremely general and popular sketch of Newton's discoveries.

But in 1738 appeared his more full and satisfactory
account of them, and it certainly does the greatest
honour to its author. This work owes its origin,
however, not more to the English residence of the
author, than to the intimacy which he formed soon
after his return to France, about the year 1730, with
the family of Du Chatelet; and before considering
the merits of the book, it may be convenient to dwell
for a little while upon the history of that celebrated
attachment.

The Marquess had married several years before a
lady of high rank, Gabrielle Emilie de Breteuil, much
younger than himself; and, according to the manners of
those times and that country, she herself had not been
consulted upon the match when her parents gave her
away. When Voltaire became acquainted with her,
she was in her twenty-fourth year, and one of the
most remarkable persons, both for beauty, talents, and
accomplishments, that adorned the French Court, or
the refined society of Paris. At first her acquaintance
with the poet was of an ordinary kind, probably formed
by the reputation of the wit and the rank of the lady.
But the literary taste of the Marchioness found so
much improvement and such constant gratification in
the great resources of his various knowledge, his versatile talents, and his inexhaustible wit, that it can be
no wonder if his society soon became necessary to a
woman of her decided inclination for literary and scientific pursuits. The fame which he had acquired as
a dramatist, and in the brilliant circles of Paris society,
would have riveted the attention of an ordinary
woman, to whom he showed a desire of devoting him-

self. But though she was herself fond of all the
common amusements of her rank and sex, lived in the
circles of the court as might be expected of a Breteuil,
and cultivated all the graces even as displayed in the
lighter accomplishments, it seems doubtful if she
would have formed so decided a predilection for the
company of any one who had not begun to cultivate
those severer sciences to which she gave a marked preference. Nor can we much question the probability
of Voltaire having, after his return from England,
turned his attention far more to these studies than he
otherwise would have done, in order to make a progress not only in philosophy, but also in the good graces
of a person so distinguished in every way, young,
handsome, noble, attractive, as well as learned beyond the ordinary measure even of man's information,
endowed with talents both solid and ornamental, and
inspired by a taste for the graver as well as the lighter
pursuits of genius. The difficulties in which he was
involved by a lettre de cachet threatened, if not issued,
on account of the ' Letters ' after his return from England, had obliged him to leave Paris. There seems every
reason to believe that the arrangement by which he became an inmate in the Marquess's house was formed
about the same time, and that he found a refuge at the
château of Cirey in Champagne, whither the literary
tastes of the Marchioness had made her resolve to withdraw from the frivolity of the court and the dissipation
of the capital, and had enabled her to prevail with the
Marquess, who yielded to this new plan of life. They
had at this time a son and a daughter; and an Abbé
named Linant was engaged as the tutor of the former,

while the Marchioness herself superintended the latter's education.

The château of Cirey, on the confines of Champagne and Lorraine, had, like most French country houses, fallen into some disrepair. Steps were immediately taken to put it in order, and a considerable addition of a gallery and a laboratory, or cabinet of natural philosophy, was made to it under Voltaire's superintendence. The elegance and even luxury of the apartments is described as very great. He likewise furnished the funds required for the improvements, by lending the Marquess 40,000 francs, and by providing a portion of the furniture, of the apparatus, and of the library, which became a sufficiently large one for all ordinary purposes. It appears, that soon after the building was finished, he reduced his claim to 30,000 francs, and agreed to take in lieu of that sum an annuity of 2000 francs. Fifteen years, however, elapsed without any payment of the annuity; and though the arrears now amounted to 30,000 francs, he agreed to receive 15,000 both for these arrears and for the remainder of his life-interest in the annuity : of this 15,000 francs it does not appear that he ever received more than 10,000—so that he gave up altogether a sum of about 2000*l.* sterling, principal and interest.* But he appears constantly to have assisted the household with money, which the careless habits of the Marquess, and the yet less worldly nature of the Marchioness, occasionally rendered necessary. The income of the Marquess

---

* A sum equal at the present time, and in England, to at least 6000*l.*

was about 40,000 francs, equal to about 6000*l.* in this country at the present time.

The family appears to have lived together in great harmony, though occasionally somewhat broken by the rather impetuous temper of the fair analyst. They led a retired, contemplative, and studious, but by no means a dull or unvaried life. Visits were occasionally made to Paris ; in Brussels and the Hague it became necessary to pass some time, partly on account of Voltaire's work then printing there, the 'Elements,' partly on account of a law-suit by which the family had been exhausted for sixty years, and of which Voltaire's active interposition obtained the amicable settlement, by payment to the Marquess of 220,000 francs.

Some of the greatest mathematicians of the age frequented the château, and assisted the Marchioness in her studies. Kœnig and his brother, disciples of the Bernouillis, passed two years there ; but also D. Bernouilli himself was occasionally a visitor ; and so was the illustrious Clairault. Maupertuis, a man of very inferior mark, but esteemed at that time, when his journey to measure a degree in Lapland caused him to be overrated, was more than once the Marquess's guest and his wife's instructor or fellow-student. The Marchioness seldom dined with the family, whose dinnerhour was twelve ; but they more frequently assembled all together to supper at eight in the evening. Though the Marchioness was chiefly engaged in her 'Commentaries on Newton,' and her able and learned translation of the 'Principia,' she could distract her mind from such studies by the pleasures of music and of the stage ; and we find Voltaire telling friends whom he is inviting to visit them, that "plays are made daily, and Jupiter's satellites observed nightly (Cor. Générale, iii. 184) ; that they will be free to pass the mornings in their own apartments, and will hear read in the evening the compositions of the day ; and that the Marchioness 'joue ou l'opéra, ou la comédie, ou la comète' " (*ib.* 312). Indeed Voltaire himself exhibited perhaps the most remarkable instance of varied and versatile talents on record, by producing, within the same three or four years, the Newtonian ' Elements,' his prize essay on ' Fire,' ' Zaire,' ' Alzire,' ' Mahomet,' ' the Discours sur l'Homme,' more than half of the ' Pucelle,' the ' History of Charles XII.,' besides an endless variety of minor pieces, and some volumes of correspondence in prose and verse. The ' Pucelle' was begun to amuse him while obliged to fly from Paris in 1734 by the persecutions he suffered on account of the ' Letters on England.'

It was at Cirey, then, with a few weeks passed in 'Sgravesande's society at Leyden, that Voltaire composed, and finally prepared for publication, his 'Elements of the Newtonian Philosophy,' as well as his ' Essay on Fire;' and of both these works we may now treat.

In order to estimate the merits of the work on Sir Isaac Newton's discoveries, we must first consider the state in which it found the Newtonian system on the Continent; next, the helps which he had in writing it.

There can be no doubt that Clairault, destined afterwards to confirm the theory of the moon's motions, though at first, with others, to undergo a temporary error upon the subject,—destined also to join with D'Alembert and Euler in explaining the disturbing forces by working out the problem of the three

bodies,—destined, finally, to bring the disturbances in
the trajectories of comets within the theory of planetary
attraction, very early, probably before Voltaire, adopted
the Newtonian philosophy; for, though only fifteen
years old when Voltaire's 'Letters' were written, he
had, when only thirteen, begun his admirable work on
Curves of Double Curvature, and it was published
very soon after the 'Letters' appeared. But it is certain
he had given nothing to the world on the theory of
gravitation.   Maupertuis had probably, in scientific
circles, professed his conversion, and intimated that he
renounced the Cartesian philosophy; but until after his
return from Lapland, in 1738, he never made any public profession of his faith, his 'Commentary,' in 1732,
being confined to the dynamical subject of the 12th Section of the 'Principia' (Book I.).   Voltaire's 'Letters,'
therefore, published in 1732, first defended generally,
and his 'Elements,' in 1738, defined in detail the new
system, and gave an explanation of it so clear and
popular, as in all likelihood neither Maupertuis nor
Clairault could have furnished.   He therefore justly
claims the glory of first making the Newtonian system accessible to the bulk of European readers, of
fully refuting the Cartesian errors, and of boldly opposing a doctrine which, of all philosophical tenets
since Aristotle's philosophy, had taken the strongest
hold of men's minds.   Indeed, the prejudices in favour
of the Vortices, like those in favour of the Aristotelian
philosophy, appear to have partaken of the zeal, and
even of the intolerant spirit, which theological dogmas
are too often found to excite.   Fontenelle, in his
'Eloge' of Newton, had shown his adhesion to Des

Cartes. The Chancellor D'Aguesseau, as I have already remarked, could never be prevailed upon to grant a licence for printing Voltaire's work; he kept the manuscript in his possession for eight months, and ended by refusing his permission—a piece of folly and bigotry worthy of that eminent and virtuous, but feeble character, which had made him also refuse the licence to print a novel, unless the hero was made to change his religion and become a Catholic. Even the 'Letters on England' had suffered persecution, partly from their opposing Des Cartes, but chiefly because, with Locke, they denied innate ideas, which the bigoted clergy deemed an approach to materialism, or at any rate, a doctrine tending to level the human mind with that of the lower animals—a doctrine, however, it must be observed, for that very reason somewhat favourable to themselves. The result of their efforts was a lettre de cachet, and Voltaire's sudden flight from Paris. Another consequence very discreditable to him was his positive and public denial of the authorship, and affirming that the letters had been written by his early patron, the Abbé Chaulieu, now no more. These letters were first published in London by his friend M. Theiriot, who caused them to be translated into English, in which language they first appeared. He was allowed to reap the whole profits of the work. Afterwards Voltaire gave a bookseller at Rouen leave to publish the original French; but withdrew his consent as soon as he perceived the trouble into which the work would bring him. His countermand, however, arrived too late, and he suffered great annoyance in consequence. It is usually represented that this book, containing his more general sketch of the Newtonian system, was written as early as 1727 or 1728; but this is certainly incorrect. The letters were in great part written while he was living at the house of Mr. Falconer at Wandsworth; but those on Sir Isaac Newton's discoveries were so far from being then finished, that they were probably not commenced; for we find in the 'Correspondance' letters as late as the autumn of 1732, in which he consulted Maupertuis upon the doctrine of attraction, and was wavering between that and the vortices. There are no less than five letters written by him on this subject; and after his objections to the Newtonian doctrine had been removed by Maupertuis, he falls back and sends him a long paper on the moon's motion, dated 5th November, 1732.* The 'Letters' at length appeared, however, and his own account of that portion of them is at once accurate and witty. "I carefully avoid entering into calculations," he says: "I am like a person who settles with his steward, but does not go to work arithmetically." The 'Elements' were written between 1732 and 1736, were finished about that time, and were published in 1738.

The other matter for consideration is the assistance which Voltaire had privately in preparing this work. It is clear that he must have begun his physical studies with a very indifferent provision of mathematical knowledge. It is equally clear that he studied natural philosophy with Madame du Chatelet, who had a particular taste for the mathematics. She had

---

* Cor. Gén., i. 244 et seq., and 259; ii. 493, 514.

received instruction from Maupertuis; some also from Clairault before he went to Lapland; but she received still more from him after he returned to Cirey. He had fully instructed her in the Newtonian philosophy, and in the method of conducting the demonstrations of the 'Principia' analytically—a most invaluable service to any student at that time, when the excellent commentary of the Jesuits* (Le Sueur and Jacquier) had not appeared: she reduced his lessons to writing, and they were afterwards published among her posthumous works.† Her 'Institutes de Physique' were published in 1740, and contain a very accurate account of the Newtonian system; and as it is clear, from Voltaire's Correspondence, that the work was written before the beginning of that year, it can admit of no doubt that she was acquainted with the Newtonian philosophy at the time he was writing his 'Elements;' the printing of which began early in 1737, and continued nearly two years. He therefore derived all the benefit that his knowledge of the subject enabled him to receive from Clairault; and Kœnig lived at Cirey the whole of the years 1738 and 1739, so as to make the revision of the book by him very possible while it passed through the press. He admits Madame du Chatelet's share in the work, in express terms, to Frederick II.‡ The access to these helps, however, does not materially lessen his

---

* They were Minimes, and not Jesuits as they are always called.

† Voltaire (Mémoires, Œuv., i. 219) erroneously ascribes this to Madame du Chatelet herself, and says it was revised by Clairault. The 'Mémoires' abound in error. Thus they make the journey to Luneville in 1749, instead of 1748.

‡ Cor. avec les Souverains, i. 60.

merits. Indeed he had the benefit of Pemberton's 'General View,' which was published as early as 1728, and is more than once referred to by him. Maclaurin's was not published till 1748.

That Voltaire had, or in consequence of sympathy with Madame du Chatelet acquired, some taste for the mathematics is certain. He even prosecuted the study with considerable assiduity. After making some progress he consulted Clairault, and asked him if he could conscientiously advise him to persevere in the pursuit—to go on with the cultivation of a science which is commonly supposed to require an undivided homage from its votaries, though D'Alembert's example negatives the assumption. We are not informed of the grounds upon which Clairault candidly gave his opinion that the science of number and quantity was not Voltaire's vocation; whether he found him ill grounded in a branch of knowledge which he had studied late, or saw in any attempts at original investigation that his genius lay not that way. It is, however, to be lamented that his advice was either given so generally, or so generally construed and followed, as to make no exception in favour of experimental philosophy, in which I am strongly inclined to think, and shall presently explain why, his acuteness, his industry, his sagacity, above all his brave contempt of received opinions, and his deep-rooted habit of judging every proposition by its own merits, would in all probability have ranked him among the discoverers of the age.

The 'Elémens' is a work of a much higher order than the 'Letters,' and does great credit both to his industry and his accuracy. It is indeed so free from errors, although it is by no means a superficial account of the Newtonian philosophy, that, with the limited knowledge of mathematics which Voltaire possessed, we can hardly conceive his having avoided mistakes, and must therefore suppose that either 'Sgravesande, with whom he passed some time at Leyden, while the work was in the press, or Kœnig, who was then living at Cirey, must have gone over and revised it. There is no greater mistake than theirs who call the ' Elements' a flimsy or superficial work. The design of it is not to enter minutely into the profound investigations of the ' Principia,' or to follow · all the exquisite inductive processes of the ' Optics,' but to give the great truths unfolded in both these immortal works, with a certain portion of the evidence on which they rest, so that the reader unacquainted with the mathematics beyond the mere definitions, and perhaps one or two of the elementary propositions in geometry, may be able to form an accurate notion of the reasoning that supports the mighty system. The design is this ; that design is executed ; and the power of explaining an abstract subject in easy and accurate language, language not in any way beneath the dignity of science, though quite suited to the comprehension of uninformed persons, is unquestionably shown in a manner which only makes it a matter of regret that the singularly gifted author did not carry his torch into all the recesses of natural philosophy. It must be added, that, beside explaining the discoveries of Newton, he has given an equally clear view of the science as it stood before those great changes were effected: The Cartesian system is fully explained, and the outline of optical science, independent of Newton's researches, is more extended and more elaborate than the account of those researches. The second part relates to the nature and action of light; the third to the system of the world; and the first part enters at some length into the general doctrines of mind, matter, force, and motion, even dealing with the doctrines of natural religion.

Whoever reads the work attentively, allowing it the full praise so justly its due, will find it wholly incapable of furnishing any proof that the author had ever read either the 'Principia' or the 'Optics.' There is no reference to those writings which at all shows that he had ever seen a line of them. In the controversy with the Cartesians, which he carried on after the 'Elements' were published, he cites the 96th proposition (meaning of the first book of the 'Principia,' although he does not mention the book); but it is only to speak of optical matters. He also refers to the *Scholium Generale*; but that has been constantly cited, and for the most part at second hand, by those who never read any other part of the work. It is further to be observed, that no account whatever is given, nor even any mention made, of the Second Book, concerning motion in resisting media;—indeed there are indications more positive of his not having drunk at the pure source itself. If he had been acquainted with the 'Optics,' in describing the induction by which the composition of white light is proved, he never surely would have omitted the *experimentum crucis.* He gives (Part ii. chap. 10) the composition of the

spectral rays by means of a lens, and their forming
white in the focus ; but he leaves entirely out the
decisive experiment of stopping different portions of
the spectrum, and then finding that the focus is no
longer white, but of the colour, or mixture of colours,
suffered to pass onward.   It is perhaps a proof of the
same kind, that he states what he certainly never could
have learnt in the 'Optics,' the blue colour of the sky
as caused by the great attenuation of the vapours arising in the atmosphere (Part ii. chap. 12).   Nor could
any one who had studied the same admirable work
have confined himself almost entirely to one portion
of it, and give scarcely any account, except the most
general, and indeed meagre, of the colours of thin
plates, and none at all of the colours of thick plates.

With respect to the 'Principia,' he gives with considerable fulness the doctrine of equal areas in equal
times ; and indeed, from his account, the demonstration
as well as the fundamental proposition itself may be
gathered.   But then comes this very summary statement of the planetary law :—" Enfin Newton a prouvé
que si la courbe décrite autour du centre est une ellipse,
la force attractive est en raison inverse du carré des
distances" (Part iii. chap. 4).   He indeed leaves us here
to infer, quite contrary to the truth, that the same
proportion is peculiar to motion in an ellipse ; and he
makes no mention whatever of the inverse problem,
the deducing the curve from the force—the more important of the two.

There is a profound view given of the irregularity in
the moon's motion caused by disturbance (Part iii.
chap. 6), and one or two other parts of the treatise

deserve the same praise. A possibility exists of these
having been written by another hand. It seems difficult to suppose the same very accurate writer could be
the author of such passages as we meet with in the de-
fences of the work against the Cartesians. Thus, in the
' Courte Réponse aux longs Discours d'un Docteur Alle-
mand,' we find him saying he had expected repose, but
now discovered that " la racine carré du cube des révo-
lutions des planètes et les carrés de leurs distances
fesaient encore des ennemis ;" in which allusion there
are three capital blunders ; the square root of the cube
is taken for the cube, the revolutions for the distances,
and the squares for the cubes.

In 1737 both Voltaire and Madame du Chatelet were
competitors for the prize of the Academy of Science.
The subject was, " The nature of fire and its propagation." Neither paper was successful, but both were
honourably mentioned by the committee of examination, and both were printed as a mark of approval.
When it is added that the illustrious Euler gained the
prize, surely we may well be permitted to say that no
discredit could result from being surpassed by such a
rival. But Voltaire's paper is of great merit. He
takes bold and original views, and describes experiments which, had he pursued them with more patience, would probably have enrolled his name among
the greatest discoverers of his age. It is impossible
to have made a more happy conjecture than he
does upon the weight acquired by metals when calcined. After describing an experiment made by him
with melted iron, " Il est très possible," says he. " que
cette augmentation de poid soit venue de la matière

repandue dans l'atmosphère : donc dans toutes les autres opérations par lesquelles les matières calcinées acquièrent du poids, cette augmentation de substance pourrait aussi leur être venue de la même cause, et non de la matière ignée." About half a century later this conjecture was verified, when the composition of the atmosphere was discovered. Had Voltaire followed up his felicitous conjecture by one or two experiments, he would very probably have discovered both the nature of oxygen and the process of oxydation, which last, indeed, he had in general terms described.

Again, how near does he approach to the true theory of fluidity, and even to the discovery of latent heat, when, speaking of the effects on the thermometer of mixing ammonia and vinegar, he says, " Il y a certainement du feu dans ces deux liqueurs, sans quoi elles ne seraient point fluides ;" and afterwards speaking of the connection between heat and permanent or gaseous elasticity, he says, " N'est-ce pas que l'air n'a plus alors la quantité de feu nécessaire pour faire jouir toutes ses parties, et pour le dégager de l'atmosphère engourdie qui le renferme ?" The experiments which he made on the heat of fluids mixed together, of different temperatures before their mixture, led him to remark the difference of the temperature when mixed from what might have been expected by combining the separate temperatures before mixture. Need I add that this is precisely the course of experiment and observation which led Black to his celebrated discovery of latent heat a quarter of a century later?

It was in these studies that the time passed at

Cirey, in these various pursuits of philosophy, of history, of poetry. But some important incidents in Voltaire's life, beside his literary successes, happened during his intimacy with the Du Chatelets. His only sister, of whom he appears to have been fond, had died while he was in England, leaving a son and two daughters. Of these, now grown up, he took a parental care, and exerted himself to marry them suitably. One, in 1737, married M. Denis, a captain in the Régiment de Champagne, who died some years after (1744), and his widow ultimately came to live with her uncle, and passed nearly thirty years under his roof. Her sister married, some years later, a M. de Fontaine. During the same period of his residence at Cirey, the Prince Royal of Prussia, afterwards Frederick II., courted his acquaintance by letter, and began a correspondence of mutual compliment and even veneration, which lasted till he became king at his father's death, in 1740. At that time he made a fruitless attempt to make Voltaire fix his residence at Berlin, and would have almost let him dictate his own terms; but as long as Madame du Chatelet lived, these offers were frankly and peremptorily refused. Voltaire being near Brussels, the King, who happened to be in that neighbourhood soon after his accession, proposed coming to wait upon the poet; but, being prevented by a severe ague, Voltaire went to him, and had his first interview while the fit was upon the royal patient in bed. He undertook to publish for him his first work, the ' Anti-Machiavel.' But unfortunately, while it was passing through the press, the death of Charles VI. left his daughter Maria Theresa in a condition of such weakness as exposed the royal combatant of Machiavel's principles to an irresistible temptation, and he made upon her province of Silesia one of the most unprovoked and unjustifiable attacks of which history has left any record. It is singular enough that, in the history which he afterwards wrote of the war, he in plain terms had stated as the cause of it, his possessing a fine army, and great treasure, which his father's recent death had left him, and his inability to resist the temptation of her weakness. Voltaire, on revising the work, struck this singular passage out of it; but, having kept a copy, he has given it in his 'Memoirs.'*

The favour which he was known to enjoy with Frederick induced the French ministry, three years after, to employ him in a secret mission, which he appears to have fulfilled with much success. He went to Berlin under cover of visiting his royal and literary correspondent, and obtained from him the assurance, that a declaration of war by France against England, then taking the Empress-Queen's part, would be fol-

---

* The passage thus erased and thus preserved is extremely curious, and for honesty or impudence has no parallel in the history of warriors :—

"Que l'on joigne à ces considérations, des troupes toujours prêtes d'agir, mon épargne bien remplie, et la vivacité de mon caractère, c'était les raisons que j'avais de faire la guerre à Marie Thérèse, Reine de Bohémie et de Hongrie,—l'ambition, l'intérêt, le désir de faire parler de moi, l'importèrent ; et la guerre fut résolue." (Mém. 238.) If every man who enters upon a voluntary war would speak out, we should have the same commentary on the lives of all the butchers who disgrace and afflict our species. Nothing, certainly, can more eloquently describe their cold-blooded wickedness than these words of Frederick.

lowed by an immediate co-operation with France on
his part. The favour which Voltaire thus obtained not only with the ministry, but with Madame
de Pompadour, then all-powerful, produced an impression which all his fine writings had failed to make.
He was allowed to enter the Academy, from which
court influence had before excluded him; he was
named gentleman of the King's chamber; and he received a pension of 2000 francs a year.

The tranquil pleasures of letters and of friendship,
which form so much the burthen of his song during
his residence at Cirey, were in the mean time suffering constant interruption, as he would represent, from
the libels of persons every way below his notice, but,
in reality, from his own irritable temper. The vehemence of the language in which he describes those
attacks, makes the reader believe that the charges
against him were of a heinous kind, and that the ac-
cusers were persons of importance; when both are
examined, they generally turn out to be equally insignificant. One attack only, which absurdly accuses
him of having failed to account for subscriptions to
the 'Henriade,' he did right in requiring a friend to
refute, who was personally acquainted with the whole
matter, having devoted to his own use part of the
money so received. He seems to have had some ground
for complaining that this gentleman, a M. Theiriot,
was slow in vindicating him; but his principal grievance is that Theiriot refused to attack the slander
in his own person, and to repeat in public what he
had so often written privately, that the accuser was
the author of other libels against them both, and was

the Abbé des Fontaines, a man of some reputation for
ability, but leading a life of scandalous libelling, and
whose ingratitude to Voltaire was sufficient to stamp
him with infamy, as to his kind exertions had been owing the Abbé's escape from a charge of the most detest-
able nature.   It is, however, a stain scarcely less deep
on Voltaire's own memory, that although he firmly believed in the man's innocence, as indeed every one else
did, he was no sooner enraged by the ungrateful return his services received, than he recurred to the
false charges in all his letters—nay, even by a plain
allusion in more than one passage of his poems, of
which we have already seen an instance in the 'Discours sur l'Homme.'   He took a more legitimate course
of punishing him by prosecuting the libel (a satire
entitled 'Voltairemanie'), and compelled the vile and
abandoned slanderer to sign a public denial of it, and
a complete disbelief of its contents.

Under the vexation which such attacks gave him,
he was comforted not only by the friendship which he
found always in his home at Cirey, but by the unvarying kindness of M. le Cidville, a respectable
magistrate of Rouen, fond of literature; by the steady
friendship of M. le Comte d'Argental, a man of large
fortune, and owner of the Isles de Rhé and Aix, off
the west coast, and his wife; by the unbroken attachment of M. d'Argenson, Secretary of State, his
brother, the War Minister, and the Duc de Richelieu.
It should seem as if Voltaire was, in his familiar
intercourse, the better for being kept under some restraint by the superior rank, or other preponderating
qualities, of his friends.   Some such calming influ-

ence was necessary for his irritable nature. Jealousy formed no part of his character; he had a rooted horror of envy, as mean and degrading ; he was always well disposed to encourage rising merit and enjoy the success of his friends, perhaps all the more readily when he aided them by his patronage and counsels; but he was easily offended, ready to believe that any one had attacked him, prone to take alarm at intended insult or apprehended combination against him; and as his nature was fundamentally satirical, he was unable to resist the indulgence of the very humour of which he could so ill bear being himself made the subject. Those who were at all dependent on him, his Theiriots and his publishers, found much less magnanimity than kindness in his temper. With his equals he rarely continued very long on cordial terms. Maupertuis, indeed, had no excuse for his proceedings ; but the extravagances of J. J. Rousseau's crazy nature might well have been overlooked, and never should have been made the subjects of such deadly warfare as Voltaire waged against him. The other Rousseau's enmity he owed entirely to himself, as we have seen; it is extremely probable that Des Fontaines was set against him by hearing of his sarcasms on a subject to which all reference was proscribed; and his persevering attacks on Le Franc de Pompignan arose from no cause beyond some general reflections on philosophers in his inaugural discourse at the Academy ; nor was he ever just enough to allow the singular merit of some, at least, of the Abbé's poetry.* It is certainly one, and a principal, cause of

---

* It might be absurd enough in Mirabeau (the elder) to exalt him

the constant disputes, the hot water he lived in, that he was always writing, generally writing something offensive of somebody; and almost as generally writing something which was likely to call down the indignation of the constituted authorities in Church and State. But had he kept his writings to himself, or only published them anonymously without any confidants, his pen would have less frequently disturbed his repose. Instead of this, he generally began by showing his compositions, often by suffering copies to be taken; sometimes these were published without his leave; but often he allowed them to be printed, and straightway complained when the authorship was discovered. His denials then knew no bounds, either for repetition or for solemnity; and we have seen in the instance of the 'Letters on England' how little scrupulous he was in what manner he confirmed his asseverations, by laying the blame upon others. To this double source of the difficulties into which his writings brought him with the government, and of the individual resentment which they occasioned, may very many of his quarrels and anxieties be traced.

But another circumstance must be mentioned, as throwing light upon his personal altercations with the friends he at various times esteemed. His nature was open and ardent; he had the irritability which oftentimes accompanies genius, but he had the warm temperament, the generous self-abandonment, the uncalculating effusion of sentiment, which is also its

into the first of modern poets, as our Locke did Blackmore; yet few passages in Voltaire's own writings can compare with the famous simile of the Egyptians, and their sacrilegious abuse of the Sun.

attendant, and which sixty years' living in the world never cured—hardly mitigated—in Voltaire. His expressions were, no doubt, stronger than his feelings; but we know that this strength of expression has a certain re-action, and excites the feelings in its turn; certainly is ever taken into the account when its object makes a bad or a cold requital, and irritates the minds from which it had proceeded, if in no other way, at least by wounding their pride. Nothing can be more extravagant than the technology of Voltaire's affections : " My dearest friend" is too cold to be almost ever used; it is " My dear and adorable friend ;" " My guardian angel ;" " My adorable friend ;" and often to the Argentals especially the union of both, " My adorable angels." All philosophers are Newtons; all poets Virgils; all historians Sallusts; all marshals Cæsars. The work of the President Henault is not certainly " *son*," but " *votre* charmante, votre immortel ouvrage :" being the most dry and least charming history that ever was penned, and which never would be read but as a convenient chronicle. The expressions of affection, of eternal, warm, even passionate affection, are lavished constantly and indifferently. Nay, to one friend, a Marshal and Duke (Richelieu), he says, addressing him as Monseigneur, "Il y a dans Paris force vieilles et illustres catins, à qui vous avez fait passer de joyeux moments, mais il n'y en a point qui vous aime plus de moi."* With all this vehemence of feeling and facility of effusion, as well as of exaggeration, there was joined an irritability that brought

---

* Corr. Gén. iv. 193.

on cold fits occasionally, and then the snow, or rather the hail, fell as easily and abundantly as the tepid showers had before descended. Nothing can exceed his affection for his nieces, especially for Madame Denis; but he must have outraged her feelings severely, to draw from her such a letter as she wrote in 1754: "Ne me forcez pas à vous haïr"—"Vous êtes le dernier des hommes par le cœur"—"Je cacherai autant que je pourrais les vices de votre cœur"—are expressions used principally on account, not of his heart, which was sound, but his temper, which was uncontrolled, and they were used to him while lying on a sick bed at Colmar, which he had not quitted for six months. I shall have occasion afterwards to speak more particularly of his quarrels with Maupertuis, Frederick II., and Rousseau; in the first of which, the chief fault lay with the mathematician; in the second, the great king claims the whole blame; and in the third, Voltaire was most censurable. At present, I have only entered upon the topics which arise during his residence at Cirey.

The same exaggeration that pervades his expressions towards others, is observable in all that he writes respecting himself, whether upon the sufferings of his mind or those, somewhat more real, of his body. He had, unhappily, a feeble constitution, and having taken little care of it in early life, he was a confirmed invalid for the rest of his days; but especially between forty and sixty. He suffered from both bladder complaints and those of the alimentary canal; and his surgical maladies, beside the pain and irritation which they directly occasioned, gave him all the sufferings and inconveniences of a bad digestion. There was therefore a sufficient foundation for frequent recourse to the state of his health. But he writes as if he was not merely in constant danger : he is generally at the point of death ; and it is observable that the more deeply he is engaged in any vexatious dispute, and the more he has, or thinks he has, occasion to complain of maltreatment, the more regularly and the more vehemently does he describe his alarming, nay, his dying condition. In such circumstances it is a figure never wanting to round a period, or to fill up the measure of his own wrongs, and his adversary's oppressions. It is singular that a man of his genius, one especially who had so well studied the human heart, and painted so strikingly the dignity of our nature, should invariably, and even with the least worthy antagonist, prefer being plaintiff to being powerful, and rather delight in being the object of compassion than of terror.

After above fourteen years had passed in the manner which has been described, accidental circumstances led to the formation of an intimacy between the family of M. du Chatelet and Stanislaus Leczinski, formerly King of Poland, and father of the reigning Queen of France. He resided at Luneville, where he kept an hospitable mansion as a great noble, rather than held his court as a Prince. He was fond of letters, and, though exceedingly devout, never departed from the principles of toleration, or the feelings of charity. In February, 1748, the Du Chatelets, accompanied by Voltaire, went to visit the King, and were so pleased with the reception which they received for some weeks,

that after a few days passed at Cirey, they returned to
Luneville ; and this Court, small, cheerful, divested
of all troublesome ceremony and cumbrous pomp, and
presenting the best instance ever known of letters
united with grandeur, and literary men patronised
without being degraded, became their residence until
the fatal event which, in the beginning of September
in the following year, severed for ever the connexion of
the parties. The Marchioness continued her studies,
and laboured with unwearried zeal in superintending
the publication of her translation of Newton. The
manuscript had been so far finished in the latter part
of 1747, that the printing had begun early in 1748;
but there were many additions and corrections to
make, and she worked on it with a degree of industry
which is supposed to have seriously injured her during
her pregnancy, extending from the month of December in the latter year. On the 4th of September,
1749, while engaged in an investigation connected
with the ' Principia,' she was so suddenly taken in
labour that a girl was born before she could be put to
bed. In the course of a few days she was no more ;
and the Marquis and Voltaire having retired to Cirey,
very soon quitted a place now gloomy with the most
painful associations, and went to Paris, where Madame
Denis, his niece, came to live with the poet. He continued to occupy the house in which the Marquis and
he had before lived together as their town residence,
when they occasionally quitted Cirey for the capital ;
and it was now, he said, endeared to him by its melancholy recollections. His niece endeavoured to distract
his attention from the dreadful loss which he had sus-

tained. It is needless to add how difficult a task this proved. For some weeks he appears to have lost the power of fixing his attention upon the occupations in which he attempted to engage. The first thing which tended to divert his mind from his affliction, was the interest he took in a comedy written by Madame Denis, ' La Coquette punie.' He admitted the talents which it showed, but was apprehensive about its success ; and after much consideration he was found to be right in his reluctance to have it produced in public. In the course of two or three months his active mind recovered its elasticity, and he was occupied with the representation of the ' Orestes,' which, partly, as is supposed, through the cabals of Crebillon, met with a reception at first most stormy, but afterwards was suffered to obtain some share of success.

Many conjectures have, of course, been raised, as at the time much scandal was circulated, respecting the nature of the attachment between Voltaire and the accomplished friend whom he thus lost. There seems upon the whole no sufficient reason to question its having been Platonic. The conduct of the husband, a respectable and honourable man, the character of the lady herself, but above all the open manner in which their intimacy was avowed, and the constant recognition of it by persons so respectable as the Argentals and Argensons, so punctilious as the Deffands and the Henaults, seem to justify this conclusion. It is well known that, both in former times and in our own, the laws of French society are exceedingly rigorous, not indeed to the exclusion of the realities, but to the saving of the appearances—" Les convenances avant tout" is the rule. It is never permitted, where a grave

suspicion exists of a criminal intercourse, that the
slightest appearance of intimacy should be seen in public
between the parties. Voltaire's letters to all his correspondents, in which he speaks of Emily to some, of
Madame la Marquise to others, of Chatelet-Newton
to others, giving her remembrances to them, and himself inviting them to the château, all seems wholly inconsistent with the rules of social intercourse observed
by our neighbours, on the supposition of her having been
his mistress. Perhaps we may add to this the proof afforded by Frederick II. always acknowledging her, and
constantly sending his regards to her. It may be recollected that when the French king's mistress, Pompadour, ventured, with many apologies, to send him a
respectful, even humble message, his good brother of
Prussia shortly and drily said, "Je ne la connais pas."*

As soon as the King of Prussia learnt Madame du
Chatelet's death, he lost no time in desiring Voltaire
to come and live in Berlin, now that the only obstacle
to this plan was removed ; but at first he could not as
yet listen to any such proposition. In the course,
however, of the next six months he began to feel the
former thraldom of the French government and clergy ;
he was once more plagued with the slanders of the
press, which did not even spare Madame du Chatelet's
memory ; he formed to himself the picture of happi-

---

* An expression which occurs in Voltaire's letter to Madame du
Deffand, announcing the Marchioness's death, seems strange. Though
it clearly proves nothing, yet it was an extraordinary thing to say
at such a moment. He asks to be allowed to weep with her for one
" qui avec ses faiblesses avait un âme respectable."—(Cor. Gén., iii.
365.) In all probability this referred to her violent temper, of
which Madame du D. might have heard him complain, as he certainly suffered much under it.

ness under a sovereign who protected letters, cultivated them himself, refused all countenance to persecutions of any sort, and had long expressed for him the warmest friendship. He believed he should at length be able to lead a tranquil life of literary occupation; he hoped to enjoy the *otium* and forgot the *dignitas;* and he set out for Berlin, where he arrived about the end of July, 1750.

The arrangements which Frederick II., enchanted with this splendid acquisition, immediately made, were of a sufficiently liberal kind. A pension of 20,000 francs a year, with 4000 for his niece should she join him and then survive him; the rank of chamberlain; the higher order of knighthood, and apartments at the palace of Potsdam, where the monarch lived ten months in the year—seemed an ample establishment, especially when added to an income already larger by a great deal than any other literary man ever enjoyed, for he possessed from his own funds 80,000 francs, or above 3000*l*., a year. The work to be done for this remuneration was to read and correct the king's writings, to be his companion at his leisure hours, and, above all, to attend his suppers, the meal at which he chiefly loved to take his relaxation after the fatigues of the day. That the society of this singularly gifted prince was captivating we cannot have any doubt. He had a great variety of information, abounded in playful and original wit, somewhat of Voltaire's own kind, was of the most easy and unceremonious manners, and had such equal spirits as cast an air of gaiety over his whole society. It is not a matter of wonder that the man whom he chiefly delighted to honour should have been enchanted with this intercourse, seasoned as it was with boundless admiration of his own genius never very coldly expressed, though always cleverly and variously, more especially when we bear in mind the fundamental fact that this host and master, who chose to make himself the poet's playfellow, was a powerful monarch, and covered with the laurels of a conqueror, as well as sustained by the troops and treasures of a prince.

Twelve months glided away in this pleasing dream; for dream after all it proved to be. That which his philosophers never forgot, it appeared that he himself, the philosopher king, forgot as little, his kingly station; and the freaks of the royal temperament, suppressed for a while, broke out on the first convenient opportunity, changing at once the whole aspect of Voltaire's position, and reducing his relation with his " royal friend " to the ordinary standard, which retains the " royal " and converts " friend " into master.

Immediately after his arrival an incident had occurred which might have opened his eyes to the claw that lurked beneath its velvet covering. Madame de Pompadour had, as has been mentioned, with many roundabout phrases, and with many humble and trembling apologies for such a liberty, ventured to offer her dutiful respects to his Majesty through Voltaire. The very unexpected answer, from one, too, whom oily words cost so little, was—" I don't know her." The unfortunate messenger would have done better to revolve this in his mind rather than very falsely write a report to the lady, in which Achilles was represented as receiving courteously the compliments of Venus. But he had not been four months at Potsdam when he had a fresh illustration of his great friend's character, and one all the more important for his own government that it related to Frederick's treatment of his dependents whom he most favoured with his professions of esteem. M. Darget's wife died; the king wrote him a letter, " touching, pathetic, even highly Christian," on the sad occur-rence; and on the same day amused himself with writing an epigram abusing the deceased. That accounts of the dissolute life secretly led by the philosophic sovereign had reached the poet cannot be doubted, as he plainly avows that had he lived in the court of Pasiphaë he would not have troubled himself about her amours.*. He afterwards entered fully into this most nauseous subject in his ' Memoirs.' Be the account there given of other parties of Frederick's day exaggerated or exact, this is plain, for here Voltaire speaks as an eye-witness, and speaks against himself: the suppers of Sans Souci (the *noctes cœnæque Deum*), so much the subject of jealousy among the scientific and literary men of the court, were disgraced by the exhibition of such brutal indecencies in the ornaments of the royal table, that it requires no small courage in any one to confess having been present a second time after once witnessing those enormities.

But after about thirteen months had elapsed of what appears to have been uninterrupted enjoyment in spite of these wrongs and these drawbacks, an enjoyment not broken by the indications he perceived.

---

* Cor. Gén., iii. 443 (17 Nov., 1750).

of the great jealousy which his fame excited among his learned brethren, it came to Voltaire's ears that his informant, La Metherie, a clever, agreeable, half-crazy physician about court, having mentioned to Frederick how great this jealousy was, the philosophic king replied, " 1 shall want him for a year longer at most; and then one throws away the rind after sucking the orange" From that moment Voltaire began to feel, as well he might, his footing insecure; and he soon found proofs of the extravagant phrases, which he had believed were exclusively applied to himself, being freely and habitually used by the king towards persons of whom he was known to have a very mean opinion. Nevertheless the enchantment continued, and would, in all probability, have lasted until he was actually dismissed, had not a quarrel, in which the intriguing, jealous spirit of Maupertuis involved him, led to a resolution that he would leave Berlin as soon as he could withdraw the funds which he had placed in the country.

Maupertuis was a man of some mathematical acquirements, but little depth, and no genius. He had originally been a captain of horse, and had, on leaving the army, cultivated science. Having acquired some reputation, he was sent, as has already been mentioned, at the head of the commission to measure a degree of the meridian in Lapland. Clairault was one of the party, and, being a very young man, was, of course, placed under Maupertuis, then much past the middle age. The successful performance of this service, a matter requiring care and patience, but nothing more, confirmed the theory of the earth being an oblate spheroid, flattened

towards the poles ; and so puffed up was the philosopher
with this poor triumph, that, after publishing a book
recording the history of the expedition, in which he
carefully suppressed all merit but his own, he actually
had himself represented in a picture, with his hands
on a globe, in the act of flattening it at the two poles.
Frederick, who was wholly ignorant of physical
science, was deceived by the noise which this person's
name, or his tongue, made in the world, and urged
him to live at Berlin, where he was named President
of the Academy which the king had founded. It is a
striking proof how perilous royal meddling in scientific
matters is, that the illustrious Euler was one of the
strangers whom his liberalities had attracted, and
that over his head was placed the flattener of the poles
and the flatterer of the king.

Such a personage was sure to be jealous of Voltaire, whose arrival occurred long after his own place
had been taken. Accordingly, we find that he gave
indications of this immediately. A month after he
came, Voltaire describes him as having become unso-
ciable,* referring doubtless to his very different behaviour when he lived for months his fellow-guest
at Cirey ; and before four months had elapsed, we
find him painted drolly enough " as taking the poet's
dimensions harshly with his quadrant," and " allowing some portion of envy to enter into his problems."
In the course of the next year this envy broke out.
Of the most intriguing disposition, he used his access
to the king for the base purpose of bearing tales

---

* Cor. Gén., iii. 411, 438.

against Voltaire. A profligate adventurer, called La Beaumelle, who had been driven from Copenhagen, where he was a popular preacher, who then came under false colours to Berlin, who had indeed originally committed a theft of Madame Maintenon's letters, and printed them, was taken up by Maupertuis, and both libelled Voltaire, pirated his works, and propagated stories of his having slandered the king. Then came a statement by Kœnig, now professor in Holland, but a member of the Berlin Academy, refuting Maupertuis' favourite doctrine of the principle of least action, and affirming, on the authority of letters from Leibnitz, that it was no new discovery. In truth, Leibnitz had refuted it, as he well might, for it rests upon an imperfect induction—chiefly on the reflection of light, and is at variance with many other phenomena, and even with the reflected motion of all bodies except light, inasmuch as no other body being perfectly elastic, the reflected line never can be the shortest possible between the point of impact and any given plane. The Courtier-President was enraged; he summoned his academicians; he had his case laid before them; he remained absent from the sitting, while an adherent proposed the expulsion of Kœnig, on the ground of his having forged the letters of Leibnitz, because the death of the person from whom he had obtained the copies prevented him from producing the originals. Nothing can well be conceived more outrageous than this proceeding on the part of a scientific body, all the members of which were paid their salaries according to the discretion of the President, and so were more or less dependent upon him. But there was yet a lower meanness behind. Maupertuis having caused Kœnig's expulsion, affected to solicit of the Academy his pardon and restitution. But this the honest Switzer's just indignation prevented ; for he insisted on retiring, having indeed sent his resignation from Holland before he could hear of the Academy's first vote. It was another, and an infamous act of this President, to employ his influence with the Princess of Orange for the purpose of depriving Kœnig of his place of librarian to that lady.

It was always an honourable distinction of Voltaire that he instinctively planted himself as a champion in the front of all who were the victims of persecution or injustice, whatever form it assumed. His feelings towards Maupertuis, whom he had formerly all but idolized, and now heartily disliked, certainly contributed to make him take Kœnig's part with extraordinary zeal, and display great bitterness against his oppressor. But we have no right to doubt that he would at all events have been found strongly on his side, the rather from having lived for so long a time under the same roof with him at Cirey. Maupertuis had, as if deprived of reason, recently published some speculations full of the most revolting absurdities, such as a proposal for penetrating to the earth's centre, and for examining the nature of the human faculties by dissecting the brains of various races of men. The field thus afforded for satire, what witty enemy could forbear to enter? Least of all, certainly, could one like Voltaire refrain. His defence of Kœnig consisted in part of a bitter satire on the President, which soon made the round of the European literary circles, was greedily devoured on account of a superscription the fittest of the age to give it currency, and was relished far more from the gratification its scurrility afforded to malice, than from any intrinsic merit which it possessed. It is among the poorest and the most tedious of its author's pieces; and when it is said to have destroyed Maupertuis' reputation, whoever reads it must feel satisfied of its utter impotence to injure any one but its author, had that reputation rested upon a solid foundation. Unfortunately for Maupertuis, he had been placed high, without any pretensions at all; he had exposed himself to just censure by his treatment of a modest, an able, and a learned man; he had covered himself with ridicule by writings which seemed to argue a deprivation of reason; and it required not the ' Diatribe of Dr. Akakia' to hurl him from the place which he usurped.*

Frederick committed on this occasion his second error respecting this unfortunate person; but it was a far more fatal one than the former. He chose to enter himself into the strife as a combatant, and he was wholly unprovided with resources. He published a pamphlet against Kœnig and Voltaire, in which he betrayed, as might be expected, entire ignorance of the subject. All scientific Europe took Kœnig's part, though it is painful to reflect that the man at the head of it sided with the King and his President; but though that man was Euler, he was one of the Academy who had been drawn into the shameful sentence

---

* It is generally said that he had at one time the misfortune to be confined in a lunatic asylum; his latter conduct certainly seems to countenance the report.

of condemnation. His authority, how venerable soever, proved of no avail ; the universal voice of the scientific world was against the whole proceedings of the confederates ; and the king was reduced to the humiliation of appealing from the reason of his readers to the authority of his prerogative. He had the incredible folly of causing Voltaire's pamphlet to be burnt by the hands of the hangman.

It was now clear that the tempest had both set in and was unappeasable. The royal disputant had received additional offence from a law-suit in which Voltaire had been obliged to arrest the Court broker, a Jew, for debt. All explanations were unavailing; he sent back his chamberlain's key and his order of knighthood, and resigned his pension. He wrote a kind of love verses with them : they were returned to him. He humbled himself in the very dust with protestations of his innocence, when charged with having libelled the King; and, among other jests at his cost, had likened his office of correcting the royal French to the functions of the laundress with the royal linen. His protestations, and his extravagant demonstrations of sorrow, were quite enough to disgrace the one party, but they failed to appease the other. A haughty and imperious answer alone was given, that " he was astonished at Voltaire's having the effrontery to deny facts as clear as the sun, instead of confessing his guilt; and that, if his works merited statues, his conduct deserved a gaol." No spark of pride, or even of ordinary dignity, was raised by this intolerable treatment, but only endless wailings as of one literally dying of a broken heart, mingled with protestations of duty, gratitude, attachment, and pitiful appeals to the compassion of his tender and benevolent nature.

Miserable as this picture of Voltaire's weakness is, we may be permitted to doubt if it is not surpassed in baseness by the flattery with which he so long fed his royal friend. He, no doubt, corrected his bad French, and often objected to his poetical errors, or the sins of his compositions against good taste. These acts of friendship, these real services, it is probable Frederick had enough of the royal author to dislike; and possibly some such feeling may have led to the exclamation respecting oranges. But assuredly he had far less right to complain, than Voltaire had to blush, at the shameful excess of adulation which could make him desire his own 'History of Louis XIV.' to be " placed under Frederick's Memoirs of the House of Branden-burgh, as the servant below the master" (Cor. avec les Souverains, i. 756); and after sitting up all night to read it, exclaiming, " Mon Dieu! que tout cela est net, élégante, précis, et surtout philosophique; on voit une génie toujours au-dessus son sujet (thus sub-jecting the owner himself of that genius) : l'histoire des mœurs, du gouvernement, de la religion, est un chef-d'œuvre" (ib. 740). And all this about the worst history that ever was written—tawdry, rambling, conceited, inflated—in a style about as near Livy's or Voltaire's own as that of Ossian's poems.

After a delay of two months the King's resentment appears to have cooled, or to have yielded to his pru-dence. The leave to depart was granted, and he desired to see Voltaire before he went. A long

interview took place, and a reconciliation; in the course
of which it is positively asserted that the king sealed
the treaty by joining, or rather originating, several
sallies against Maupertuis. During the week that
followed before his departure Voltaire supped every
night at the royal table, and on the 26th of March,
1753, he set out. After passing a month at the Court
of Saxe Gotha he arrived at Francfort on the Maine,
where his niece, Madame Denis, met him. Here they
were both unexpectedly and rudely arrested at the
instance of a Prussian agent, who demanded, by the
King's authority, the delivery of the key, the ribbon,
and a volume of his Majesty's poetry. This volume
was a privately printed collection; only a few copies had
been struck off; and it contained a poem—'Le Palla-
dium,' in the style of the 'Pucelle,' but attacking
living characters. As Voltaire's baggage had gone by
another route to Paris, both the uncle and niece
were detained for some time till the book was recovered; and they were then, and apparently without
any pretence of authority, seized, upon leaving Francfort,
at the instance of another of the Prussian authorities.
They were now imprisoned, under a guard, for twelve
days, with every circumstance of insult, to the extent
of Madame Denis being forced to sleep the whole time
of their imprisonment in a room with four soldiers
standing sentinel round her bed, and without any
female attendant. It must be observed that the King
had written a letter desiring these effects to be returned
to him two months before Voltaire left Berlin;
but the reconcilement which had afterwards taken
place naturally enough led to the belief that this

requisition was countermanded. The exactions to which he was exposed during this detention, and the sums taken from his trunks, are stated by him as amounting to the whole money which he had received during all his service at Berlin. This treatment made, and naturally made, an impression upon his mind which no time seems ever to have removed.* Had he remained near the King, the same resentment would not have kept possession of him; but he was now beyond the reach both of the royal seductions and the royal power; and he vented his indignation in that scandalous chronicle of Frederick's life and manners, which was plainly his main object in the autobiography, composed as soon as he quitted Francfort, and not destroyed after the second reconcilement, which took place in 1757.

The style of the correspondence afterwards, when Frederick had him not in his power, and when distance enabled him to see with more impartial eyes the character of his royal friend, affords a contrast to all that preceded, quite refreshing to the admirers of genius. We at last have Voltaire writing like a man, and no longer either fawning like a courtier parasite, or whining like a child in his addresses to the king. Frederick, on his part, never ' forgets his alleged grievances; he constantly refers to them, but he does full justice to the merits of his illustrious correspondent, in whom he at length finds the more dignified qualities of an independent mind. As to Maupertuis, stung to madness by the merited contempt into which

---

* See Cor. Gén., v. 67 (1757), but it breaks out often afterwards.

he had fallen through his own folly and misconduct, and discovering how little the alliance of a monarch can avail the party to philosophical controversy, he vented his spleen in a challenge, which he sent after Voltaire, who received it at Leipzig, and returned it such an answer as it deserved; though no sarcasm could now make the poor man more ridiculous than he had made himself. There seems no ground for believing the random charge thrown out by Collini, Voltaire's secretary, in his ' Memoirs,' that Maupertuis had a hand in the shameful transaction of Francfort. Indeed the blame of that appears to fall much rather upon the low agents employed than even upon Frederick himself, though he grossly neglected his duty in not bringing them to condign punishment.

Madame Denis left her uncle and returned to Paris as soon as he was safe in Alsace, where he had a mortgage or rent charge on the Duke of Wirtemberg's estates; and he remained at Colmar for several months, which he chiefly passed in bed, suffering very much under a complication of diseases. He had no difficulty in going to Paris, had he been so disposed; for there was not any prohibition; the king had overlooked his going to Berlin, and had even continued his pension and his situation in the household, though he had taken away the place of historiographer. But it seemed as if the cabals he so much dreaded were still at work; and feeling that he could not be sure of a quiet as well as a distinguished reception in the capital and at court, where he had put forth several feelers, and been ready enough to worship Madame Pompadour, he remained in Alsace for nearly two years, only

going for a few weeks to the waters of Plombières,
where his niece and the Argentals came to meet him.
He also went to Lyons, where Cardinal Tencin, the
archbishop, saw him, and considered himself under the
necessity of avoiding his society, notwithstanding his
being uncle of Voltaire's dearest friend, M. Argental's
wife. The people, however, took another view of the
matter, and held festivals in honour of the great poet
and wit, by inviting him to their theatre and playing
his tragedies before him with the most enthusiastic
acclamations. He was now ordered to try the waters
of Aix in Savoy, and for this purpose he must pass
through Geneva. There he consulted the famous
Dr. Tronchin, who at once forbade that mineral, and
he purchased sixty acres of land near the town, where
he was made to pay twice as much as it would have
cost him near Paris. He afterwards bought the villa of
Tournay, since called Ferney, in the French territory,
and about a league from Geneva. In summer he went
to a house which he purchased near Lausanne, called
Monnier; and in these retreats, agreeable for their
scenery in summer, but subject to the curse of a
rigorous climate in winter, he spent the remaining
portion of his life.

Frederick was reconciled to him in 1757. He wrote
him a kind letter in August of that year, when he had,
in consequence of his disaster at Kolin on the 18th of
June, been reduced to great straits. This renewed
their correspondence. In September he was so much
more desperate that he wrote to Voltaire, declaring his
resolution to kill himself should he lose another
battle; and he said the same thing in the poem which

he addressed to M. d'Argens, then in his employ. He became more resigned after this, and resolved to brave all dangers. He says, in one of his poems addressed to Voltaire, 9th October,

> " Je dois, en affrontant l'orage,
> Penser, écrire, et mourir en Roi."

Immediately after (5th November) he gained the battle of Rosbach, in which the French army under Soubise were seized with a panic and fled disgracefully. But aware of his difficulties, he wished to renew the nego- tiations for peace which he had two months before in vain attempted to open with the Duc de Richelieu, then commanding in Westphalia. The Cardinal Tencin, still a minister, though superseded in active influence by the Abbé, afterwards Cardinal Bernis, had always been averse to the Austrian alliance, which Madame Pompadour, from personal resentment towards Frederick, mainly aided in bringing about; and he employed Voltaire's intimacy with the Margravine of Baireuth, Frederick's sister, to open a negotiation. The letters passed through Voltaire and that princess. Frederick readily acceded to the suggestion. The letter from the margravine on her brother's part was sent in this manner to the cardinal, who wrote, en- closing it, to the king of France. He received a dry answer, that the Secretary for Foreign Affairs would communicate his intentions. That secretary, the Abbé Bernis, did so; he dictated to the cardinal an answer to the margravine, refusing to negotiate, and the car- dinal is represented by Voltaire (Mém., Œuv., i. 295) as having died of mortification in a fortnight. The sudden change of tone in Frederick towards Voltaire, happening at so peculiar a moment, the very fortnight before he endeavoured to draw M. de Richelieu into a negotiation, leaves no doubt that he intended to avail himself of the poet's known intimacy with the General in furtherance of this scheme. Voltaire had, some days before this revival of friendly relations, been writing of him as he usually did. On the 6th of August, 1757, he had, in one of his letters, said, " L'ennemi publique est pris de tous côtés. Vive Marie Thérèse!" (Cor. Gén., v. 21.)*

During the two years of his residence in Alsace Voltaire had done little more than correct his works, and publish the 'Annales de l'Empire,' a history undertaken at the request of the Grand Duchess of Saxe Gotha, and upon the plan of the President Henault's dull work. But at Berlin he finished his ' Siècle de Louis XIV.,' the materials of which he had brought with him from Paris. He also began at that time his correspondence with Diderot and D'Alembert, then engaged in editing the famous ' Encyclopédie,' the effects of which he very early foresaw, and to encourage it gave his best efforts, both while at Berlin and after his establishment near Geneva. Whatever we may deem respecting the tendency of the work (on its merits there cannot be two opinions), it is impossible not to have our admiration excited as well as to take a lively interest in the zeal and untiring activity which the aged philosopher displayed in encouraging

---

* It is the humour of Voltaire and his Parisian correspondents to call Frederick always " *Luc.*" This was probably the name of some noted knave at the time. The term is plainly used *dyslogistically*.

his young correspondents. On this remarkable occasion he put forth all those qualities which form a party chief and gain over the warm support of his followers —ardour, good humour, patience, courage, tolerance, activity, knowledge, skill. The 'Encyclopédie,' as is well known, was, after a few years, no longer suffered to appear openly in France. In 1751, and the following years, the first seven volumes appeared at Paris under Diderot and D'Alembert; in 1758 it was stopped, at a time when its sale had reached no less than 3000 ('Cor. Gén.,' v. 127), and the remaining ten volumes were published in 1765 at Neufchâtel under Diderot alone. The four volumes of Supplement were published in 1776 and 1777 at Amsterdam. All the eleven volumes of plates were published at Paris between 1762 and 1772, and the supplemental volume of plates in 1777. The whole of this great work thus consisted of thirty-three folio volumes. Some of Voltaire's articles are clever, and abound with good reflections. The greater number of them are too light, having the fault which he certainly imputes to many of the other contributors in his 'Letters,' when he observes that they are fitter for a magazine than an encyclopædia.

The quarrel with Frederick appears to have raised in Voltaire's mind the admiration with which, while in England, he had been smitten for Swift's writings, especially his immortal 'Gulliver.' He had, while at Cirey, written the 'Voyage de Scarmentado,' and the 'Zadig.' 'Micromegas' was added soon after his return to France. A careful revision of all these was the fruit of this revived taste for the philosophical and satirical romance. Soon after his establishment at Geneva he finished his great historical work, of all his writings the most valuable, and perhaps the most original, the ' Essai sur les Mœurs des Nations ;' and he then produced the composition which in originality comes next to it, and in genius is the most perfect of all his performances, the celebrated ' Candide.' The ' Essai' had been in great part written at Cirey, but being printed much later, it was first published in 1757,* the ' Candide' early in 1759. The former, of course, was avowed, but the latter was studiously denied even to the Theiriots and Thibouvilles, his most familiar friends, though Frederick II. appears to have been intrusted with the secret at the very date of these denials.†

The two master-pieces which I have now mentioned in one respect differed materially : the design of the History was quite original ; of the Romance there had been examples before. But in the execution both possessed a very high merit, and a merit of the very same kind—-the truth with which great principles were seized, and the admirable lightness of the touches by which both the opinions and the comments upon them were presented to the mind.

---

* It was the fate of many writings left by Voltaire at Cirey, and among others, of some critical dissertations and translations for the Essay, to be burnt by the base fanaticism or low jealousy of the Marquess's brother, after Madame du Chatelet's death. The ' General Dissertation on History' was written in 1764, and published the year after. Voltaire, in the advertisement prefixed to it in an edition of his works, erroneously mentions it as written at Cirey.

† Cor. avec les Souv., i. 796.—Cor. Gén., v. 225, 329.

Before Voltaire's, there was no history which did not confine itself to the record, more or less chronological, more or less detailed, of wars and treaties, conquests or surrenders; the succession, by death, or usurpation, or marriage, of princes; and the great public calamities, as plague, or inundation, or fire, which afflicted mankind from natural causes. The proceedings of councils, or synods, or parliaments, were referred to, but chiefly as connected with the wars of the countries in which they met, or the succession or the deposition of the sovereigns that ruled over them. No measure or proportion was observed between the events thus chronicled, in respect of their various degrees of importance, still less was their influence upon the condition of the people described, or even noted. To deliver the facts, to describe the scenes and the actors, relating the events, and giving an estimate of their characters, with perhaps a few moral reflections or inferences occasionally suggested by the narrative— was deemed the proper, and the only office of history. The ancients, our masters in this as in all other walks of literature, painted both scenes and men with a vivid pencil; they gave, too, chiefly in the form of speeches, supposed to have been made by the personages whose actions were related, their own reflections upon events, or the sentiments of those personages which actuated their conduct. The same thing was done by modern historians more formally, as dissertations interspersed with the story. But in all these writings there was one common cardinal defect, one omission equally to be lamented. First, the same particularity of detail, which was desirable when important transactions or interest-

ing occurrences were to be recorded, became tedious,
and only loaded the memory with useless facts, when
matters of usual occurrence, or of inferior interest,
were to be related ; yet the historian's duty was understood to require that none should be left out.   Next,
there was no account given of the manners and habits
of the people, the bearing of events upon their condition, the influence of men's character upon their
fortunes ; it was even very rare to find the conduct of
nations described, unless in so far as it might be connected with the conduct of some distinguished individuals ; and generally speaking, all that happened to a
people while enjoying the blessings of peace—their
arts, their commerce, their education, their wealth,
their prosperity or decline, their civilization—all was
either wholly neglected, or passed with scarcely any
notice, while the most careful attention was given to
every detail of battles, and sieges, and individual exploits in arms, of which the importance was often
wholly insignificant, and the interest died with the relation.   There had at all times, indeed, been some
pictures, or rather descriptions, expressly devoted to
figuring forth the manners and customs of a particular
people.   Cæsar had thus described, in a portion of his
'Commentaries,' both the Germans and the Britons :
Tacitus had written a work expressly on the German
manners and character.   But these were either works
apart from history, or episodes in its course ; the history of a nation was never considered to be anything
but the story of its wars and its rulers ; and, what is
still more material, these works, excellent and valuable
as they are, only give a description, and not a narrative ;

only a picture without any motion ; only the representation of a people's manners and condition at a given
time, and not the history of the changes which those
manners undergo, and the varying and progressive
alteration in that condition.

Voltaire, whose daring genius was never trammelled
by the precedents of former times, or the works of preceding writers, at once saw how grievous was the error
thus committed in both its branches; and he resolved
to remedy it by writing a history of nations, giving, in
his narrative of events, their spirit and their tendency
rather than their details. For we shall greatly err if
we suppose that he only supplied the second defect now
pointed out, and joined with ordinary history the
account of the manners and condition of nations at different stated periods of their progress. He undertook to
banish the servile presentation of all events in all their
details, according to their succession in order of time ;
to separate the wheat from the chaff, and the ore from
the dross ; to seize on the salient points, the really important parts of each period, giving as it were the cream
only, and preserving the true spirit of history ; and with
all this to give, at every step and in every relation, whether of particular occurrences or of general subjects in
any one country, a comparative view of similar occurrences and similar subjects in other countries, or the
contrasts which the analogous history of these other
countries presents to the view of the philosophical historian. This last characteristic of the work is, in some
respects, the most distinguishing and the most remarkable of the whole; for it should seem as if the author
never deals with any subject in the history of any one

country but he has present to his mind, by the extraordinary reach of his memory, the history of every other
which stands in any relation, whether of resemblance or
of diversity, to the matter immediately under review.

This work has thus become the true history of human society, indeed of the human race. He limits
himself, no doubt, in time, beginning with the age of
Charlemagne; but he fixes no bounds of space to his
survey. From that period, the middle of the eighth
century, to the middle of the seventeenth, upwards of
nine centuries, he tráverses the whole globe, to gather
in each quarter, at each time, all the changes that
have taken place in society—all the events that have
happened among men—the story of all the eminent
individuals that have flourished—all the revolutions
that have affected the fortunes of nations or of princes;
and neglecting everywhere the trivial matters, however authentically vouched, he fixes our attention only
on the things which deserve to be remembered as having
exerted a sensible influence upon the destinies of the
world. In proportion to the real intrinsic importance
of each event, or to the interest which it is calculated
to excite, is the minuteness with which its circumstances are detailed. But no event is given in detail
merely because it is fitted to excite a vulgar and ignorant wonder; while those things are recorded which
are of real moment, although their particulars may
seem to create little interest. To the work was prefixed a treatise on the 'Philosophy of History,' but the
whole book might justly be designated by that name.

Such was the design; the execution of it has already
been characterised as marked by the peculiar felicity of

the author in seizing upon the more remarkable features of each subject, and conveying both the accounts
of events or of individuals, and the reflections to which
they justly lead, at once with great brevity and with
striking effect. But it is also to be remarked that in
the two great qualities of the historian he eminently
excels—his diligence and his impartiality. To take an
example of the former, we may observe that it would
not be easy anywhere to find a more accurate account
of the Council of Trent than in the 172nd chapter ;
and there are, in various other parts of the work, marks
to be perceived of his having consulted even the least
commonly-known writers and authorities for the materials of his narrative or subjects of his reflections. A
testimony of the greatest value was, indeed, borne to his
learning and accuracy by no less an authority than
Robertson, himself the most faithful of historians, according to Gibbon's description. Speaking of "that extraordinary man whose genius no less enterprising than
universal has attempted almost every species of literary
composition, in many excelled, and in all, save where
he touches religion, is instructive and agreeable ;" the
great historian adds that had Voltaire only given his
authorities, "many of his readers who only consider
him as an entertaining and lively writer, would have
found that he is a learned and well-informed historian."

Voltaire in no part of his work disguises his peculiar
opinions, but in none can he fairly be charged with
making his representation of the facts bend to them.
It would not be easy to imagine subjects upon which
he was more likely to be warped by those opinions than

in relating the conduct of Luther and Calvin, in describing Leo X. and the other Popes; yet full justice is rendered to the character and the accomplishments of Leo, as well as to his coarse and repulsive antagonists: and with all the natural prejudice against a tyrannical Pontiff, a fiery zealot, and a gloomy religious persecutor, we find him praising the attractive parts of the Pope's character, the amiable qualities of the apostle's, and the rigid disinterestedness of the intolerant reformer's, as warmly as if the former had never domineered in the Vatican, and the latter had not outraged, the one all taste and decorum by his language, the other all humanity by his cruelty.

But it is a merit of as high an order, and one which distinguishes all Voltaire's historical writings, that he exercises an unremitting caution in receiving improbable relations, whether supported by the authority of particular historians or vouched by the general belief of mankind. Here his sagacity never fails him—here his scepticism is never hurtful. The admirable tract in which he assembled a large body of his critical doubts under the appropriate title of ' Le Pyrrhonisme de l'Histoire,' is only a concentrated sample of the bold spirit in which he examined all the startling narratives to which our assent is so frequently asked, and which used, before the age of Voltaire, to be as unthinkingly yielded. In the article ' History' of the ' Encyclopédie,' we find much of what is now the general faith upon the early history of Rome, but in those days was never dreamt of. The same unflinching boldness and the same unfailing acuteness pervade all the work of which we have now been discoursing. We may safely affirm that no historical treatise was ever given to the world more full of solid and useful instruction. That there should have crept into the execution of so vast a design, perhaps the most magnificent that ever was conceived, errors of detail, is of no consequence whatever to its general usefulness, any more than the petty inequalities on the surface of a mirror are sufficient to destroy its reflecting, and, if concave, its magnifying power; because we read the book not for its minute details, but for its general views, and are not injured by these faults any more than the astronomer is by the irregularities of the speculum which might impede the course of an insect, as these inaccuracies might the study of one who was groping for details when he should have been looking for great principles. But whoever has studied history as it ought to be studied, will confess his obligations to this work, holding himself indebted to it for the lamp by which the annals of the world are to be viewed.

The example so happily set by the 'Essai' was soon followed by the other great writers of the age. It had the most important and salutary effect upon the great æra of historical composition which now opened. Hume's first volume, 'The Stuarts from the Accession of James I. to the Death of Charles I.,' had been published in 1754, and had contained a most able appendix, giving a general account of the government, and manners, and condition of the country at James's death. Whether he had seen the imperfect and partial copies of the 'Essai' which had been surreptitiously printed as early as the winter of 1753, some months before his own was published, or the still more imperfect publications of many chapters in the 'Mercure de France' several years earlier, we have no means of ascertaining. Voltaire himself, in a panegyrical notice of Hume's plan ('Remarques sur l'Essai No. 3,' in vol. v. of the work, p. 355), assumes that he had adopted his plan of writing history; and, in fact, the 'Siècle de Louis XIV.,' of which nearly one-fourth is written on the plan of Hume's appendix, had been published as far back as 1751, and was in such universal circulation as to have been repeatedly pirated. But there can be no doubt that Robertson's celebrated view of society (forming the first volume of Charles V.) was suggested by the 'Essai,' for he intimates that the occasion for his work would have been superseded by the 'Essai' had Voltaire's authorities for the facts been referred to. That Gibbon, Henry, Watson, Rulhières, all adopted the new system is clear.

On his other histories we need not dwell; they are in every respect performances of an ordinary merit. The 'Charles XII.' is the best; the 'Peter the Great' the worst. The former has the great merit of a clear, equable, and interesting narrative, apparently collected from good sources, and given with impartiality. The latter, beside its flimsy texture, was written in too close communication with the Russian court to be very trustworthy; and it is not only glaringly partial on points which, while independent and unbiassed, he had treated with honesty, but it falls into the most vulgar errors on the merits of Peter's proceedings.* The 'Siècle de Louis XIV.' holds a middle rank

---

* A contemptuous denial of the charge of poisoning his son, and an elaborate vindication of the Czar's conduct (part ii. chap. 10), is at complete variance with the 'Anecdotes' previously published. He had also in his 'Charles XII.,' written in 1727, thirty years before

between the two, and it has some of the merits of the
general or philosophical history. But how far it can
be relied on for perfect fairness is another matter.
He himself admits that it was necessary to write at a
distance from France, a work which treated of men's
conduct whose near relations still lived in the society
which he frequented at Paris. "To what," he asks,
"should I have been exposed at home? Thirty different correspondences even here have I been obliged to
carry on after my first edition was published, all owing
to the difficulty of satisfying the distant cousins of
those whose history I had been relating." But if any
proof were wanting that his distance did not wholly
protect him from bias—and, indeed, every one must see
that he was likely to feel such motives if he did not
mean his banishment from Paris to be perpetual—we
have the evidence in such letters as that in which he
complains that such a one is not satisfied, but has made
remonstrances, and says that of another applicant's
ancestor he has not been able to speak so favourably as
was desired, but yet that he had gone a good deal out
of his way to embellish them (*enjoliver*) as was

---

his correspondence with the Empresses Elizabeth and Catherine,
described the Czar as " cutting off heads in a drunken debauch to
show his dexterity" (liv. i.). In both the ' Charles XII.' and
' Peter I.' we find nearly the same unaccountable credulity as to
the wonders related of his studies—his learning watchmaking, sur-
gery (to be able to dress wounds in the field), handicrafts, mathematics—all at the same time ; and Voltaire, who would, in any other
case, have been the first to ridicule these articles of popular belief,
and to expose the folly of a sovereign learning such things to fit him
for reigning, falls headlong into all the common errors on this subject. Peter's quarrels with his clergy, and his subduing their authority, had some hand in producing such errors by captivating Voltaire's esteem ; but he adopts them far more implicitly after his intercourse had begun with the Court of Petersburgh.

desired.* His admiration of Louis XIV. was no doubt
very sincere, and it was not perhaps necessary, in the
pursuit of court favour under his successor, to soften
the harsher features of his character. Yet there is some
partiality to him shown throughout the work. Thus
the atrocious butchery and havoc in the Palatinate could
not be passed over, and, if mentioned, must be blamed ;
but the historian censures it as slightly as possible
when he says, that at a distance, and in the midst of
his pleasures, the king only saw " an exercise of his
power and his belligerent rights, while, had he been
on the spot, he would only have seen the horrors of
the spectacle," (Ch. xvi.)

The best of the Romances are ' Zadig,' one beautiful
chapter of which our Parnell has versified and improved in his ' Hermit ;' the ' Ingénu ;' and, above all,
' Candide.' Some are disposed to place this last at the
head of all his works ; and even Dr. Johnson, with all
his extreme prejudices against a Frenchman, an
unbeliever, and a leveller, never spoke of it without
unstinted admiration, professing that had he seen it,
he should not have written ' Rasselas.'† It is indeed a
most extraordinary performance ; and while it has such

---

* Cor. Gén., iv. 113.—" Je ne ferai pas certainement de Valen-
court un grand homme ; il était excessivement médiocre ; mais j'enjoli-
verai son article pour vous plaire." It appears (ib. 44) that his
first publication was a most imperfect sketch, and written when he
was without sufficient materials. These afterwards poured in from
all quarters, and he extended the next edition a third. But how
much matter must have been sent to him of a more than suspicious
quality !

† There was an interval of several months, as my learned friend
Mr. Croker has clearly ascertained, between the two works ; but
Johnson had never seen ' Candide ' when he came by a singular coin-
cidence on the very same ground.

a charm that its repeated perusal never wearies, we are left in doubt whether most to admire the plain, sound sense, above all cant, of some parts, or the rich fancy of others; the singular felicity of the design for the purposes it is intended to serve, or the natural yet striking graces of the execution. The lightness of the touch with which all the effects are produced—the constant affluence of the most playful wit—the humour wherever it is wanted, abundant, and never overdone— the truth and accuracy of each blow that falls, always on the head of the right nail—the quickness and yet the ease of the transitions—the lucid clearness of the language, pure, simple, entirely natural—the perfect conciseness of diction as well as brevity of composition, so that there is not a line, or even a word, that seems ever to be superfluous, and a point, a single phrase, sometimes a single word, produces the whole effect intended; these are qualities that we shall in vain look for in any other work of the same description, per- haps in any other work of fancy. That there is a cari- cature throughout, no one denies; but the design is to caricature, and the doctrines ridiculed are themselves a gross and intolerable exaggeration. That there occur here and there irreverent expressions is equally true; but that there is anything irreligious in the ridicule of a doctrine which is in itself directly at variance with all religion, at least with all the hopes of a future state, the most valuable portion of every religious system, may most confidently be denied. We have already seen Voltaire's sober and enlightened view of this subject in his moral poems, and those views agree with the opinions of the most pious Christians, as well as the most enlightened philosophers, who, unable to

doubt the existence of evil in this world, or to account
for its inconsistency with the Divine goodness, await
with patient resignation the light which will dawn
upon them in another state of being, and by which all
these difficulties will be explained.*

The residence of Voltaire, first at the Délices, near
Geneva, and, when the Calvinist metropolis obliged
him to part with that place at a heavy loss, at Ferney within the French frontier, was for the remainder
of his life far more tranquil and agreeable than during
the more passionate and irritable period which preceded.   His literary occupation was as incessant as
ever; and, beside some of his lesser poems, the greater
portion of his philosophical and critical works were
written during this latter time.†   His relaxation was

---

* He appears to have disavowed this admirable work even more
carefully than any of his far more exceptionable productions.   To
his most familiar friends we find him exceeding all the fair limits of
denial within which authors writing anonymously should confine
themselves.   To M. Vernes, pastor at Geneva, with whom he was
intimate, he writes, " J'ai lu enfin ' Candide;' il faut avoir perdu
le sens pour m'attribuer cette coïonnerie: j'ai, Dieu merci! de meil-
leurs occupations" (Cor. Gén., v. 229).   To Thibouville he says,
" J'ai lu enfin ce ' Candide,' dont vous m'avez parlé; et plus il m'a
fait rire, plus je suis fâché qu'on me l'attribue" (ib. 258).   Even
to his confidant and tool Theiriot he says—" Dieu me garde d'avoir
eu la moindre part à cet ouvrage!" (ib. 258).

† About twenty-eight of his works, beside some of the romances
and some of the minor poems, were written and published after
the year 1758; of the ' Dictionary,' eight volumes; of the ' Philosophy' all the six, except half a volume; of the ' Mélanges Litté-
raires,' more than one; of the 'Mélanges Historiques,' two;
' Dialogues,' two; ' History of the Parliaments of Paris,' one; nearly
all the volumes of ' Facéties;' all but half a volume of the three on
' Politics and Legislation,' including his writings on the cases of

the society of his friends and the amusements of the
stage, a small theatre being formed in the château,
and his niece, and occasionally himself, acting in the
different pieces represented. Madame Denis had some
talents for the stage, but he greatly exaggerated her
merit, and even amused Marmontel, who relates the
anecdote in his 'Memoirs,' with telling him on one occasion how much she had excelled Clairon. "J'avoue,"
says he, "j'ai trouvé cela un peu fort." Voltaire himself had very humble pretensions as an actor, and
laughs at himself, with much good humour, in his
letters for these exhibitions. The Genevese purists
were scandalised at the near neighbourhood of private
theatricals, but they occasionally formed part of the
audience in spite of Rousseau's exhortations against
the stage. They also visited Voltaire without scruple
at Ferney. He kept a hospitable house, befitting his
affluent circumstances and generous disposition; he
received strangers who were properly introduced, and
it may well be imagined that the inexhaustible resources
of his learning and his wit, as varied as it was original,
gave extraordinary delight to his guests. He was fond
of assisting persons in distress, but chiefly young persons
of ability struggling with difficult circumstances: thus
the niece of Corneille, left in a destitute condition, was
invited, about the year 1760, to Ferney, where she

Calas and Debarre; nearly the whole of the three volumes of
'Commentaries on Dramatic Works.' Beside these volumes there
are eight or more thick volumes of his Correspondence; and beside
finishing and correcting some of his other historical works, he wrote
the 'Peter the Great' and the 'Age of Louis XV.' during the
same last twenty years of his life; so that he wrote forty volumes
during that period of his old age.

remained for several years, and received her education. But, above all, he was the protector of the oppressed, whether by political or ecclesiastical tyranny. His fame rests on an imperishable foundation as a great writer—certainly the greatest of a highly polite and cultivated age; but these claims to our respect are mingled with sad regrets at the pernicious tendency of no small portion of his works. As the champion of injured virtue, the avenger of enormous public crimes, he claims a veneration which embalms his memory in the hearts of all good men ; and this part of his character untarnished by any stain, enfeebled by no failing, is justly to be set up against the charges to which other passages of his story are exposed, redeeming those passages from the dislike or the contempt which they are calculated to inspire towards their author.

During the winter of 1761-62, a scene of mingled judicial bigotry, ignorance, and cruelty was enacted in Languedoc, the account of which reached Ferney, where the unhappy family of its victims sought refuge. A young man, twenty-eight years of age, Marc Antoine Calas, the son of a respectable old Calvinist, was found dead, having, it appears, hanged himself. There arose a suspicion nearly amounting to insanity in the mind of a fanatical magistrate of the name of David, that the young man had been hanged by the father to prevent him from becoming a Catholic. There was another son already converted, and whom the father, so far from repudiating, supplied with a handsome allowance. There was a visitor of the family, a youth of nineteen years old, present at the time when the murder was supposed to have been committed ; as were the mother and brothers of the deceased, all of whom must have concurred in the diabolical act. The father had for some time, beside his age of sixty-nine, been reduced to great weakness by a paralytic complaint. The deceased was one of the most powerful men in the country, and nearly six feet high. He was also of dissolute habits, involved in pecuniary difficulties, and possessing and fond of reading books that defended suicide. Finally, it was certainly known that the notion of his wishing to become a Catholic was a pure fiction, and that he had never given the least intimation of such a desire. In the face of all this, amounting to proof of the magistrate's fancy being an absolute impossibility, he ordered the whole family to be cast into prison together with the father, as accomplices in the supposed murder. The populace immediately took up the subject thus suggested to them by authority, and considered the deceased as a martyr. The brotherhood of the White Penitents (Voltaire says at the desire of the magistrate) celebrated a mass for his soul, exhibiting his figure with a palm-branch in one hand as the emblem of martyrdom, and a pen in the other, the instrument wherewith, as was represented, he intended to have signed his recantation of Calvinism. A report was industriously spread abroad that the Protestants regard the murder of children by their parents as a duty when they are minded to abjure the reformed faith; but that, for the sake of greater certainty, and to prevent the escape of the convert, the sect assembles in a secret place, and elects at stated times a public executioner to perform this office. The court before whom the case was brought,

at first was disposed to put the whole family to the
torture, never doubting that the murder would be
confessed by one or other of them ; but they ended
by only condemning the father to be broke alive upon
the wheel. The Parliament of Toulouse, by a narrow
majority, confirmed this atrocious sentence; and the
wretched old man died in torments, declaring his perfect innocence with his latest breath. The rest of the
family were acquitted—an absurdity the most glaring,
inasmuch as they were all his accomplices of absolute
necessity if he was guilty.

Loaded with grief, and suffering under the additional
pangs of their blasted reputation, the wretched family
came to Geneva, the head-quarters of their sect, and
immediately applied to Voltaire. He at once devoted
himself to their defence, and to obtaining the reversal
of perhaps the most iniquitous sentence that ever a
court professing or profaning the name of justice
pronounced. He was nobly seconded by the Duc de
Choiseul, then Minister. The case was remitted to a
Special Court of Judges appointed to investigate the
whole matter. The preparation of memorials, the
examination of evidence, a long correspondence with
the authorities, were not the philosopher's only
labours in this good cause : he revised all the pleadings
of the advocates, made important additions to them,
and infused a spirit into the whole proceedings the
fruit of his genius, and worthy of his pious design.
In 1765 the decree was reversed ; Calas was declared
innocent, and his memory restored (*réhabilité*) ; and
the Minister afforded to the family an ample pecuniary

compensation, as far as any sum could repair such cruel wrongs.* This took place in the spring of 1766. The Parliament of Languedoc was, unfortunately, not compelled to recognise the justice of the act which reversed its decree, and it had the wretched meanness to refuse obstinately the only reparation it could make—indeed, the only step by which its own honour could be saved.

When we hear considerable persons, as we used to hear Mr. Windham, argue from the example of the French tribunals that judicial places may safely be sold, let the case of Calas not be forgotten. No men who had risen to the Bench by their professional talents ever could have joined the ferocious David in committing this judicial murder. For him a signal and a just retribution was reserved. The reversal of the sentence either stung him with remorse, or, covering him with shame, affected his reason, and he died soon after in a mad-house. The efforts of Voltaire, crowned with success, gained him universal applause. Since the revocation of the Edict of Nantz, the Huguenots had never felt any security against persecution. They now felt that they had a champion equally zealous, honest, and powerful. Indeed, the zeal which he displayed knew no rest ; his whole soul was in the cause. He was wont to say, that during the three years that the proceedings lasted he never smiled without feeling that he had com-

---

* 36,000 francs was bestowed by the King, on the representation of the Court which reversed the abominable sentence. (Œuv. de Pol. et Lég., i. 315.)

mitted a crime. The country never forgot it. When, during the last days of his life, in the spring of 1778, he was one day on the Pont Royal, and some person asked the name of "that man whom the crowd followed?"—" Ne savez vous pas" (answered a common woman) " que c'est le sauveur des Calas ?" It is said that he was more touched with this simple tribute to his fame than with all the adoration they lavished upon him.*

About the same time with this memorable event of Calas, there was an attempt made by the same fanatical party in Languedoc to charge a respectable couple, of the name of Sirven, with the murder of their daughter, a young woman who had been confined in a monastery, under a lettre de cachet, obtained by the priests, and, having suffered from cruel treatment, and made her escape, was found in a well drowned. Sirven and his wife escaped upon hearing of the charge: he was sentenced to death *par contumace ;* she died upon the journey, and he took refuge in Geneva. Voltaire exerted himself as before ; and though it was necessary that the party should expose himself to the risk of an unjust condemnation by appearing to answer the accusation in the Court of

---

* Some unreflecting person has lately been endeavouring to reverse the public judgment in favour of Calas and of Voltaire, by examining the records of the Courts in Languedoc ; and has published an assertion, that the original sentence on Calas was right. Was any one silly enough to suppose that these Courts would preserve any evidence of their own delinquency ?

Toulouse, so much were men's minds improved since the former tragedy, that the great efforts of the advocates, acting under Voltaire's instructions and with his help, succeeded in obtaining a complete acquittal.

This happened in the year 1762. The year after another horrid tragedy was acted in the north, although here Voltaire's great exertions failed in obtaining any justice against the overwhelming weight of the Parliament of Paris, which basely countenanced the iniquity of the court below. A crucifix was found to have been insulted in the night, on the bridge of Abbeville. Two young men, D'Etallonde and the Chevalier La Barre, were accused of this offence on mere vague suspicion, by the spite of a tradesman who owed them some grudge. The former made his escape; the latter, a youth of seventeen, and highly connected, ventured to stand his trial. Other charges were coupled with the main accusation, all resolving themselves into alleged irreverent behaviour at taverns, and in other private societies. The court pronounced La Barre guilty, and sentenced him to suffer the rack, to have his tongue torn out, and then to be beheaded. This infernal sentence was executed upon the miserable youth. The courage shown by Voltaire in exerting himself for La Barre was the more to be admired, that one of the charges against the Chevalier was the having a work of his own in his possession, and treating it with peculiar veneration. This proved, however, to be a groundless suggestion. It was infinitely to Frederick's honour, that when Voltaire asked his countenance and protection for the other young gentleman who had fled and been condemned *par contumace*, he gave

him a company, promoted him as an engineer, settled
a pension upon him, and afterwards made his fortune
in the Prussian army.*

It would be gratifying could we assert with truth,
that the same love of liberty and justice marked every
part of his conduct during the latter years of his
illustrious life. One great exception is to be found in
the correspondence with Frederick and the Empress
Catherine of Russia, at the period of their execrable
partition of Poland in 1772. He treats that foul
crime not only with no reprobation, but even with
flattering approval; and, in one of his letters, he
describes the Empress's share in it as " noble and useful, and consistent with strict justice."†

We have examined the history of his two celebrated
quarrels, those with Frederick and Maupertuis; and
have now contemplated his humane and charitable exertion for the Calas, the Sirvens, and the La Barres : but
his other quarrel reflects less honour on him. His
behaviour towards Rousseau cannot be said to do much
credit either to his temper or his humanity. Rousseau,
younger by eighteen years than Voltaire, and dazzled

---

* In addition to the other atrocities of this case, was the incom-
petency of the Abbeville tribunal. Of the three judges, one was
connected with the prosecutor ; another had quitted the profession
and become a dealer in cattle, had a sentence against him, and was
afterwards declared incapable of holding any office.

† See his verses about kings dividing their cake (Cor. avec les Souv.,
ii. 92), and his rejoicing in having lived to see " the great event"
(93). To Catherine he says, she has, by her " parti noble et utile,
rendu à chacun ce que chacun croit lui appartenir, en commençant
par elle-même" (ib. ii. 618). Again he says, " Le dernier acte de
votre grande tragédie parait bien beau." (ib. 627.)

by his brilliant reputation, had paid him a court by no
means niggardly, yet not subject to the charge of
flattery. Voltaire had returned his civilities, as was
his wont, with good interest. Rousseau, on the Lisbon
poem appearing, wrote an answer in a long, eloquent,
and ill-reasoned letter to Voltaire, which he never
made public, but it came into print by some accident
yet unaccounted for. Voltaire had, in a note, half
jocose and quite kind, declined the controversy, as he
had before declined to discuss the benefits of civilization
and learning with the same antagonist. Rousseau had,
previously to the letter appearing, written an attack
upon the Theatre, and was supposed by Voltaire to have
stirred up the people of Geneva against him, partly on
that account, and partly because of his infidel opinions.
Rousseau now, in 1760, addressed a letter to him full
of bitter complaints, laying to his door the moral
destruction, as he calls it, of Geneva (meaning by the
Ferney theatricals), his own proscription there, and
his banishment from his native country, rendered
insupportable by the neighbourhood of Ferney (Confessions, Part ii., book x.). To this letter Voltaire very
properly returned no answer; he treats it as the
effusion of a distempered mind, in all the allusions to
it which we find among his letters. But he always
asserted, that the charge of injuring the writer of it
was so far from being well founded, that he had
uniformly supported him among his bigoted countrymen. Be this as it may, we find ever after the most
unmeasured and unmerciful abuse of Rousseau as often
as he is mentioned; and the dull but malignant poem,
'Guerre civile de Genève,' contains a more fierce and

cruel attack upon this poor man than is to be found upon any other person in that or any of Voltaire's satires. It is not to be forgotten that the constant undervaluing of Rousseau's genius can scarcely be ascribed to anything but jealousy, if not of his talents, yet of his success. He can see no merit whatever in any of these writings, except the 'Profession de Foi,' in the ' Emile ;' and of that he only speaks as an exception to their general worthlessness ; whereas we know that he felt the greatest jealousy of the courage which it displayed in attacking religion openly, while he had himself never ventured upon any but covert, anonymous assaults, always disavowed as soon as repelled or reprobated. Rousseau's conduct towards Voltaire was a great contrast to this. To the end of his life he avowed the most unrestrained admiration of that great genius ; he subscribed to his statue erected at Lyons— an act which Voltaire was silly enough to resent, affecting to think that the Duc de Choiseul, whose name was at the head of the subscription, might not like being in such company. Finally, when ' Irène,' his last composition, was represented a few weeks before his death, Rousseau generously declared, on some one mentioning the decline of genius which it indicated, that it would be equally inhuman and ungrateful in the public to observe such a thing, even if it were unquestionably true.

That the genius of the poet had in some degree suffered by the lapse of so many years, who can doubt ? Yet the ' Irène,' finished two months before his death, and the ' Agathocles,' which he had not finished when he died, contain passages of great splendour and beauty ;

nor was there ever, it may truly be asserted, a poet at the age of eighty-four capable of so signal an exertion. It is, indeed, only one of the many proofs which remain of the inextinguishable activity of his great mind. He added a passage to the introductory chapters of his ' Louis XIV.,' which shows that it was written a few weeks before his decease, for it gives an account of Hook's publication which appeared in 1778.*

After an absence of above seven and twenty years he revisited Paris with his niece, who, at the beginning of 1778, wished to accompany thither a young lady, recently married to M. Vilette. Voltaire had just finished ' Irène,' and had a desire to see its representation. The reception he met with in every quarter was enthusiastic. He had outlived all his enemies, all his detractors, all his quarrels. The Academy, which had, under the influence of court intrigues, now long forgotten, delayed his admission till his fifty-second year, seemed now anxious to repair its fault, and received him with honours due rather to the great chief than to a fellow-citizen in the commonwealth of letters. All that was most eminent in station or most distinguished in talents—all that most shone in society or most ruled at court, seemed to bend before him. The homage of every class and of every rank was tendered to him, and it seemed as if one universal feeling prevailed, the desire of having it hereafter to say—" I saw Voltaire." But, in a peculiar manner, his triumphant return was celebrated at the theatre. Present at the third night of ' Irène,' all eyes were

---

* Siècle de Louis XIV., i. p. 25.

turned from the stage to the poet, whose looks, not those of the actors, were watched from the rising to the falling of the curtain. Then his bust was seen on the stage; it was crowned with chaplets, amidst the shouts and the tears of the audience. He left the house, and hundreds pressed forward to aid his feeble steps as he retired to his carriage. No one was suffered to sustain him above an instant—all must enjoy the honour of having once supported Voltaire's arm. Countless multitudes attended him to his apartments, and as he entered they knelt to kiss his garments. The cries of " *Vive Voltaire!*" " *Vive la Henriade!*" " *Vive Zaire!*" rent the air. The aged poet's heart was moved with tenderness. " On veut" (he feebly cried)—" on veut me faire mourir de plaisir! On m'étouffe de roses!"

Franklin was in Paris on Voltaire's arrival, as envoy from the revolted colonies, and was soon presented to him. Voltaire had long ceased to speak our language, but he for some time made the attempt, and added, " Je n'ai pû résister au désir de parler un moment la langue de M. Franklin." The philosopher presented his grandson, and asked a blessing: "God and liberty," said Voltaire, " is the only one fitting for Franklin's children." These two great men met again at a public sitting of the Academy, and when they took their places side by side, and shook hands together, a burst of applause involuntarily rose from the whole assembly.

During his short stay at Paris Voltaire showed his unwearied activity of mind, increased, if possible, by the transports with which his fellow-citizens everywhere received him. He planned an antidote to the errors which the admitted probity as well as the rare opportunities of the Duc de St. Simon were calculated to propagate in his 'Memoirs,' still kept secret, but destined soon to see the light. He worked at his 'Agathocles;' he corrected many parts of his historical works; and he prevailed upon the Académie Française to prepare its 'Dictionary' upon the novel plan of following each word in the different senses given it at successive periods, and illustrating each by choice passages from contemporary authors. He proposed that each academician should take a letter, and he began himself strenuously to work upon letter A. These labours, and the excitement of the reception at the theatre, proved too much for his remaining strength, and he was seized with a spitting of blood. A new exertion, made in the hope of obviating certain objections taken at the Academy to his plan of the 'Dictionary,' brought on sleeplessness, and he took opium in too considerable doses. Condorcet says that a servant mistook one of the doses, and that the mistake was the immediate cause of his death, which happened on the 30th of May, 1778. He was in the eighty-fifth year of his age.

We have preserved, and in his own hand, the few lines he wrote to Lally Tolendal, four days before his death, that he died happy, on hearing the reversal of the iniquitous sentence against his father, in whose cause he had exerted himself twelve years before with his wonted zeal and perseverance. Some very good verses, addressed ten days before to the Abbé de l'Atteignant, in the same measure in which he had written some verses to Voltaire, attest the extraordinary vigour in which his faculties remained to the last.*

While in his last illness the clergy had come round him; and as all the philosophers of that period appear to have felt particularly anxious that no public stigma should be cast upon them by a refusal of Christian burial, they persuaded him to undergo confession and absolution. He had a few weeks before submitted to this ceremony, and professed to die in the Catholic faith, in which he was born—a ceremony which M. Condorcet may well say gave less edification to the devout than it did scandal to the free-thinkers. The curé (rector) of St. Sulpice had, on this being related, made inquiry, and found the formula too general; he required the Abbé Gauthier, who had performed the office, to insist upon a more detailed profession of faith, else he should withhold the burial certificate. While this dispute was going on, the dying man recovered, and put an end to it. On what proved his real death-bed, the curé came and insisted on a full confession. When the dying man had gone a certain length, he was required to subscribe to the doctrine of our Saviour's divinity. This roused his indignation, and he gave vent to it in an exclamation which at once put to flight all the doubts of the pious, and reconciled the infidels to their patriarch. The certificate was refused, and he was buried in a somewhat clandestine, certainly a hasty manner, at the monastery of Scellières, of

---

* Cor. Gén., xi. 627, 628.

which his nephew was abbot. The bishop of the
diocese (Troyes) hearing of the abbé's intention, dispatched a positive prohibition ; but it arrived the day
after the ceremony had taken place.

The notion which some have taken that Voltaire
was ignorant of, or at least imperfectly acquainted with
the English language, and into which an accomplished
though somewhat prejudiced critic has among others
been betrayed, is purely fanciful : he had as thorough
a knowledge of it as could be acquired by a foreigner ;
perhaps a greater familiarity and easier use of it than
any other ever had. He wrote it with ease, and with
perfect correctness, in the earlier part of his life, hardly
making any mistakes—certainly none which a little care
would not have prevented. I have lately seen a letter
of his, thanking an author for the present of his book,
probably Sir H. Sloane ; and there is but one word,
lectors for *readers,* wrong ; nor is there the very least
restraint in the style, which is also quite idiomatic, as
when he speaks of his " crazy constitution." *Ills* for
maux, meaning complaints, has the authority of Shakspeare, if indeed any authority were required to justify
this use of the word. The Gallicism or mistake of *lectors*
proves that he himself wrote this letter, and sent it without any one revising it. While visiting England, in 1727,
he published an essay on the ' Civil Wars of France,'
with remarks on the ' Epic Poetry of all Ages,'—a small
octavo, or large duodecimo volume, intended to illustrate the ' Henriade,' of which, as has been observed,
an edition was published at that time by subscription.
The English is perfectly correct, and the diction quite
easy and natural. There is a copy in the British Mu-
seum, with these words on the title-page, in his own

hand—" To Sir Hanslone (Hans Sloane), from his obedient servant, Voltaire." In his latter years he spoke English with great difficulty, and seldom attempted it; but that he retained his familiarity with the language, and could easily write it, we have the clearest evidence in two excellent lines which he wrote when in his eightieth year to Dr. Cradock, who had sent him a copy of his drama, ' Zobeide,' chiefly borrowed from Voltaire's ' Scythes :'—

" Thanks to your muse, a foreign copper shines,
    Turn'd into gold, and coin'd in sterling lines."

Nor is our admiration of this facility of English diction lessened by the consideration that the idea is in some degree imitated from Roscommon. H. Walpole has indeed said, with a gross exaggeration, respecting his letter to Lord Lyttelton, that not one word of it is tolerable English; but he may late in life have lost the facility of writing in a language not acquired while a child, as we know that both with Lord Loughborough and Lord Erskine the Scottish accent returned in old age, though they had got entirely rid of it during the middle period of life.

After the details of his life, and the full consideration of his various works, it would be a very superfluous task to attempt summing up the character of Voltaire, either as regards his intellectual or his moral qualities. The judgment to be pronounced on these must depend upon the details of fact and the particular opinions already given, and no general reflections could alter the impression which these must already have produced.

One part only of his composition has had no place, and derived no illustration from the preceding pages—

his convivial qualities, or colloquial powers. These
are on all hands represented as having been admirable.
He was of a humour peculiarly gay and lively; he
had no impatience of temper in society ; his irritability
was reserved for the closet, and his gall flowed only
through the pen. Then his vast information on all
subjects, and his ready wit, never failing, but never
tiring, added to his having none of the fastidious taste
which prevents many great men from enjoying the
humours of society themselves, while it casts a damp
and a shade over the cheerful hours of others—all
must have conspired to render his company a treat of
the highest order. His odd and unexpected turns
gave his wit a zest that probably never belonged to
any other man's. His writings give us some taste of
this; and there are anecdotes on record, or at least
preserved by tradition, of jokes of which they who read
his works at once recognise him as the author. When
the Dijon academicians presented him with the place
of an honorary member, observing that their academy
was a daughter of the Parisian body—" Eh! oui:"
said he, "eh! et une bonne fille, je vous en réponds,
qui ne fera jamais parler d'elle."—When at some family
party the guests were passing the evening in telling
stories of robbers, and it came to his turn—" Once
upon a time (he began)—Jadis, il y avoit, un fermier-
général——ma foi, Messieurs, j'ai oublié le reste."

When St. Ange, who plumed himself on the refined
delicacy of his flattery, said, on arriving at Ferney,
" To-day I have seen Homer; to-morrow I shall see
Sophocles and Euripides, then Tacitus, then Livy:"
" Ah! Monsieur," said his ancient host, alarmed at the

outline of a long visit, which he seemed fated to see filled up, "Ah, Monsieur ! je suis horriblement vieux. Ne pourriez vous pas tâcher les voir tous le même jour ?" The sketch probably was left unfinished by this interruption. So when an English traveller who had been to see Haller, heard Voltaire speak loudly in his praise, and expressed admiration of this candour, saying Haller spoke not so well of him: "Hélas!" was the admirable answer, "il se peut bien que nous avons tort, tous les deux." A graver rebuke was administered by him to an old lady who expressed her horror at finding herself under the same roof with a declared enemy of the Supreme Being, as she was pleased to term Voltaire :—" Sachez, madame, que j'ai dit plus de bien de Dieu dans un seul de mes vers que vous n'en penserez de votre être."

A striking picture of his powers of conversation is given by Goldsmith, who passed an evening in his company about the year 1754. He describes it, after saying generally that no man whom he had ever seen exceeded him ; and Goldsmith had lived with the most famous wits of the world, especially of his own country— with Burke, Windham, Johnson, Beauclerk, Fox. There arose a dispute in the party upon the English taste and literature. Diderot was the first to join battle with Fontenelle, who defeated him easily, the knowledge of the former being very limited on the subject of the controversy. " Voltaire," says Goldsmith, " remained silent and passive for a long while, as if he wished to bear no part in the argument which was going on. At last, about midnight, he began, and spoke for nearly three hours, but in a manner not to

be forgotten—his whole frame was animated -- what
eloquence, mixed with spirit—the finest strokes of
raillery — the greatest elegance of language — the
utmost sensibility of manner! Never was I so much
charmed, nor ever was so absolute a victory as he
gained."*

To enter further on any general description, when
all the particulars have been gone over, would be absurd.
It is, however, fit to remark that the odium which has
cast a shadow on a name that must otherwise have
shone forth with pure and surpassing lustre, is partly
at least owing to the little care taken to conceal his
unpopular opinions, which is no sufficient ground of
blame. But in part, it is owing to that which is exceedingly blameable, the unsparing bitterness of his invective
on all the honest prejudices (as even he must have
deemed them) of believers, and the unceasing ribaldry
of his attacks on those opinions, which, whether he
thought them true or not, had at any rate the sanction
of ages, the support of established institutions, and the
cordial assent of the vast majority of mankind. The
last twenty years of his life were devoted to a constant
warfare with these sentiments. Had he confined himself to discussion, had he only brought the resources
of his universal learning and acute reasoning to bear
upon the religious belief of his contemporaries, no one
would have had a right to complain, and no rational
Christian would ever have complained, if the twenty
volumes which he thus wrote had been multiplied
twenty fold, or even so as " that all the earth could not

* Prior's Edition of O. Goldsmith's Works, iii. 223.

K

have held the books which should have been written."
But there is a perpetual appeal from the calm reason of
the reflecting few to the laugh of the thoughtless many;
a substitution often, generally an addition, of sneer,
and gibe, and coarse ridicule, to argumentation; a
determination to cry down and laugh down the dogmas
which, with his learning and his reason, he was also
assaulting in lawful combat. And the consequence
has been, that although nothing can be more inaccurate
than the notion that he never argues, never produces
any proofs which make their appeal to the understanding, yet he passes with the bulk of mankind for a profane
scoffer, and little more. The belief of D'Alembert
was exactly the same with his own; he has left
abundance of letters which show that he had as much
zeal against religion as his master, and entered with
as much delight into all his endless ribaldry at the
expense of the faith and the faithful;* but because he
never publicly joined in the assault, we find even those
who most thoroughly knew his opinions, nay, bishops
themselves, concurring in the chant of his praises, as the

---

* See especially such letters as that in which he speaks of the
'Dictionnaire Philosophique,' calling it the Dictionnaire de Satan :
—" Si j'avais des connaissances à l'imprimerie de Belzebuth, je m'em-
presserai de m'en procurer un exemplaire ; car cette lecture m'a fait
un plaisir de tous les diables." He says he has swallowed it,
" Gloutonnement, en mettant les morceaux en double ;" and adds—
" Assurément si l'auteur va dans les états de celui qui a fait impri-
mer cet ouvrage infernal, il sera au moins son premier ministre : personne ne lui a rendu des services plus importans." (Cor. d'Al., 274.)
The flippancy of this work, which threw D'Alembert into such rap-
tures, is nearly equal to its great learning and ability. Thus, vol. vi.
p. 274 :—" Bon jour, mon ami Job ! tu es un des plus grands ori-
ginaux," &c. &c.

most inoffensive, and even moral of men ; while Voltaire, who never said worse than D'Alembert freely but privately wrote, raises in their minds the idea of an emanation from the father of all evil. It may be hard to define the bounds which should contain the free discussion of sacred subjects. Those who are the most firmly convinced of religious truth are, generally speaking, the most careless to what extent the liberty of assailing it, in examining its grounds, shall be carried ; but without attempting to lay down any such rule, we may safely admit that Voltaire offended, and offended grievously, by the manner in which he devoted himself to crying down the sacred things of his country, whether we regard the interests of society at large, or the interests of the particular system which he desired to establish.

But though it would be exceedingly wrong to pass over this great and prevailing fault without severe reprobation, it would be equally unjust, nay, ungrateful, ever to forget the immense obligations under which Voltaire has laid mankind by his writings, the pleasure derived from his fancy and his wit, the amusement which his singular and original humour bestows, even the copious instruction with which his historical works are pregnant, and the vast improvement in the manner of writing history which we owe to him. Yet great as these services are—among the greatest that can be rendered by a man of letters—they are really of far inferior value to the benefits which have resulted from his long and arduous struggle against oppression, especially against tyranny in the worst form which it can assume, the persecution of opinion, the infraction of the sacred right to exercise the reason upon all subjects, unfettered by prejudice, uncontrolled by authority, whether of great names or of temporal power. That he combated many important truths which he found enveloped in a cloud of errors, and could not patiently sift, so as to separate the right from the wrong, is undeniably true; that he carried on his conflict, whether with error or with truth, in an offensive manner, and by the use of unlawful weapons, has been freely admitted. But we owe to him the habit of scrutinizing, both in sacred matters and in profane, the merits of whatever is presented for our belief, of examining boldly the foundations of received opinions, of making probability a part of the consideration in all that is related, of calling in plain reason and common sense to assist in our councils when grave matters are under discussion; nor can any one since the days of Luther be named, to whom the spirit of free inquiry, nay, the emancipation of the human mind from spiritual tyranny, owes a more lasting debt of gratitude. No one beyond the pale of the Romish church ever denies his obligation to the great Reformer, whom he thanks and all but reveres for having broken the chains of her spiritual thraldom. All his coarseness, all his low ribaldry, all that makes the reading of his works in many places disgusting, in not a few offensive to common decency,* and even to the decorum proper to the

---

* See particularly his abominable sermon at Wittenberg, on marriage, actually preached, and of so immoral a tendency, as well as couched in such indelicate language, that it can only be referred to without translation, by Bishop Bossuet and others; also his ' Tabletalk,' in those parts where he treats of women, and describes with

handling of pious topics, all his assaults upon things which should have been sacred from rude touch, as well as his adherence with unrestrained zeal to some of the most erroneous tenets of the Romish faith—all are forgiven, nay, forgotten, in contemplating the man of whom we can say "He broke our chains." Unhappily the bad parts of Voltaire's writings are not only placed as it were in a setting by the graces of his style, so that we unwillingly cast them aside, but embalmed for conservation in the spirit of his immortal wit. But if ever the time shall arrive when men, intent solely on graver matters, and bending their whole minds to things of solid importance, shall be careless of such light accomplishments, and the writings which now have so great a relish, more or less openly tasted, shall pass into oblivion, then the impression which this great genius has left will remain; and while his failings are forgotten, and the influence of his faults corrected, the world, wiser and better because he lived, will continue still to celebrate his name.*

---

ribaldry the most filthy his conflicts against the devil. Nothing in Rabelais is more coarse. Indeed these are passages unexampled in any printed book; but the original sermon must be consulted, for no translator would soil his page with them, and accordingly Audin and others give them only by allusion and circumlocution. 'Titzen-Rede,' p. 306 and 464, must itself be resorted to if we would see how the great Reformer wrote and spoke. His allowing the Landgrave of Hesse to marry a second wife while the first was living, and the grounds of the permission, are well known; and the attempt to deny this passage of his life is an entire failure.

* The edition of Voltaire referred to in this 'Life' is that of Baudouin, at Paris, 1828, in 75 volumes.

APPENDIX I.

It would be improper to dismiss the subject of Voltaire without adverting to the somewhat ambitious work which Condorcet has written under the somewhat inaccurate title of his 'Life.' This is a defence and panegyric throughout; no admission of blame, or even error, is ever made; and there is a scorn of all details, facts, dates, which takes from the book its whole value as a biographical, while its unremitting partiality deprives it of all merit as a philosophical composition. Considering the importance of the subject, and the resources of the writer for either recording facts or giving a commentary, it may safely be asserted that there is no greater failure than this work, appealed to as it so often is, out of mere deference to the respectable name it bears. Condorcet was a man of science, no doubt, a good mathematician; but he was in other respects of a middling understanding and violent feelings. In the revolution they called him "le mouton enragé," by way of describing his feeble fury. He belonged to the class of literary men in France whose intolerance was fully equal to that of their pious adversaries—those denouncing as superstition all belief, these holding all doubt to be impious. Rather enamoured of Voltaire's irreligion than dazzled with his wit or his fine sense, he makes no distinction between his good and his bad writings in point of moral worth, nor indeed ever seems to admit that in point of merit one is or can be inferior to another. Witness his panegyric of the 'Pucelle,' which, after some passages were erased, he pronounces to be "a work for which the author of 'Mahomet' and 'Louis XIV.' had no longer any reason to blush" (Vie de Voltaire, 100). His credulity on material things is at least equal to his unbelief on spiritual. He gravely relates that hopes were held out from the court of Madame de Pompadour of a cardinal's hat for Voltaire when he was instructed to translate some psalms, a task which he performed with such admirable address, though in perfect good faith, that they excited a general horror, and were condemned to be burnt. It is none of the least absurd parts of Condorcet's work, that he, being so well versed in physical and mathematical science, passes without any particular observation the writings of Voltaire on physical subjects, when he was so competent to pronounce an opinion upon their merits. But the strangest part of the matter is, that the author of Voltaire's 'Life' should apparently never have read his voluminous and various correspondence, from which alone the real materials for such a work are to be obtained. He might as well have undertaken the 'Life' of Rousseau without reading the 'Confessions.'

The publication in 1820 of Madame de Grafigny's 'Letters,' while residing for six months at Cirey, entitled, not accurately, 'Vie privée de Voltaire et de Madame du Chatelet,' adds some curious particulars to our former knowledge of Madame du Chatelet and of her household, always supposing that we can entirely rely on the testimony of a woman whose own character was very far from respectable, and who professedly acted the very unworthy part of an eaves-dropper for so considerable a time, pleading only as her excuse the extreme penury from which the hospitality that she violated afforded her a shelter. On Voltaire's character it casts no new light whatever, except that it tends to raise our admiration of his talents, if that be possible, and also of his kindly disposition. Of Madame du Chatelet it gives a far less amiable picture.

APPENDIX II.

I HAVE been favoured, by the great kindness of Mr. Stanford, F.R.S., with part of a series of letters which Voltaire wrote to the Duchess Louisa of Saxe Gotha, grandmother of the late Duke, and of which his Serene Highness was graciously pleased to allow him to make a copy. By Mr. Stanford's permission I am enabled to add some of them; and I have selected the six following, which are now for the first time made public. They will be found very interesting.

No. I.

MADAME, À Swetzingen, près de Manheim, 1754.

Je m'approche du midy à pas lents en regrettant cette *Turinge* que votre Altesse Sérénissime embelissait à mes yeux, et on elle faisait naître de si beau jours, qu'il semble que vos bontez aient donné : j'ai trouvé à la cour de Manheim une image de ces bontez, dont j'ai été comblé à Gotha : cela ne sert qu'à redoubler mes regrets ; je les porterai partout. Il faut enfin aller à Plombières suivant les ordres des médecins et des rois, deux espèces très respectables, avec lesquelles on prétend que la vie humaine est quelquefois en danger ; mais je supplie votre Altesse Sérénissime de considérer combien je luy suis fidèle : il n'y a point d'ancien chevalier errant qui ait si constamment tenu sa promesse. J'ai achevé Charles Quint tantôt à Mayence, tantôt à Manheim ; j'ai été jusqu'au Chimiste Rodolphe Second ; j'ai songé de cour en cour, de cabaret en cabaret, que j'avais des ordres de Madame la Duchesse de Gotha ; je voiage avec des livres comme les héroïnes de roman voiageaient avec des diamants et du linge sale ; je trouverai à Strasbourg des secours pour achever ce que mon obéissance à vos ordres a commencé ; mais, Madame, qu'il sera dur de vous obéir de si loin !

Je ne ferai jamais qu'une seule prière à Dieu : je luy diray, Donnez moy la santé pour que je retourne à Gotha. Je me flatte que la Grande Maîtresse des Cœurs me conserve toujours ses bontez ; qu'elle me protège toujours auprès de votre Altesse Sérénissime. Je me mets à vos pieds, Madame, avec quarante Empereurs, préférant assurément la vie heureuse de Gotha à toutes leurs aventures. Je serai attaché le reste de ma vie à votre Altesse Sérénissime, avec le plus profond respect, et une reconnaissance inalterable. Permettez moy, Madame, de présenter les même sentimens à Monseigneur le Duc et à votre auguste famille.

V.

No. II.

MADAME,   À Colmar, 30 Juillet, 1754.

. . . .

. . . . Ce que votre Altesse Sérénissime me dit d'une certaine personne* qui se sert du mot de "rappeler" ne me convient guères ; ce n'est qu'auprès de vous, Madame, que je peuve jamais être appelé par mon cœur ; il est vray que c'est la ce qui m'avait conduit auprès de la personne en question ; je luy ay sacrifié mon temps et ma fortune ; je luy ay servi de mâitre pendant trois ans ; je luy ay donné des leçons de bouche et par écrit tous les jours dans les choses de mon métier.   Un Tartare, un Arabe du désert, ne m'auroit pas donné une si cruelle récompense.   Ma pauvre nièce, qui est encor malade des atrocitez qu'elle a essuiées, est un témoignage bien funeste contre luy.   Il est inoui qu'on ait jamais traitté ainsi la fille d'un gentilhomme, et la veuve d'un gentilhomme, d'un officier des armées du Roy de France ; et j'ose le dire une femme très respectable par elle-même, et qui a dans l'Europe des amis.   Si le Roy de Prusse connaissait la véritable gloire, il aurait réparé l'action infame qu'on a faitte en son nom.   Je demande pardonne à votre Altesse Sérénissime de luy parler de cette triste affaire ; mais la bonté qu'elle a de s'intéresser au sort de ma nièce me rappelle tout ce qu'elle a soufert.   Je m'imagine que votre Altesse Sérénissime est actuellement dans son palais d'Altembourg avec Monseigneur et les princes ses enfans : je me mets à vos pieds et aux leurs.

On m'a envoyé de Berlin une relation moitié vers et moitié prose du voyage de Maupertuis et d'un nommé Cogolin : ce n'est pas un chef-d'œuvre.

Recevez, Madame, mes profonds respects et ma vive reconnaissance.   V.

No. III.

MADAME,   Aux Délices, 23 Août, 1758.

L'optimisme et le tout est bien recoivent en Suède de terribles échecs : on se bat sur mer, on se menace sur terre ;

---

* Frederick II.

heureuse encor un fois la terre promise de Gotha, où l'on est
tranquille et heureux sous les auspices de votre Altesse
Sérénissime. Elle a donc lu les lettres de cette femme sin-
gulière, veuve d'un poète burlesque et d'un grand Roy,
qui naquit Protestante, et qui contribua à la révocation de
l'Edit de Nantes ; qui fut dévote, et qui fit l'amour. Je ne sçais,
Madame, si vous aurez trouvé beaucoup de lettres intéres-
santes. A l'égard des mémoires de La Beaumelle, c'est l'ouvrage
d'un imposteur insensé, qui a quelque fois de l'esprit, mais qui
en a toujours mal-à-propos ; ses calomnies viennent de le faire
enfermer à la Bastille pour la seconde fois : c'était un chien
enragé qu'on ne pouvoit plus laisser dans les rues : c'est une
étrange fatalité que ce soit un pareil homme qui ait été
cause de ce qu'on appelle mon malheur à la cour de Berlin.
Pour moy, Madame, je ne connais d'autre malheur que d'être
loin de votre Altesse Sérénissime. On est grand nouvéliste
dans le pays que j'habite. On prétend qu'il y a dans une partie
de l'Allemagne des orages prêts à crever : heureusement ils
sont loin de vos états. Je n'ose, Madame, vous demander si
votre Altesse Sérénissime pense qu'il y ait guerre cette année :
il ne m'appartient pas de faire des questions, mais je sçais
que votre Altesse Sérénissime voit les choses d'un coup d'œil
bien juste ; son opinion déciderait en plus d'une conjoncture
de ce qu'on doit penser ; plus d'un particulier est intéressé aux
affaires générales. Qu'elle me pardonne de lui en parler, et
qu'elle daigne recevoir avec sa bonté ordinaire mon profond
respect.   V.

[In another letter it is stated that the greater part of La
Beaumelle's publication of Madame Maintenon's letters referred to in No. III. proved to be a fabrication.]

No. IV.

MADAME,   Aux Délices.
    J'ai également à me plaindre de la guerre et de la
nature : l'une et l'autre conspirent à me priver du bonheur
de faire ma cour à votre Altesse Sérénissime. La vieillesse,
les maladies, et les houzards sont de cruels ennemis : j'ay

bien peur, Madame, que ces houzards ne demandent un peu
de fourrage à vos états, et qu'ils payent fort mal leur diner
et celuy de leurs chevaux. Du moins, Madame, votre beau
Duché, reste d'un Duché encore plus beau, n'aura rien à
reprocher à la cavalerie Française : je crois que depuis Rosbach
elle a perdue l'idée de venir prendre respectueusement du
foin dans vos quartiers. Il me parait que le Roy de Prusse,
qui, attaquant à droit et à gauche autrefois, comme le bélier
de la vision de Daniel, est totalement sur la deffensive : pour
nous, nous sommes sur l'espectative ; et Paris est sur
l'indifférence la plus gaie ; jamais on ne s'est tant réjoui—
jamais on n'a inventé tant de plaisanteries, tant de nouveaux
amusements. Je ne sçais rien de si sage que ce peuple
de Paris, accusé d'être frivole : quand il a vu les malheurs
accumulez sur terre et sur mer, il s'est mis à se réjouir, et
a fort bien fait ; voyla la vraie philosophie. Je suis un vieillard
très indulgent : il faut en plaignant les malheureux applaudir
à ceux qui ignorent leurs malheurs.

Je renouvelle mes remerciments très humbles à votre
Altesse Sérénissime : sa protection au sujet des paperasses
touchant le Czar fait ma consolation. Je me mets à ses pieds
avec le plus profond respect : je suis, &c.

V.

No. V.

MADAME,   Au Château de Tourney, par Genève, 21 Février, 1760.

La nature nous fait payer bien cher la faveur qu'elle
nous fait de changer l'hiver en printemps. Votre Altesse Sérénissime a été malade, et la Princesse sa fille a été attaquée de
la petite vérole : ce qui est encore très cruel, c'est qu'on est un
mois entier dans la crainte, avant de recevoir une nouvelle con-
solante. Vous daignez, Madame, me mander du 10 Février que
j'ay à trembler pour votre santé et pour celle de la Princesse ;
mais quand daignerez vous rassurer le cœur qui est le plus sensible à vos bontez, et le plus attaché à votre bien-être ? Quand
apprendrai-je que la petite vérole a respecté la vie et la beauté
d'une Princesse née pour vous ressembler, et que votre Altesse

Sérénissime a recouvré cette belle santé que je luy ai connue, cet air de fraicheur et de félicité? Madame, il y faut renoncer jusqu'à la paix. J'apprends, et Dieu veuille qu'on me trompe, qu'on foule encore vos états, et qu'on exige des fournitures pour aller faire ailleurs des malheureux. Il faut avouer les Princes chrétiens et les peuples de cette partie de l'Europe sont bien à plaindre ; on met en campagne quatre fois plus de trouppes pour disputer une petite province que le Grand Turc n'en a pour conserver ses vastes états. Les causes de vos guerres sont toujours très minces, et les effets abominables: vous êtes le contraire de la nature, chez qui l'effet est toujours proportioné à la cause. On ruine cent villes, on engage cent mille hommes, et qu'en résulte-t-il?—rien. La guerre de 1741 a laissé les choses comme elles étaient: il en sera de même de celle-cy : on fait, on aime, le mal pour le mal, à l'imitation d'un plus grand Seigneur que les Rois, qui s'appelle le Diable. On dit que nos Suisses sont sages : leur pays est en paix. Oui! mais ils vont tuer et se faire tuer pour quatre écus par mois, au lieu de cultiver leur champs et leur vignes. Le Roy de Prusse vient de m'envoier deux cent vers de sa façon, tandis qu'il se prépare à deux cent mille meurtres ; mais que dire des Jesuittes, Messieurs R. de Matos et Jéronimo Emmanuel, qui ont fait assassiner le Roi de Portugal au nom de la Vierge Marie et de St. Antoine.

Profond respect et inquiétude sur la santé de votre Altesse Sérénissime.　　　　　　　　　　　　　　　　　　　V.

Je crois que la Grande Maîtresse des Cœurs n'a guère dormi.

No. VI.

MADAME,　　　　　　　　　　　　À Ferney, 22 Juillet, 1762.

C'en est trop ; votre générosité est trop grande, mais il faut avouer que votre Altesse Sérénissime ne pouvoit mieux placer ses bienfaits que sur cette famille infortunée :* il n'en a

---

* The family of Sirven, for whom Voltaire was then exerting himself in every direction, and for whom he appears to have asked the Grand Duchess's charity.

presque rien coûté pour l'opprimer, pour luy ravir les aliments,
et pour faire expirer la vertueuse mère, presque dans mes
bras, et il en coûte de très fortes sommes avant qu'on se soit
mis seulement eu état de lui faire obtenir une ombre de justice : on fait même mille chicanes au généreux Le Beaumont
pour l'empêcher de publier l'excellent mémoire qu'il a com-
posé en faveur de l'innocence. On persécute à la fois par le
fer, par la corde, et par les flammes, la religion et la philosophie ; cinq jeunes gens ont été condamnes au bûcher pour
n'avoir pas oté leur chapeau en voyant passer une procession
à trente pas ! Est-il possible, Madame, qu'une nation qui
passe pour si gaye et si polie soit en effet si barbare ?

L'Allemagne n'a jamais vu de pareille horreurs : elle sait
conserver sa liberté, et respecter l'humanité. Notre religion
est prêchée en France par des bourreaux. Que ne puis-je venir
achever à vos pieds, le peu de jours qui me restent à vivre, loin
d'une si indigne patrie ? C'est moy qui suis le trésorier de ces
pauvres *Sirvens :* on peut tout m'envoyer pour eux que votre
âme si belle leur destine. Madame, qu'elle me console de toutes
les abominations dont je suis témoin ! Mon cœur est pénétré
de la bonté du votre. Daignez agréer mon admiration, mon
attachement, mon respect pour vos Altesses Sérénissimes.

Je n'oublierai jamais la Grande Maîtresse des Cœurs.

V.

APPENDIX III.

THE following singular anecdote has never, it is understood,
been made public, and it comes from a respectable quarter
entitled to credit. Nothing can more strongly illustrate Voltaire's peculiar humour : the contrast between his habitual
reverence for the Deity, and his habit of scoffing at the sacred
things of Religion, is here presented in a remarkable manner :—

"Une matinée du mois de Mai, M. de Voltaire fait demander
au jeune M. le Comte de Latour s'il veut être de sa promenade
(3 heures du matin sonnaient). Etonné de cette fantasie,

M. de L. croyait achever un rêve, quand un second message vint confirmer la vérité du premier. Il ne hésite pas à se rendre dans le cabinet du Patriarche, qui, vêtu de son habit de cérémonie, habit et veste mordorés, et culotte d'un petit gris tendre, se disposait à partir. 'Mon cher Comte,' lui dit-il, 'je sors pour voir un peu le lever du soleil ; cette Profession de Foi d'un Vicaire Savoyard m'en a donné envie . . . voyons si Rousseau a dit vrai.'

" Ils partent par le temps le plus noir ; ils s'acheminent ; un guide les éclairait avec sa lanterne, meuble assez singulier pour chercher le soleil ! Enfin, après deux heures d'excursion fatigante, le jour commence à peindre. Voltaire frappe ses mains avec un véritable joie d'enfant. Ils étaient alors dans un creux. Ils grimpent assez péniblement vers les hauteurs : les 81 ans du philosophe pesant sur lui, on n'avançait guère, et la clarté arrivait vite ; déjà quelques teintes vives et rougeâtres se projetait à l'horizon. Voltaire s'accroche au bras du guide, se soutient sur M. de Latour, et les contemplateurs s'arrêtent sur la sommet d'une petite montagne. De là le spectacle était magnifique ! les roches pères du Jura, les sapins verts, se découpant sur le bleu du ciel dans les cimes, ou sur le jaune chaud et apre des terres ; au loin des prairies, des ruisseaux ; les milles accidents de ce suave passage qui précède la Suisse, et l'annonce si bien, et enfin la vue se prolonge encore dans un horizon sans bornes, un immense cercle de feu empourprant tout le ciel. Devant cette sublimité de la nature, Voltaire est saisi de respect : il se découvre, se prosterne, et quand il peut parler ses paroles sont un hymne ! ' Je crois, je crois en Toi !' s'écriat-il avec enthousiasme ; puis décrivant, avec son génie de poète, et la force de son âme, le tableau que reveillait en lui tant d'émotions, au but de chacun des véritables strophes qu'il improvisait, 'Dieu puissant! je crois!' répétait-il encore. Mais tout-à-coup se relevant, il remit son chapeau, sécoua la poussière de ses genoux, reprit sa figure plissée, et regardant le ciel comme il regardait quelquefois le Marquis de Villette lorsque ce dernier disait une *naïveté*, il ajoute vivement, ' Quand à Monsieur le Fils, et à Madame sa Mère, c'est une autre affaire.' "

ROUSSEAU.

From an original Picture by Latour,
in the possession of Mr. Fordis, at Paris.

ROUSSEAU.

THE life of Rousseau neither requires so full a consideration as that of Voltaire, nor affords the materials
for it. Mankind are not divided upon his character
and his merits, nor ever were. That he was a person
of rare genius within limited, nay, somewhat confined,
bounds, of a lively imagination, wholly deficient in
judgment, capable of great vices as well as virtues, and
of a mind so diseased that it may possibly be doubtful if
he was accountable for his actions, is the opinion which
his contemporaries formed of him during his life,
which has ever since prevailed, and which, indeed, was
confirmed by his own testimony, produced after his
decease, and calculated to show that he would not
have either dissented from the sentence or have hesitated to join in pronouncing it. His history and his
writings are of a kind that unavoidably interest us ;
but the one affords too few events, the other too little
variety, to detain us very long in examining either.

Jean Jacques Rousseau was born at Geneva, on the
28th of June, 1712. His father was a watchmaker ;
his mother the daughter of M. Bertrand, a Protestant
minister; and her brother, an engineer, married the

---

* The edition of Rousseau referred to in the text is that of
Lefèvre, Paris, 1839, in eight large volumes.

sister of old Rousseau, who appears to have been a
man of exemplary virtue, of considerable abilities,
some information, and of a very feeling heart. He
had gone to Constantinople about seven years after the
birth of his eldest and then his only son, but he returned
on being apprized by his wife that she was beset by
the attentions of the French Resident, to whom she
had given every possible repulse. This gentleman,
M. de la Clôsure, showed, at a distance of thirty years,
some kindness to the son, and was moved to tears in
speaking of his mother, who died when she had given
him birth, ten months after her husband's return
from the East. His grief was excessive ; and he used
for some years after to take a mournful pleasure in
speaking of her, and weeping over her memory with
his child. He read with him all her books, which
were chiefly novels and romances, and in devouring
these they would frequently sit up whole nights. The
stock being exhausted, they betook themselves to a
more wholesome food ; the library of her father
having, on his death, come to them, and containing
historical and other useful books. An extraordinary
enthusiasm for the Greek and Roman characters, and
especially the eager perusal of ' Plutarch's Lives,' and
the Roman history, was the consequence of this new
course of reading. Young Rousseau could not abstain
from the subject, and one day alarmed the family at
dinner, while he was relating the fable of Scævola, by
running to the chafing-dish and holding his hand on
it. When he was eight or nine years old, his father
had a quarrel with a French officer, and to avoid
being cast into prison, left Geneva and settled at

Lausanne, where he afterwards married a second wife advanced in years, and had no children by her. His eldest son, seven or eight years older than Jean Jacques, had never been the favourite, though bred to his father's business; he took a dissipated course, left the place, and went into Germany. Little pains were taken to stop or to trace him; he never wrote to any one after his flight, and what became of him is not known. In all probability, he died before his brother's name became well known, else he probably would have discovered himself.

Beside the love of modern romances and of ancient history, accident gave him a fondness for music, which, with the other passion, accompanied him through life. His aunt, who took care of him, sang a great number of simple airs, chiefly popular ones, with a sweet small voice, which, aided by his attachment to her, made a deep impression upon him, and formed his taste in song as well as imbued him with a sensibility to its charms. After his father's departure for Lausanne, he was left to the care of his uncle Bertrand, who sent him for two years to Boissy, near Geneva, where he remained under the tuition of M. Lambercier, a pastor, and appears to have learnt a little Latin; but when the Abbé Gouvon, in whose service he afterwards was, at Turin, treated him rather as a secretary than a footman, and read Latin with him, he was found to be very ill grounded, and wholly unable to construe Virgil. He acknowledges, indeed, that he never was tolerably acquainted with the language, though he repeatedly attempted to gain it. His statement to this effect, twelve years after he had translated the first

book of Tacitus's 'History,' and translated it exceedingly well, in most passages correctly, in some with
great felicity, is one of the exaggerations in which he
indulges both of his merits and his defects. [But he
learnt whatever he knew comparatively late.] Nothing
could possibly be worse than the education of a man
who made it a principle through life to cry down
learning, not because he never possessed it, but because
he found it was hurtful to the character and inconsistent with sound wisdom and true virtue.

After quitting the school at Boissy, he was apprenticed to an engraver, who seems to have treated him
harshly.   But his conduct was already bad.   He had
a habit of lying on all occasions, whether moved by fear
to conceal some misconduct, or incited by some appetite
he wished to gratify, or actuated by some other equally
sordid motive.   A strong disposition to thieving was
likewise among his propensities, and this continued to
abide by him long after he grew up, and even when
he lived in society he never could entirely shake it off.
His temperament, too, was vehement, and his timidity
and shyness equally strong.   The indulgences into
which he was thus seduced, he has himself described ;
but to embellish such subjects, or even to veil them so
as to hide their disgusting aspect, would require the
magic of that diction in which he has clothed his own
story, and of which he never seems to have been a
master in any of his other writings.   After serving
through half his apprenticeship, he was surprised one
Sunday evening in an excursion with his companions,
out of the town, by the shutting of the gates; and
there wanted no more to make him elope.   He went

to the parsonage of a Savoyard curé (rector) at Carouges, two leagues from Geneva, who received him hospitably in the hopes of converting him, and gave him letters of introduction* to Madame de Warens, a Swiss lady, who having left her husband, had become a Catholic, and lived on a pension from the devout King of Sardinia. She received him kindly, and sent him to Turin, where he was entertained at the seminary of Catechists, established for converting heretics. In this religious establishment he found manners of the most dissolute and even abominable kind ; he was feebly reasoned with by the brethren on the errors of his belief; he does not seem in reality to have been convinced ; but a provision in the Church had been placed before his eyes as the probable reward of his apostacy, and he embraced publicly the Catholic religion. It was, however, soon discovered by the officers of the Inquisition that he was not sufficiently orthodox in his faith, for he would not avow his belief that his mother had been numbered among the damned. He was, therefore, turned out of the seminary, with a present of twenty francs from the sum collected at the exhibition of his abjuration.

After living obscurely in Turin in a lodging-house for common people at half a sous a night, he now entered as a footman the service of the Countess de Vercellis, and wore livery with the rest of the servants. In the course of a few months this lady died, and the servants were of course dismissed. It was found that

---

* The common accounts say that the Bishop of Annecy gave him this introduction. It was M. de Pontverre, Romish curé, in Savoy.

a ribbon had been stolen; all were interrogated, and
Rousseau, in whose possession it was found, and who
was in fact the thief, had the wickedness to charge it
upon an innocent girl; he persisted in averring that she
had stolen it to give him, there having been some little
love-making between them. The ruin of this poor girl
was the consequence, and he describes the bitter agonies
of remorse which he ever after endured in reflecting
upon the crime thus committed. He endeavours to
explain it in a refined, absurd, and false manner, by
saying that his love for Marian caused it all, because
he had stolen it to give her, and this put it into his
head to think of accusing her of the same intention.
But the truth is, that his cowardice, the parent of lies,
caused it all. He never would have dared charge a
man with the offence. He thought he could escape
exposure and perhaps punishment (though he affects to
say he dreaded not that) by laying the blame on an
innocent young girl who had shown a liking for him
which he returned. He also tries to represent himself
as only a child then,* and, writing in 1766 or 1767,
speaks of forty years having elapsed. But this is not
true. He came to Annecy in 1728, sixteen years old,
having left Geneva in July or August, and after several
months' residence in Turin and the seminary, and
three in the Countess's house, he must have been seventeen when she died, instead of fourteen or fifteen, which
his calculation of forty years would make him. He
expressly says that he had attained the age of sixteen
before he ran away from his master, and he was born

* " La faute d'un enfant."—(Conf., part i. liv. 2.)

on the 28th of June. Indeed, if he remained in his next place less than a year, as he was uncertain when he left it, he must have been eighteen when he committed the offence. Nothing therefore like an excuse, or extenuation from his youth, can be urged on this head.

He was now to prove himself as foolish as he had been found wicked. Received as footman in the great family of Solar, an accident showed him to be superior in reading to the other servants, and one of the house, the Abbé de Gouvon, a man of great accomplishments and of a kindly disposition, made him a sort of secretary, taking much pains also with his education ; so that, though he could not master Latin, he became a good Italian scholar. Suddenly the fancy seized him of quarrelling with the good people, and returning on foot to Geneva with a good-for-nothing young rake from that town, named Bacler, whose acquaintance he had made, and whose low buffoonery he could not refrain from relishing, and even envying, as he uniformly did whatever qualities he observed to attract the admiration of the multitude. He showed the utmost insolence and ingratitude to the Solars, and was all but kicked out of their palace, where he had been cherished as a child of the family, and had been offered the sure means of making his fortune. A plaything, which in his extreme ignorance he calls *fontaine d'heron*, but which is well known as the fountain of Hiero (fontaine d'Hiéron), had been given him by his patron. His childish delight in this bauble was unbounded, and he expected by showing it off on the road to make his way for nothing, a journey of ninety leagues. With this ridiculous pro-

ject he set out, and with his warm attachment for his
new acquaintance; but as he came near Annecy, and
once more hoped to be received into Madame de
Warens' house, he felt he could not take Bâcler
with him, and so he began to affect a great coldness,
that he might shake him off. This he soon contrived
to do, and he was kindly taken into her hospitable
family, where he became domesticated.

By the account of her, which exposes all her failings
with great minuteness, as a reward for her undeviating
kindness towards him, Madame de Warens appears to
have been a woman of some accomplishments, of considerable personal charms, of attractive manners, of a
most kind and charitable disposition, and of very loose
principles. This latter particular he endeavours to
gloss over by insisting on her peculiar notions of what
was fit and allowable. One of her peculiarities was to
make herself uniformly the mistress of all her men
servants, beside having occasionally deviations into a
superior rank of life. To be sure, he maintains that
she only adopted this course as the means of attaching
these domestics the more to her service; and he holds it
quite clear that she neither sought nor found any gratification whatever in this odd kind of family intercourse. Nevertheless he records that his own successor was a tall, ignorant, ill-bred young man of the
lowest rank, a hairdresser's apprentice, who domineered
over the household, maltreated her shamefully, and
brought her to ruin by his extravagance. Her constant and most delicate kindness to Rousseau himself
was repaid by much ingratitude, of which the worst
part is his committing to paper every detail of his con-

nexion with her. He desired, indeed, that the book should not be published before 1800, and it was given to the world by a breach of trust in 1788. But the lady's family were still alive, had it been withheld the full period prescribed, and her memory was something, or should have been something, in the estimation of a pure sentimentalist, of one who was preparing his own history for the very purpose of gratifying a perverted, unnatural love of posthumous distinction by publishing his weakness and his shame to the scorn of future ages. He could hardly conceive that any other person than himself had a similar propensity for self-slander. But even he himself would not easily have borne to be slandered by any pen but his own.

Madame de Warens endeavoured to procure for him orders in the church, and sent him with a pension given by the Bishop of Annecy to the seminary, where after some months it was found impossible to make him learn Latin enough for a priest. She then made a M. le Maître, the director of the cathedral music, take him as a pupil and helper. He passed near a year with him, and was treated with the utmost kindness. A profligate, unprincipled young man from Provence, called Venture de Villeneuve, came to Annecy, and from his cleverness, his skill in music, and his excessive impudence, made some sensation in the society of that place. He soon captivated Rousseau for that reason, and to save him from so ruinous an association, as well as to assist Le Maitre, who had quarrelled with the chapter, he was desired to accompany him to Lyons. Thither he went, and was still most kindly treated by Le Maitre, whose only fault seems to have been his

misfortunes, and his being subject to epileptic fits.
Rousseau took the opportunity one day, when he fell
down in the street, of leaving him to his fate, and
escaping in the crowd. Such was his return for the
favours received from a kind master. He stole back to
Annecy, and found Madame de Warens had left the
place on a secret expedition, which proved to be a residence of some time at Paris.

He now wandered about Switzerland, and at one
time he settled in Lausanne as a music master. He
must needs call himself Vaussure de Villeneuve,* in
imitation of the creature he was last taken with; and
as it should seem, in a fit of insanity, being wholly incapable of composing, he wrote a concerto which was
given before a large company at a law professor's house,
he himself directing the orchestra. The hideous discords
and absolutely incoherent nonsense of the piece created,
of course, unbounded and universal ridicule. His scholars soon dropped off; indeed he was fain now to confess himself an impostor, and to own that he had undertaken to teach what he was himself profoundly ignorant
of. He began, however, to learn music, and had made
some progress when another impostor like himself came
to Lausanne, and induced him to go as his secretary
and interpreter. This was a man pretending to be an
Archimandrite of the Greek church, come to beg aid
for repairing the holy sepulchre. He accompanied
this knave, and on one occasion made a speech for him
to the senate of Bern, who bestowed a considerable sum
on the unworthy pair. The French ambassador, who

---

* Vaussure was a kind of anagram of Rousseau.

had been in the East, discovered the trick, and Rousseau was employed by him on a mission to Paris; from whence he returned, and passing through Chambery, found Madame de Warens, or Maman as he always called her, established there.

Received again kindly, again he committed his ordinary follies. Madame de Warens obtained for him a comfortable place in a public office (the Cadastre). He kept it two years, and then resigned in order to be a music-master. His skill was fortunately become considerable, and he had a number of scholars. His patroness now promoted him to the rank of lover, but without discarding the servant Claude Anet, who also took care of her botanical as well as her amorous concerns; he was a man of considerable merit and great conduct, and became a kind of governor to Rousseau, who more than any child of six years old stood in need of a master. He was succeeded by a young hairdresser's apprentice, as Rousseau found on his return from a few months passed at Montpelier for his health; the young man supplanted both Claude Anet and Jean Jacques, and continued with this kind-hearted but imprudent woman until, ruined by his extravagance and her own projects, she died in a state of wretchedness over which Rousseau has drawn a veil. He saw her, after an absence of fifteen years, in 1754, at Chailly; and she came to see him for the last time near Geneva soon after. He had helped her with such sums as he could spare. She now, in receiving a small pittance, showed her constitutional tenderness of heart and that generosity of disposition which no penury could eradicate; she took off her finger a ring, her only remaining

trinket, and pressed it upon the woman through whom
the money had been sent. Rousseau charges himself
with black ingratitude for not having gone with her
and saved her from wretchedness; he could not quit
a new attachment which he had formed, and he declares
that the reflection on his conduct had haunted him with
remorse greater than any other passage of his life could
inflict.

But we have anticipated in the narrative. From
Chambery he removed to Lyons, where his kind pro-
tectress obtained for him an employment as preceptor
in M. Mabillon's family. Soon he, as usual, left this
place, returned to Chambery, found he could no longer
be comfortable in Madame de Warens' house, and set
out to seek his fortune in Paris with a 'Discourse on a
new Theory of Music,' or rather Musical Notation,
which he had written. It had some success at the
Academy, where it was read; he became introduced to
many persons of note; he accepted the place of secretary to Count de Montaigue, ambassador at Venice, and
was on his arrival, as he represents, made secretary of
the embassy. Here his conduct was, for the first time in
his life, prudent, and he reaped the fruits of it in the re-
spectability which he enjoyed. He remained performing
with satisfaction all the duties of his station, which the
utter incapacity of the ambassador made heavier than
they otherwise would have been; and after a variety of
the meanest attempts on his Excellency's part to share
his perquisites, and repeated acts of maltreatment, at last
amounting to the insolence and fury of a madman, this
ambassador compelled him to resign. The madness
had, however, some method, for the salary was with-

held, and in lieu of it the most absurd charges were brought against him. The senate, the council, all the French inhabitants, and all the diplomatists took his part, and he returned to Paris, where he never could get even an answer to his just complaints, being told that a foreigner, like him, could not be regarded when charging a French functionary with injustice ; for the government very consistently forgot that if foreigners are to be employed in the public service, their not being natives affords no defence whatever to those who maltreat them, and obstruct them in the performance of their official duties.

On his return to Paris he went to live at an inferior hotel, or rather lodging-house, near the Luxembourg, and there dining at the table with the family, he became acquainted with a female servant, a girl from Orléans, where her father had held a place in the mint and her mother had been a shopkeeper, but both were reduced to distress. Their name was Le Vasseur, and the girl's Theresa. She was about twenty-three, of modest demeanour, and so much without education that even after living with him for many years she never could read the figures on the dial-plate of a clock, or tell in what order the months succeeded each other.* He became attached to her ; she cohabited with him, and bore him five children, all of which he sent one after the other to the Foundling Hospital, regardless of the poor mother's tears ; and after twenty-five years of this intercourse he married her. The mother, a vulgar and affected woman, lived with them ; and the father, whom she could not endure, but

---

Couf., part ii. liv. 7.

of whom Theresa was very fond, was, on pretext of economy, sent at the age of 80 to the workhouse, where the disgrace of this treatment immediately broke his heart.

After the battle of Fontenoy, in 1745, the Court gave several theatrical entertainments, and Voltaire contributed the 'Princesse de Navarre,' of which the famous Rameau had composed the music ; it was now changed into the 'Fête de Ramire,' and Rousseau being employed to complete the adaptation, which required considerable alteration both of words and airs, Voltaire was extremely pleased with his work and with his flattering letter respecting it. Rousseau composed his own opera of 'Les Muses Galantes' the same year ; but after one or two rehearsals, apprehensive of its fate, he withdrew it. The death of his father enabled him to obtain a small sum which belonged to his mother, and which the father had enjoyed for his life. A small portion, which he sent to Chambery, was at once devoured by the knaves who surrounded Madame de Warens, and lived by pillaging her.

The kindness of his steady friend M. Francueil, Receiver-General of Finance, placed him in the office of his cashier (*caissier*), one of great trust, which he dreaded, and of considerable emolument, which, because he was starving and complained of being forced to send his children to the Hospital, he altogether contemned. He resigned it in a few weeks, on the ground that its duties were irksome, and prevented him from fully enjoying himself as he liked, at a time when he believed he had only a few months to live. Self-indulgence appears to have been erected by him into a kind of principle, or rule of conduct. He therefore betook himself to copying music, which he did very carelessly, and very ill.

In 1749 he wrote his 'Essay on the Mischiefs of Science,' the subject proposed by the Academy of Dijon, as if on purpose to frustrate Voltaire's remark already mentioned in his 'Life;' for assuredly it was a slip in a scientific body to make it a question whether science corrupted or improved the morals of mankind. Next year it obtained the prize. He justly thought very meanly of its arrangement and reasoning, nor did he himself think highly of its composition; yet partly by the brilliancy and power of the declamation, and partly by the boldness of the paradoxes, it attracted the greatest notice, both made converts and raised adversaries against its doctrines. He has described his manner of writing it: he lay in bed with his eyes closed, revolving and finishing his periods, which he always did very slowly and with much difficulty. He slept little, and on rising in the morning the act of dressing would drive the greater part of what he had composed out of his head. He therefore used to make Theresa's mother come and write under his dictation. The success of his 'Essay' was followed by one more brilliant still. He composed the little opera of the 'Devin du Village' in about six weeks, and it was performed with prodigious success before the King, in his private theatre at Fontainebleau, in 1751. A message was sent next morning to desire his attendance, and it was confidently believed about Court that a pension was to have been granted him; but he was far too much alarmed, and had far too little command of

himself, or power of crossing his inclinations, to undergo this scene, and he very indecorously as well as
very foolishly ran away to Paris early in the morning.
From the Court, however, and the musical engravers,
he received between two and three hundred louis, as
much as the 'Emile' afterwards brought him, for the
fruit of twenty years' labour. The piece deserved its
success. Nothing can be more light and gay than both
the simple plan, the pretty songs, and the lively, graceful
airs. It seems to have all the excellence that a performance of this inferior class can well attain. Next year
his 'Narcissus,' a drama, was given at the 'Français;'
and though borne for two nights, he was himself
so tired of it, and so convinced of its failure, that
he could not remain to the end of the performance,
but came out, ran to a coffee-house, and announced
its certain fate, avowing himself at the same time
to be the author, a circumstance which had been
carefully concealed. In 1753-4 he wrote a second
'Essay on the Inequality of Human Conditions,' also
for the Dijon Academy. It had the faults of the first,
with more of paradox, and also better composition;
but its want of novelty, and its inferior eloquence, prevented it from succeeding.

In the summer of 1754 he was, with Theresa, taken
by a friend, M. Gauffecourt, a tour to Geneva, where
he remained some months. He went by Chambery, to
see Madame de Warens, and he was received with
great distinction by all the families whom he had
known; but as he approached Geneva he felt the annoyance to which he was subjected by having lost his
civic rights, in consequence of his quitting the Protes-

tant Church. He soon resolved to remove this only obstacle which stood in the way of his regaining them ; and abjuring Romanism with as much reflection and as much disinterestedness as he had formerly Calvinism, he was once more a Protestant, and became a citizen of Geneva. Among the reasons which chiefly influenced him in not retiring thither for the rest of his life was the near neighbourhood of Voltaire, whom he regarded as destroying the place by corrupting its inhabitants.* This was in 1754; while to all outward appearance he was bowing to the idol of the day, and expressing his entire admiration of his genius.

On the establishment of the ' Encyclopédie,' D'Alembert and Diderot, with whom he was acquainted, engaged him to write some articles; and this increased his intimacy with Diderot, whose habits were loose, as well as introduced him to Diderot's friend Grimm, a man of letters, in the service of the Duke of Saxe Gotha, and employed by him for many years as a kind of literary and philosophical Resident at Paris. The letters which he wrote in that capacity, his despatches, as it were, have been since published, and are well known. When he came to Paris, being a man of wit as well as letters, he was successful in society, and became dissipated and even profligate in his manners ; but he does not appear either to have indulged in any vulgar excesses, or to have offended against the conventional laws of honour which bind the polite world. Rousseau always represents himself as his introducer into the Parisian circles, and as having been

---

* Conf., part ii. liv. 8.

supplanted there by his superior address and habits of the world. Among others he had presented him to the family of M. d'Epinay, Fermier-Général, who kept a very hospitable house, where the Encyclopédists were familiar, as they were still more at the Baron d'Holbach's. Grimm became the professed lover of Madame d'Epinay, whose sister-in-law, Madame d'Houdetot, made a still deeper impression on the heart of Rousseau; but her avowed lover was his friend St. Lambert. The Epinays had a country house, Chenettes, in the fine valley of Montmorency; and Rousseau, when visiting there, was greatly taken with the retirement of a cottage and garden called the Hermitage, in its neighbourhood, and likewise belonging to the family. Hither he transferred his residence, in the spring of 1756, and it was his home for the next six years of his life.* Theresa's mother came with him as well as herself, and nothing can be more disgusting than the details of her mean, sordid, double-dealing conduct, to obtain money and other things from him, through the agency of her daughter. But she was of some use in the management of his house, for which her daughter was as unfit as himself.

At the Hermitage, for the first year or two of his residence, he seems to have suffered for want of the society which he had quitted, though this is the last thing he will confess. He admits that his imagination was excited

---

* It is only another instance of his inattention to dates that he totally omits the several years passed at Neufchâtel, when he speaks of Montmorency as his constant residence, and represents it as such after his visit to England in 1766.

by the recollection of past scenes of enjoyment in a more sensual kind; and the void left by these gratifications, now past, or only existing in his memory, he filled up with creations of his fancy, embodying beings of a lovely and excellent nature, and placing them in situations of lively interest, which, if his own experience and recollections failed to suggest, it cost his imagination, sometimes sentimental, sometimes prurient, nothing to invent. This was the origin of the 'Nouvelle Héloïse,' of all his works the most renowned, and of all, except his posthumous 'Memoirs,' the best, though certainly very greatly overrated both by the public opinion and by his own. He describes the delight he had in composing it as approaching to an actual enjoyment, though it only consisted in the pleasures of an indulged fancy. He wandered all day in the forest of Montmorency; he had his pencil and note-book with him; Theresa walked calmly by. In the afternoon returning home, he wrote what had occurred on the finest paper, sanded with gold and blue dust, bound with bright-coloured ribbons; and he read at night the produce of the day to the mother, who entered not into it with any comprehension, much less tasted it with any relish, but said "Monsieur, cela est bien beau;" and to the daughter, who entered not into it at all, but sighed and sobbed when she saw him appear to be moved.

To deny the great merit of this work would be absurd; the degree in which it has been overrated, owing chiefly to its immorality, and in part also to its vices of taste, not unnaturally leads to its depreciation when the critic soberly and calmly exercises his stern and

M

ungrateful office.   But the conception of the piece is,
for its simplicity and nature, happy, with the exception which may be taken especially to the unnatural
situations of the lovers on meeting after Julie's marriage, to the extravagant as well as dull deathbed scene,
and to the episode, the adventures of the English Lord.
The descriptions of natural scenery are admirable—far
superior to the moral painting ; for Rousseau's taste in
landscape was excellent, while with his moral taste,
his perverted sentiments, so wide from truth and
nature, always interfered.   The interest of the story
is quite well sustained, and the turns in it are well
represented by the successive letters.   The passions are
vividly painted, and as by one who had felt their force,
though they are not touched with a delicate pencil.
The feelings are ill rendered, partly because they are
mixed with the perverted sentiments of the ill-regu-
lated, and even diseased mind, in which they are
hatched into life, partly because they are given in the
diction of rhetoric, and not of nature.   The love which
he plumes himself on exhibiting beyond all his predecessors, nay, as if he first had portrayed, and almost
alone had felt it. is a mixture of the sensual and the
declamatory, with something of the grossness of the
one, much of the other's exaggeration.   As this is the
main object of the book, therefore, the book must be
allowed to be a failure.   It charmed many ; it enchanted both the Bishops Warburton and Hurd, as
we see in their published correspondence ; it still holds
a high place among the works which prudent mothers
withhold from their daughters, and which many daughters contrive to enjoy in secret ; it makes a deep im-

pression on hearts as yet little acquainted with real passion, and heads inexperienced in the social relations ; it assuredly has no great charms either for the experienced or the wise, and is alike condemned by a severe taste in composition and a strict judgment in morals.

It would be endless to support these remarks by examples ; but let us only take, as the fairest test by which to judge the ' Nouvelle Héloïse,' its author's own favourite piece, the ' Elysée' and the ' Voyage on the Lake,' at the end of Part iv. They are Letters xi. and xvii. of that part ; and he denounces a woe upon whosoever can read them without feeling his heart melt in tenderness.*

Now the greater part of the first (Letter xi.) is mere description of place ; it is landscape painting, not history painting ; and, with the exception of an extremely unnatural reprimand, given by M. de Wolmar to St. Preux, for speaking of the shrubbery where he and Julie used to ramble, and into which since her marriage she never went, there is really not one touch of sentiment in the whole : unless, indeed, it can be reckoned such, that on revisiting the Elysée next morning, when he expected to be melted with seeing the walks she had made and used, the flowers she had planted, &c., he recollects the terrible reprimand of the evening before, and no longer can think of any thing except the happiness of a future state. All this is well written, but it is mere rhetoric ; the sen-

---

* " Quiconque, en lisant ces deux lettres, ne sent pas amollir, et se fonder son cœur dans l'attendrissement qui me les dictât, doit fermer le livre ; il n'est pas fait pour juger les choses de sentiment."— (Conf., part ii. liv. 9.)

timents are cold, they are unnatural; the reprimand of yesterday never would have stifled the passion of to-day. The last effect that this letter, filled with admirable description of a garden and an aviary, could ever produce, is assuredly that of melting the heart in tenderness; and as far as this first letter goes, the woe denounced in the ' Confessions' must attach on all who read it.

The other (Letter xvii.) is of a much more ambitious character; but, with one single exception, it is liable to the remark to which every part of the ' Nouvelle Héloïse' justly gives rise—that it is rhetoric, not elo-quence; it is declamation, not true expression of sentiment. The most laboured passage, beyond all doubt, is the speech which St. Preux addresses to Julie on taking her to the grove and the rocks where he had passed his time when separated from her, and when only thinking of her and writing to her; it is a very long speech, full of set phrases, and describing the icicles on rocks, and snow festoons on trees, and the cold only made bearable by the fire in his heart; touching also on ornithology, as well as meteorology : "le vorace épervier; le corbeau funèbre; l'aigle terrible des Alpes" (a phrase, by the way, which no one living among the Alps would ever use); and then ending in a rant of "Fille trop constamment aimée! Oh toi pour qui j'étais né!" &c. She interrupts him with "Allons nous en; l'air de ce lieu n'est pas bon pour moi." Now this is certainly better than the speech, but it is as certainly not pathetic. What follows in the boat is much finer; and is both well conceived, excepting at first, and well executed. He

feels his situation so bitterly, that he is tempted
for a moment to plunge into the water, dragging her
after him; but he rushes away from her side, and
weeps violently in the prow. All this is nothing;
and indeed the violence of the scene is revolting; but
we are recompensed by what follows and closes it.
He comes and sits down again by her;—" Elle tenait
son mouchoir; je le sentis fort mouillé. Ah! lui dis-je
tout bas, je vois que nos cœurs n'ont jamais cessé de
s'entendre!" She admits it in a faltering voice, and
desires their hearts may never more so commune.
They then speak calmly, and he afterwards observes,
on landing and coming to the light, that she had
been weeping—her eyes were red and inflamed. This
is finely done; but with two great faults, the worst
which such painting can have—a piece of wit and an
overdone and a needless description. An epigram, almost
a pleasantry, is introduced, when he says—and it is the
working up of the whole—that their hearts had plainly
never ceased to hear or to understand each other; she
answers with a repartee. Instead of stopping at " Il est
vrai," or saying nothing, being unable to speak, which
would have been better, she goes on, " Mais que ce
soit la dernière fois." Even there she might have
ended, giving the moral rebuke; but she goes on,
" Mais que ce soit la dernière fois qu'ils auront parlé
sur ce ton." Then what reason was there for his
" J'aperçus à la lumière, qu'elle avait les yeux rouges et
forte gonflés, et elle ne dût pas trouver les miens en meil-
leur état," after the wet handkerchief and faltering
voice in the boat, and his own agony in the prow? Such
scenes as these require the very greatest care and the

most rigid abstinence in the moral artist. Particulars, details, circumstances, must be given, and given when the moral excitement is at its pitch; but the selection is of infinite moment, and there must be no superfluity, no ornament, nothing flowery, nothing, no, absolutely nothing, introduced of an opposite, an inconsistent character. The superfluity surfeits, and sickens, and weakens all effect; the foreign substance inserted causes as it were, a fermentation to cast the intruder forth.

The less delicate and more vehement portions of the work are certainly very inferior, faulty as even the best parts are. Nothing can be less refined, nothing, indeed, more vulgar, than a lover writing to his mistress at all about his transports on obtaining possession of her. But St. Preux begins, "from the first kiss of love," to hold up her weakness in her own face, and that happens no later in the piece than the fourteenth letter. He holds her conduct up, too, in coarse terms, by way of making the offence less out-rageous : " Je suis ivre—mes sens sont troublés par ce baiser mortel."—" Un doux frémissement." — " Ta bouche de roses—la bouche de Julie—se poser sur la mienne, et mon corps serré dans tes bras."* This may not possibly be the only instance of an innocent girl suffering such a liberty for the first time in her life without resistance, nay, meeting her lover more than half-way; but assuredly it is the only instance of his telling her in plain terms what a forward, abandoned wanton she proved. After this, we are well pre-pared for a letter, in which she says that all difficulties

---

* Part I., let. xix. : Œuv. ii. 5.

only give her more spirit and boldness, and that if his courage is equal to her own, he may come in the night, when she will "acquitter ses promesses, et payer d'une seule fois toutes les dettes de l'amour." She then exclaims, " Non, mon doux ami! non! nous ne quitterons pas cette courte vie sans avoir un instant goûté du bonheur;" and to leave no doubt of the kind of happiness she had in her eye, she adds, " Viens avouer, même au sein des plaisirs, que c'est du sein des cœurs qu'ils prirent leur plus grand charme;" of which very bold avowal the chasteness of the diction is on a par with the purity of the morals: for " âme de mon cœur" and " vie de ma vie" are, especially the former, expressions of a moderate correctness. Then follow the two very celebrated letters in consequence of the lady's invitation being accepted. One is written in the ante-room of Julie's bed-chamber, and is of an incomparable absurdity in the design, for which no felicity in the execution could ever compensate. But is the execution less bad than the conception in such lines as these?—"O désirs! O crainte! O palpitations cruelles!—On ouvre! on entre!—C'est elle, c'est elle! Mon faible cœur, tu succombes!—Ah! cherchez des forces pour supporter la félicité qui t'accable."* Of the other letter the following day, absolutely insulting to the poor girl, little needs be said. The scheme of writing it is revolting enough; but less so, perhaps, than the language its execution is couched in. He actually speaks of " ces baisers qu'une voluptueuse lan- gueur nous faisaient lentement savourer, et ces gé-

---

* Part I., Let. liv.: Œuv. ii. 127.

missemens si tendres durant lesquels tu pressais sur
ton cœur, ce cœur fait pour s'unir à lui."* He calls
her "divine Julie." It certainly was another epithet
originally; I remember to have first read it "incon-
cevable Julie," and to have thought it the best word
in the whole book.

There is no concealing the truth that a volume of
love-letters must naturally be tiresome to the very
verge of not being readable. Their interest to the
parties is only exceeded by their indifference in all
other eyes. Hence the 'Nouvelle Héloïse,' which pro-
fesses chiefly to consist of this kind of material in its
most interesting portions, must have been dull, had
there been no digressions to relieve it. The marriage
of Julie, and the Parisian sojourn of St. Preux, his
return to La Meillerie, and Julie's death, afford those
varieties, and enable the book to proceed through its
very considerable length.

At l'Ermitage, he very soon fell in love with Madame d'Houdetot, M. d'Epinay's sister, and he declares that this was the only love he ever felt in
his life. How often the same thing had been avowed
to others by the man of pure heart, who deemed
sincerity as above all other virtues, who could excuse all
vices save the want of perfect simplicity and honesty,
we have no means of judging. That he had before
been on such terms with some seven or eight women
as must have led to similar declarations of attachment,
unless he avowed that he treated them as brutes, as

---

* Part I., Let. lv.: Œuv., ii. 127.

mere instruments of sensual pleasure, is certain from his own account. But he declares, with perfect solemnity, that this passion was "la première et l'unique de toute sa vie."* The lady treated him with kindness, apparently as a child; his friend St. Lambert did not much relish the matter, being unable to adopt his singular habit of several lovers at one and the same time intimate with one mistress; and she became in consequence reserved and distant. An open quarrel took place with Madame d'Epinay, her sister-in-law, like many of Rousseau's quarrels, without any intelligible ground, except his taking offence at something which he had imagined, and then writing abusive letters. He wrote to say he should leave l'Ermitage; she answered that if he chose to do so he was welcome. He replied that after such a hint he could not remain a week. He removed to another house near Montmorency, and there he remained, taking very properly the opportunity of this removal to get rid of Madame le Vasseur, whom no entreaties of her daughter could induce him to keep about him any longer. With Grimm and Diderot he quarrelled irreconcileably; and his book is filled with attacks upon them both, but especially upon Grimm. He charges them, as usual, with a conspiracy, the overt acts of which were their sometimes seeing and conversing with Theresa's mother, the improper purpose of which he never could describe, or even inform us what he suspected it to be. He had some vague, half-crazy notion that they wanted to direct and guide him, and to injure his fame and to

---

* Conf., part ii. let. 9: Œuv., i. p. 423.

make him do foolish things,—as if they could have any conceivable interest in his degradation, or could possibly drive him to do more foolish things than he perpetually did of his own accord. Next to his quarrel with Hume, nothing so betokened a diseased mind as his suspicions of these two friends. One letter which he received from Grimm he says contained an avowal of hating him, or at least a throwing off of his friendship; but he says he never read more than the beginning of it, and that he sent it back with a violent answer.*
But, unfortunately, Madame d'Epinay in her 'Memoirs' published the letter, and it contains nothing like what Rousseau complained of till the very end. Nothing, therefore, can be more inconsistent than his account of the whole transaction; and indeed his furious passion at other letters of the most indifferent kind, which he cites in his 'Confessions,' shows sufficiently that his mind laboured under morbid delusions in all this epistolary intercourse.

In his new residence he wrote the letter to D'Alembert on the article 'Genève,' of the 'Encyclopédie,' the subject of which is an attack upon theatrical entertainments. He says he composed it in three weeks of a severe winter, sitting in an open summer-house at the end of the garden, without fire or shelter. It had very great success, and it is written with much power. The sale of this work, with that of the 'Nouvelle Héloïse,' published in 1759, gave him 3000 francs to spare. The latter work had been printing in Holland above two years, and had frequently been read in

---

* Conf., part ii. liv. 9: Œuv., i. p. 467.

manuscript to persons of distinction, such as the
Maréchal de Luxembourg, and the Maréchale who
now had the Château de Montmorency, and with whom
he formed a great intimacy, insomuch that they
gave him a convenient summer-house, near their
orangery, where he lived occasionally. The avidity
with which the work was at first read may be judged of
from this, that it was lent out by the booksellers at
twelve sous an hour; and instances are cited of prin-
cesses ordering their carriages at night to attend an
opera or ball, and being found absorbed in the book at
two in the morning so as to send their carriages away.

The 'Emile' was published in the spring of 1762,
and the 'Contrat Social' a few weeks before it. The
'Contrat,' which he appears, with the wonted soundness
of an author's judgment on himself, to have valued beyond all his other works, and to have elaborated the
most, is an irrefragable proof of his unfitness for all political discussion, as his 'Discourse on Political Economy'
for the 'Encyclopédie' proves his equal unfitness for
economical studies. It is not that he bewilders himself in all the errors and inconsistencies of an original
compact, for Locke and Somers had done so before
him, though he flounders in the mire very differently
from Locke; but he, who pretends to write in
modern times upon government, denies all virtue
to the great improvement of modern policy, the representative system, declaring that the people are slaves,
and the state is near its ruin, when the rights and
duties of rulers are performed by any but the whole
body of the citizens (lib. iii. ch. 15); that the English "are slaves, are nothing, except a few days in

six or seven years."* His capacity of defining with logical precision is shown by his reckoning an elective aristocracy as one form of that polity, and of course preferring it to either a natural or an hereditary aristocracy, nay, apparently to any other kind of government, without perceiving that it is nothing like an aristocracy at all, but is, in truth, a form of the representative government which he condemns (Lib. iii. ch. 5). His power of dealing with particular constitutions is seen in his comments on that of Poland, the subject of a separate treatise which he published in 1772. He considers the radical vice of the Polish government to be the extent of the country, and recommends either a federal union or the abandonment to neighbouring powers of some part of its dominions—a plan which those powers full soon caused to be adopted. The election of the sovereign he holds to be a good principle, under wise restrictions; and the one which he proposes is the selection by the whole people of one from among the noblemen of the first class, to be chosen by lot,—an absurdity unexampled in political reveries. ('Considérations sur le Gouvernement de Pologne,' ch. v. xiv.)

The merits of the 'Emile' are of a much higher order; for together with wild theories, mere fantastical dreams of education, it contains a great deal of striking, though certainly not pure, composition, sometimes of a

---

* "Le peuple Anglais pense être libre: il se trompe fort; il ne l'est que durant l'élection des membres du Parlement; si tôt ils ont élu, il est esclave, il n'est rien. Dans les courts momens de sa liberté, l'usage qu'il en fait mérite bien qu'il la perde" (liv. iii. ch. 15).

sentimental, sometimes of a declamatory kind; and it abounds in remarks, the result of personal experience or actual observation, and so entitled to much attention. The religious portion, the 'Profession de Foi d'un Vicaire Savoyard,' is that which naturally excited most attention at the time of its publication, and which still possesses the most interest. His long letter in the 'Nouvelle Héloïse' (Liv. v., Let. 3) contains his thoughts on the subject of education, powerfully though more concisely given; but nothing of an infidel cast was given before the 'Emile.' It is true Wolmar, a perfect character, is made first an atheist, and then a sceptic, owing to his contempt for the ceremonies of the Greek and Romish churches; and that Julie's religion is rather pure, exalted, impassioned theism, than Christianity (Liv. vi., Let. 5; Liv. xvi., Let. 7, 8), yet the Scriptures are spoken of with Christian reverence (Œuv., ii., p. 622); and both Julie dies a Christian death, and Wolmar is, in consequence, about to be converted when the curtain falls. But the 'Emile' at once declares against Revelation; it does not indeed substitute, for the Christian scheme dogmatically rejected, a dogmatical theism, but it denies the credibility of the Gospel dispensation as recorded in the Scriptures, and it substitutes a moderate but humble scepticism. There is no sarcasm, no dogmatism, no ribaldry, no abuse; the feelings of the Christian reader are consulted, and not outraged; the weapons of attack are reasoning and sentiment, not ridicule; the author's errors are to every candid reader his misfortune, not his fault; and he gives the impression to a charitable mind of having wished to be a believer, and failed.

Nevertheless a storm ensued upon the publication of the book. M. de Malesherbes, first President of the Cour des Aides, and at the head of the Censorship (Librairie), had given it his official sanction, and it had in consequence been published at Paris and Amsterdam about the same time. But the Courts of Law interfered, and a decree of arrest was issued. Rousseau had notice through the kindness of his excellent friends the Lux- embourgs, and by their aid he escaped to Neufchâtel, where Lord Marischal (Keith), the Prussian governor, protected and befriended him. Theresa followed, and appears to have in no degree increased the com- forts of his residence. She soon grew tired of the solitude in which they lived—the manners of the inhabitants would not tolerate kept women ; and there is every reason to think, that after feeding his suspicious mind with alarms, and making him believe that his life was in danger from the bigotry of the people, she strengthened her exhortations by pretending that his house was one night during the fair attacked by the mob He gives a minute account of the " quarry of stones" found in the house next morning, alleging that they were thrown through the windows. But M. Servan ('Réflexions sur les Confessions') states his having been particularly informed, by a respectable person who saw the house the same day, that the holes in the windows were smaller than the stones found on the floor ; and Comte d'Eschery, a passionate admirer of Rousseau, and who doubled the prize offered by the Académie Française, in 1790, for his ' Eloge,' affirms, in his 'Mélanges de Littérature' (vol. iii., p. 35 and 154), not only that Theresa, who had made herself

detested by her violent and slanderous tongue, was the
principal author of the trick, but that Rousseau himself must have been her accomplice, in the hope of
giving an excuse, and a colour of persecution, to his
departure from Neufchâtel. The whole was reduced on
examination to "a single pane of glass broken by a
stone thrown from the outside in the night." The
Count gives other anecdotes showing how completely
Rousseau was the dupe of his own fancies. One is,
that when they passed a night together in the mountains, lying on some new-mown hay, and asked one
another how they had slept, Jean Jacques said " he
never slept;" and Col. de Pury, one of the party,
stopped him by saying *he* had envied him the whole
night, as he lay awake, owing to the fermenting of the
hay beneath him, while the sleepless philosopher
snored without any intermission. Of Theresa the
Count speaks with constant scorn and dislike, as
of a most silly, vulgar, and mischievous person, having
only the one accomplishment of being a very good cook.
But Rousseau never suffered her to sit at table, though
he was continually taking the most ignorant and stupid
things she said for proofs of her natural sense.

It seems here the place to observe that Rousseau
distinctly admits his never having felt for a moment the
least love for this poor creature (Confessions, Part ii., liv.
ix.: Œuv., i., 378)—" la moindre étincelle d'amour."
Whatever she may have felt for him, he tells us
had become nearly extinguished long before 1768, when
he married her ; indeed his treatment of her, as well
by forming other attachments as by tearing her five
infants from her on their birth, and while she was

in the first weakness of childbearing, was quite enough
to make her weary of him, if his temper had been far
less irritable than a diseased bladder, bad stomach, and
half crazy brain, allowed it to be. That he had a
great contempt for her understanding, and no confidence in her virtue or her disposition, is quite plain
from a letter which he wrote her in 1769, and which is
preserved. Her complaints of the tiresome life they led,
and her constant threats of leaving him, appear to have
given rise to this letter, together with a complaint of
a less delicate kind to which he adverts in plain terms
enough, but which no other pen can well touch upon.
Her conduct in England gave the greatest offence to
Mr. Davenport ; and, among other tricks to which she
resorted for the purpose of making Rousseau suspect
everybody, and thus resolve to quit Wootton, of which
she as easily tired as she did of Switzerland, she broke
open his letters, and made him fancy that his enemies
had done it.

After they quitted Neufchâtel, in 1765, they went to
live for a few months in the Isle St. Pierre, an islet
in the Lac de Bienne, belonging to the hospital of
Bern. Here he indulged in his botanical pursuits,
and fancied that he led a quiet wild life, as in a state
of nature. The invitation sent through Madame de
Boufflers, from David Hume, to visit England, brought
him from his solitude, and he accompanied the philosopher thither. Mr. Davenport soon afterwards
invited him to inhabit his convenient mansion of
Wootton in Derbyshire. A pension of £100 a-year
was obtained for him through Mr. Hume's influence
with the Conway family, and it appears to have been

the only overt act of the conspiracy in which he soon
believed Mr. Hume had joined to ruin his character for
ever. Another suspicion proved quite as groundless.
Horace Walpole having written a jeu d'esprit which
amused the Parisian circles—a letter from Frederick
inviting him to Berlin, but warning him that he never
would gratify him by any of the persecution he so
greatly delighted in—Rousseau fancied Hume had
written this, in which he had no hand whatever.

That actual insanity had now undermined his reason, was become quite apparent. The most indifferent
things were converted into proofs of a conspiracy, the
object of which was, if possible, more utterly incompre-
hensible than that of Grimm and Diderot. In the
'Confessions' he refers to this English plot, and says,
that "he sees marching towards its execution, without
any resistance, the most black, the most frightful conspiracy that ever was devised against a man's memory,"
(Conf., part ii., lib. xi. ; Œuv., i. 550.) He also fancied
that the government, a party to it by granting the pension, was preventing him from leaving the country ;
nay, he wrote to General Conway, then Secretary of
State, that he was aware his departure never could be
suffered. That letter, indeed, is as completely the
production of a madman as any that ever was penned
within the walls of Bedlam. He wrote it from Dover,
whither he had gone by a rapid journey from Spalding, in Lincolnshire, having first gone to Spalding
from Wootton, to escape his enemies and the agents
of government. After living ten months in England,
he came over to France, changing his name to Renou,
and went to Amiens, where, though he was received

with high distinction by every one, and even by the authorities of the place, he still felt suspicious and uneasy. In autumn, 1767, he went to Trye le Château, a place of Prince de Conti's, where he remained a year in the same irritable and suspicious state of mind. It must be added to these undoubted symptoms of mental disease, that, some years after, and when his mind had regained composure, he really admitted his having been so affected. No man confesses madness in terms, even after it has ceased. We find George III., in a letter to Lord Eldon, in which, after his recovery (1804), he refused to have his mad doctor still about him, only says, that "patients in a ' *nervous fever*,' when well, cannot bear the presence of those who had the care of them in their illness." (Twiss's Life, vol. i., p. 382.) So Rousseau softened his admission, when conversing with Bernardin de St. Pierre:—" J'ai mis trop d'humeur dans mes querelles avec M. Hume ; mais le climat d'Angleterre, la situation de ma fortune, et les persécutions que je venais d'essuyer, tout me jetait dans la mélancolie." (L'Arcadie, Préambule.)

When he quitted Trye, in June, 1768, he went to Grenoble, and soon after to Bougoin, in the Lyonnais. That vanity was at the bottom of his malady, no one could doubt, even did no proof exist under his hand. But he scrawled, when passing through Lyons, a number of sentences on the door of his bedroom, and afterwards sent a copy of them to a lady there : they show that he considered the whole world as occupied with him, and all but kings, bishops, and the higher nobility, as his bitter enemies. (Cor., ii. 380.) From Bougoin he went to Monguin, a village in the neighbourhood, at the beginning of 1769, and there chose to fall acquainted with a retired officer, M. St. Germain, on whom he forced his most confidential friendship, and who told him plainly, that, seeing the disordered state of his fancy, he preferred his own plain sense to all his philosophy. This worthy man, however, though very religious, and as different from him as possible in his character, conceived that warm friendship which so many people felt for him, chiefly from the pity which his weakness and misery inspired, partly from the infantine openness of his heart. His letters at this time are all dated in a cypher, like those of the Quakers;* and he begins each letter with four bad verses, about men being poor creatures. Nothing can be more dull than his correspondence during the two years which he spent in this neighbourhood. He could, however, no longer refrain from the food which Paris offered to his vanity; and after resolving to visit Chambery, partly, he said, to weep over the recollection of Madame de Warens, who had died while he was at Neufchâtel, partly to discomfit his enemies, because they would not know he was there, he all at once says, " Ne parlons plus de Chambery: l'honneur et le devoir crient, et je n'entends plus que leur voix." So away he goes to Paris, where he creates, by his arrival, some sensation, and more by his reading the ' Confessions' in select circles ; and this is all the explanation ever given of what he meant by the calls of honour and duty. From July, 1770, when he returned, to March, 1778, when he removed to Ermenonville, he remained at

---

* Thus for 15th January, 1769. $\frac{1}{15}$ 1769.

Paris. With M. St. Germain he never had a minute's
difference of any kind; yet he entirely gave over
writing to him for the last seven years of his life.
With all his former friends he quarrelled; and half
a year before his death he wrote and sent a circular, representing himself and his wife as so much reduced that they could no longer live out of a workhouse, and begging to be sent to some hospital, where
their little income might be used for their support. It
is plain that he would have greatly wished some friend,
some of the supposed conspirators, to send him there
without his asking it; but as no one thought of doing
so, the circular was issued. It was all a pretence.
At Ermenonville, he immediately became so much
pleased with the place, that he began writing, and
seemed as contented as his nature would allow him
to be. Two friends, much attached to him, and
alarmed by the tone of the circular, ascertained that it
was all a trick—there is no other word to give it—a
trick to attract pity, and make his persecutions be cre-
dited. Nor can any one doubt, that had he been
taken at his word, he would have proclaimed the
grand plot as having reached its consummation. He
died suddenly, on the 2d of July, 1778, apparently of
apoplexy, having immediately before come home ill
from a walk, and complained of a pain in the head.
He had only been at Ermenonville six weeks. He was
buried, at his own request, on the island in the lake
there. The report of his suicide was utterly without
foundation, though Madame de Staël, in her clever
' Essay' on his genius, gives it countenance. It has
been again and again completely disproved.

In 1790 the National Assembly bestowed a pension of 1200 francs on his widow, which the Convention, in 1793, increased to 1500, ordering also a statue to his memory. The following year his remains were transferred to the Pantheon, with those of Voltaire, and others of the great men to whom the simple and striking inscription of that noble edifice refers.* The example of Paris was followed in the other towns which he had at any time honoured with his residence. His statue was erected at Geneva; and at Lyons, Grenoble, Montpelier, almost wherever he had dwelt, celebrations in honour of his memory were had.

The pension, and the interest of considerable funds (nearly 40,000 francs) which the different publishers owed her husband, amply provided for his widow. But that worthless creature, immediately after his death, formed a connexion with an Irishman, a groom of M. Girardin, owner of Ermenonville. With him she lived until he had spent all her money, and she was in her old age reduced to beggary. In that state she used to take her stand and beg at the door of the theatre. She died in 1801, at the age of 80.

All Rousseau's works, except his posthumous memoirs, the 'Confessions,' we have had occasion already to consider. But that is, beyond any question, and very much beyond any comparison, his masterpiece. There is no work in the French language of which the style is more racy, and, indeed, more classically pure. But its diction is idiomatical as well as pure. As if he had lived long enough away from Geneva to lose not only

---

* Aux Grands Hommes, la Patrie Reconnaissante.

all the provincialisms of that place, but also to lose all
its pedantry and precision, he writes both with the
accuracy and elegance of a Frenchman, and with the
freedom of wit and of genius, even of humour and
drollery—yes, even of humour and drollery; for the
picture of the vulgar young man who supplanted him
with Madame de Warens shows no mean power of
caricature; and the sketches of his own ludicrous situations, as at the concert he gave in the Professor s
house at Lausanne, show the impartiality with which
he could exert this power at his own proper cost and
charge.   The subject is often tiresome ; it is almost
always his own sufferings, and genius, and feelings; always, of course, but of that no complaint can be justly
made, of his own adventures ; yet we are carried irre-
sistibly along, first of all by the manifest truth and
sincerity of the narrative which the fulness of the humiliating confessions at every step attests, and then,
and chiefly, by the magical diction,—a diction so idiomatical and yet so classical—so full of nature and yet
so refined by art—so exquisitely graphic without any
effort, and so accommodated to its subject without any
baseness,—that there hardly exists another example of
the miracles which composition can perform.   The
subject is not only wearisome from its sameness, but,
from the absurdities of the author's conduct, and
opinions, and feelings, it is revolting ; yet on we
go, enchained and incapable of leaving it, how often
soever we may feel irritated and all but enraged.
The subject is not only wearisome generally, revolting
frequently, but it is oftentimes low, vulgar, grovelling,
fitted to turn us away from the contemplation with

aversion, even with disgust; yet the diction of the great magician is our master; he can impart elegance to the most ordinary and mean things, in his description of them; he can elevate the lowest, even the most nasty ideas, into dignity by the witchery of his language. We stand aghast after pausing, when we can take breath, and can see over what filthy ground we have been led, but we feel the extraordinary power of the hand that has led us along. It is one of Homer's great praises, that he ennobles the most low and homely details of the most vulgar life, as when he brings Ulysses into the swineherd's company, and paints the domestic economy of that unadorned and ignoble peasant. No doubt the diction is sweet in which he warbles those ordinary strains; yet the subject, how humble soever, is pure unsophisticated nature, with no taint of the far more insufferable pollution derived from vice. Not so Rousseau's subject: he sings of vices, and of vices the most revolting and the most base—of vices which song never before came near to elevate; and he sings of the ludicrous and the offensive as well as the hateful and the repulsive, yet he sings without impurity, and contrives to entrance us in admiration. No triumph so great was ever won by diction. The work in this respect stands alone; it is reasonable to wish that it may have no imitators.

But is it as faithful in all particulars as it is striking and attractive—as scrupulously faithful as the awful eloquence of its commencement ought to have kept it throughout? In the great majority of instances, it certainly is entitled to this praise; but exceptions,

it must be admitted, there are. One has been noted
respecting his age when he committed the great crime
against his fellow-servant at Turin; though this is
rather apparent than real, inasmuch as he himself has
furnished the means of detection.—But the 'Correspondence' frequently indicates suppressions in the 'Confessions,' especially his letter 1732 to his father, and
1735 to his aunt; for he there speaks of grave faults
which he had committed, and of which the 'Confessions' give no intimation.—It is also certain both that
his friends represent his manner of living with Theresa
differently from himself, and that his letter to her
after their marriage gives an idea of her wholly different from that conveyed by the 'Memoirs.'—The story
of the attack upon his house at Neufchâtel, too, is
quite a fiction, and must have been, by the evidence of
l'Eschery, a wilful one.—The account of his bold and
resolute conduct towards Count de Montaigue, at
Venice, is probably much exaggerated. Nothing can be
more unlike the rest of his life; and his letters to the
Foreign Department omit every portion of it, though
they are very full on all the other circumstances.*—
The letter he wrote to Voltaire, too, in 1765, saying
he was " an impudent liar" if he represented him as
having been a servant instead of Secretary of Embassy
at Venice, seems somewhat too strong, when we find
him, in his own letters to the Foreign Department,
plainly calling himself, over and over again, a " domes-

* Compare Conf., Part ii., lib. vii. (Œuv., i. 299), and Corresp.,
i. (Œuv., vii.)

tique," and though sometimes a secretary, yet speaking of the relations between master and domestique in plain terms.* He drew the distinction between domestique and valet, indeed; but surely he could not after this complain of any one doubting whether he ever had been Secretary of Embassy.—It is another great discrepancy between his book and his 'Correspondence,' that while he complains to the Foreign Office of being left penniless at Venice, and without the means of returning home, he states, in his 'Confessions,' that at the Consul's, where he dined the day he quitted the Embassy, "every purse at table was opened to him," and he accepted a sum which he mentions, forty sequins, for the necessary expenses of his journey; and he also gives the names of the two persons who lent him the money.†—The remark seems quite fair, too, as well as obvious, that from the moment when he first formed the plan of reading his book to select circles, we lose the entire confidence inspired by the earlier parts of the book; and though he may not, till after he grew tired of England, and returned to Bougoin, have intended to give these readings at Paris, he probably had, for some time before, an idea that he should at one period or other read or show, if not publish, them.

Of his character it is almost as easy to speak with confidence as of his writings. It seems certain that so much genius never was in any other man united to

---

* Compare Cor., ii. (Œuv., viii., p. 71) and i. (Œuv., vii. 53, p. 53–59).

† Conf. and Cor., ib.

so much weakness. The fruits of an education exceedingly neglected, nay, in his earlier years very ill
directed, were gathered from his youth upwards at
each stage of his progress; but many men have been
as much neglected, and many more spoilt in their
childhood and boyhood, without ever becoming what
he was. We are to add, therefore, to the causes of his
misery, perhaps of his misconduct, an hereditary disposition to melancholy, to brooding sadly over realities,
and to indulging in the sad miseries of the imagination.
Nor was this all: he formed a kind of system or
principle for himself of the most unsound nature and
dangerous consequences. He seems to have thought
that the free indulgence of the feelings was a duty as
well as a privilege, and never to have doubted that
those feelings which naturally arise in the breast are
therefore innocent and right. The only evil which
he could perceive was in their restraint; and as even
to regulate them is to restrain, he not only regarded
such self-government as superfluous, but as hurtful.
The current was in his view pure and harmless; the
obstacles which broke its course, the dykes which confined it, the canals which guided it, were the only objects of aversion and of blame. It is obvious to ask if
he who had undertaken to write upon education a work
of much length and elaboration, had ever observed the
workings of our nature in infants, in very young children. It is a branch of the subject which he seems
never to have studied; else he must have seen how
the mere animal predominates at that age. At first
pure selfishness prevails, and indulgence of every appetite is the rule. Next succeeds, with nearly equal

selfishness, fear as soon as any restraint is applied, and
fear invariably gives rise to the protection of falsehood.
All natural propensities are eagerly indulged; all restraint is distasteful. Among others, the love of truth
is a restraint imposed by tuition, and like all restraints,
it is a violence to natural propensities. Now Rousseau
erected into his rule of conduct the self-indulgence
which the rules of reason and virtue proscribe alike.
The divinity he worshipped was sentiment, feeling,
often amiable, often reasonable, sometimes contrary to
reason, sometimes inconsistent with virtue ; and always,
when indulged in excess, offending against reason, and
leading to offences against virtue. Whoever reads his
' Confessions' must perceive that he never could conceive
he was acting wrong when he was following the bent
of his feelings ; scarcely that he was acting imprudently
when he was sacrificing to them his own plainest and
highest interests. To such a pitch was his folly on
this point, this cardinal point, carried, that we find
him unable to conceive how any one could ever reproach a man with his worst crimes after he had once
openly avowed them, or rather after he had allowed
certain things to be wrong ; for, having admitted in
the ' Emile' that whoever under any pretext or from
any motive whatever withdrew from the performance
of his parental duties, must expect ever after to weep
bitterly over his fault (*sa faute*), he declares that it
"was surprising any person after such an avowal could
ever have the courage to reproach him with the fault"
(*faute*) of sending his five infants to the Foundling
Hospital. He altogether forgets that the courage of
making such confessions, even had they been much more

full and specific, instead of being any defence to ward off the punishment of universal reprobation, was a virtue of an equivocal kind, and might be taken as easily for callous impudence as for sincere penitence.

The natural result of the system on which his moral feelings were built, was that the most undeviating selfishness took possession of his whole soul. Self-indulgence was his rule—self-restraint his abhorrence. The sophistry with which he so constantly seeks to cover over this vice is pitiable when it is not ridiculous. For many years he had almost ceased even to write to Madame de Warens; and for above two years after his removal to Neufchâtel, the last years of her miserable life, she was, as he too well knew, plunged in the depths of misery—she who had supported him while she had a farthing to give—she to whom he owed his whole existence for the first ten years and the most destitute of his life—she for whom he had so often avowed, and also felt, the most tender affection, and who had ever treated him like an anxious mother—not only did he remain for those two years a day's journey from her residence without ever repairing to see and to console, if he could not relieve and reclaim her, but he never gave her the comfort of a letter to show he still bore her image in his heart—and why? " because he feared to sadden her heart (*contrister son cœur*) with the story of his disasters!"*—As if she had not real disasters of her own—as if the straw on which she was perishing of want offered not wherewithal to touch her more nearly than the tale of his fancied wrongs

---

* Conf. and Cor., 600.

and trumpery persecutions! The least sagacity is
enough to pierce through this flimsy veil of hypocritical cant. Every one sees that he was unwilling to interrupt his own enjoyments by the sight of her misery,
and therefore did not repair to Chambery—that he
was unwilling to interrupt his walks, or his readings,
or his writings, or his musings, and therefore did not
write letters that might have led to asking assistance
which he did not choose to give.

The sentiment of religion, if not its principles, was
deeply impressed on his mind; he never could endure
the infidelity of the d'Holbach circle, nor even the
modified infidelity of Voltaire. It is indeed made the
main ground of his charges against him. Though he
himself aimed deadly blows, and with malice afore-
thought, at Revelation, he was as intolerant of Voltaire's sneers and scoffs as if he had been the most pious
of men; and as if of too pure eyes to behold such iniquity, he refused even to read ' Candide,' though he says
it was written in answer to his own ' Letter on Evil.'
To trifle with so sacred a subject, therefore, was in
his eyes a crime of a deep dye. To shelter himself
from temporal power by spiritual, to make a gain by
belief, was to him a vice of a more vile and sordid
aspect still. Yet did he, with his eyes open and his
understanding uncontrolled, change his religion twice
—becoming a Catholic for the hope of an income, a
Protestant for the rank of a burgess, when probably he
neither at the one change nor the other was a Christian
at all; and at a subsequent period, long after he had
proclaimed his unbelief to the world, he went through
the mockery of taking the sacrament in the hope of

screening himself from annoyances or of reconciling
himself to the favour of the Calvinists at Geneva. No
more selfish and unprincipled conduct can be easily cited
of any man who had Rousseau's deep feelings of the importance properly attached to all religious subjects.

The crime of his life which is most dwelt upon, and
can never be held up to sufficient execration, has been
already more than once referred to; it was entirely the
result of the same selfish disposition, the same confirmed
incapacity to see or feel any other existence than his own.
What incurable folly to suppose that any one could be
duped, or that he was himself duped, by the pretence
of his having an insufficient income, and being unwilling that his children should be brought up in penury!
How could a man of ordinary reflection avoid perceiving a refutation of his defence each time that he swallowed a morsel more palatable than bread and water?
How could a man of ordinary feeling avoid tasting in
each such morsel the bitterness of an asp's gall? But
his circumstances mended—he became possessed of
money—did he endeavour to repair the mischief he
had done? He hardly allowed Madame de Luxembourg to make inquiry as to one of his exposed children, and after none of them did he himself ever inquire. He was determined to lead his own life of
misery, and vanity, and self-indulgence, uninterrupted
by the cries or the claims of a family, the bringing of
whom into the world was his own act, also an act of
self-indulgence.

A part of this his moral nature, and a material part
of it, was his vanity, perhaps greater than ever had
dominion over a highly gifted mind. That this was

the point, as not unfrequently happens, upon which
the insanity turned which clouded some of his later
years, is certain; but no less certainly may we perceive
its malignant influence through the whole of his
course. He laboured under a great delusion upon this
subject; for he actually conceived that he had less
vanity than any other person that ever existed; and
he has given expression to this notion. The ground
of the delusion plainly was, that he often forgot this
indulgence in pursuit of others; and also, that he had
less shame than other men in unveiling his faults and
frailties, when their disclosure ministered to any ruling
propensity, not seldom when it fed that same vanity
itself. But no one can read his account of the fancies
he took in his early years, and not perceive how strikingly the love of distinction prevailed in him even
then, and while his existence was perfectly obscure.
The displays that captivated him, excited his envy, and
even led to his uncouth attempts at imitation, were not
the solid qualities or valuable acquirements of those he
saw at Annecy or at Turin, but the base tricks and
superficial accomplishments of a Bacler and a Venture,
performers of the lowest order, but who, he perceived,
were followed by public applause. Later in life he
seems to have been almost insensible to any existence
but his own, or when he could believe in that of external objects, it was always in reference to himself; and
at last this feeling reached the morbid temperature of
fancying that he and his concerns were the only thing
about which all other men cared, and with which
all were occupying themselves; thus absorbing in self-

contemplation all the faculties and all the feelings of
his own mind.*

That with all his failings and all his faults, he could
win his way to many hearts, is easily to be understood;
for, beside the genius, and latterly the fame, which
dazzled beholders, some of his weaknesses were of a
kind that interested benevolent natures, partly through
compassion, partly from the openness and infantine
simplicity with which they were attended ; and as long
as he did not conceive the suspicions which generally
broke out sooner or later, none of those weaknesses
were of a kind which offended others. The interest
which not only kindly natures, like that of the Lux-
embourgs, and such good-humoured companions as
David Hume, but such stern personages as St. Lambert,
St. Germain, Lord Mareschal, took in him and his
fortunes, is a sufficient illustration of these remarks;
but it may be doubted if that interest could have survived such a full disclosure as we now have of his
defects since his death.

In society he must have been, when his mind was
sound and his irritability calmed, and his painful constitutional maladies soothed or intermitted,† a very

---

* Perhaps the most extraordinary creation of fancy in which his
morbid vanity indulged, was his believing that he perceived a marked
increase of Hume's popularity at Paris in consequence of his having
asked Rousseau's company on his journey to London (Œuv., viii.
166, and again in his crazy letter to Hume himself, ib. 186), and
this while he was complaining of having no supporters, and of all
men being his enemies !

† He had not only a bladder complaint and a hemorrhoidal malady, but was for years supposed to have the stone. On his being

pleasing mixture, possibly a delightful companion. He greatly underrates himself in this particular. It is true, as he frequently says, that his shyness often made him appear dull, often gave birth to absurd sayings, and even grotesque conduct; it is also possibly true that he was not ready in repartee, which he expressed by saying "Qu'il avait l'esprit un quart d'heure après tout le monde." Yet we have a strong testimony to the charms of his conversation in the words of a respectable witness, M. Dussaulx, who, speaking of a party he gave to Rousseau, among others, in 1771, exclaims "A quelque nuages près, mon Dieu, qu'il fut aimable ce jour là!—tantôt enjoué, tantôt sublime. Avant le diner il nous donnait à quelquesuns les plus innocentes anecdotes consignées dans les 'Confessions.' Plusieurs d'entre nous les connaissaient déjà; mais il sût leur donner une physiognomie nouvelle, et plus de mouvement encore que dans son livre. J'ose dire qu'il ne se connaissait pas lui-même lorsqu'il prétendait que la nature lui avait refusé le don de la parole. La solitude sans doute avait concentré ce talent en lui-même; mais dans ces moments d'abandon, et lorsque rien ne l'offusquait, il débordait comme un torrent impétueux que rien ne résiste."*

It is never permitted to vindicate, or even to palliate, crimes by citing the defects of physical tempera‚ ment; no course can be more dangerous to virtue; and where the reason is only undermined by indulgence,

---

sounded, in 1762, this was found to be a mistake: he was, however found to have a scirrhous prostate gland.

* De mes Rapports avec J. J. Rousseau. p. 99.

O

by weaknesses which exertion and self-restraint might
in time have extirpated or counteracted, the excuse
which is sometimes made of mental disease likewise
fails.   Rousseau's malady was probably of this description ; but weaknesses are to be palliated, if not pitied,
by a view of bodily sufferings such as he certainly endured ; and as far as irritable temper and restless disposition are concerned, let no one severely blame them,
or even look down too proudly on the conduct which
they prompted, without reflecting charitably and com-
passionately upon the diseased state in which much of
his life was passed, and considering in common fairness how much less impatient and irritable he would
himself have proved under the same infliction.

APPENDIX.

It appears from the whole correspondence with M. de St.
Germain, which I have seen, that two or three letters not
published were written to him by Rousseau after his arrival
in Paris, 1770 and 1771.   From that time to his death, in
1778, none appear.
    The following epitaph on Voltaire by Rousseau has not, as
it seems, ever before been published.   It may appear somewhat to qualify the praise bestowed on the latter for his treatment of that great man ; and though written with spirit, is extremely unjust.

> " Plus bel esprit que grand génie,
>   Sans loi, sans mœurs, et sans vertu ;
>   Il est mort comme il a vécu,
>   Couvert de gloire et d'infamie."

DAVID HUME.

From a Print by L. Smith, after
a Picture by Allen Ramsay

H U M E.

GREATLY distinguished as the people of Great Britain had ever been for their achievements in all the other walks of literature and science, it is certain that there never had appeared among them any historian of eminence before the middle of the eighteenth century. The country of Bacon, of Newton, of Locke, of Napier— the country of Milton, of Shakspeare, and Buchanan —of Dryden, Swift, Bolingbroke—had as yet nothing more to produce as the rival of ancient historical fame than the crude and partial annals of Buchanan, great only as a poet, and the far more classical and less prejudiced political Memoirs rather than 'History' of Clarendon. While Italy had her Davila and Guicciardini, and France her Thuanus (Du Thou), this island was nearly unknown for any native annals, and a Frenchman (Rapin de Thoyras) had provided the only 'History of England' which any one could find readable, nor in reading that could he affect to find pleasure. It was reserved for two natives of Scotland to remove such an unhappy peculiarity, and to place our fame in this important walk of literature upon a level with our eminence in all its other departments. Mr. Hume first entered the field; and though his is by no means the work on which the historical

merit of the country mainly rests (for he had neither
the impartiality nor the patience of the historical
office), yet he is decidedly to be praised as having been
the first to enter the field with the talents of a fine
writer, and the habits of a philosophic inquirer.

David Hume was born at Edinburgh, in April,
1711. He was the younger son of Mr. Hume of
Ninewells, in the county of Berwick, and related to
Earl Hume's, or Home's, family; his mother was the
daughter of Sir David Falconer, Lord President, and·
niece of Lord Halkerston, one of the Judges, of the Court
of Session. His father dying soon after his birth, his
guardians intended him for the bar; but he tells us that
while "he was supposed to be poring over Voet and Vin-
ning, he was secretly devouring the pages of Cicero and
Virgil." He neglected Greek in his early years, and had
to make up for this deficiency, with some labour, in after
life.

The fortune of his father, to which his eldest brother Joseph succeeded, was inconsiderable; and his own
portion being necessarily very small, it was deemed expedient, as he refused to be a lawyer, that he should exert
himself in some other way to provide for his support.
He was therefore sent to a mercantile house at Bristol,
in 1734; but he found the drudgery of this employment intolerable, and he retired to Rheims, in the
north of France, determined, while he prosecuted his
favourite studies, to supply, by rigorous economy and
a life of abstinence, the want of fortune. From
Rheims he removed to La Flèche, in Anjou, and there
wrote his 'Treatise on Human Nature.' It was published in 1737, and fell, as he says, still-born from the

press. He afterwards distributed it into separate 'Essays,' which, with additions, he published in 1742, and it had more success.

After his first publication he retired to his brother's house, and lived so happily there among his books that he afterwards says, in a letter to Dr. Robertson, that he should never have left it, had not his brother's marriage made a change in the family. Although he appears to have felt much more and much earlier than Robertson the love of literary fame, his first work having been published when he was only 26, while the 'History of Scotland' only appeared in the author's 38th year, yet manifestly the same love of literary pursuits for their own sake, the desire of knowledge, the indulgence of a speculative turn, and meditating on the events of past times and on the systems of former inquirers, appears to have been the mainspring of both their movements ; and Hume was happy in being allowed to gratify these strong propensities of his nature.

The last Marquess of Annandale was a person of weak intellect. Though neither insane nor idiotic, he required the company of a friend, as his imbecility excluded him from society, and he was not ill enough to require the care of a keeper. Mr. Hume, in 1745, accepted this situation, as a large salary was very naturally given to induce him. But after a year's residence, finding, as we see from the late publication of some querulous letters very little like his ordinary correspondence, that he could no longer submit to such a life, he left this occupation, and was fortunate enough to receive an invitation immediately after of a very different

kind. It was to attend, as private secretary, General
St. Clair (uncle of Lord Loughborough, and great-
uncle of the late Lord Rosslyn), whose family has
always been honourably distinguished by their love of
literary society. The General was appointed to command an expedition, at first destined for the conquest
of Canada, but afterwards very unwisely, and with no
result any more than any rational design, diverted to
the folly of making an incursion on the coast of
France. The following year, 1747, he accompanied
the General on his embassy to the courts of Vienna
and Turin. This mission was of a military nature,
and the philosopher tells us that he was not only
Secretary, but Aide-de-camp, with two military men
—Captain, afterwards General, Grant, and Sir Henry
Erskine, afterwards a General officer also, and who married the Ambassador's sister. These two years, 1746
and 1747, formed the only interruption ever given to
his studies; but they appear to have satisfied him in
one important particular; for, "not only," he says, " I
passed this period of time agreeably and in good company, but my appointments with frugality had made
me reach a fortune which I called independent, though
most of my friends were incited to smile when I said
so; in short, I was now master of near a thousand
pounds."

While he was at Turin, his ' Inquiry concerning the
Human Understanding' was published in London. It
was the 'Treatise on Human Nature' presented in a new
form, and was not much more successful than its predecessor; but he nevertheless began to perceive symptoms of his books coming into notice; " for," says he,

"I found, by Dr. Warburton's railing, that they are beginning to be esteemed in good company." Returning to Scotland, he again resided with his brother, and wrote his ' Political Discourses,' which were published in 1752, and immediately excited much attention. "The work was," he says, " well received both at home and abroad." But he published, the same year, the ' Inquiry concerning the Principles of Morals,' which " came," he says, " unnoticed and unobserved into the world;" though he adds, that "in his own opinion it is incomparably the best of all his writings, historical, philosophical, or literary." It is plain, then, that neither in their original forms of treatises, forms three times varied, nor when broken down into separate essays, did his metaphysical and theological speculations succeed so far as even to obtain any attention. This is the more surprising, that beside the great ingenuity and novelty of some theories which they contain, they are tinged throughout with an excessive scepticism upon all subjects of a religious nature, and upon some with an openly professed unbelief, which might have been expected to excite indignation, and so rescue the writings from neglect. The ' Essays, Moral and Metaphysical,' are the form in which we now read these speculations, and a life of Hume which should not speak of their merits would be imperfect, as they certainly have long obtained the full share of celebrity which was at first denied them.

To refuse these well-known Essays the praise of great subtilty, much clever argument, some successful sarcasm, and very considerable originality, is impos-

sible; but a love of singularity, an aversion to agree
with other men, and particularly with the bulk of the
people, prevails very manifestly throughout the work;
and we may recollect that it is the author's earliest production, the 'Treatise on Human Nature,' which formed
the basis of the whole, having been written before
his six and twentieth year, at an age when the distinction of differing with the world, the boldness of
attacking opinions held sacred by mankind at large, is
apt to have most charms for vain and ambitious minds.

Accordingly, he finds all wrong in the opinions
which men generally entertained, whether upon moral, metaphysical, or theological subjects, and he
pushes his theories to an extreme point in almost
every instance. Thus, that we only know the connexion between events by their succession one to another in point of time, and that what we term causation, the relation of cause and effect, is really only the
constant precedence of one event, act, or thing to
another, is now admitted by all reasoners; and we
owe to Mr. Hume the discovery, it may be well called,
of this important truth. But he will not stop here:
he must deny that there can be such a thing as
one act, or effect, or event causing another: he must
hold that there can be no such thing as causation, no
such thing as power; he must discard from our
belief those ideas which all men in all ages have
held so distinctly, and so universally, as to have given
them names, specific appellations, in all languages.
He denies all connexion, all influence, all power, and
holds it impossible that any such things should be—
that any rational meaning should belong to such words.

—In like manner, every one is ready to admit the solidity of the distinction which he takes between the impressions of memory and those of imagination. But this won't satisfy him; he will have all belief to consist merely in this difference, and that we only believe or disbelieve any thing or any event according as our minds have a more or less vivid idea of it from memory, or from sensation, than from imagination.—In like manner, while no objection could be taken to his holding that a miracle is, *prima facie,* to be regarded incredible, because it is much more likely, and much more according to the laws of nature, that human testimony should deceive us, even that men's senses should delude them, than that those laws should be suddenly and violently suspended, yet he will not be satisfied unless we go a great step farther, and admit not merely the improbability but the impossibility of miracles, as if the weight of testimony never could be so accumulated as to make it more unlikely, more a miracle, that it should be false, than that the alleged deviation from the laws of nature should have taken place.* Indeed, had he lived to see the late discoveries in Fossil Ostelogy, he would have been placed in a complete dilemma; for these plainly show, that at one remote period in the history of the globe there was such an interposition of creative power as could alone form man and other animals not previously existing; and thus he must either have distrusted the evidence of thousands

---

* In the first part of the 'Essay' this qualification is introduced, but the second part roundly asserts the absolute impossibility, on the ground of the laws of nature being broken.

now alive, and even of his own senses, the phenomenon
being visible daily, or he must have admitted the miracle
of creation; that is, the interposition of a being powerful to
suspend the existing order of things, and make a new one.

It is by no means correct to affirm, as some do, and
Mr. Hume himself among the number, that his writings are only sceptical. Many of them amount merely
to doubts; but some, under the mask of doubts, are
essentially dogmatical. Indeed, some of his speculations are upon subjects which cannot be treated scepti-
cally; for the question in these cases being whether
we have evidence or not of the position, whoever
maintains the negative denies the position. Thus, to
take the most important example of all, the argument
upon Providence and a Future State is of this very
character. The question, and none other equal in importance can exercise the human faculties, is, whether
we have or not, by the light of nature, sufficient evidence to make us believe in a Deity and the Soul's
Immortality. His argument is, not that there is any
doubt on the subject, but that we have no such evidence; consequently his position must be that there
is no ground for believing in a God or a Future State.
It is easy to say Mr. Hume was not an atheist; and
that neither he nor any man can in one sense of the
word be an atheist is certain. If by denying a God we
mean believing that his non-existence is proved, there
neither is nor can be an atheist, because there cannot
possibly be conceived any demonstration of that negative proposition. To prove that a man asserted to be
in existence, exists not, we must either show that he
once existed, and has ceased to exist, or that he never

existed, but more certainly the former than the latter, because the former alone can be considered to leave the proposition quite certain. Now, clearly this kind of proof is inconceivable as to a Deity; consequently no man in this sense can be an atheist, if his understanding be sound. But we really mean by atheist as contradistinguished from sceptic, one who holds that there exists no evidence of a Deity, as contradistinguished from him who only entertains doubts on the subject — doubts whether there be evidence or no. Mr. Hume's argument, if solid, shows that there is no evidence, and not that there are doubts : consequently the inference from his argument is, not that we have reason for doubting whether or not there is proof, but that we have no proof, and, therefore, if consistent with ourselves, admitting his argument, we must not believe; that is, we must disbelieve. In the ordinary sense of the word, and as far as it is possible for the thing to exist, this is atheism, not scepticism. On miracles, no one has ever contended that the author's doctrine amounted only to scepticism. He does not doubt at all—he denies, and not only denies negatively that any miracle was ever proved by evidence, but affirms positively that none ever can be so proved. His whole argument goes to this; and between the impossibility of a miracle ever having been performed, and the total want of evidence of a Deity by the light of nature, we are left not to doubt, but to deny both providence and a future state. The one argument shows supernatural evidence to be impossible ; it shuts out light from above : the other shows natural evidence to be non-existent; it shuts out light from the world around

us. The two together amount to plain and practical
atheism, as far as such a belief is compatible with
sanity of mind.

Of the ' Political Discourses' it would be difficult
to speak in terms of too great commendation. They
combine almost every excellence which can belong to
such a performance. The reasoning is clear, and unin-
cumbered with more words or more illustrations than
are necessary for bringing out the doctrine. The
learning is extensive, accurate, and profound, not only
as to systems of philosophy, but as to history, whether
modern or ancient. The subjects are most happily
chosen; the language is elegant, precise, and vigorous; and so admirably are the topics selected, that
there is as little of dryness in these fine essays as if
the subject were not scientific ; and we rise from their
perusal scarce able to believe that it is a work of philosophy we have been reading, having all the while
thought it a book of curiosity and entertainment.
The great merit, however, of these discourses, is their
originality, and the new system of politics and political economy which they unfold. Mr. Hume is, beyond
all doubt, the author of the modern doctrines which
now rule the world of science, which are to a great
extent the guide of practical statesmen, and are only
prevented from being applied in their fullest extent to
the affairs of nations, by the clashing interests and the
ignorant prejudices of certain powerful classes ; for no
one deserving the name of legislator pretends to doubt
the soundness of the theory, although many hold that
the errors of our predecessors require a slow recourse to
right principle in conducting the practical business of

the world. The peculiar felicity of the author in distributing his doctrines as the subjects of separate essays,
whereby he avoided the repulsive forms of a treatise,
and yet moulding these separate treatises into one
body and one harmonious system, cannot be too much
admired. We read them as different and as short
works on various subjects; but we perceive at each
step that we are guided by the same genius,—that one
spirit of inquiry pervades the whole—one view of
human society and of national interests is taken
throughout—one sagacious unfolder of truth, one
accurate and bold discoverer of popular error, is at
work in each discourse; and it is certain that Dr.
Smith's celebrated work, with all its great merits, is
less of a regular system than the detached essays of
Mr. Hume. The originality of the latter's opinions is
wholly undeniable: they were published full fourteen
years before the ' Wealth of Nations.'

As for his 'Inquiry concerning the Principles of
Morals,' of which he had himself formed so high an
estimate, this is indeed a very excellent work, and appears well to deserve the opinion pronounced upon it
by the author, although his 'Political Discourses'
may be superior in the originality and importance of
their views. But the composition of the ' Inquiry ' is
more careful and better elaborated than that of his
other philosophical writings, at the same time that
it loses none of the ease or grace by which his manner is always so remarkably distinguished. There is
in this treatise a copiousness and felicity of illustration rarely anywhere else to be found; and it is
full of learned allusions and references, showing

the various and extensive reading in which he
had indulged. Nor is it the least remarkable feature of the work, that though preferred by him
before all the other productions of his genius, it
contains nothing at all even bordering upon sceptical opinions. On the contrary, he reprobates the
selfish system of morals, and is a strenuous advocate of
that which recognises the benevolent feelings, and
traces human conduct to a desire of enjoying their
gratification. Of utility he largely states the importance,
but rather as one leading motive than as the sole source
of either our actions or our judgments upon them; and
assuredly both in this and the other branches of the
argument a wider departure from the commonly
received standard of morals may be seen in the philosophy of Paley than in that of the ' Inquiry.'

In the same year that he published the ' Political Essays,' 1752, he was appointed their librarian by the Faculty of Advocates. He obtained this
place after a very severe contest, in which the utmost force of the party opposed to his known opinions
was brought to bear in favour of his antagonist. The
emoluments of the office were not above fifty pounds
a-year; but the violence of the parties was propor-
tioned to their zeal for and against the principles of
the candidates; and I find in his unpublished letters
curious indications of his anxiety for success, and of his
delight at the victory which he gained, chiefly, he says,
through the assistance of the younger members of the
Scottish bar and of the ladies of Edinburgh. " There
is nothing," he says, in a letter to his intimate friend
Dr. Clephane, then a physician in London, " since the

rebellion (1745), that ever so much drew the attention of this town, except Provost Stuart's trial ; and there is scarce a man whose friendship or acquaintance I could desire, who has not given me undoubted proofs of his concern and regard." His adversary was Mr. Kenneth Mackenzie, professor of civil law in thé University of Edinburgh.*

Although the salary of the office which he thus obtained was inconsiderable, the situation for a literary man was very desirable. He thus had constant and easy access to an excellent library. This induced him to undertake a work which he thought much wanted, a classical history of England; but he was afraid of attempting it on so extensive a scale as to begin at the earliest period, and continue it for seventeen centuries ; and he therefore confined himself at first to the Stuarts, commencing with the accession of James I., and closing with the expulsion of his grandson James II., at the revolution of 1688. This work made two volumes, of which one was published in 1754, and another in 1756. He entertained a sanguine expectation that his first volume, containing the reigns of James I. and Charles I., would have met with a favourable reception ; and we find the grounds of his confidence stated in one of his letters to Dr. Clephane. His election was in February, 1752, and in the following January he must have made great progress; for he thus describes his having already consulted his friends

---

* It is singular that a contest and a victory which once so much occupied him, and which he regarded as the battle and the triumph of his free opinions over bigotry, is not even glanced at in his ' Life' of himself.

upon his performance:—" As there is no happiness," he says, " without occupation, I have begun a work which will employ me several years, and which yields me much satisfaction. 'Tis a history of Britain, from the union of the crowns to the present time. I have already printed the reign of King James. My friends flatter me (by this I mean that they do not flatter me) that I have succeeded. You know that there is no path of honour on the English Parnassus more vacant than that of history. Style, judgment, impartiality, ease, every thing is wanting to our historians; and even Rapin, during his latter period, is extremely deficient. I make my work very concise, after the manner of the ancients. It divides into three very moderate volumes—one to end with the death of Charles I., the second at the Revolution, the third at the Accession, 1714; for I dare come no nearer the present times. The work will neither please the Duke of Bedford nor James Frazer, but I hope it will please you and posterity."—" I was, I own," he says in his account of his life, " sanguine in my expectations of the success of this work. I thought I was the only historian that had at once neglected present power, interest, and authority, and the cry of popular prejudices; and as the subject was suited to my capacity, I expected proportionate success."

But whatever might be the want of such a work, and how much soever he relied on his superior qualifications for the task, he was doomed to a bitter disappointment. "I was assaulted," says he, " by one cry of reproach, disapprobation, and even detestation. English, Scotch, and Irish, Whig and Tory, church-

man and sectary, freethinker and religionist, patriot
and courtier, united against the man who had presumed to shed a generous tear for the fate of Charles I.
and the Earl of Strafford." But the singularity of
the case, and the great mortification of the author,
was this : that with all the universal clamour, all the
storm did not save him from neglect; it subsided
as quickly as it had been raised, and the 'History' sunk
into oblivion. In a year's time, only five and forty
copies were sold, at least in London ; and although he
tells us in another letter, that " at Edinburgh no
book was ever more bought, or furnished more
subject of conversation," yet in London it was otherwise. The author's discouragement was great; he
was disgusted with belonging to a country so subject
to the tyranny of faction and the clamours of the mob,
while it boasted so constantly, and blustered so loudly, about its liberties: he even entertained serious
thoughts of leaving it for ever, changing his name,
and passing the rest of his days in some French provincial town, far from those braggarts and intolerant
brawlers. Nor does he appear to have been deterred
from this project, excepting by the obstacles to its
execution which the war, breaking out immediately
after, interposed. The only encouragement which
he received under his disappointment was from the
two Primates, Herring and Stone, who approved of
the book, and sent him messages, bidding him not to
be cast down by the temporary failure.

During the interval between the first and second
volume appeared his 'Natural History of Religion,'
which so far attracted notice, that Bishop Hurd wrote

an answer to it; and about as elegantly feeble as might
be expected from that moderate prelate, unless that
some part of it came from the more haughty and
vigorous pen of his patron Warburton, and redeemed
the tract from the imputation of candour, toleration, and
temper.   The second volume of the 'Stuarts' "happened to give less offence to the Whigs than the first," he
says, "and being therefore somewhat better received,
helped to buoy up its unfortunate brother." Three years
after he published the 'House of Tudor,' which containing his account of ecclesiastical matters in Elizabeth's reign, and of Queen Mary's conduct, revived the
clamour raised against the first volume, and, like that,
was soon neglected and forgotten.   In 1761 he
finished the work by publishing the two volumes containing the earlier history : "they had," he says, "tolerable, and but tolerable, success."   It is, however, also
stated by him, as an indication of growing popularity,
that all the clamour and all the neglect did not prevent
the booksellers from giving him more money when
they purchased the copyrights than had ever before
been paid in England ; so that, with his sober habits
and moderate desires, he was become not only independent, but opulent.   It is to be observed that, for his
'History of Scotland,' Dr. Robertson had only received
600*l.*, the publishers having cleared 6000*l.*   For
'Charles V.' he received 3,600*l.*, and for 'America'
2,400*l.* (being in the same proportion), while, no
doubt, 50,000*l.* at the least must have been realised by
those works.

In considering the merits of the 'History of England,' we must first of all observe upon the great

difference which appears between the pains bestowed
upon this celebrated work and those which the rival
historian was wont to bestow upon his writings. Dr.
Robertson's 'Scotland,' consisting of about a volume
and a half (for the rest of the second volume is composed of original documents printed as an appendix),
occupied his almost undivided attention for above six
years.* Hume's first volume could not have been the
work of above a year or fifteen months; for it was
begun when he went to the Advocates' Library early
in 1752, and it was published in 1754. The second
volume succeeded in 1756, but he had written half
of it when the first was published ; and in 1755 there
appeared also his 'Natural History of Religion.' Consequently we are positively certain that he wrote more
of his 'History' in less than two years than Dr.
Robertson wrote of his in above six ; and that his whole
'History of the Stuarts' could not have taken above
three years to prepare and to write. It is impossible
to doubt that this mode of writing history must leave
no room for a full investigation of facts and weighing
of authorities. He had no right to number "care"
among the items of superiority to his predecessors,
upon which he had plumed himself in his letter to
Dr. Clephane. The transactions of James's time com-
prised perhaps the most important period of our
constitutional history, because the struggle between

* Though by his letter to Lord-Hailes he seems only to have
begun it in 1742, yet I have heard his eldest sister often say that
he had a whole room full of books to read or consult for some time
before at Gladsmuir, where she lived with him.

the Crown and the Commons then began, and occupied the greater part of his reign. It was impossible
to examine the period too closely, or in too minute
detail. The struggle continued in Charles's time, and
ended in the quarrel between the King and the people,
in the usurpations of the Parliament, and in the over-
throw of the Monarchy. The Commonwealth then
followed, and the Cromwell usurpation. Now there
is hardly one passage in all this history, from 1600 to
1650, which is not the subject of vehement controversy
among parties of conflicting principles, and among
inquiring men of various opinions; yet all this was
examined by Mr. Hume in less than two years, and
his history of it was actually composed, as well as
his materials collected and his authorities investigated
and compared and weighed, within that short period
of time. No one can be surprised if, in so short a time
allotted to the whole work, far more attention was
given to the composition of the narrative than to the
preparation of the materials. It was altogether impossible that, in so short a period, the duty of the
historian should be diligently performed. The execution
of the work answers to the mode of its performance.

But if the ' History' be not diligently prepared, is it
faithfully written? There are numberless proofs of
the contrary; but we have the most express evidence
in the author's own statement to prove this position.
The temper in which his work was written upon all
the constantly recurring points in contest between the
two opposing parties may be judged of with accuracy,
and towards himself with perfect justice, by the avowal
which he makes respecting the alterations introduced

after the first publication. "Though I had been taught," he says, "that the Whig party were in possession of bestowing all places, both in the State and in literature, I was so little inclined to yield to their senseless clamour, that in above a hundred alterations, which further study, reading, or reflection, engaged me to make in the reigns of the two first Stuarts, I have made all of them invariably to the Tory side." We have here indeed a double confession. To the first volume is confined the reign of the first two Stuarts, and to that consequently is this remarkable admission limited. Now, if that volume had been written with any " care," could subsequent reading and reflection have suggested above a hundred alterations, all admitted to be material, by the statement that they affected the complexion of the political opinions conveyed in those passages? But again, if the author's mind was in a state of impartiality when he thus finally composed his book, how could it happen that every one of his corrections should be on one side, and not a single correction on the other, unless he had written the work originally with a strong bias towards the Whig side, instead of which his bias is, on all hands, allowed to have been strongly the other way?

The 'History of the Tudors' has the same cardinal imperfection of carelessness and haste, but in a lesser degree, because he had fewer controverted points to consider, and a smaller mass of authorities to examine. He had also less temptation to give his narrative and reflections a bias from the leaning of his opinions, because, excepting the questions relating to Mary Queen of Scots, there are few passages from Henry VII. to

Elizabeth subject to much controversy between the
Whig and the Tory parties. The earlier period before
the Conquest, and from the Conquest to Richard III.,
is wholly free from questions of this description; but
also it must be observed that the historian's diligence
did not increase as he approached the termination of
his labours; the Anglo-Saxon history is in every
respect the most meagre and superficial part of the
whole work. We shall afterwards see how his friends
explained this inferiority (*Life of Robertson*).

The bias of Mr. Hume's mind, from which his chief
partialities proceed, was the prejudice which he had
conceived against Whig, and generally against popular,
principles. This arose, in great part, from his contempt of vulgar errors, and his distrust of the more
numerous and ignorant classes of the community, whom
those errors chiefly may be supposed to affect. His
acquaintance with antiquity, too, had not tended to
lessen his belief of the giddiness and violence of multitudes when they interfere directly in the conduct of
affairs. To these considerations must certainly be
added the connexion between the Whig party in the
State and the fanatical party in the Church. The
Roundheads were religious bigots in his eyes, and
were, in fact, deeply tinged with superstition; and
they were the original of the Whigs both in England
and in Scotland. The Cavaliers held cheap all such ob-
servances, regarding religious enthusiasm with mingled
dislike and derision; and from them came the Tories
in both parts of the island. Nor was the connexion
merely genealogical or historical. As late as the
times of Addison and Bolingbroke, we find the friends

of the Hanoverian succession distinguished by their respect for religion, and the Jacobites chiefly giving in to the fashionable deism, or the latitudinarian principles, of Catholic countries in modern times.

A contempt of popular rights, a leaning towards power, a proneness to find all institutions already established worthy of support, a suspicion of all measures tending towards change, is thus to be seen prevailing through Mr. Hume's reflections, and influencing both his faith in historical evidence and his manner of conducting the narration of facts. A bias of the like kind is plainly perceptible in his remarks and in his recital, wherever the Church, the sects are concerned, and generally wherever religion forms the subject of either. Independent of the testimony which he has unwittingly borne against himself, in respect of his Tory partialities, the proofs of his perverting facts, especially in the last two volumes of his work, have been multiplied by the industry of succeeding historians, till the discredit of the book, as a history, has become no longer a matter of any doubt. It is of no avail that he himself and his admirers cite the disrepute and even odium into which his account of the Stuarts fell with the Jacobites, as much as with the Whigs, from its first appearance. That party's unreasonable demands upon our faith would be satisfied with nothing short of absolutely acquitting all the Stuarts of all guilt and of all indiscretion; and they probably felt more disappointed, because they were certainly more injured, by the admissions of one manifestly ranged on their side, when he was compelled to stop short of their pure and perfect creed. Afterwards the Tudor history completed their discontent; but it affords no proof whatever of his impartiality. He had, of course, far too much sense and too penetrating a sagacity to doubt the guilt of Queen Mary during the Scottish portion of her life, admitted as the greater part of the charges against her were, by her own conduct in the open profligacy of her connexion with her husband's murderer; and the prejudice which this unavoidable conviction raised in his mind, extended itself to the more doubtful question of her accession to Babington's conspiracy, a question which he appears to have examined with much less patience of research, though it belonged to his own subject, than he had applied to the Scottish transactions of the queen, which, in their detail at least, had far less connexion with his work.

If patient investigation of the subject be a merit—and next to fidelity it is the chief merit of history—Mr. Hume's work is here most defective. The time taken to compose it sufficiently proves this, as has already been shown; but there is continual proof that he took what he found set down in former works without weighing the relative value of conflicting authorities, and generally resorted to the most accessible sources of information. There have been instances without number adduced of his inaccuracy in citing even the authorities to which he confined his researches.

Nor can we acquit him on another charge not rarely brought against him, and partaking of the two former —neglect or carelessness about the truth, and infidelity in relating it. He loved effect in his narrative, and studied it. Unmindful of the ancient critic's golden

rule, "Historia tanto robustior quanto verior,"* he occasionally adorned and enlivened his page by excursions
into the field, to the historian forbidden, of fancy;
and either perverted or forgot the facts of the true
story. Sometimes he overlooked inconsistencies in
matters within his own knowledge, as when he made
Charles I. be disturbed in his sleep by the erection of
the scaffolding for his execution, when he is proved to
have known that Charles suffered by cold in the walk
across the park from St. James's, where he really slept.†
As for his picturesque description of sudden deaths and
female miscarriages being occasioned by the execution,
and of equally violent effects produced by the Restoration, these appear to be mere fancy pieces, no authority
whatever being cited to support them.

If from the cardinal virtues of fidelity, research, and
accuracy, we turn to the great but secondary accomplishments of the historian, we can scarcely find expressions too strong to delineate the merit of Mr.
Hume. His style is altogether to be admired. It is
not surpassed by Livy himself. There is no pedantry
or affectation, nothing forced or far-fetched. It flows
smoothly and rapidly, according to the maxim of the
critic, "Currere debet et ferri."‡ It seems to have the
"lactea ubertas"§ of Livy, with the "immortalis
velocitas"‖ of Sallust. Nothing can be more narra-

---

* Quinct. ii. 4, 2.

† His marks are upon Lord Herbert's narrative in the Advocates'
Library at Edinburgh; but he prefers citing Walker's 'History of
the Independents,' which contains the false statement, although the
very next page mentions his coming from St. James's.

‡ Quinct. ix. 4, 18.   § Ib. x. 1, 32.   ‖ Ib. x. 1, 102.

tive; the story is unbroken, it is clear, all its parts distinct, and all succeeding in natural order; nor is any
reflection omitted where it should occur, or introduced
where it would encumber or interrupt. In both his
narrative and his descriptions there is nothing petty, or
detailed more than is fit or needful; there is nothing
of what painters call spotty—all is breadth and bold
relief. His persons are finely grouped, and his subjects
boldly massed. His story is no more like a chronicle,
or his views like a catalogue of particulars, than a fine
picture is like a map of the country or a copy of the subject.
His language is more beautiful and powerful than correct. He has no little tendency to Gallicisms. He has
many very inaccurate, some ungrammatical phrases. In
this respect he is far behind Robertson. The general
effect, however, of his diction is unequalled. He cannot
be said to write idiomatic English, being indeed a
foreigner in that sense; but his language is often, nay,
generally, racy, and he avails himself of the expressions,
both the terms and the phrases, which he finds in
older writers, transferring them to his own page. In
this he enjoys a great advantage over Robertson, who,
resorting necessarily to Latin, or to foreign or provincial authors, could not manage such transfers, and
was obliged to make all undergo the digestive and
assimilating process, converting the whole into his own
beautiful, correct, and uniform style. Another reach
of art Hume has attained, and better than any writer
in our language : he has given either a new sense to
expressions, or revived an old, so as never to offend us
by the neology of the one process or by the archaism
of the other. With this style, sustained by his pro-

found philosophy, there can be nothing more beautiful than some of his descriptions of personal character, or of public feeling, or of manners, or of individual suffering; and, like all great masters of composition, he produces his effect suddenly, and, as it were, with a single blow.

Who that has read can ever forget his account, fanciful though it be, of the effects produced on the people by Charles's death and his son's return? Or his picture of the French Ambassador at his first audience of Elizabeth, after the massacre of St. Bartholomew, proceeding "through the palace,—silence, as in the dead of night, reigning through all the chambers, and sorrow sitting on every face—the courtiers and ladies clad in deep mourning, ranged on each side, and allowing him to pass without affording him one salute or favourable look:" Or Cromwell's state of mind when "society terrified him, surrounded by numerous, unknown, implacable enemies; solitude astonished him by withdrawing the protection necessary for his security:"† Or the groups of great men who subverted the monarchy, when " was celebrated the sagacity of Pym, more fitted for use than ornament; matured, not chilled by age "—when "was displayed the mighty ambition of Hampden, taught disguise, not moderation, from former constraint; sustained by courage, conducted by prudence, embellished by modesty"—when "were known the dark, ardent, and dangerous character of St. John, the impetuous spirit of Hollis, violent, open, and entire in his enmities

---

* Chap. xl. † Chap. lxii.

and in his friendships; the enthusiastic genius of young
Vane, extravagant in the ends which he proposed,
sagacious and profound in the means which he employed, incited by the appearances of religion, negli-
gent of the duties of morality."* These are the strokes
of a master's pencil, and beauties such as these would
make this the first of histories, if the grace of form
could atone for the defect of substance; if the trans-
gressions against fidelity and the want of diligence
could be covered over by the magical power of diction.

The sagacious reflections and spirit of profound philosophy must not be passed over; they are another praise
of this work. These rarely fail the author, whether in
judging of the connexion and the influence of events;
or in estimating the value of conflicting accounts, where
he will give himself the trouble of comparison; or in
noting the errors and the merits of the policy pursued
by statesmen. It is to be observed, however, that as
in treating of ecclesiastical affairs he generally suffers
his peculiar religious opinions to be superseded by the
received principles of those rulers whose conduct he
describes, and of their subjects; so does he not often
obtrude his sound and enlightened views of public
policy, especially of economical science, upon his reader,
rather conforming himself to the vulgar errors on the
subject, as when he speaks of the balance being for or
against a commercial state. Perhaps, too, in ranking
Galileo above Bacon he made the same kind of sacrifice, though certainly his disrespectful remarks on
Shakspeare run counter to the critical faith commonly

---

* Chap. lix.

received in England; and the contempt with which he treats the political writings of Locke and Sidney in his concluding chapter is a sacrifice of his own taste as well as of his reader's feelings to the prejudices of his party. It must be added—because great mistakes have been committed in this matter—that though the whole work was written in too short a time to give an opportunity for investigating the subject, yet the composition was exceedingly careful, and anything rather than hasty. He is represented as having written with such ease that he hardly ever corrected. Even Mr. Stewart has fallen into the error;* and Mr. Gibbon commends as a thing admitted the "careless, inimitable beauties" of Hume's style. It was exactly the reverse, of which evidence remains admitting of no doubt and no appeal. The manuscript of his reign before that of Henry VI., written after the ' History of the Stuarts and the Tudors,' is still extant, and bears marks of composition anxiously laboured, words being written and scored out, and even several times changed, until he could find the expression to his mind. The manuscript of his 'Dialogues' also remains, and is written in the same manner. Nay, his very letters appear by this test to have been the result of care and labour. The maxim of Quinctilian—"Quæramus optimum, nec protinus offerentibus gaudeamus"—seems always to have been his rule as to words; and his own testimony to the same effect is to be found in a letter which I have obtained.† Certainly it would have been well if he had not adopted the opposite principle as to

---

* Life of A. Smith.　　　　† See Appendix.

facts and authorities. It is remarkable, however, that he
hesitated much as to the subject he should choose for his
historical labours, and more strange still that he should
have balanced between England and the Church.
From this he was dissuaded chiefly by the strong
recommendations of Adam Smith and Sir Gilbert
Elliott. I have this fact upon the authority of Dr.
Robertson, who, in relating it to the late Lord
Meadowbank, added, "It would, at any rate, have
suited me had he adhered to the plan he himself proposed, as the 'History of England' would have thus
been left open, which fell in with an early plan of my
own."

After the publication of his 'History' was closed in
1761, being now fifty years old, and possessed of an
ample competency, Mr. Hume resolved, he tells us,
"never more to set his foot out of his native country,
enjoying the satisfaction of never having asked a
favour, or made advances to any great man's acquaintance." In less than two years, however, a great
man's repeated solicitation to him changed his plan
of life; and he accompanied Lord Hertford, the
British Ambassador, to Paris, with the immediate
prospect of being appointed Secretary of Embassy.
This was realized; and in 1765, when the Ambassador went to Ireland as Lord Lieutenant, the philosopher was for part of the year chargé d'affaires.
His station, his agreeable manners, but above all his
philosophical, including his irreligious, fame, were
well suited to make a deep impression upon the society
of the Paris circles. He was as popular among the
wits, the philosophers, the coteries, and the women,

as Franklin was at a later period, when his name was given to articles of fashionable attire. One of his letters gives an amusing account of the Dauphin, afterwards Louis XVI., then a child, having paid him court at his presentation, by speaking familiarly of his works, and of his younger brother, afterwards Louis XVIII., having followed in the same complimentary strain. The charms, however, of such society as Paris then presented, the elegance of the manners, the easy good humour of the inhabitants, the freedom from all coarse dissipation, and, above all, from factious brawls, naturally made a pleasing contrast with that which he had left behind him at home. There certainly was nothing in this country more alien to his nature, and less suited to his taste, than our political violence; and the intolerance of our religious feelings, as well as the rudeness of our manners, he had some right to complain of, when a man like Dr. Johnson could be found to roar out " No, Sir !" in his presence, on being asked by a common friend to let him present the Historian to the Moralist. Upon a subsequent occasion the same intolerant believer behaved with personal insolence and vulgar rudeness to Dr. Smith,* as good a Christian as himself, and a man of purer moral life, merely because he had, while afflicted with Mr. Hume's recent death, vented his grief in a touching panegyric upon his undoubtedly profound wisdom, and his virtue free from all re-

---

* Mr. Smith came to a company, of which Professor Millar, the relater of the fact, was one, and seemed to be much disturbed. It turned out that Dr. Johnson had just said to him, before another company, with great rudeness, " *You lie.*"

proach. This model of bigotry and rudeness had, notwithstanding, met at dinner, with perfect satisfaction, and conversed for hours, with Wilkes, whose life was as abandoned as his faith was scanty, who had been convicted of blasphemy and obscenity in a court of justice, and who held in bitter scorn every one of the sturdy moralist's religious and political principles. But Wilkes was English, Hume Scotch. From the country of the Johnsons, the latter deemed that he had made a happy escape, when he found himself among the gay, the polite, the tolerant French; and he remained there happy, and respected, and beloved, till 1766, when he was diverted from his project of settling in Paris for the rest of his life, by being appointed Under-Secretary of State in General Conway's ministry, who was Lord Hertford's brother. He held that office for about two years, and in 1769 returned to Edinburgh with an income of a thousand a-year, the produce of his own honest industry, " healthy," as he says, " but somewhat stricken in years, with the prospect before him of long enjoying his ease, and of seeing his reputation increase."

During the first few months of his residence at Paris he was not Private Secretary, as he tells one of his correspondents whom he chides for making that mistake, as will be seen in the Appendix; and he adds that he performed all the duties of the Secretary of Embassy, Sir Charles Bunbury, who was the brother-in-law of Lord Holland and the Duke of Richmond, and who, being thus protected, did nothing beyond receiving the salary. Lord Hertford, however, exerted his influence to obtain Mr. Hume's appoint-

ment in the room of Sir Charles ; and Marshal Conway
being Secretary for Foreign Affairs, he prevailed over
Sir Charles's family interest. Mr. Hume was appointed
2d July, 1765 ; and, on Lord Hertford's immediately
after being removed to Ireland as Lord-Lieutenant, he
became Chargé d'Affaires until the Duke of Richmond's
arrival as Ambassador in the month of October. By
Lord Aberdeen's kindness I have been allowed to
examine the correspondence of the Embassy with Marshal Conway during these four months; and it is
highly creditable to the philosopher's business-like
talents, and his capacity for affairs. The negotiations of
which he had the sole conduct related to the important and interesting discussions of Canada ; matters
arising out of the cession by the Peace of Paris ; and to
the demolition of the works at Dunkirk, also stipulated
by that treaty. His dispatches, some of them of great
length, most of them in his own hand, are clearly and
ably written. The course which he describes himself
as pursuing with the very slippery and evasive ministers against whom he had to contend, particularly the
Duc de Praslin, appears to have been marked by firmness and temper, as well as by quickness and sagacity.
His memorials, of which two or three are given,
show a perfect familiarity with diplomatic modes and
habits, and they are both well written and ably
reasoned. His information must have been correct ;
for he obtained a knowledge of the secret proceedings of
the Assembly of Clergy, which, though convoked for
the purpose of obtaining the usual *don gratuit*, chose
to enter upon the discussion of all the clerical grievances, while they kept their deliberations carefully

Q

secret, and were opposed by the Parliament of Paris as soon as their proceedings became known. Mr. Hume obtained a very early though somewhat exaggerated account of these things through two of the foreign ambassadors; and when he communicated it to the Bishop of Senlis, he was treated with contempt, as if nothing could be so wild, and as if some enemy of the Church had invented the fable to discredit her. Marshal Conway appears by his dispatches (which are also excellent) to have rested his hopes of these differences passing off on the prevailing irreligious spirit in France, where " the Dauphin alone," he says, " has any care for such matters; and he has of late taken a military turn." In a short time the whole ferment was allayed by the prudent and able conduct of Brienne, Archbishop of Toulouse; the *don gratuit* was voted; and the Assembly was prorogued to the following May. Mr. Hume praises Brienne very highly on this, as indeed he did on all occasions. In John Home's Journal of his excursion with the historian to Bath, in his last illness (1776), we find the same opinion expressed; Hume considering him as the only man in France fit to be minister, and relating several instances of his great ability.* It was the same prelate, thus highly commended, who proved so insufficient to meet the tempest of the Revolution, when, twelve years later, he was placed in the situation for which the partiality of the historian had early predicted his exclusive fitness.†

---

* Mackenzie's Life of John Home, p. 170.

† One writer has taken upon him to decide against Mr. Hume's

While Mr. Hume lived in Paris, he was applied to by some friends of Rousseau, who had become tired of his fantastic plans of solitude in Switzerland, and who was doubtful of his reception in French society, as others naturally were of his power to demean himself so as to make himself bearable in it ; and intending shortly to remove from France, and settle in England, he expressed his readiness to take charge of the "interesting solitary," as he was called, whose writings he admired in common with the rest of the world. He wrote to Rousseau, and offered to take him over to England ; the offer was immediately accepted, with the warmest expressions of gratitude. He came to Paris, on a permission of the Government to pass through France, notwithstanding the decree of arrest still in force against him. On his arrival, in December, 1765, he chose to parade himself daily in the neighbourhood of his hotel, in his ridiculous Armenian dress. The insolence of this proceeding in a person only by sufferance at large, made the police intimate that he must leave the country ; and he accompanied Mr. Hume to London, at the beginning of January. He does not deny that he was

---

talents for public business, certainly in perfect ignorance of the subject. After saying that it would be superfluous to inquire in what manner he executed the duties of his office as Under Secretary, he adds, "Certain it is that the state papers of those times evince no extraordinary marks of splendid abilities" (Ritchie's Life of Hume, p. 281); as if the Under Secretary of State had any connexion with these papers—or as if this writer had carefully examined them, when he had just said the inquiry would be superfluous ! But he who so discharged the similar—nay, the same duties of Ambassador, must have acted with equal ability as Foreign Under Secretary.

treated with the utmost kindness, and that every thing was done which friendship could devise to render his stay in London and its neighbourhood agreeable. Mr. Hume then, finding that he was resolved to live at a distance from society, and had intended going into Wales, introduced him to Mr. Davenport,* who kindly offered him the use of his house at Wootton, in Derbyshire. The silly, misplaced pride of the poor man would not suffer him to accept this without paying an equivalent; and he was allowed to sit at an almost nominal rent of thirty pounds.

He went to Wootton about the 20th of March, 1766. His letters to Mr. Hume, of the 22nd and 29th, are full of gratitude and affection, though he had seen three weeks before the supposed letter of Frederick II.; for he speaks of it to his friend De Peyron, 11th March; and he says, that on asking Hume if it was Horace Walpole's, "he neither said yes nor no," a silence afterwards made one of his charges against Hume. On the 5th of April he writes to Madame de Boufflers, still full of gratitude to Mr. Hume, who, he says, had obtained for him the comfort and pleasure of his retreat in Derbyshire. Two days after, 7th April, he writes to a friend not named, and sends a contradiction of Frederick's letter to a newspaper: Rousseau's letter speaks of secret enemies, under the " mask of perfidious friendship, seeking to dishonour him ;" and on the 9th he writes his accusation of Mr. Hume to Madame de Boufflers, so that it is clear he had all at once, between the 5th and 7th,

---

* Grandfather of Lady Williams, wife of Mr. Justice Williams.

by exciting his warm and feverish imagination, suddenly broke with his benefactor and " dear patron," as he before called him. His proofs of the conspiracy, and of Mr. Hume's secret enmity, are truly the workings of a sick brain, and sick with vanity ; as appears, among other symptoms, from his declaring how happy it made him to observe the popularity Hume had gained at Paris by his kindness to Rousseau ; and as also appears, by his roundly asserting that his own popularity and following in England was extraordinary, until this plot was concocted to decry him. The letter is at the bottom of it all.*   He at once pronounced that he knew it from its style to be D'Alembert's, and was enraged when told that it was certainly written by Horace Walpole—" as if," said he, " it were possible I could mistake D'Alembert's style, and imagine an Englishman's French to be his." Then D'Alembert was a friend of Hume's ; and though D'Alembert had no more to do with the joke than Rousseau himself, this was made the foundation of a quarrel; for not only was D'Alembert Hume's friend, but a M. Tronchin was Hume's landlord, whose father had slandered Rousseau at Geneva ; and others of his enemies, real or supposed, turned out to be Hume's friends also.   This was, he gravely asserts, a clear case of conspiracy made out against Hume, who must have inveigled him over to England in order to ruin his reputation. One of the overt acts of this plot was the obtaining, through General Conway, a pension for him who was starving, of a hundred a-year. But it is to

---

* See these letters in Œuv., vol. vii., p. 138, 139, 148 et seq.

be remarked, that the only part of the whole statement
which he at once willingly disbelieved, although it was
the only part that had a real foundation, was Hume's
helping him to the pension.   Therefore, having in the
heroics of his first indignation thrown it up, he at once
offered afterwards to take it back, and complained of
the whole arrears not having been paid.

Mr. Hume hearing that this frantic creature was
writing constantly to Paris complaints of being deceived and persecuted by him, wrote to desire he would
specify his grounds; and then came a letter, full of the
most ridiculous charges, ascribing to Mr. Hume's most
indifferent acts, even to his looks, the most black designs; a letter plainly proving that the writer was
deranged in one region of his mind, and that vanity
was, if not the main cause of his malady, certainly the
pivot on which it turned.   No one can read that letter without a feeling of indignation; for it shows
throughout quite reason enough to make its writer
answerable for his pure selfishness and his unbearable
suspicions.   It is a source, too, of irritation to the reader,
that of the many persons whom he called in as arbi-
trators, by sending them copies of his favourite production, not any one appears to have had the manly
firmness, the true and rational friendship for Rousseau
himself, of at once plainly declaring, what all of them
must needs have felt when they read it, that the
whole was a fiction of the man's own brain.   Lord
Marischal seems, indeed, to have perceived that any
communication with such a creature was unsafe; and
he let him know that henceforth they must no
longer correspond.   But for this notice, he no doubt

would have been the plotter of the next conspiracy; for Rousseau had for some years desired to consider him as a father, and always addressed him, a steady old soldier and political intriguer, wholly void of any sentiment beyond those of heat and cold, hunger and thirst, by that endearing and ridiculous title.

It is known that Rousseau, a year or two after his return to France, admitted that the foggy climate of England had produced in him a mental affection, and that he had been to blame in his quarrel with Hume;* but he never had the common fairness and gratitude to address this confession to his benefactor, or to any of those whose ears he had sought to poison with his malignant slanders.

Contrary to his invariable practice, when attacked for his writings, Mr. Hume very unadvisedly gave himself the trouble, and underwent the anxiety, of writing an answer to this silly and malignant individual. He published a short but detailed statement of all that had passed between them. This step he took contrary to the earnest advice of Adam Smith, whose letter remains, strongly dissuading him from taking any notice of Rousseau's slanders. He appears to have been overpowered by D'Alembert and D'Holbach, who, living in the gossip and slander-loving credulity of Paris society, were afraid lest Rousseau's constant letter-writing might produce an effect

---

* See Bernardin de St. Pierre's statement of his conversation (L'Arcadie, Préambule), or Appendix aux Confessions, Œuv., vol. i., p. 642. The passage is given in the Life of Rousseau, which immediately precedes the present piece.

unfavourable to their friend. Certain it is, that
Hume's publication, wholly superfluous to all men of
ordinary sense and common candour, was insufficient
to convince such ill-natured and silly people as the
Deffands and their flatterers, who were anxious to
have a pretext for levelling their malice at the Englishman and the philosopher; and though despising
Rousseau from the bottom of their hearts, were willing
enough to make his fancied grievances a cloak for their
attacks upon Mr. Hume. It seems plain that his own
subsequent reflection upon the matter brought him over
to Mr. Smith's opinion: for in the sketch which he
has left of his own life, he makes not the least allusion
to his quarrel with Rousseau, although, in his pamphlet, he says that it gave him more trouble and annoyance than any thing that had ever happened to him.

Mr. Hume returned to Edinburgh in 1766, but
early next year he was appointed Under-Secretary of
State under Marshal Conway, and held that office
above a year. In 1769, some time after he resigned
it, he returned to Edinburgh, and took a house in
the only part of the new town then built, St. Andrew's Square. With the exception of a journey to
Harrowgate for his health, and another to Bath the
year he died, he lived in his native country during
the remainder of his life, enjoying the constant society
of his old friends; and himself the delight of their
circles by his abundant spirits, his never-failing good-
humour, and even temper, and the kindness as well
as the uprightness of his character. In the spring
of 1775, he tells us, he was seized with a disease in
his bowels. "At first," he says, "it gave me no

alarm, but has since, as I apprehend it, become mortal and incurable. I now," adds the philosopher, reckon on a speedy dissolution. I have suffered very little pain from my disorder, and what is more strange, have, notwithstanding the great decline of my person, never suffered a moment's abatement of my spirits ; insomuch that, were I to name the period of my life which I should most choose to pass over again, I might be tempted to point to this latter period. I possess the same ardour as ever in study, and the same gaiety in company. I consider, besides, that a man of sixty-five, by dying, cuts off only a few years of infirmities ; and though I see many symptoms of my literary reputation breaking out at last with additional lustre, I could have but few years to enjoy it. It is difficult to be more detached from life than I am at present."

While he continued to decline by a gradual exhaustion, he continued to see his friends about him as usual, and his gaiety was never clouded by the prospect before him now drawing to a close. A few weeks before his death, when there were dining with him two or three of his intimate companions, one of them, Dr. Smith, happening to complain of the world as spiteful and ill-natured, "No, no," said Mr. Hume, " here am I, who have written on all sorts of subjects calculated to excite hostility, moral, political, and religious, and yet I have no enemies ; except, indeed, all the Whigs, all the Tories, and all the Christians."

When his strength gradually failed, he was unable to remain so long as before in the company of his friends. By degrees he became confined to his room the greater part of the day, and at last altogether. But his intellect and his calmness continued to the last. A letter to Madame de Boufflers remains, written only five days before his death, and occasioned by the decease of the Prince de Conti, her great friend. "I am," he says, "certainly within a few weeks, and perhaps a few days, of my own death; yet I cannot help being struck with the Prince's, as a great loss in every particular."—"I see death," he adds, "approaching gradually, without anxiety or regret. I salute you with great affection and regard, for the last time." This was written on the 20th of August; on the 25th he was no more. On that day he gently expired, without a struggle, in the sixty-fifth year of his age. He was buried in the cemetery on the Calton Hill, where a conspicuous monument is erected to his memory.

He had shown a feverish anxiety for the publication of one work, his 'Dialogues on Natural Religion;' and he left this with his other manuscripts to Dr. Smith; but giving positive injunctions to publish this work, and allowing no discretion whatever upon the subject. Nay, he left a legacy of two hundred pounds, to be paid on the publication, though all the other legacies were made payable at the first term after his death : that is, Whitsuntide or Martinmas, according to the prevailing habit of the Scotch in their money arrangements. Smith refused to publish them; and there exists a curious correspondence between him and Mr. Hume of Ninewells, the philosopher's brother, on the subject. Smith, about the same time, stopped a publication of all the 'Essays,' which included one on the 'Immortality of the Soul,' and another, both believed to be spurious. The 'Dialogues' were so constantly corrected in his own hand, that they appear as if wholly re-written : a specimen of this is given in the Appendix. His nephew, afterwards Mr. Baron Hume, published them in 1779.

Having spoken of his writings at large, it remains to add that, though respecting these men may form various opinions, and especially respecting his philosophical works, of his character as a man there never was, nor could there be, but one. His great capacity all admit ; his genius for metaphysical inquiries, those who most differ with him, even those who most lament the use to which he directed it, confess to have been of the highest order—at once bold, penetrating, original. His talents for political speculation were of as brilliant a description, and were so admirably and so usefully applied, that his works are as yet unrivalled in that most important department of practical science ; and he may justly be deemed the father of the liberal, enlightened, and rational system of national polity which has the general approval of statesmen, and would be everywhere adopted but for conflicting interests, and popular ignorance.

But universal as is the assent to these positions, the judgment is no less unanimous which must be pronounced upon his character as a member of society, unless we reject all the testimony of all his contemporaries, supported as it is by the tone and spirit of all his correspondence which has come down to us. He was a man of perfectly honest and single heart, of the kindest nature, of unequalled good-humour in the intercourse of society, carrying the same placid disposition into those controversies which are most apt to ruffle or to sour the temper; and even under disappointments which would have embittered the existence of most men, and disheartened almost all, neither losing his general good will towards others, nor suffering himself to be cast down. The party violence and delusions to which the failure of his 'History' was in part owing, he often has exposed, but certainly in no other terms than he would have used had his work succeeded: for he employed the same language in writing the portion first published at a time when he made sure of its success; and he never afterwards troubled himself with doing more than uttering a good-humoured exclamation, or, perhaps, passing a joke at the expense of those who make themselves the tools of others by being the slaves to their own factious prejudices or propensities. But the reception of the 'History' was not his only disappointment, though it was the most severe. It would not be easy to find any instance of conduct more truly worthy of a philosopher than his bearing up against the repeated failures of the works he most esteemed, and the mortifying neglect which at first all his writings experienced, with but one exception. He looked steadily forward, with a confidence truly surprising and amply justified by the event, to the time when, probably after his course was run, his fame would shine out with surpassing lustre. Even in his latter hours, when he had, in some measure, seen the failure of the injustice under which he originally suffered, he retained a confident belief that his renown had not yet nearly reached its highest pitch; and that most admirable

passage above cited from his 'Life,' written a few weeks
before his death, makes a touching reference to the
prospects which then cheered him, but which he
knew were never, while he lived, to be realized. They
were the only prospects, unhappily for him, which
shed light around his dying couch; yet such was the
truly admirable temper of his mind, that no believer
could possess his spirit in more tranquil peace, in contemplation of the end which he saw fast approaching,
nor meet his last hour with more cheerful resignation.

It is to be observed that the charges made against
Mr. Hume for his sceptical writings, and for the irreligious doctrines which he published to the world, are
in almost every respect ill-founded. He never had recourse to ribaldry, hardly ever invoked the aid even of
wit to his argument. He had well examined the subject
of his inquiries. He had, with some bias in favour of the
singularity or the originality of the conclusions to which
they led, been conducted thither by reasoning, and
firmly believed all he wrote. It may be a question,
whether his duty required him to make public the results of his speculations, when these tended to unsettle
established faith, and might destroy one system of belief
without putting another in its place. Yet if we suppose
him to have been sincerely convinced that men were
living in error and in darkness, it is not very easy to deny
even the duty of endeavouring to enlighten them, and to
reclaim. But it is impossible to doubt that, with his
opinions, even if justified in suppressing them, he never
would have stood excused had he done anything to
countenance and uphold what he firmly believed to be
errors on the most important of all questions. Nor is

it less manifest that he was justified in giving his own
opinions to the world on those questions if he chose,
provided he handled them with decorum, and with the
respect due from all good citizens to the religious opinions of the State. There are but one or two passages
in them all, chiefly in the ' Essay on Miracles,' which
do not preserve the most unbroken gravity, and all
the seriousness befitting the subject.

In his familiar correspondence he was a little less
precise, though even here he was very far from resembling the Voltaire school. In his conversation he
seldom alluded to the subject, but occasionally his
opinions were perceivable. Thus, when one of the
University, the late Mr. John Bruce, professor of
logic, asked him to revise the syllabus of his lectures,
he went over the proof-sheets with him; and on
coming to the section entitled ' Proofs of the Existence of the Deity,' Mr. Hume said, " Right ; very
well." But the next section was entitled ' Proof of
the Unity of the Deity,' and then he cried out, " Stop,
John, stop : who told you whether there were *ane* or
mair?" The same professor met him one day on
the staircase of the College Library, where the inscription " *Christo et Musis has ædes sacrarunt cives
Edinenses*" drew from the unbeliever an irreverent
observation on the junction which the piety rather
than the classical purity of the good town had made
between the worship of the heathen and our own.

That his conversation, however, was habitually free
from all irreverent allusion, there can be no more
complete proof than his uninterrupted intimacy with
a man who never would have tolerated the least devia-

tion from perfect decorum in that particular, Dr. Ro-
hertson. The reflection which naturally arises from
their friendship is, first, that so venerable an authority
has pronounced in favour of his friend's conduct; that
he never deemed his writings an offence against even
the ecclesiastical laws of his country, much less against
good morals; that he regarded those speculations which
he the least approved and the most lamented, as justified by their author's honest sincerity of purpose; and
that he considered the conduct of his argument as
liable to no reprobation even from himself, a sincere
believer, a pious Christian, a leading Presbyter of a
Church whose discipline is peculiarly strict, a man
above almost all other men regardful of decorum in
his own demeanour, professional and private. It is
another reflection, suggested by the same fact, that such
bigots as Dr. Johnson are exposed to our reprobation,
almost to our contempt, for being unable to bear the
presence of a man with whom Robertson deigned, and
even loved, to associate. Assuredly the English layman had not a more pious disposition than the Scottish
divine; the historian of the Reformation had rendered
as valuable service to the cause of religion as the essay-
ist. The man who had passed his nights with Savage
in the haunts of dissipation, and whom a dinner could
tempt to sit for hours by Wilkes, might well submit to
the society of a man through his whole life as pure in
morals, as blameless in conduct, as those others were
profligate and abandoned. But Robertson's faith was
founded on reason and inquiry, not built upon the
blind devotion to established usages; and his piety,
while charity tempered it, was warmed at the genial

fire of a learned and inquiring philosophy, and proceeded from his reason, not, like the dogmatical zeal of
Johnson, inspired by fierce passions, matured by hypo-
chondriacal temperament, stimulated by nervous fears.
The one could give a reason for the faith that was in
him—the other believed upon trust; the one believed
because he could argue—the other because he was
afraid; the one grounded his religion upon his learning—the other upon his wishes and his temper. The
intolerant layman seemed to betray in his demeanour
his soreness, in his horror of discussion a lurking suspicion that all was not sound in the groundwork of his
system. The tolerant and philosophic divine showed
a manly confidence in the solidity of the altar at
which he ministered. While Johnson was enraged at
the foundations of his ill-understood, unexamined belief
being scrutinized for fear they should be shaken, Robertson, who well comprehended on what his faith rested,
defied the utmost inquiry and most active efforts of his
adversaries, well assured that out of the conflict, however fiercely sustained, the system to which he was attached, because he understood it, must come with new
claims to universal acceptation.

APPENDIX.

I HAVE been favoured with some unpublished letters of Mr.
Hume by the kindness of my learned kinsman Lord Meadowbank and other friends. By the following part of a letter to Dr.
Clephane, we may perceive that he had once, at least, gone out
of his line, and attempted something purely fanciful, apparently
in verse. From the sample of his imaginative writing in the
Essays, the 'Epicurean' especially, little room is left for lamenting that he did not further pursue this deviation from his appointed walk. The letter is dated 18th February, 1751. His
low estimate of Shakspeare breaks out in this letter; but he
became convinced in the sequel, that his kinsman's tragedy,
'Douglas,' to which he alludes, deserved the success which he
justly predicts; for we find him afterwards, to the same friend,
giving his opinion, after reading the tragedy, and he terms it
"a singular as well as fine performance, steering clear of the
spirit of the English theatre, not devoid of Attic and French
elegance." He seems to have formed a very low estimate of the
English genius in those days; for, speaking of Lord Lyttelton's
'Henry III.,' which he hears is to be in three quarto volumes,
he exclaims, "O magnum, horribile, et sacrum libellum !—
the last epithet probably applicable to it in more senses than
one"—and adds, "however, it cannot well fail to be readable,
which is a great deal for an English book now-a-days."

"Ninewells, near Berwick, 18th February, 1751.

. . . "But since I am in the humour of displaying my wit,
I must tell you that lately, at our idle hours, I wrote a sheet
called the 'Bellman's Petition,' wherein (if I be not partial,

which I certainly am) there was great pleasantry and satire.
The printers in Edinburgh refused to print it (a good sign,
you'll say, of my prudence and discretion). Mr. Mure, the
member, has a copy of it: ask it of him if you meet with him,
or bid the Colonel, who sees him every day in the house, ask
it; and, if you like it, read it to the General, and then return
it. I will not boast, for I have no manner of vanity. But
when I think of the present dulness of London, I cannot
forbear exclaiming, ' Rome n'est pas dans Rome : c'est partout où je suis.'

"A namesake of mine has wrote a tragedy, which he ex-
pects to come on this winter. I have not seen it, but some
people commend it much. It is very likely to meet with
success, and not to deserve it; for the author tells me he is a
great admirer of Shakspeare, and never read Racine.

" If you answer this any time within the twelvemonth, it is
sufficient; and I promise not to answer your next at less than
six months' interval. And so, as the Germans say, ' Je me
recomante à fos crâces.'

" Yours,

" DAVID HUME."

The following, to the same correspondent, gives an account
of his establishment after his election as librarian :—

" Edinburgh, 5th February, 1752.

" I must now set you an example and speak of myself; by
this I mean that you are to speak to me of yourself. I shall
exult and triumph to you a little that I have now at last, being
turned of forty, to my honour, to that of learning, and to that of
the present age, arrived at the dignity of being a householder.
About seven months ago I got a house of my own, and completed a regular family, consisting of a head, viz. myself, and
two inferior members, a maid and a cat. My sister has since
joined me, and keeps me company. With frugality I can
reach, I find, cleanliness, warmth, light, plenty, and content-
ment. What would you have more? Independence? I
have it in a supreme degree. Honour? That is not altogether
wanting. Grace? That will come in time. A wife? That

is none of the indispensable requisites of life. Books? That
is one of them, and I have more than I can use. In short, I
cannot find any blessing of consequence that I am not possessed of in a greater or less degree; and without any great
effort of philosophy, I may be easy and satisfied.

"As there is no happiness without occupation, I have
begun a work which will employ me several years, and which
yields me much satisfaction."

The following is his letter introducing the future Chancellor,
then a young man of twenty, going for the first time to
London, which he visited before he was admitted an advocate
in Scotland :—

"DEAR DOCTOR,   "Edinburgh, 6th March, 1753.
      "This is delivered to you by my friend Mr. Wedder-
burn, who makes a jaunt to London, partly with a view to
study, partly to entertainment. I thought I could not do him
a better office, nor more suitable to both these purposes, than
to recommend him to the friendship and acquaintance of a
man of learning and conversation. He is young;

> ' Mais dans les âmes bien nées
> La vertu n'attend point le nombre des années.'

"It will be a great obligation both to him and me if you give
him encouragement to see you frequently; and after that, I
doubt not but you will think that you owe me an obligation,

> ' Ha in giovanile corpo senile senno.'

But I will say no more of him, lest my letter fall into the same
fault which may be remarked in his behaviour and his conduct
in life—the only fault which has been remarked in them—
that of promising so much that it will be difficult for him to
support it. You will allow that he must have been guilty of
some error of this kind when I tell you, that the man with
whose friendship and company I have thought myself very
much favoured, and whom I recommend to you as a friend
and a companion, is just twenty.

              "I am, dear Doctor,
                    "Your affectionate friend and servant,
  "Dr. Clephane."   "DAVID HUME.

There is a long letter to Dr. Clephane anxiously desiring his opinion upon the true causes of his 'History' having so entirely failed, and indicating his own notion that this was owing to his freedom in treating religious and ecclesiastical subjects, but expressing his surprise that such a tone should not rather have recommended his book to the favour of one class and the hostility of another, than have made it sink into oblivion and neglect. In a letter to Colonel Edmonstone he treats the same disappointment in a more jocose manner, indicating what he conceives to be the taste of the public, and their fondness for worthless writings.

" Edinburgh, 25th September, 1757.

" I am engaged in writing a new volume of history from the beginning of Henry VII. till the accession of James I. It will probably be published in the winter after next. I believe I shall write no more history, but proceed directly to attack the Lord's Prayer, and the Ten Commandments, and the Single Catechism, and to recommend suicide and adultery, and persist until it shall please the Lord to take me to himself. " Yours ever,

"D. H."

To ANDREW MILLAR, the Bookseller.

" 12th April, 1755.

" The second volume of my ' History' I can easily find a way of conveying to you, when finished, and corrected, and fairly copied. Perhaps I may be in London myself about that time. I have always said to all my acquaintance, that if the first volume bore a little of a Tory aspect, the second would probably be as grateful to the opposite party. The two first princes of the House of Stuart were certainly more excusable than the two second. The constitution was in their time very ambiguous and undetermined, and their parliaments were in many respects refractory and obdurate. But Charles the Second knew that he had succeeded to a very limited monarchy. His Long Parliament was indulgent to him, and even consisted almost entirely of Royalists, yet he could not be quiet nor contented with a legal authority. I need not mention the oppressions in Scotland, nor the absurd conduct of King James the Second: these are obvious and glaring points. Upon the whole, I wish the two volumes had been published together ; neither one party nor the other would in that case have had the least pretext for reproaching me with partiality.

" I shall give no further umbrage to the godly ; though I am far from thinking that my liberties on that head have been the real cause of checking the sale of the first volume : they might afford a pretence for decrying it to those who were resolved, on other accounts, to lay hold of pretexts.

" Pray tell Dr. Birch, if you have occasion to see him, that his story of the warrant for Lord Loudon's execution, though at first I thought it highly improbable, appears to me at present a great deal more likely. I find the same story in Scotstarvel's ' Staggering State,' which was published here a few months ago. The same story, coming from different channels, without any dependence on each other, bears a strong air of probability. I have spoke to Duke Hamilton, who says I shall be very welcome to peruse all his papers. I shall take the first opportunity of going to the bottom of that affair; and if I find any confirmation of the suspicion, will be sure to inform Dr. Birch. I own it is the strongest instance of any which history affords of King Charles's arbitrary principles.

" I have made a trial of ' Plutarch,' and find that I take pleasure in it, but cannot yet form so just a notion of the time and pains which it will require, as to tell you what sum of money I would think an equivalent. But I shall be sure to inform you as soon as I come to a resolution. The notes requisite will not be numerous, nor so many as in the former edition. I think so bulky a book ought to be swelled as little as possible, and nothing added but what is absolutely requisite. The little trial I have made convinces me that the undertaking will require time. My manner of composing is slow, and I have great difficulty to satisfy myself."

The conclusion of this letter is extremely interesting, as proving the truth of the assertion in the ' Life' respecting his careful and deliberate manner of composing. This Appendix gives further proofs from the MS. of his Works.

To Andrew Millar.

"Edinburgh, 22nd September, 1756.

"Mr. Strachan in a few days will have finished the printing this volume; and I hope you will find leisure before the hurry of winter to peruse it, and to write me your remarks on it. I fancy you will publish about the middle of November. I must desire you to take the trouble of distributing a few copies to my friends in London, and of sending me a few copies here; the whole will be fifteen copies.

"Notwithstanding Mr. Mallet's impertinence in not answering my letter (for it deserves no better a name), if you can engage him, from yourself, to mark, on the perusal, such slips of language as he thinks I have fallen into in this volume, it will be a great obligation to me: I mean that I shall lie under an obligation to you; for I would not willingly owe any to him.

"I am, dear Sir,

"Your most humble Servant,

"DAVID HUME."

To Andrew Millar.

"DEAR SIR,   1758 or 1759.

"I am very glad that Mr. Robertson is entering on terms with you. It was, indeed, my advice to him, when he set out for London, that he should think of no other body; and I ventured to assure him that he would find your way of dealing frank, and open, and generous. He read me part of his 'History;' and I had an opportunity of reading another part of it in manuscript about a twelvemonth ago. Upon the whole, my expectations, both from what I saw, and from my knowledge of the author, are very much raised, and I consider it as a work of uncommon merit. I know that he has employed himself with great diligence and care in collecting the facts. His style is lively and entertaining, and he judges with temper and candour. He is a man generally known and esteemed in this country; and we look upon him very deservedly as inferior to nobody in capacity and learning. Hamilton and Balfour have offered him a very unusual price,—no less than five hundred pounds for an edition of two thousand ; but I own that I should be better pleased to see him in your hands. I only inform you of the fact, that you may see how high the general expectations are of Mr. Robertson's performance. It will have a quick sale in this country, from the character of the author; and in England, from the merit of the work, as soon as it is known.

" Some part of the subject is common with mine ; but as his work is a History of Scotland, mine of England, we do not interfere ; and it will rather be an amusement to the reader to compare our method of treating the same subject. I give you thanks, however, for your attention in asking my opinion."

It is not without some reluctance that I add the following letter, because it is likely to give an unfavourable and also an unfair impression of the writer's principles. But let it be remembered that he sincerely believed in the unhappy dogmas of infidelity, and consequently held the whole subject of religious opinions cheap. To have done so in public would have been exceedingly blameable; in private, it seemed to his mind a necessary consequence of his indifference or contempt, that he should fall into the lax morality of the ancients on this point, and give an exoterical conformity to what he esoterically disbelieved. In my very clear opinion this course is wholly repugnant to sound morals ; and is to be reprobated, whether in the excess to which Mr. Hume carried it, or in the lesser degree to which such reasoners as Dr. Paley have adopted it. The suppression of such a letter would have appeared inconsistent with the plan of writing Mr. Hume's life historically, and not merely composing a panegyric upon him.

To Colonel Edmonstone.

" Dear Edmonstone,   Not dated, but supposed, 1764.

" I was just projecting to write a long letter to you, and another to Mr. V., when your last obliging epistle came to hand. I immediately put pen to paper to assure you that the report is entirely groundless, and that I have not lost, nor ever could have lost, a shilling by Fairholm's bankruptcy. Poor John Adams is very deeply engaged with him; but I had a letter last post from Dr. Blair which informs me that he will yet be able to save fifteen or sixteen thousand pounds. I am glad to give you also this piece of intelligence.

" What—do you know that Lord Bute is again all-powerful? —or rather that he was always so, but is now acknowledged for such by all the world? Let this be a new motive for Mr. V. to adhere to the ecclesiastical profession, in which he may have so good a patron, for civil employments for men of letters can scarcely be found. All is occupied by men of business, or by Parliamentary interest. It is putting too great a respect on the vulgar, and on their superstitions, to pique oneself on sincerity with regard to them. Did ever one make it a point of honour to speak truth to children or madmen? If the thing were worthy being treated gravely, I should tell him that the Pythian oracle, with the approbation of Xenophon, advised every one to worship the Gods νομῳ πολεως. I wish it were still in my power to be a hypocrite in this particular. The common duties of society usually require it; and the ecclesiastical profession only adds a little more to an innocent dissimulation, or rather simulation, without which it is impossible to pass through the world. Am I a liar because I order my servant to say I am not at home when I do not desire to see company?

" How could you imagine that I was under-secretary to Lord Hertford, or that I would ever be prevailed on to accept such a character? I am not secretary at all, but do the business of secretary to the embassy without any character. Bunbury has the commission and appointment—a young man of three or four and twenty, somewhat vain and ignorant, whom Lord Hertford refused to accept of, as thinking he would be of no use to him. The King gave me a pension of 200*l.* a-year for life to engage me to attend his Lordship. My Lord is very impatient to have me secretary to the embassy, and writes very earnest letters to that purpose to the ministers— and among the rest to Lord Bute. He engaged me somewhat

against my will to write also to such of my friends as had credit
with that favourite, Oswald, Elliot, Sir Harry Erskine, and
John Hume of Douglas. The King has promised that my
Lord Hertford shall soon be satisfied in this particular; and
yet I know not how, I suspect that some obstacle will yet in-
terpose, though nothing can be more scandalous than for a
man to enjoy the revenue of an office which is exercised by
another. Mr. Bunbury has great interest, being married to
a sister of the Duke of Richmond, and sister-in-law to Lord
Holland. The appointments of this office are above 1000*l.*
a-year, and the expense attending it nothing; and it leads to
all the great employments. I wait the issue with patience,
and even with indifference. At my years, and with my fortune, a man with a little common sense, without philosophy,
may be indifferent about what happens.

> " I am, dear Edmonstone,
>   " Yours sincerely,
>   " DAVID HUME."

The following fac-simile extracts from the MS. of the ' History' prove two things :—*First,* that Hume carefully composed
and diligently corrected his composition; but *secondly,* that
the finer passages having more occupied his attention, he had,
before committing them to paper, more attentively elaborated
and more nearly finished them. The characters of Alfred
and of Edward III. are of this description, so is the earlier
part of the magnificent description of the Romish Interdict's
operation. The MS. of the ' Dialogues ' affords an example of
his repeated correction in his more ordinary passages. In the
second edition of his works he again and again corrected; and
even his familiar letters appear to have been laboured with
similar care :—

" The ~~personal be character~~ of this Prince, both ~~personal~~
(merit) (in private life,)
& public ∧ may with advantage be set in opposition to
~~that which~~ (any) that of any Monarch or citizen, which the Annals

of any age or any Nation, can present to us. He seems indeed to ~~ha~~ be the compleat model of that perfect character, which, under the denomination of a Sage or Wiseman, the Philosophers have ~~ever~~ ~~■■framed,~~ been fond of delineating rather as a fiction of their imagination, than with the hopes of ~~ever~~ ever seeing it reduc'd to Practice: so happily were all his virtues temper'd together: so ~~nicely~~ justly were they blended: and so powerfully did each prevent the other from exceeding its proper Bounds. He knew how to conciliate the boldest enterprize with the coolest moderation: the most obstinate Perseverance with the easiest Flexibility: the most severe justice with the greatest lenity: the most rigorous command with the ~~most affable~~ greatest affability of deportment: the highest capacity ⌃and inclination for ~~knowledge~~ science with the most shining talents for action. His civil and his military virtues are almost equally the objects of our admiration: except⌃ing only, that the former, being more rare among princes, as well as more useful seem chiefly to challenge our applause. Nature also, as if desirous, that so bright a production of her skill shoud be set in the fairest light, had ~~endowed~~ ⌃ ~~with~~ ⌃ bestowed on him all bodily accomplishments, vigour of limbs, Dignity of shap and air, and a pleasant, engaging, and open countenance. Fortune, alone. by throwing him into that barbarous age, deprived him of historians worthy to transmit his Fame to Posterity: and we wish to see him ~~painted~~ delineated in more lively ~~strokes~~ colours, and with more ~~lively colours,~~ particular strokes that we may at least ~~see see~~ perceive some of those small Specks and Blemishes, from which, as a man, it is impossible he coud be entirely ~~free~~ exempted."

" The sentence of Interdict was at that time the great instrument of Vengeance and Policy employd by the Court of Rome: was pronounc'd against sovereigns for the lightest offences: and ~~for the guilt of one person~~ made the guilt of one person involve the Ruin of Millions, even in their spiritual and eternal Welfare. The execution of it was artificially calculated to strike the senses in the highest degree, and to operate ~ on the superstitious minds. [with irresistable force] The Nation was of a sudden deprivd of all exterior exercise of its religion. The altars were despoild of ~~all~~ their ornaments. The crosses, the relicts, the images, the statues of the saints were laid on the ground, and as if the air itself were profan'd and might pollute them by its contact, the priests carefully cover'd them up, even from their own approach and veneration. The use of bells entirely ceas'd in all the churches. The bells themselves were removd from the steeples and laid on the ground with the other sacred utensils. Mass was celebrated ~~in the church~~ [* ▬▬ churches] with shut doors, and none but the priests were ~~allow'd to attend~~ [admitted to] their holy institution. ~~No rite of religion was practicd~~ [The laity partook of no religious rite] except baptism to new born infants, and the communion to the dying. The dead were not ~~allowed to be~~ interred in consecrated ground. They were thrown into ditches, and bury'd in common fields : and the obsequies were not attended with prayers or any hallow'd ceremony. Marriage was cele- brated in ~ churchyards, and that ~~no~~ [the] every action in life might bear marks of this dreadful situation, the people were ~~forbid~~ [prohibited] the use of meat, as in lent or ~~the~~ times of the highest penance, were debarrd from all pleasures and entertainments, and were forbid even to salute each other, or so much as to shave their beards and give any decent attention to their person and apparel. Every circumstance ~~bere the marks~~ [carryd the symptoms] of the deepest distress, and of the most ~~dreadful expectation~~ [immediate] apprehensions of divine vengeance and indignation."

---

* Illegible.

HENRY III.

"I reckon not among the violations of the great charter
some ~~practices~~ _{arbitrary} ∧ Exertions of Prerogative, which Henry's
necessities oblig'd him to practice, and which ∧ _{without producing any discontents} were uniformly
~~practiced~~ _{continued} by all his successors till the last century. As the parliament often refusd him supplies, and ∧ _{that ~~sometimes~~ in a manner somewhat} ~~often in a very~~ rude
and indecent ~~manner~~, he obliged his opulent subjects, parti-
cularly the citizens of London, to grant him loans of money:
and it is natural to imagine, that the same ~~necessities~~ _{want of economy} which
~~obliged him to borrow~~, _{reduced him to the necessity of borrowing} would prevent ~~but~~ _{him from} being very ~~regular~~
in ~~the~~ _{their} payment ~~of his debts~~ ∧ _{He demanded benevolences, or pretended voluntary contributions from his nobility & prelates.} He was the first King of
England since the Conquest who could be fairly said to
lye under the restraint of law: and he was ∧ _{also} the first who
practicd the dispensing power, and employ'd the famous
clause of *non obstante* in his grants and ~~charters~~ _{Patents}. The Princes
of Wales ∧ _{notwithstanding the great power of the monarchs, both of the Saxon & Norman line} still preserved authority in their ~~mountains~~ _{own country} and
tho' they ~~continued to do homage~~ _{had often ~~had~~ been constraind to pay tribute} to the crown of England,
they were with difficulty retaind ~~in subjection~~ _{in subordination or even in peace} and almost
~~in~~ _{throughout} every reign since the conquest had infested the English
frontiers with petty incursions and sudden ~~incursions~~, _{inroads} which
seldom ~~merited to have place~~ _{~~deserved to be mentioned~~ merited to have place} in a general history."

"The behaviour of John show'd him not unworthy of
this ∧ ~~generous~~ _{courteous} treatment. His present abject fortune ∧ _{never} made him
~~never~~ forget a moment that he was a King. More sensible
to ~~his the Princes~~ _{Edward's} generosity than to his own calamities, he

confess'd, that, notwithstanding his Defeat and Captivity, his
Honour was still unimpair'd : and that, if he yielded the
victory, it was at least gain'd by a Prince of such consummate
Valour and Humanity."

EDWARD III.

" The prisoners were everywhere treated with Humanity and
were soon after dismissd on paying moderate Ransoms to the
Persons into whose hands they had fallen. The extent of their
fortunes was consider'd, and no more was exacted of them,
that* what woud still leave them sufficient to enable them
for the future, to take the field in a manner suitable to their
rank & ~~station.~~ ^{quality} Yet so numerous ~~and such a~~ were the
noble Prisoners, that these Ransoms ~~were sufficient to enri~~
join'd to the spoils of the ~~Battle~~ ^{Field} were sufficient to enrich
the Princes army : and as they had sufferd very little in the
action, their ~~triumph~~ ^{joy & exultation} was complete."

DIALOGUES ON NATURAL RELIGION.

" Now *Cleanthes* said *Philo,* with an air of Alacrity &
Triumph—Mark the consequence. *First* By this Method of
Reasoning, you renounce all ~~Pretensions~~ ^{claim} to Infinity in any of
the attributes of the Deity. For as the Cause ought only to be
proportion'd to the Effect, and the Effect so far as it falls under
our cognisance : what Pretensions ~~youll say~~ , upon your supposition have we to ascribe
that ~~Epithet~~ ^{Attribute} to the Divine Being ? ^{You will still resist that, by} ~~By~~ removing him so
much from all similarity to human creatures, we ^ ~~destroy~~ all ^{hypothesis} ~~by th~~ give into the most arbitrary ~~suppositions~~ & at the same time weaken
Proofs of his Existence.

---

* *Sic.*

"This Theory, I own, replyd *Cleanthes*, has never before occurd to me, tho' a pretty·natural one; and I cannot readily ~~deliver any opinion about it~~ _{deliver any opinion with regard to it} upon so short an examination & reflection ‸. You are very scrupulous indeed, said

_{Were} _{examine}

Philo : ~~and were~~ I to ~~start objections and difficulties to~~ any system of yours, I should not have acted with half that _{in starting objections & difficulties to it} caution and reserve ‸. However, if any thing occur to you, _{will} you~~ll~~ oblige us by proposing it.

_{between}

"I allow of your comparison ~~betwixt~~ the *Stoics* & *Sceptics*, _{may} ~~as just,~~ replyd *Philo*. But you ~~must~~ observe, at the same time, that the mind cannot in Stoicism, support the highest Flights of Philosophy, yet even when it sinks lower, it still retains somewhat of its former Disposition; & the

_{The Stoics}   ~~the Stoics~~
~~his The Stoic his~~ will   his

effects of ~~its~~ ‸ Reasoning ‸ appear in ‸ ~~its~~ conduct in common _{thro'}   _{his}
Life, and ‸ the whole Tenor of ~~its~~ actions. The Antient

~~the school the school of~~
~~that~~

schools, particularly ~~that of~~ ‸ *Zeno*, produced examples of Virtue & Constancy which seem astonishing to present times."

It is necessary to correct a very gross misstatement into which some idle or ill-intentioned person has betrayed an ingenious and learned critic respecting the papers of Mr. Hume still remaining and in Edinburgh. "Those who have examined the Hume papers, which we know only from report, speak highly of their interest, but add that they furnish painful disclosures concerning the opinions then prevailing among the clergy of the northern metropolis ; distinguished ministers of the Gospel encouraging the scoffs of their familiar friend, the author of the 'Essay on Miracles,' and echoing the blasphemies of their associate the author of the 'Essay on Suicide.'" These Edinburgh clergymen are then called "be-

trayers of their Lord," and much more is added of a like kind.*
Now this heavy charge against some of the most pious and
most virtuous men who ever adorned any church, Dr. Robertson, Dr. Blair, Dr. Jardine, Dr. Drysdale, and others, seemed
eminently unlikely to be well founded. I have caused
minute search to be made; and on fully examining all that
collection, the result is to give the most unqualified and
peremptory contradiction to this scandalous report. It is inconceivable how such a rumour should have arisen in any
quarter.

A severe, and we may well be permitted to add, a singularly
absurd observation of Archbishop Magee is cited in the same
criticism.† His Grace describes Hume's heterodox writings as
" standing memorials of a heart as wicked and a head as weak as
ever pretended to the character of philosopher and moralist."

Now I have no right to complain of the Most Reverend
Prelate for forming so low an estimate of Mr. Hume's understanding, and entertaining so bad an opinion of his heart; an
estimate and an opinion not confined by his Grace to one class
of his writings, though undeserved by any. Yet it does appear
somewhat strange that merely because one of the most able
men that ever lived, and one of the most virtuous, unhappily
entertained religious opinions very different from those of the
Archbishop, therefore he must be proclaimed both a dunce and
a knave. It may also be permitted us to wish that the disciples
of the religion in which " the greatest of these things is
charity," and in which erring mortals are forbidden " to judge
lest they be judged," should emulate the candour and the
charity of unbelievers; for assuredly if Mr. Hume had lived to
read the Archbishop's work on the 'Atonement,' though he
might not have been converted by it, he would freely have
confessed the great talents and the unspotted virtue of its
author.

---

* Quarterly Review, vol. lxxiii. p. 556.　　† Id., p. 552.

ROBERTSON.

JOINED in friendship and in fame with the great man whose life and writings we have been contemplating, and, equally with him, founder of the reputation of our country for excellence in historical composition, was William Robertson, also a native of Scotland. His father, a learned, pious, and eloquent divine, was settled for several years as minister of the Scotch church in London Wall, but had returned to Scotland before his marriage with Miss Pitcairn of Dreghorn, in the county of Edinburgh, and was settled at Borthwick, in the same county, at the time of the historian's birth, on the 19th of September, 1721. I have been curious to ascertain the kind of genius which distinguished his father beside his talent for drawing, of which I possess a specimen showing some skill,* and by the kindness of a kinsman I have had the great

---

* It is a miniature in Indian ink of James, Earl of Seafield, one of the forfeited Lords, to whom he was believed to be distantly related. A tradition prevailed in the family that they descended from John Knox. The historian professed himself quite unacquainted with the reasons of this rumour which connected him with "the rustic Apostle," whose character and conduct he has described most faithfully and strikingly.

satisfaction of receiving a copy of the only sermon which he ever published, as well as of two or three hymns, translations, and paraphrases from the Hebrew of the Old Testament. The sermon is able, judicious, correctly composed, both for accuracy of diction and severity of taste, and contains passages of great beauty and effect. It resembles what in England would be called an Ordination Sermon or Charge, being delivered at the opening of the Metropolitan Synod in May, 1737, and is a full description of the duties of ministers, the title of it being that "they should please God rather than men." The poetry is elegant and classical. Both productions plainly show that good taste, as well as strong but sober reason, came to the great historian by descent as well as by study. But that his father held opinions more strict on some subjects than the relaxed rigour of the Presbyterian rule prescribed half a century later, may be seen from his requiring his son's promise never to enter a play-house. This was stated by him in reference to his father, when debating the question of John Home's having written the play of 'Douglas.' It is needless to add that, however much he differed with his father on this subject, he strictly adhered through life to the promise thus given, insomuch that when Garrick and Henderson at different times visited him, they entertained and interested him by exhibiting to him in private specimens of the art in which both so eminently excelled. The traditional character of the venerable person whom I have mentioned, in his family, was anything rather than sour or stern, how severe and unbending soever may have been his moral feelings. For the sweetness of his placid temper, and the cheerfulness of his kindly disposition, I have heard him spoken of in terms of the warmest enthusiasm by such of his children as were old enough at the time of his decease to recollect him distinctly. The idea of again meeting him in another state was ever present to my grandmother's mind, (who was his eldest daughter,) and especially when stricken with any illness. It was with her a common source of argument for a future state, as proved by the light of nature, and in her pious mind a confirmation of the truth of Christianity, that, believing in the Divine goodness, she could not conceive the extinction of so much angelical purity as adorned her parent, and so fine an understanding as he possessed. Their mother was a woman of great ability and force of character; but like many of that cast, women especially, she was more stern, and even severe, than amiable; and this contrast, unfavourable to the one, redounded to the augmented love of the other. It cannot be doubted that the son's character derived a strong tincture from both parents, but that while he was mild and gentle in his temper, and of an engaging demeanour, his firmness and decision, nay, his inclination towards the Stoical system of morals, and even to a certain degree of Stoical feeling too, was derived from his mother.

The death of these two excellent persons was singularly melancholy, and served to impress on the minds of their family a mournful recollection of their virtues. Mr. Robertson had been removed to the Old Grey Friars Church of Edinburgh in 1733; and ten years afterwards, both he and his wife, seized with putrid fever,

died within a few days of one another, leaving eight
children, six daughters and two sons, of whom William was the elder. He had been educated first at the
school of Dalkeith, under a very able teacher of the
name of Leslie, a gentleman at that time of the greatest eminence in his profession. On his father's removal
to Edinburgh, he was taken thither and placed at the
University, though only twelve years old. His diligence in study was unremitting, and he pursued
his education at the different classes for eight years
with indefatigable zeal. He had laid down for himself
a strict plan of reading; and of the notes which he
took there remain a number of books, beginning when
he was only fourteen, all bearing the sentence as a
motto which so characterised his love of learning, indicating that he delighted in it abstractedly, and for its
own sake, without regarding the uses to which it might
be turned—" *Vita sine litteris mors.*" I give this gloss
upon the motto or text advisedly. His whole life was
spent in study. I well remember his constant habit of
quitting the drawing-room both after dinner and again
after tea, and remaining shut up in his library. The
period of time when I saw this was after the ' History
of America' had been published, and before Major Ren-
nell's map and memoir appeared, which he tells us
first suggested the ' Disquisition on Ancient India.'
Consequently, for above ten years he was in the course
of constant study, engaged in extending his information, examining and revolving the facts of history,
contemplating ethical and theological truths, amusing his fancy with the strains of Greek and Roman
poetry, or warming it at the fire of ancient eloquence

s 2

so congenial to his mind, at once argumentative and rhetorical; and all this study produced not one written line, though thus unremittingly carried on. The same may be said of the ten years he passed in constant study from 1743, the beginning of his residence in a small parish, of very little clerical duty, to 1752, when we know from his letter to Lord Hailes he began his first work. But, indeed, the composition of his three great works, spread over a period of nearly thirty years, clearly evinces that during this long time his studies must have been much more subservient to his own gratification than to the preparation of his writings, which never could have required one half that number of years for their completion.

Translations from the classics, and especially from the Greek, of which he was a perfect master, formed a considerable part of his labour. He considered this exercise as well calculated to give an accurate knowledge of our own language, by obliging us to weigh the shades of difference between words or phrases, and to find the expression, whether by the selection of the terms or the turning of the idiom, which is required for a given meaning; whereas, when composing originally, the idea may be varied in order to suit the diction which most easily presents itself, of which the influence produced manifestly by rhymes, in moulding the sense as well as suggesting it, affords a striking and familiar example.* His translations, however, were not wholly confined to their purpose of teaching composi-

---

* I may mention that both he and his son, the Judge, prescribed this exercise to me, and, among others, made me translate all the ' History ' of Florus.

tion; he appears to have at the same time industriously completed the work of rendering some ancient
treatises, which peculiarly interested him. He had even
prepared for the press a translation of Antoninus's ' Meditations,'* having thus early felt a strong leaning
towards the Stoical philosophy. The appearance of a
very poor translation at Glasgow prevented the execution of this design, but the work remains : I have it
now in my possession, and shall give one or two passages in the Appendix. In elocution he acquired facility and correctness by attending a society which met
weekly to debate literary and philosophical questions.
This society gave rise many years later to another,
which was frequented by the men who in after life
proved the most distinguished of their countrymen :
Hume, Smith (neither of whom ever took part in debate), Wedderburn (afterwards Chancellor), Ferguson, Home (Lord Kames), were of the number. But
his thirst of knowledge was not confined to these its
more easy and more inviting walks. He had deeply
studied some branches of the severer sciences. It is
not, therefore, without good cause that he speaks of
mathematical subjects (in his preface to the work on
India) as having been embraced in his course of study,
though not having been carried so far as a discussion
of the Brahminical astronomy might require.

In 1741, according to the constitution of the Scotch
Church, he was licensed by the Presbytery of Edinburgh to preach; orders being only conferred upon a

---

* Marc. Aurel.: Των εις εαυτον.

presentation to a living or Kirk. Two years after, he
was appointed minister of Gladsmuir, a country parish
in East Lothian ; and this event happened fortunately
on the eve of the irreparable loss sustained by the
family in the death of both their parents, which left his
brother and his sisters wholly without provision. He
immediately took the care of them upon himself, and
would form no connexion in marriage until he had seen
them placed in situations of independence. He thus
remained single for eight years, during which his eldest
and favourite sister superintended his family. In her
sound judgment he always placed the greatest confidence; for he knew that to great beauty she added a
calm and a firm temper, inherited from their mother,
but with greater sweetness of disposition. An instance
of her fortitude and presence of mind was sometimes
mentioned by him, though never alluded to by herself,
that a swarm of bees having settled on her head and
shoulders while sitting in the garden, she remained
motionless until they took wing, thus saving her life,
which was in imminent jeopardy. She was married in
1750, and the year after he married his cousin, Miss
Nesbit.

While at Gladsmuir, where he remained fifteen
years, his life was passed in constant study, and in the
duties of his sacred profession. He rose very early,
and devoted the whole morning to his books. Later
in the day he had ample time for visiting the sick and
the poor generally; and he gave great attention to the
important duty of examining and catechising the young
people under his care. But nothing can be more
absurd than the statement in some of the lives which

have been published, as if his whole time after break-
fast was devoted to these duties. It would have been
utterly impossible to find subjects for his visits in
that small country parish, not containing two hundred
families.

It is remarkable that, with all the love of study
which formed so striking a feature of his character, nay,
with the contemplative disposition which histhirst of
knowledge for its own sake plainly indicates, he should
have joined an extraordinary fitness for the less
speculative pursuits of active life, and a manifest
willingness to bear a part in them. The rebellion of
1745 afforded an occasion on which he conceived that
the dangers surrounding civil and religious liberty
called for the exertions of all good citizens in its
defence. On the news of the rebels marching towards
Edinburgh he quitted his parsonage (manse) and joined
the volunteers of the capital. How far they marched
is not known; but that they must have proceeded
towards the Highlands, and for some time remained
under arms, is certain from this, that he always mentioned the effect of the first coal fire on his head after
he had been for some time accustomed to burn peat
only. When Edinburgh was surrendered he joined a
small body of persons from the city, who offered their
services at Haddington to the Commander-in-Chief.

Soon after his marriage he was returned as a member
to the General Assembly, and again his capacity and
his inclination for active life appeared. He devoted
himself assiduously to the business of that body; and,
having a very strong and clear opinion in favour of lay
patronage, the great question which divided the Church

of Scotland in that day, as, in truth, it again does in
our own, he assumed the lead of its advocates. At first
they formed a small minority of the Assembly; but,
by degrees, reason enforced by eloquence had its course,
and he gained ultimately a complete victory over his
adversaries.

The persecution of John Home, by the fanatical
party, for writing the moral and innocent and even
pious tragedy of 'Douglas,' gave another occasion to
show Dr. Robertson's liberal and rational sentiments.
Such of the clergy as had attended the theatre to
witness the representation were involved in the same
bigoted outcry. Home himself bent to the storm, and
resigned his living ; Robertson's judicious but spirited
defence saved the rest from more than a rebuke to
some, and a few weeks' suspension to others. He manfully explained why he had never attended himself, saying, that it was only owing to the promise already mentioned ; but he avowed that he saw no harm in the attendance of his brethren whom no such promise bound.

He was now looked up to as the acknowledged
leader of the moderate party ; and, as they soon after
became the ruling body in the Church, he must be
considered as the leading minister of that venerable
body during all the time he continued in the Assembly.
Of the lustre with which his talents now shone forth
all men are agreed in giving the same account. I have
frequently conversed with those who could well remember his conduct as a great party chief, and their
uniform observation was upon the manifest capacity
which he displayed for affairs. " That he was not in
his right place when only a clerical leader or a literary

man, but was plainly designed by nature, as well as formed by study, for a great practical statesman and orator," is the remark which seems to have struck all who observed his course. His eloquence was bold and masculine ; his diction, which flowed with perfect ease, resembled that of his writings, but of course became suited to the exigencies of extemporaneous speech. He had the happy faculty of conveying an argument in a statement, and would more than half answer his adversary by describing his propositions and his reasonings. He showed the greatest presence of mind in debate ; and, as nothing could ruffle the calmness of his temper, it was quite impossible to find him getting into a difficulty, or to take him at a disadvantage. He knew precisely the proper time of coming forward to debate, and the time when, repairing other men's errors, supplying their deficiencies, and repelling the adverse assaults, he could make sure of most advantageously influencing the result of the conflict, to which he ever steadily looked, and not to display. If his habitual command of temper averted anger and made him loved, his undeviating dignity both of demeanour and of conduct secured him respect. The purity of his blameless life, and the rigid decorum of his manners, made all personal attacks upon him hopeless ; and, in the management of party concerns, he was so far above any thing like manœuvre or stratagem, that he achieved the triumph so rare, and for a party chief so hard to win, of making his influence seem always to rest on reason and principle, and his success in carrying his measures to arise from their wisdom, and not from his own power.

They relate one instance of his being thrown somewhat off his guard, and showing a feeling of great displeasure, if not of anger, in a severe remark upon a young member. But the provocation was wholly out of the ordinary course of things, and it might well have excused, nay, called for, a much more unsparing visitation than his remark, which really poured oil into the wound it made. Mr. Cullen, afterwards Lord Cullen, was celebrated for his unrivalled talent of mimicry, and Dr. Robertson, who was one of his favourite subjects, had left the Assembly to dine, meaning to return. As the aisle of the old church, consecrated to the Assembly meetings, was at that late hour extremely dark, the artist took his opportunity of rising in the Principal's place and delivering a short speech in his character, an evolution which he accomplished without detection. The true chief returned soon after ; and, at the proper time for his interposition, rose to address the house. The venerable Assembly was convulsed with laughter, for he seemed to be repeating what he had said before, so happy had the imitation been. He was astonished and vexed when some one explained the mystery—opened as it were the dark passage where Mr. Cullen had been acting. He said he saw how it was, and hoped that a gentleman who could well speak in his own person would at length begin to act the character which properly belonged to him.*

That great additional weight accrued to him as ruler

---

* A somewhat similar scene occurred in the House of Commons on the publication of Mr. Tickell's celebrated jeu d'esprit, ' Anticipation.' It only appeared on the morning of the day when the session opened, and some of the speakers who had not read it verified it, to the no small amusement of those who had.

of the Church, from the lustre of his literary fame, cannot be doubted; and that the circumstance of his connexion with the University always securing him a seat in the Assembly, while others went out in rotation, tended greatly to consolidate his influence, is equally clear. But these accidents, as they are with respect to the General Assembly, would have availed him little, had not his intrinsic qualities as a great practical statesman secured his power. He may be said to have directed the ecclesiastical affairs of Scotland for more than a quarter of a century with unexampled success, and without any compromise of his own opinions, or modification of his views of church policy; and he quitted the scene of his brilliant career while in the full vigour of his faculties, and the untarnished lustre of his fame.

At the latter end of George II.'s reign, that Prince, or his advisers, deemed it expedient to make a proposal, having for its object the elevation of this eminent person to a high rank in the English Church. The particulars are not known; but Mr. Stewart, who probably had some intimation of them, says that the offer was met with "a rejection, in terms which effectually prevented a repetition of the attempt." Probably he considered it as, in substance, an insult to his character for sincerity as well as independence; for though no man was less tainted by narrow-minded bigotry, and none probably could regard less than he did the differences, rather political than religious, which separate the two churches as matters of con- science, he yet had declared his aversion to Episcopacy on grounds not to be shaken, at any rate not to be shaken by a proposal accompanied with temporal advantage, and he would have deemed his entertaining it for an instant a corrupt sacrifice of his principles to the gratification of his ambition.

While the conflict was raging in the Church Courts on Patronage, he had given to the world his first published works—his historical articles contributed to a periodical work established by Smith, Wedderburn (afterwards Chancellor), Jardine, Blair, Russell, and others, under the name, since become more famous, of the Edinburgh Review, and a sermon preached before the Society for promoting Christian Knowledge, in January 1755. The Review contained many able and learned papers, and reached a second number, when its conductors were obliged to give it up, in consequence of the fanatical outcry raised against a most justly severe criticism upon a wretched production of theological bigotry and intolerance which had just disgraced the extreme party in the Church.* The subject of the sermon is one peculiarly suited to his habits of inquiry—the situation of the world at the time of our Saviour's appearance as connected with the success of his mission. The merits of this piece, as a sermon, are very great; and it is admirable, as an historical composition, in that department which Voltaire first extended to all the records of past times. It was

---

* This criticism was from the elegant pen of Dr. Jardine, one of the most pious ministers of the Church, and a very intimate friend of the Principal. The papers of the latter appear to have been chiefly written on subjects which he had occasion to consider as incidental to his historical researches, and he does not seem to have put forth his strength in their composition. They are slight as compared with Adam Smith's review of Johnson's Dictionary, and his excellent letter to the editors on the General State of Literature, recommending an enlargement of their plan, which was confined to Scottish publications.

written and published before the appearance of the
'Essai sur les Mœurs;' though, as has been already
said,* detached portions of that work had appeared in
a Paris periodical work.

As a preacher he was most successful. His language, of course, was pure, his composition graceful,
his reasoning cogent, his manner impressive. He spoke
according to the custom of the Scottish Church, having only notes to assist his memory. His notions of
usefulness, and his wish to avoid the fanaticism of the
High Church party (what with us would be called the
Low Church, or Evangelical), led him generally to
prefer moral to theological or Gospel subjects. Yet
he mingled also three themes essential to the duties of a
Christian pastor. He loved to dwell on the goodness
of the Deity, as shown forth not only in the monuments of creation, but the work of love in the redemp-
tion of mankind. He delighted to expatiate on the
fate of man in a future state of being, and to contrast
the darkness of the views which the wisest of the heathen
had, with the perfect light of the new dispensation. He
oftentimes would expound the Scriptures, taking, as is
the usage of the Kirk, a portion of some chapter for
the subject of what is called *lecture* as contradistinguished from sermon; and in these discourses, the
richness of his learning, the remarkable clearness of his
explanation, the felicity of his illustration, shone forth,
as well as the cogency and elegance of his practical
application to our duties in life, the end and aim of all
his teaching. I have heard him repeatedly, occupying
as he did from 1759 to his death the pulpit of the Old

---

* Life of Voltaire.

Grey Friars, where his father had been minister before
him. But one sermon, though I was very young at the
time, I never can forget. The occasion was the celebra-
tion (5th November, 1788) of the centenary of the Revolution, and his sister, considering that to have heard
such a man discourse on such a subject was a thing to
be remembered by any one through life ever after, took
me to hear him. It was of singular and striking interest, for the extreme earnestness, the youthful fervour
with which it was delivered. But it was in some passages upon a revolution which he expected and saw
approaching, if not begun, as well as upon the one
which was long past, and almost faded from the
memory in the more absorbing interest of present
affairs. I well remember his referring to the events
now going on on the Continent, as the forerunners of
far greater ones which he saw casting their shadows
before. He certainly had no apprehensions of mischief,
but he was full of hope for the future, and his exultation was boundless in contemplating the deliverance
of "so many millions of so great a nation from the
fetters of arbitrary government." His sister and I
often afterwards reflected on this extraordinary discourse with wonder, and I feel almost certain of some
such expressions as these having been used, and of his
foretelling that our neighbours would one day have to
celebrate such an event as had now called us together.
We dined with him the same day on leaving the
church, for it was the afternoon service that he had
performed. His eldest son, afterwards Lord Robertson, was of the company; and when the Principal
expressed his satisfaction at having had his presence at
church (a thing by no means of weekly occurrence),

the answer was, " Aye, sir, if you'll always give us such sermons, you may make it worth our while." "Ah," answered he, "you would like it, as the boys say," referring to a vulgar school taunt. I have again and again asked my learned kinsman to show me the sermon, which he admitted he possessed among his father's papers, fairly written out. His answer was that he wished to avoid giving it publicity, because, in the violence of the times, the author of it would be set down for a Jacobin, how innocent soever he was at the day of its being preached. Those times have happily long since passed away. I cannot believe that any one has ventured to destroy this remarkable production, though hitherto it has not been found.*—I return to the course of his life.

From 1752 to 1758 he had been diligently occupied with the 'History of Scotland;' in 1759 it appeared. The success of this admirable work was as immediate and as universal as it was deserved. The whole edition, though of two quarto volumes, was exhausted in less than a month. There was but one voice in every part of the country, and among all ranks and descriptions of men, both upon its pure and beautiful composition, its interesting narrative, and its anxious and conscientious accuracy. A murmur was heard from the Jacobite party, who in Scotland

---

* My kinsman, executor of Lord Robertson, has at length, after many a fruitless search, succeeded in finding the sermon, and it now lies before me, written in his own hand. I can see the places where he added remarks made on the inspiration of the moment, particularly the one above cited, of which I am the more certain from the subsequent conversations of his sister, who heard it with me.

were more wild and romantic, and more unreasoning, than in the southern parts of the island. Not satisfied with the far less harsh view of Mary's conduct which he had taken compared with Hume's, partial as Hume was to the Stuarts, it was the fashion of this little set of enthusiasts to say that he had "cut her with a razor dipped in oil." It was no little concession to have acquitted her of all part in Babington's conspiracy, to have left her share in Darnley's murder hanging in doubt, to have pronounced a decisive judgment against Elizabeth, for her whole conduct both towards the Scots and their Queen. These silly persons would not be appeased unless, in the face of all her own conduct and her own words, she was acquitted of the outrage on common decency of wedding her husband's murderer, and screening his accomplices from punishment. But the clamour, though it produced a book or two in support of this most desperate cause, spread very little even in Scotland; and the national vanity was inexpressibly gratified by this great triumph in the most important and most popular of all the walks of polite learning. The delight of his friends was of course still more lively. Aware of his merits, as they always had been, and somewhat impatient of the length of time which he had suffered his known capacity to remain barren, now that they saw the abundant fruits crowning his works, they exulted as if they gathered in the rich harvest in common, and confessed that the postponement had not stunted the growth, but, like a fallow, made it more plenteous and more rich. In truth, the discipline of so many years' study to which he had subjected himself, the long delay which he had interposed, though all the while thoroughly versed in all the arts of composition, had the salutary effect of making his first work as mature as his latest production. This is perhaps a singular instance of one who had from his early youth been studying diction, who had been constantly writing, and had for long years been almost as expert as he ever became, withholding himself from employing the faculty which he had acquired, except to render himself still more dexterous in its use, and continuing four and twenty years ere he appeared before the world, nay, eighteen years before he even began to write the work which should lay the foundation of his fame. He was eight and thirty when he published it. But then it is another singularity as great, that considerable doubt remains if any of his subsequent works surpassed this first production.

Among his exulting friends, David Hume deserves to be singled out for the heartiness of his disinterested joy. Far from not bearing a brother near the throne, he entirely rejoiced in his rival's success, and even in the uniting of all testimonies to his merits, so strongly contrasted with the universal clamour for some years raised against his own 'History,' and the niggard praise which, even after five years, that work received. Among other kind acts, he encouraged some literary men at Paris to translate the new 'History;' and he thus jocosely touches upon the loss of his undivided superiority as an historian: "I warn you, however, this is the last time I shall ever speak the least good of it. A plague take you! Here I sat

near the historical summit of Parnassus, immediately
under Dr. Smollett,* and you have the impudence to
squeeze yourself past me, and place yourself directly under his feet! Do you imagine that this can be agreeable to me? and must not I be guilty of great simplicity to contribute by my endeavours to your thrusting
me out of my place both at Paris and in London?
But I give you warning that you will find the matter
somewhat difficult, at least in the former city. A
friend of mine who is there, writes home to his father
the strangest accounts of that kind, which my modesty
will not allow me to repeat, but which it allowed me
very deliciously to swallow."

Just before the ' History ' was published, the author
visited London for the first time; and his merit having been made known to some persons of eminence
and of good taste, who had been allowed to peruse portions, at least, of the proof sheets, his reception was of
a distinguished kind. I have now before me some letters
of his to his bosom friend, and steady coadjutor in
ecclesiastical politics, Dr. Jardine, and it is pleasing
to mark the natural expression of his satisfaction with
his visit.

The first letter which I shall give begins with
a good deal of narrative upon the success of John
Home's ' Agis.' At that time the violence and folly of
the fanatical party made the subject of this elegant
and amiable writer's dramas doubly interesting to his
friends. The tragedy, so successful at first, chiefly be-

---

* He of course had the lowest opinion of this writer's parts as
an historian.

cause of its predecessor, ' Douglas,'* having succeeded
through merit, and partly because of high patronage,
is a very middling performance, and, like all Mr.
Home's plays, except ' Douglas,' has long since sunk
into deserved oblivion.   Dr. Robertson's amiable zeal
for his friend, and his exultation at the success of his
piece, is very striking in this letter.

" MY DEAR SIR,   " Thursday, March 16th.
  " When I wrote you the history of ' Agis,' I certainly
foresaw some of the purposes for which it would serve, and
that you would naturally employ it for an use of mortification
to the wicked, as well as of comfort to the pious. I could not,
however, have any presage either of the absurdity of the
players, or of the malice and credulity of Home's enemies,
which rendered my account doubly seasonable. I now put
it in your power to mortify them with still fuller accounts
of the triumphs of ' Agis.' Never were there more crowded
houses than during the whole run of the play. The Prince
of Wales was present no less than three different nights, one
of which a benefit night. Such honourable distinction was
never formerly bestowed upon any new piece. The snarlers
and small critics are somewhat enraged at this, and every one
against Lord Bute; though I can assure you, the frequency of
the Prince's attendance was his own proper motion, and proceeded from his admiration of ' Agis.' But what is still more
honourable for Home, since the ninth night, ' Agis' has been
acted twice, and both times the house was more crowded (if
possible), and the applause louder than ever. There has ap-

---

  * ' Douglas' was the second in date of composition, though the first
performed.   Garrick had rejected it peremptorily; and it was
brought out with great success at Edinburgh. Garrick had also
rejected all Home's other pieces; until Lord Bute and other persons
of distinction patronised the poet, when the manager, following his
ignoble nature, suddenly became the zealous and forward patron of
all he wrote, and joined those noble supporters in forcing the very
poor tragedy of ' Agis' on the public.

peared a critic on 'Agis,' one Henerden. I am persuaded
Home has hired him, and given him a crown to write such
execrable stuff. Every body laughs at it; and, in the wicked
language of this town, it is called a d——d tame piece of nonsense. Wedderburn makes all the progress we could wish:
even the door-keeper of the House of Peers tells me that 'he
is a d——d clever fellow, and speaks devilish good English.'
This very morning he was retained in a Plantation cause
before the Privy Council, which is a thing altogether extraordinary for so young a man. You cannot imagine what odd
fellows his rivals are, and how far and how fast he is likely
to go.

"I can't say so much about my own progress. I unluckily
have but one copy of my 'History,' otherwise I might advance
with more rapidity. I have been with Horace Walpole, a son
of Sir Robert's, a very clever man, and of great leading among
the literary people of fashion. We had much conversation about
Mary. He is one of the greatest critics I ever met with, as
to the facts in the period. Our notions jumped perfectly.
Part of my papers are in his hands; the Duke of Argyle has
another; Scott, who was preceptor to the Prince of Wales, a
third; and Lord Royston a fourth. I have got from this last
a vast collection of original papers; many of them are curious.
I am advised by several people to transcribe as many as will
swell the book to a guinea price. The taste of this town is
such, that such an addition will be esteemed very meritorious;
and though it cost me little but having an amanuensis, it will
add to the price in proportion to the increase of bulk. You
see I begin to learn the craft of authorship. I have hitherto
industriously avoided meeting with booksellers, but shall soon
begin my operations with them. I have had a great offer
from Hamilton and Balfour, which you'll probably have heard
of. I can scarcely believe that even the effrontery of
W——r's roguery could have seriously set his face to such a
scheme as that you mention. I scarce think it necessary,
upon such a surmise, to write to Lord Milton; but I shall
drop a line to Mrs. Wedderburn or Miss Hepburn, in order
to prevent any such foolish measure being heard with patience.
I have not yet seen either Dr. Chandler or the Lions. All the

other scenes you recommend to me I have seen. I have heard the Bishops of Salisbury and Oxford. There was some elegance, a spice of drollery, and not a little buffoonery in the sermon of the latter; and his audience admired and laughed, and were edified. Blair is but a ninny of an orator; he makes his hearers serious, and sets them a-crying; but here they go to heaven, laughing as they go. You cannot imagine what strange characters I have met with, which I cannot now take off. I am a sort of domestic with Dr. Campbell, the best of all the authors I have seen.* I am often with Tucker of Bristol. I dined and drank claret with Douglas, the murderer of Bower."—" There were nine other persons in company (at another dinner), all of them retainers to the author or bookseller; and I will draw you such a picture of that night, that you shall say the seeing of it alone was worth my coming to London. I wrote Bruce a long letter about news some days ago: you would probably meet with him and hear its contents. The Hanoverians are still making progress, as you will read more at large in the 'Chronicle.' The only thing which engrosses the talk of politicians is the flight of Bonneville. He was the officer who dissuaded the landing at Rochefort, and who, before the court-martial, gave evidence directly opposite to Clerk's. He went over to Holland; was seen often at d'Affry's, the French Ambassador's: he told him, 'Sir, I do possess some merit; I saved one town to France, and three generals to England.' His evidence acquitted Mordant, &c. From Holland he went over to France. You may believe Pit† and Colonel Clerk, &c., enjoy this adventure, which is indeed a remarkable one. Last day I was in the House of Commons, of which I am made free by "——

Unfortunately the MS. breaks off just as he was about to describe the debate.

---

* The able author of the fine historical pieces in the edition 1740 of Harris's 'Voyages.' Dr. R. always used to mention his Presbyterian horror of the "profane expletives" which he found formed a part of all English colloquial discourse in those days.

† Sic.

The following letter gives a further account of the historian's progress in preparing for the publication of his work. It is written to the same friend, Dr. Jardine :—

"MY DEAR JOHN,   "London, 20th April, 1759.

"I write this in the British Coffee-House,* in the middle of a company playing at cards and drinking claret. After this preamble, you are not to expect either a very long or a very distinct epistle. As to your letter, I postponed writing an answer to it, in expectation of hearing some account of the transactions of the Haddington Presbytery; but as that has not come to hand, I must proceed to write without it. I am as much interested as you can possibly be in preventing the intended elevation of Turnstill to the Moderator's chair. But how could it possibly enter into the head of such a politician as you are, and one who has seen London too, that there was any method of engaging our laymen here to take part in a question about which they (laymen) are totally indifferent? At the same time, I am earnest in giving opposition, and I think it may be made with great probability of success; but I should be apt to imagine that neither Dick nor Hamilton are the proper candidates. You know neither of them stand well with Lord Milton ;† and if either you or I should give our interest or solicit for them, you know what a handle might be made of it. If Morrison, or some such grave, inoffensive, ecclesiastical personage could be set up, I join you with all my vigour. You must make the choice as well as you can. Why may you not stand yourself? At any rate, fix upon some feasible man. Write a few letters, and endeavour to raise the jealousy of the brethren against a perpetual moderator, and I don't doubt of our defeating the Doctor. If we can discomfit him by our own strength, this will render him inconsiderable : all other methods of doing so would be ineffectual.

---

* Much frequented then, as it still is, by Scotchmen. The gentlewoman who at that time kept it was sister to Bishop Douglas, and a person of excellent manners and abilities.

† Then a kind of minister for Scotland, being Lord Bute's uncle.

"I have now brought my offers to a conclusion with Andrew Millar. After viewing the town, and considering the irresistible power of a combination of booksellers, I have agreed to sell him the property for £600. This, you see, is the sum I originally fixed upon as the full price of my work, and is more than was ever given for any book except David Hume's. You cannot imagine how much it has astonished all the London authors, nor how much Andrew Millar was astonished at the encomiums of my book which he got from people of rank. I have got some of the best puffers of England on my side. Mr. Doddington, Horace Walpole, Lady Hervey, and the Speaker are my sworn friends; and you will wonder, even in this great place, how I have got Mary Queen of Scots to be a subject of conversation. Every body here approves of the bargain I have made with Millar, and I am fully satisfied of the prudence of my own conduct; but of this I shall have full leisure to talk with you soon. The exploits which Carlyle and I have performed among the Dissenters are beyond belief. Poor Dr. Chandler is humbled to the dust, and he feels it as much as other quack doctors feel their mortification. This day I signed my contract with Andrew Millar, and am, according to your advice, to be a Doctor of Divinity within six months, so that I shall take place immediately after Dr. Blair, as he taketh place immediately after Dr. Turnstill. What great things have I to say of Mr. Pit,* who yesterday brought all the Tories to approve of continental measures as the only thing for the good of old England! Yesterday I dined with Mr. Garrick, in spite of John Hyndman† and the Presbytery of Dalkeith. To-morrow I go to Portsmouth, to wait on Admiral Hawke and see the Royal George. How much have I to tell you! I ever am yours,

" W_M. R."

The rank of the 'History of Scotland' stands very high indeed among the most eminent of historical compositions. The philosophical spirit which per-

---

* Sic.   † A leader among the fanatical party in the Kirk.

vades it, the enlarged views of polity in which it
abounds, the sober and rational, but bold speculations
with which it is variegated, and the constant references
to authorities which accompany it, place it above the
works of antiquity, deficient in all these particulars,
altogether wanting in some of them. The skilful and
striking delineations of individual character which are
mingled with the narrative, but never overlaying it, and
the reference to the histories of other countries which
is introduced wherever it became necessary or instructive, forms another high merit of the work. But
it is as a history, and a history of Scotland, that its
execution must mainly be regarded, and in this it is
truly a great performance. It is difficult to admire
sufficiently the graphic power which the historian
displays in bringing before us the rude and stormy
period he has chosen to describe—the strange mixture
of simple barbaric manners in some classes with artificial refinement in others—of poverty in the country
with splendour at court, and among the chiefs—of
great crimes with striking virtues—the morality of
unprincipled and ferocious men with the vehement
religious opinions of fanatics—the spectacle of a nation
hardly half-civilized, barely emerging from a rude state,
conducted by rulers, and disputed by factious leaders,
with all the refinements and corruption of statesmen
bred in the Italian courts. In the great staple of all
historical excellence, the narrative, it has certainly
never been surpassed. There is nothing obscure or
vague, nothing affected or epigrammatic, nor is any
sacrifice made of the sense to the phrase; the diction
is simple and pure, and soberly, if at all, adorned; but

it is also striking; the things described are presented
in the clearest light, and with the most vivid, natural,
and unambitious colouring, without exaggeration, apparently without effort; like the figures of Raphael,
which, for this reason, never captivate us so much on the
first view as after we have repeatedly gazed upon them
with still increasing wonder. The even flow of the story,
the last perfection and the most difficult which the narrative art attains, is likewise complete. If not overlaid
with ornament, nor disfigured by declamation, nor
studded with points and other feats of speech, so neither
is it broken by abrupt transitions and unseemly pauses,
but holds its clear, simple, majestic course uninterrupted and untroubled. The story of Livy does
not more differ from that of Tacitus in all these essen-
tials than the simple but striking narration of the
Scotch historian from the tinsel, the epigram, the
word-catching of Gibbon.

For examples to illustrate the high merits of this
narrative, we need not have recourse to a curious selection of remarkable scenes or events, because the texture
of the 'History' in the ordinary portions of its fabric
where the mere common annals are related, would be
sufficient. There may, however, be no harm in noting the singular effect of the story when Rizzio's
murder is related, or Gowrie's conspiracy, or Mary's
execution. The artistlike selection of particulars is to
be marked in all these cases; as in the first, Ruthven's
figure clad in armour, and ghastly pale from his late
illness; in the second, the trembling of the mysterious
armed man with a dagger near him, and a sword in
the small study whither the Earl had led the King,

closing the doors behind them, and up a staircase; in
the third, the Queen's majestic air and noble dress, the
pomander chain of her Agnus Dei round her neck, the
beads at her girdle, the crucifix of ivory in her hand.
By all these skilful selections we are made to see, as it
were, the things represented to us, and the pen of the
great historian produces the effect of the great artist's
pencil, while its pictures are not subject to the destroying influence of time.*

There seems considerable reason to lament that an
intimate acquaintance with the great scenes and celebrated characters of history, in all ages, should have
made the historian too familiar with the crimes on a
great scale of importance, and therefore of wickedness,
perpetrated by persons in exalted stations, so that he
suppresses in recounting or in citing them the feelings
of severe reprobation to which a more pure morality,
a more strict justice, would certainly have given vent.
It is painful to see him fall into the vulgar and pernicious delusion which secures for the worst enemies of
their species the praise and the increase of worldly
greatness.   It is equally painful to see the worst crimes,
even of a more ordinary description, passed over in
silence when they sully the illustrious culprit.   Let us

---

* Hume, as well as Robertson, has given this scene of Mary's
death ; the latter with by far greater effect.   But it is singular that
he should have left out her noble remonstrance with the commissioners when refused the assistance of her servants.   It has a great
effect in Hume.   The observations of the latter on the trial are
really beneath contempt.   The gross errors into which he falls on
the principles of evidence seem hardly credible, and arise from his
careless habits, and from his undertaking rashly to deal with matters
of which he was ignorant.

only, by way of example, and for explanation, survey
the highly-wrought and indeed admirably composed
character of Queen Elizabeth. It opens with enrolling
Henry V. and Edward III. among "the monarchs
who merit the people's gratitude ;" nay, it singles them
out from among the list on which William III., Edward I., and Alfred himself stand enrolled, and holds
them up as the most gratefully admired of all for the
" blessings and splendour of their reigns." Yet the
wars of Henry V. are the only, and of Edward III.
almost the only deeds by which we can know them ;
or if any benefit accrued to our constitution by these
princes, it was in consequence of the pecuniary difficulties into which those wars plunged them, but
plunged their kingdoms too, so that our liberties made
some gain from the dreadful expense of blood and of
treasure by which those conquerors exhausted their
dominions. Then Elizabeth is described as " still
adored in England ;" and though her " dissimulation
without necessity, and her severity beyond example,"
are recorded as making her treatment of Mary an
exception to the rest of her reign, it is not stated that
her whole life was one tissue of the same gross falsehood whenever she deemed it for her interest, or felt it
suited her caprices, to practise artifices as pitiful as they
were clumsy. But a graver charge than dissimulation
and severity as regards her connexion with the history of
Mary is entirely suppressed, and yet the foul crime is
described in the same work. It is undeniable that
Elizabeth did not cause her to be executed until she had
repeatedly endeavoured to make Sir Amyas Paulett and
Sir Drue Drury, who had the custody of her person,

take her off by assassination.   When those two gallant
cavaliers rejected the infamous proposition with indignation and with scorn, she attacked them as " dainty " and
" precise fellows," " men promising much and performing nothing ;" nay, she was with difficulty dissuaded
from displacing them, and employing one Wingfield in
their stead, " who had both courage and inclination to
strike the blow."   Then finding she could not commit
murder, she signed the warrant for Mary's execution ;
and immediately perpetrated a crime only less foul than
murder, treacherously denying her handwriting, and
destroying by heavy fine and long imprisonment the
Secretary of State whom she had herself employed to
issue the fatal warrant.   History, fertile in its records of
royal crimes, offers to our execration few such characters
as that of this great, successful, and popular princess.
An assassin in her heart, nay, in her councils and her
orders ; an oppressor of the most unrelenting cruelty
in her whole conduct ; a hypocritical dissembler, to
whom falsehood was habitual, honest frankness strange
—such is the light in which she ought to be ever held
up, as long as humanity and truth shall bear any value
in the eyes of men.   That she rendered great services
to her subjects ; that she possessed extraordinary firmness of character as a sovereign, with despicable weakness as an individual ; that she governed her dominions
with admirable prudence, and guided her course
through as great difficulties in the affairs of the state,
and still more in those of the church, as beset the path
of any who ever ruled—is equally incontrovertible ;
but there is no such thing as " right of set-off" in the
judgments which impartial history has to pronounce—

no doctrine of compensation in the code of public
morals; and he who undertakes to record the actions
of princes, and to paint their characters, is not at
liberty to cast a veil over undeniable imperfections, or
suffer himself like the giddy vulgar to be so dazzled by
vulgar glory that his eyes are blind to crime.*

A few months previous to the publication of his
'History,' Dr. Robertson, who had before received the
degree of Doctor in Divinity from the University of
Edinburgh, removed to that city, being presented to
the kirk of the Old Grey Friars. In 1759 he was
made one of the chaplains royal, a sinecure in the
Scotch Church; in 1762 he was appointed Principal
of the University, and a proposition was now made, proceeding from the King through his favourite minister,
Lord Bute, who communicated it to Lord Cathcart, and
he to the Principal, that if he would undertake to write
the History of England, every source of information
which the government could command would be laid
open to his researches, and such provision settled upon
him as might enable him to bestow his whole attention
and time upon this important work without the inter-
ruptions occasioned by his professional duties. This
plan was so far favourably received that he expressed
his willingness now to undertake the subject, as he could

---

* Hume's highly-wrought character of Elizabeth, perhaps the
finest of all his historical portraits, is liable to the same grave objection; somewhat mitigated by the circumstance that he seemed to
lend less implicit credence to Davidson's testimony against her than
Robertson does. It is remarkable that neither historian has remarked
in Mary's vindication the undoubted right she had, without committing an offence against the law or against morals, to join in any measures of hostility against Elizabeth, who held her in an illegal custody.

not any longer come into conflict with his friend Mr.
Hume, whose work would have been all published
many years before the new 'History' could appear. His
former objection of Mr. Hume's 'History' being then in
progress when a similar plan was pressed upon him by
the booksellers had thus been removed; and though he
declined on any account to lay down his clerical character, and withdraw from his station in the church, he
had yet no objection, if he could still retain his connexion with that venerated establishment, to be relieved
from the parochial labours connected with the cure of
souls; and provided Edinburgh should continue to be his
place of residence, he purposed passing each year two
or three months in London for the benefit of the
collections offered to be placed at his service. It is
probable that the retirement of Lord Bute from office,
which happened soon after, put an end to this important negotiation; important in a very high degree to
the literature, and, indeed, to the constitutional interests of the country. Nothing more seems to have
resulted from the correspondence except the reviving
in his favour the place of historiographer for Scotland,
to which he was appointed in 1764. But who that
values the accuracy of historical narration, and sets a
right estimate upon the benefits derived to our political
system from a thorough investigation of the records
and the events of former times, during which our
mixed government was slowly formed and gradually
matured, can avoid deeply lamenting that the subject
of English history had not fallen into the hands of
him who was, by a competent judge, though a rival
author, justly called " the most diligent and most

faithful of penmen?" We should then have possessed
a work of which the brilliant outside gloss being sustained by the intrinsic value of the coin, it would no
longer have been necessary for the student to read one
narrative for its dramatic effect, while he sought in
another the real facts of the story, and to refuse giving
the first praise of an historian to the first master of
historical composition. Nor would the acquisition of
an English history, at once readable and credible, have
been purchased by the sacrifice of the other works with
which this great writer, after the failure of the treaty,
enriched our literature. It was part of the conditions
which he imposed that he should first be allowed to finish
his ' Charles V. ;' and when we reflect on ten years having
elapsed after he finished his ' America,' without resuming
his pen, there seems no reason to doubt that he could have
written this and the English history also during the period between 1769, when ' Charles ' was published, and
1789, when he began the ' Disquisition on Ancient
India.' The failure of the treaty, therefore, is a matter
of unmingled regret; and is one of the worst of the
many mischiefs which we owe to the English plan of
conducting government by the conflict of adverse
parties, with the consequence inevitably flowing from
it, of all the principles, and all the measures, and all the
designs of one ministry becoming, as a matter of course,
an object of suspicion, and even of dislike, to their
successors.

It is probable that he did not begin his second work
for some little time after the publication of the first;
but from the correspondence just now referred to, we
learn that in July, 1762, a third part of it was finished,

and that he reckoned two years more sufficient for its
completion. In this he was deceived, whether it be that
he underrated the labour required by the portion of his
task still before him, or that he was interrupted in it (as
has been supposed) by the fierce dissensions which during
that period raged in the Scottish Church, and which
must no doubt have occupied some portion of his leisure,
though with so severe an economist of his time, and a
mind so little liable to be disturbed, there seems little
reason to think that these proceedings could seriously
distract his attention from his studies for any considerable portion of the year. At length the public impatience was gratified by the appearance of the work
in 1769, exactly ten years after his 'Scotland.' Its
success was not a matter of doubt, and it fully answered the expectations which had naturally been
formed. The prevailing opinion places this work at
the head of his writings; and certainly, if the extent
and importance of the subject be regarded, and the
great value be considered of a clear and distinct narrative, embracing the history of Europe during the
period when its different states assumed the position
with relation to each other in which they now stand,
and most of them also adopted the political system
which is established for the government of their several
affairs, there can be no comparison between this and
any other of his works; to which must doubtless be
added, the far greater difficulty of executing so vast a
plan, tracing the complicated parts of the great European commonwealth in their connexion with each
other, and drawing, as Mr. Stewart has happily expressed it, a meridian line through modern history, to

which all the branches of separate annals may be referred. But though the same felicitous narrative is in this work to be always found, and though the first book contains the most perfect example of general or philosophical history anywhere to be seen, yet I hesitate greatly in preferring it as an historical composition to either its predecessor or its immediate successor. There are more remarkable beauties of a purely historical kind in both of these, according to my humble judgment. As a whole, as a history of a country for a given period, I am much disposed to place his ' Scotland' first; while I conceive that the ' America' presents particular passages, feats of narrative excellence, unrivalled by anything in either of the other works, perhaps not to be matched, and certainly not exceeded, by any other historical composition of any age.

In proof of this last position I will refer to the fascinating account of Cortez's arrival at Mexico, and of his subsequent bold and masterly, though most cruel and profligate measures; to the romantic history of Pedro de la Gasca's quelling by his individual wisdom and firmness the great rebellion of Peru; but, above all, to the grand event, the most important recorded in the annals of our race, the discovery of the New World by Columbus. The skill with which this last narrative is managed, and the conduct of the story, may truly be pronounced matchless. I am now speaking merely of the composition. The dramatic effect of the whole is extraordinary. We are at first interested in Columbus's sagacity, and boldness, and science, by which he was led, through a course of private study

and contemplation, to form the adventurous and novel
opinion that the East Indies was to be reached by
steering a westerly course from Europe across the At-
lantic. His difficulties in obtaining the assent of his
contemporaries to so strange a doctrine are then described, and our interest in his theory is increased.
But the successive obstacles which he had to encounter
in his efforts to obtain the assistance of various sovereigns, that he might be enabled to test his theory by
navigating the unknown and pathless ocean, wind up
our anxiety to the highest pitch. We follow him to
the Genoese senate, to the court of Portugal, to England, whither he had dispatched his brother, whose
strange adventures among pirates and his utter indi-
gence in London so as to make it necessary he should
subsist by selling maps till he could scrape together
enough to purchase decent clothes wherein he might
appear before Henry VIII., form a striking episode in
the narrative. Finally, we have his own arrival in Spain,
and his constant repulses for twelve long years in all his
attempts to make that country the richest and most
glorious on the face of the earth.   All these wander-
ings and disappointments for so vast a portion of this
great man's life create a breathless impatience for his
success, when our wishes are at length crowned by the
warm support of his steady patroness Isabella ; and he
finally sets sail on the 3rd of August, 1492.—Such is
the man whose fortunes we are to follow, now far past
the middle age, for he was in his fifty-sixth year, of
which above twenty had been spent in preparing for
his magnificent enterprise ; but full of the vigour of
youth, in the height of his powerful faculties, and in-

spired with the sanguine temper which enables genius to work its wonders.

The voyage is related with absolute clearness as regards all its nautical details, which are given so as to fix our attention without wearying it, and elucidate the narrative without encumbering it. But in the incidents of the passage we take the greatest interest, placed, as we feel ourselves to be, in the position of the navigators, to whom every occurrence was of moment, because everything was of necessity new. Their conduct and their feelings, however, occupy us still more, for beside our sympathy with them, upon them the fate of the great enterprise depends.

But one figure ever stands out from the group; it is the great Captain who guides the voyage through the unknown ocean, and whom, beside his past history, we all the while feel by anticipation to be piercing through the night of ages to bring into acquaintance with each other the old world and the new. Upon his steady courage, undismayed by the dark uncertainty of all his steps, upon his fortitude which no peril can shake, his temper unruffled by all opposition, upon his copious resources under every difficulty, we dwell with the most profound attention; sometimes hardly venturing to hope for his successful conquest over so many difficulties. The voyage meanwhile proceeds, and the distance from any known portion of the world becomes tremendous, while nothing but sea and air is on all hands to be discerned. At length some slight indications of approach to land begin to be perceived; but so slight that universal despondency creates a general resistance, breaking out into actual mutiny.

Our anxiety for the result, and our interest in the great admiral, is now wound up to the highest pitch, when he obtains a promise of his crew persevering, "watching with him" yet three days. The indications of land being not far off now become less doubtful; and from among them are selected the more striking, closing with this picturesque passage :—" The sailors aboard the Nina took up the branch of a tree with red berries, perfectly fresh. The clouds around the setting sun assumed a new appearance ; the air was more mild and warm, and during the night the wind beca meunequal and variable." When we are thus in painful suspense, comes the crowning victory—at once of the great navigator who has happily traced the unknown ocean, and of the great historian who has strictly pursued his path, but so as to give the well-known truth all the interest and all the novelty of a romantic tale now first told.

I beg any one who thinks these remarks overrate his merit, to mark the exquisite texture of the following sentences, in which the grand result, the development of the whole, is given; and to mark the careful simplicity of the diction, the self-concealed art of the master, and his admirable selection of particulars, by which we, as it were, descend and perch upon the deck of the great admiral :—" From all these symptoms Columbus was so confident of being near land, that on the evening of the 11th of October, after public prayers for success, he ordered the sails to be furled, and the ships to lie-to, keeping strict watch, lest they should be driven on shore in the night. During this interval of suspense and expectation no man shut his eyes; all kept upon deck, gazing intently towards that quarter whence they expected to discern the land which had been so long the object of their wishes." It is a judicious thing, though it seems trivial, that he here breaks off, as it were, and begins a new paragraph; and mark well its structure :—

"About two hours before midnight Columbus, standing on the forecastle, observed a light at a distance, and privately pointed it out to Pedro Guttierez, a page of the queen's wardrobe. Guttierez perceived it, and calling to Salcedo, comptroller of the fleet, all three saw it in motion, as if it were carried from place to place. A little after midnight the joyful sound of *Land! Land!* was heard from the Pinta, which kept always ahead of the other ships. But having been so often deceived by fallacious appearances, every man now became slow of belief, and waited in all the anguish of uncertainty and impatience for the return of day. As soon as the morning dawned, all doubts and fears were dispelled. From every ship an island was seen about two leagues to the north, whose flat and verdant fields, well stored with wood, and watered with many rivulets, presented the aspect of a delightful country. The crew of the Pinta instantly began the *Te Deum*, as a hymn of thanksgiving to God, and were joined by those of the other ships, with tears of joy and transports of congratulation. This office of gratitude to Heaven was followed by an act of justice to their commander. They threw themselves at the feet of Columbus with feelings of self-condemnation mingled with remorse. They implored him to pardon their ignorance, incredulity, and injustice, which had created him so much unnecessary disquiet, and had so often obstructed the execution of his well-concerted plan; and passing in the warmth of their admiration from one extreme to another, they now pronounced the man whom they had so lately reviled and threatened, to be a person inspired by Heaven with sagacity and fortitude more than human in order to accomplish a design so far beyond the ideas and conception of all former ages."

In like manner is the landing and the meeting with the natives painted rather than described. The impression made, for instance, by the Spaniards on the minds of these simple folk shows that the great writer can place himself in the position of the savage as well as the sage. "The vast machines in which they had traversed the ocean, that seemed to move upon the waters with wings, and uttered a dreadful sound like thunder, accompanied with lightning and smoke, struck them with such terror, that they began to respect their new guests as a superior order of beings, and concluded that they were children of the sun, who had descended to visit the earth."

The simple language of these passages, to make but one observation, is remarkable; and their dignity is with this perfect plainness perfectly sustained. It is always in such language that a master of diction will make his impression; and the near approach of any catastrophe, whether awful or pathetic, may always be suspected when the language becomes very simple, and the particulars begin to abound. There is but one word above the most homely style of the most ordinary conversation in all that I have cited. The fields are "verdant," not green; and this word is correctly chosen for the rhythm, which would not allow a monosyllable. Possibly "descend" was unnecessary; "come down" would have been sufficiently sustained. The technical words "lie-to" and "ahead" were in like manner necessary, because there is ridicule attached to speaking of a ship "stopping," or one being before another, as on the road; besides that these phrases have been imported from nautical language, and are now naturalised on shore.

The effect which the passage adverted to is calculated to produce on readers of understanding and of feeling was once remarkably seen by me, when I made my illustrious and venerated friend Lord Wellesley attend to it. He told me next day that he had never been so much moved by any modern writing; that he had shed tears while he read it, and that it had broken his rest at night.

If the word dramatic has been applied to this narrative, it has been advisedly chosen; because no one can doubt that, with the most scrupulous regard to the truth, and even to the minute accuracy of history, this composition has all the beauties of a striking poem. To judge of its merits in this respect, I will not compare or rather contrast it with the Histories of Oviedo, or Herrera, or Ferdinand Columbus, or even with the far better composition of Dr. Campbell, or whoever wrote the history of the discovery in Harris's 'Bibliotheca Itinerantium,'* nor yet with the ambitious but

---

* This work, in two folio volumes, contains some admirable historical pieces. Burke's 'European Settlements' is very much taken from it. I refer to the edition of 1740, by Dr. Campbell, whose acquaintance Dr. Robertson appears by his 'Letters' above cited to have had great pleasure in making when he visited London.

worse written narrative of Mr. Washington Irvine, in his 'Life and Voyages of Columbus;'* but I will refer to a poetical work written purely for effect, and

---

* It is no part of my intention to underrate the merits of this very popular author; but I speak of the manner in which he has treated the subject; and coming after so great a master, it was not judicious in him to try after effect, instead of studying the chaste simplicity of his predecessor. These are a few of his expressions :—The ships " were ploughing the waves ;" Columbus was " wrapped in the shades of night ;" he " maintained an intense watch ;" he " ranged his eye along the dusky horizon ;" he beheld " suddenly a glimmering light." Robertson had never thought of saying " suddenly," as knowing that light must of necessity be sudden. Then the light has " passing gleams ;" his feelings " must have been tumultuous and intense," contrary to the fact, and to the character of the man ; " the great mystery of the ocean was revealed ;" " what a bewildering crowd of conjectures thronged on his mind !" All this speculation of the writer to insure the effect, Dr. Robertson rejects as fatal to effect, and gives only what actually happened. Finally, he was possibly to find " the morning dawn upon spicy groves, and glittering fanes, and gilded cities." Surely no one can hesitate which of the two pictures to prefer. If the one is not absolutely tawdry, the other is assuredly more chaste. To compare the two pieces of workmanship is a good lesson, and may tend to cure a vitiated taste (Book iii. chap. 3). To take only one instance :—" About two hours before midnight, Columbus, standing on the forecastle, observed a light at a distance, and presently pointed it out to Pedro," &c. Thus Robertson. Irvine says, " Wrapped from observation in the shades of night, he maintained an intense and unremitting watch, ranging his eye along the dusky horizon. Suddenly, about ten o'clock, he thought he beheld a light glimmering at a distance." Can any one doubt which of the two passages is the most striking—the chaste and severe, or the ornamented and gaudy and meretricious? The account of Robertson makes the ships lie-to all night. Irvine either makes them lie-to, and afterwards go on sailing rapidly, or the lying-to was the night before, and they sailed quicker the nearer they came to land, and in the dusk. The one makes them only see the shore after dawn ; the other makes them see it two leagues off, in a dark night, at two in the morning, within the tropics.

of which the author was at full liberty to indulge his fancy in selecting, or indeed in imagining the facts and the scenes he represented. That author, too, is a poet of no mean fame, the late Mr. Southey, who has sung the discovery of America by Madoc; and his verse is much less fine, and as a poem, than the history which I have been asking the reader to contemplate. The poet leaves out all the most picturesque matters, the truly poetical matters; and instead of them all, after a mutiny he raises a storm, which so cripples the ships that the seamen cannot sail back if they would. All he says of the discovery is, that the commander watched upon deck till dawn, and then saw the distant land arise like a grey cloud from the ocean. He also makes the sea shallow, though at such distance as that the land looks like a cloud. It really should seem as if he had refrained from looking at Robertson's 'History' because he was to write a poem on the subject, as he tells us he did from reading Voltaire's poem before, and, indeed, also after he wrote 'Joan of Arc.'

There is one reflection which arises very naturally on examining the rare excellence of such narratives as that of Pedro de la Gasca and Columbus's voyage. The subject of the latter is altogether free from warlike interest; of the former, nearly so; and of neither scene is the effect at all heightened by the vices or the excesses of the actors. Then who can find any more interesting narrative of events where great crimes are the subject, and who can doubt that the same pen which could so admirably paint the scenes, peaceful and guiltless, which compose the subject of such historical pictures, could in like manner have lent an interest

to others of a like kind, without exalting, at the expense
of public virtue, the merits of wicked men? But
if it be said that the quieting a great republic, or discovering a new hemisphere, are acts of such interest as
lend themselves to the historian's pen, and are easily
made to rivet our attention, surely the same pen which
described them can represent even the wars that deso-
late the earth, and the crimes that disgrace humanity, in
such colours as shall at once make us see the things perpetrated, and yet lament the wretchedness of the events,
and execrate the cruelties or scorn the perfidies of the
criminals, instead of making us, with a preposterous
joy and a guilty admiration, exult in the occurrence of
the one, and revere the memory of the other. Reference has been made already to the Plantagenet Prince
and the Tudor Princess, so much the theme of admiration with historians for great capacity, crowned with
dazzling success. But why could not the diction of
Hume and of Robertson have been employed for the
far more worthy purpose of causing men to despise the
intrigues and execrate the wars of such rulers? The
same events had then studded their page, the same
picturesque details given it striking effect, the same
graphic colours added life to it, and yet the right
feelings of the reader would have been exerted and
cherished ; nor would the historians have made themselves accomplices with the vulgar in the criminal
award of applause and of fame, by which the wicked
actions of past times are rewarded, and the repetition of the same offences encouraged.

Historians, too, are capricious and uncertain in their
panegyrics. Some princes of undoubted genius, of great

courage, of singular skill in conquest and in government, nay, even who have rendered services to mankind, notwithstanding their vices, are set apart to be loaded with obloquy—quite just in their instance, but inconsistent enough with the suppression of all reprobation in other cases of less atrocity, indeed, yet of deep shades of guilt. The Borgia family are proverbial for profligacy and cruelty ; yet both father and son showed talents of the highest order, to which the latter added great bravery, while the family were generous protectors of learning, especially of the study of jurisprudence, and do not seem to have misgoverned the people of their states more than others of the same age and country, their violence being exhausted on foreign princes and on their own feudal barons.* Of them, however, all anecdotes without evidence are believed. So the least credible stories of our Richard III. are easily received without proof, and he is universally regarded as a monster living in the habitual commission of murder ; yet his capacity and his courage were universally admitted to be of the very highest order, and his reign conferred great advantages on the jurisprudence of England, while the nobles only, and not the community at large, suffered from his tyranny. Is it not somewhat inconsistent in the same historians who are so hostile to these great bad men that they can discover no merit in them, to be so dazzled by the battles of the Plantagenets and the policy of the Tudors that they can discover no blame in the sanguinary ambition of

---

* Livy's character of Hannibal has been, and not unjustly, likened by Hume to Guicciardini's account of Alexander VI.

the one and the tyranny and perfidy of the other?
Henry VIII., indeed, by his cruelty to his wives, has
been deprived of much palliation which otherwise his
abilities and his accomplishments would have obtained
for his despotic life, his numerous judicial murders
actually perpetrated, as well as his plot for an ordinary
assassination, that of Cardinal Beaton, only prevented
by his own decease. But his daughter, who was as
tyrannical to the full, and only restrained by the religious difficulties of her position, who was a model of
falsehood in all its more hateful and despicable
forms, who had all the guilt of murder on her head,
and was only saved from its actual perpetration by having a Paulett for her agent, whom she would fain
have suborned to commit it, instead of a Tyrrel, is
loaded with the praise due to the most pure and virtuous of sovereigns, because she had talents and firmness and ruled successfully in difficult times.

It is not, however, merely by abstaining from
indiscriminate praise, or by dwelling with dispro-
portioned earnestness upon the great qualities, and
passing lightly over the bad ones, of eminent men,
and thus leaving a false general impression of their
conduct, that historians err, and pervert the opinions
and feelings of mankind. Even if they were to give a
careful estimate of each character, and pronounce just
judgment upon the whole, they would still leave by
far the most important part of their duty unperformed,
unless they also framed their narrative so as to excite
our interest in the worthy of past times; to make us
dwell with delight on the scenes of human improvement; to lessen the pleasure too naturally felt in con-

templating successful courage or skill, whensoever these
are directed towards the injury of mankind ; to call
forth our scorn of perfidious actions, however successful;
our detestation of cruel and bloodthirsty propensities,
however powerful the talents by which their indulgence was secured. Instead of holding up to our
admiration the " pride, pomp, and circumstance of
glorious war," it is the historian's duty to make
us regard with unceasing delight the ease, worth, and
happiness of blessed peace ; he must remember that

" Peace hath her victories,
No less renown'd than War :"*

and to celebrate these triumphs, the progress of science
and of art, the extension and security of freedom, the
improvement of national institutions, the diffusion of
general prosperity—exhausting on such pure and
wholesome themes all the resources of his philosophy, all the graces of his style, giving honour to
whom honour is due, withholding all incentives to
misplaced interest and vicious admiration, and not
merely by general remarks on men and on events, but
by the manner of describing the one and recording the
other, causing us to entertain the proper sentiments,
whether of respect or of interest, or of aversion or of
indifference, for the various subjects of the narration.

It is not to be denied, that history written in this
spirit must differ materially from any of which we
have as yet the experience : it is only to be lamented
that those great masters, whose writings we have been
contemplating, did not consecrate their mighty talents

---

* Milton.

to so good a work. To the historians of all ages
joining with the vulgar, and, indeed, writing as if
they belonged themselves either to the class of ambitious warriors and intriguing statesmen, or to the
herd of ordinary men whom successful crimes de-
frauded at once of their rights and their praises,
may be ascribed by far the greater part of the encouragement held out to profligate conduct in those
who have the destinies of nations in their hands. At
all events, this is certain: if they could not eradicate
the natural propensity in the human mind towards
these errors when unrefined, they might have enlightened it, and have gradually diffused a sounder
and better feeling.

So deeply have I always felt the duty of attempting
some such reformation in the historical character and
practice, that I had begun to undertake the reigns of
Henry V., of Elizabeth, and of Alfred, upon these
great principles. A deep sense of the inadequate
powers which I brought to this hard task, would
probably have so far grown upon me as its execution
advanced, that I should have abandoned it to abler
hands; but professional, and afterwards judicial, duties
put an end to the attempt before it had made any
considerable progress. Nevertheless, I found no
small reason to be satisfied of success being attainable,
when I came narrowly to examine the interesting
facts connected with national improvement and virtuous conduct; and I am sure, that whoever may
repeat the attempt will gather encouragement from
the proof, which I have drawn from the master-piece
we have been contemplating, that the events and

characters of past times lend themselves to an affecting narrative, conducted on right principles.

The last work of Dr. Robertson, and which he published little more than two years before his death, was his 'Disquisition concerning India.' It is an able and most learned inquiry, critical and historical, into the knowledge of India possessed by the ancient nations who dwelt on the Mediterranean Sea. Nothing can be more unjust than the notion that this work is so incorrect, or grounded on information so imperfect, as to have been superseded by more full and accurate books since published. There is no doubt that the account of the native customs and manners given in the Appendix has been rendered less useful by the more copious details since obtained, and that some dispute has been made of the views which the author occasionally takes in that Appendix; but the Disquisition itself remains perfectly untouched by any controversy; and so far is it from having been superseded, that no other work has ever been since given to the world on the same subject. It is, from its accuracy, its knowledge of the ancient writings, its judicious reasoning and remarks, as well as its admirable composition, quite worthy of a place by the author's former and more celebrated writings; and it proves his great faculties to have continued in their entire vigour to the latest period of his life.

It remains to speak of Robertson's style. No one ever doubted of its great excellence, but it has sometimes been objected to as less idiomatic and more laboured than is consistent with the perfection of composition. The want of purely idiomatic expressions

is the almost unavoidable consequence of provincial
education and habits. Many forms of speech which
are English, are almost entirely unknown in the
remote parts of the kingdom; many which are perfectly pure and classical, a person living in Scotland
would fear to use as doubting their correctness. That
Robertson, however, had carefully studied the best
writers, with 'a view to acquire genuine Anglicism,
cannot be doubted. He was intimately acquainted
with Swift's writings; indeed, he regarded him as
eminently skilled in the narrative art. He had the
same familiarity with Defoe, and had formed the same
high estimate of his historical powers. I know, that
when a Professor in another University consulted him
on the best discipline for acquiring a good narrative
style, previous to drawing up John Bell of Antermony's
'Travels across Russia to Tartary and the Chinese
Wall,' the remarkable advice he gave him was to read
'Robinson Crusoe' carefully; and when the Professor
was astonished, and supposed it was a jest, the historian said he was quite serious: but if 'Robinson
Crusoe' would not help him, or he was above studying
Defoe, then he recommended 'Gulliver's Travels.'

The works of Dr. Robertson involved him, as was
to be expected, in some controversy of considerable
violence; but as all men have done ample justice to his
diligence in consulting his authorities, and as all candid
men have testified to his strict impartiality, the attacks
which were made upon him, and to which he never
would offer any answer, proceeded from two unworthy
sources—the bitter zeal of party, and the still more
bitter enmity of personal spleen. The Jacobites have

ever regarded Queen Mary's honour as an integral part of their political faith; and they could not forgive any one who, with whatever leaning towards a princess the victim of such cruel treatment, and the sufferer under misfortunes so long and so heavy, and with whatever disposition to free her from any charges unsupported by evidence, had yet performed faithfully his duty as an historian and as a moralist, of condemning profligate conduct, and exposing gross imprudence amounting to absolute infatuation even if guilt be denied. Nothing could have satisfied the blind zeal of this faction, neither respectable from number, nor distinguished for ability, but acquitting Mary of every charge that she did not herself confess, and then approving of her marriage with the murderer of her husband within three months of his assassination. By far the ablest of the writings which the controversy produced, was the 'Inquiry' of Mr. Tytler, a lawyer by profession, a man of strong prejudices, but equally strong understanding, and a very diligent and accurate investigator of particular facts. The most learned, but the most repulsive from its dogmatism and its overbearing tone, was the 'Vindication' of Mr. Whittaker, a clergyman of the Church of England, settled in Cornwall, and remarkable for his industrious study of ancient British antiquities. With Mr. Hume Dr. Robertson likewise differed, but it was in an opposite direction: he could not yield to that able writer's arguments in proof of Mary's having been accessary to the Babington conspiracy; and though he minutely considered both the new evidence supposed to be printed in Murdin's 'State Papers' since the 'History of Scotland' was composed, and also carefully examined again all his authorities on the points on which he had been assailed by the Jacobite forces, yet, with the exception of a few unimportant errors or oversights, which he corrected, he adhered to his original statements, well weighed and maturely framed as they had, in all instances, been.

The personal resentment of an able but unprincipled man was the cause of the most unworthy and unmeasured attacks, both on his 'Scottish History' and on his subsequent publications. Gilbert Stuart was a person of undoubted parts, but of idle and dissipated habits. An able and learned work which he had published at a very early age, on the 'History of the British Constitution,' made the University of Edinburgh give him the degree of Doctor of Laws, when little more than one and twenty; and he soon after published his 'View of Society in Europe,' being an historical inquiry concerning laws, manners, and government. Immediately after this he was a candidate for the Professorship of Public Law, in the University, and he fancied that he owed his rejection to the influence of the Principal. Nothing could be more fitting than that such should be the case; for the life of Stuart was known to be that of habitual dissipation, in the intervals only of which he had paroxysms of study. To exclude such a person from the professor's chair would have been a duty incumbent upon the head of any university in Christendom, whatever, in other respects, might be his merits; but no admission

was ever made by the Principal's friends that he had
interfered, or indeed that the opinions and inclinations
of the magistrates, who are the patrons, rendered any
such interference necessary. But the disappointed
candidate had no doubt upon the subject, and he set no
bounds to his thirst of revenge. He repaired to London, where he became a writer in reviews, and made
all the literary men of Edinburgh the subjects of his
envious and malignant attacks, from 1768 to 1773;
the editors of these journals, as is usual with persons
in their really responsible situation, but who think
they can throw the responsibility upon their unknown
contributors, never inquiring whether the criticisms
which they published proceeded from the honest judg·
ment or the personal spite of the writers. He returned
to Edinburgh, and set up a magazine and review, of
which the scurrility, dictated by private resentments,
was so unremitting that it brought the work to a close
in less than three years, when he returned to London,
and recommenced his anonymous vituperation of Scottish authors through the periodical press. He also
published in 1779, 1780, and 1782, three works: one
on the ' Constitutional History of Scotland,' being an
attack on Dr. Robertson's first book; another on
the ' History of the Reformation in Scotland;' and the
third on the ' History of Queen Mary,' being also an
elaborate attack upon the Principal. The ability and
the learning of these works, and their lively and even
engaging style, has not saved them from the oblivion
to which they were justly consigned by the manifest
indications prevailing throughout them all, of splenetic
temper, of personal violence, and of a constant disturb-

ance of the judgment by these vile, unworthy passions.* The same hostility towards the person of the Principal even involved this reckless man in a quarrel with his eldest son; it led to a duel, in which neither party was hurt. An accommodation having taken place on the field, I have heard Stuart's second say that he was obliged, knowing his friend's intemperate habits, to oppose the proposal which he made with his usual want of conduct, and indeed of right feeling, that all the parties should dine together on quitting the field. That second, an able and an honourable man, always admitted Stuart's unjustifiable conduct towards the historian, one of whose nieces he (the second) afterwards married. Stuart's dissipation continued unbroken, excepting by his occasional literary work, and he died of a dropsy, in 1786, at the early age of forty.

Others, far more deserving of attention, have raised an objection to the ' History of America,' from which it is difficult to defend it. There is induced by the narrative, in the mind of the reader, far too great sympathy with the conquerors of the New World.

---

* Next to the Principal no one was more bitterly assailed than my late venerated friend and master, Dr. Adam, rector of the High School. His admirable ' Grammar' was received universally by the literary and didactic world (by the scholar as well as the teacher) with the approbation which it so well deserved. But it had one fault—it was on a subject on which Stuart's cousin, Ruddiman, had published a book. This was enough to enlist Stuart's ferocity against both the work and the writer. He published anonymous reviews without end, and he also published, under the name of Busby, a bitter attack upon the personal peculiarities of Dr. Adam. Every one felt unmingled disgust at such base and unprincipled proceedings, and the Rector, like the Principal, gave the unworthy author the mortification of leaving his assaults unanswered.

This may in part be palliated by the feeling so difficult for any historian to avoid, and which leads him
to paint in interesting, if not in attractive colours,
the deeds and the heroes of his story. But the atrocious crimes of those Spanish invaders, who, with a
combination of fanatical violence and sordid avarice,
subjugated or extirpated unoffending millions because
of their pagan ignorance and their precious mines,—
those bigoted furies who poured out the blood of men
like water, in order to establish the Gospel of peace
and good will towards man,—those monsters of cruelty,
who, after wearying themselves with massacre, racked
their invention for tortures, which might either glut
their savage propensities or slake their execrable thirst
of gold,—all ought to have called for reprobation, far
more severe than any which the historian of their
guilt has denounced against them. This is a great
stain upon the work, and it can only be palliated by
the excuse already offered,—an excuse by which the
stain never can be wiped out.

After the Principal's publication of ' Charles V.,' and
while he was writing the ' America,' no event of importance occurred in his life, which was tranquil and
dignified, occupied only with his duties as head of the
University, where the habitual deference of his colleagues rendered the administration of its concerns
easy and prosperous, diversified also with his conduct
of the Scottish church, now under his guidance, un-
opposed by any rival. He occasionally visited London,
where he was received by all the more distinguished

characters, whether statesmen or men of letters, with
the highest distinction; and the charms of his conversation, at once easy, lively, good-humoured, and yet
perfectly dignified as became his sacred profession and
his elevated position, added greatly to the interest that
naturally arose from his literary renown.

In 1778, the concessions to the English and Irish
Roman Catholics, by repealing the most oppressive parts
of the penal laws, suggested to those of Scotland the
obtaining a similar boon, or rather a similar act of justice. The Principal approved and supported their claims.
An alarm was excited, and the Puritanical party in
the General Assembly urged the adoption of a remonstrance against the proposed measure, but the Principal's salutary interference occasioned its rejection.   The
alarm was, however, stimulated by all the means to
which the unscrupulous fury of religious faction has
recourse; and so great a dread of violence was excited,
that the Catholics at once abandoned their attempt.
Their concessions, however, came too late to allay the
popular ferment which the Puritans had raised ; and a
fanatical mob attacking the Protestant chapels at
Edinburgh, burnt one and pulled down another, then,
proceeding to the college, were about to assail the
Principal's house, which they beleaguered, with the
most savage imprecations against him, but having had
notice of their approach he had withdrawn his family,
and a body of soldiers stationed there saved the building and the rest of the university.   At the next
Assembly in 1780 he made a speech of singular eloquence, declaring his unaltered opinion on the justice
of the measure, but adding that before the riots he

had been disposed to recommend a postponement of it until time should be given to enlighten the public mind, and free it from the gross delusions under which it had been brought through the acts of unprincipled men. This speech is given with tolerable fulness in the Scotch Magazine for that year, and it fully justifies the exalted opinion traditionally entertained of the Principal's oratory. He declared on this memorable occasion his intention to withdraw from public life, and stated that his friends well knew this resolution had been taken some time before the late controversy.

Nothing memorable occurred to this eminent and virtuous person after the period to which reference has now been made. A matrimonial alliance between his eldest daughter and Mr. Brydone, the celebrated traveller, a gentleman, too, known for his scientific pursuits, as well as distinguished for his amiable manners and kindness of disposition, had contributed materially to her father's happiness; and he liked to pass a few weeks in the summer or autumn at the delightful residence of Lennel on the southern border, where that excellent person lived, and where as late as 1814 he ended his days.

In the autumn of 1791 the Principal's health first began to fail; and a jaundice, proceeding from an affection of the liver, brought him early in 1793 to a state of weakness which left no hope of his recovery. He bore his infirmity with entire patience, and beheld the prospect of death, which was for many months before him, with unshaken fortitude. A month or two previous to his decease, he was removed to Grange House, in the neighbourhood of Edinburgh. Profes-

sor Stewart there saw him more than once; and far
from avoiding the subject, he said it would be satisfactory to him that his friend should write the account
of his life—it being, according to the usage of the
Royal Society (of Edinburgh), customary to give in their
' Transactions' the lives of deceased members who have
attained distinction by their works. On another occasion an observation was made on the fruit-trees then in
blossom ; and he alluded, with cheerful composure, to
the event which must happen before they came to
their maturity, and prevent him who now looked upon
the flower from seeing the fruit. His strength of
body gradually declining, though his mind remained
quite entire, he died on the 11th June, 1793, in the
72nd year of his age. His funeral in the Grey Friars
church-yard was attended by the professors, the magistrates of the city, the heads of the law, and many
of the other respectable inhabitants of Edinburgh.
It was, as I can testify, a scene peculiarly impressive
to all who witnessed it, from the sterling virtue as
well as the great celebrity and intrinsic merits of the
illustrious deceased.

The history of the author is the history of the individual, excepting as regards his private life and his
personal habits : these were in the most perfect degree dignified and pure. Without anything of harshness
or fanaticism, he was rationally pious and blamelessly
moral. His conduct, both as a Christian minister, as
a member of society, as a relation, and as a friend, was
wholly without a stain. His affections were warm,
they were ever under control, and therefore equal and
steady. His feelings might pass for being less strong

and lively than they were, partly because he had an insuperable aversion to extremes in all things, partly because, for fear of any semblance of pretension, to which he was yet more averse, he preferred appearing less moved than he really was, in order to avoid the possibility of feeling less than he externally showed. But he was of opinions respecting conduct which led to keeping the feelings under curb, and never giving way to them ; he leant in this towards the philosophy and discipline of the Stoics ; and he also held, which was apt to beget the same mistake as to the warmth of his heart, that exhibitions of sorrow, any more than of boisterous mirth, were unfit to be made ; that such emotions should as far as possible be reduced to moderation, even in private ; but that in society they were altogether misplaced and mistimed. He considered, and rightly considered, that if a person labouring under any afflictive feelings be well enough at ease to go into company, he gives a sort of pledge that he is so far recovered of his wound, or at least can so far conceal his pains, as to behave like the rest of the circle. He held, and rightly held, that men frequent society, not to pour forth their sorrows, or indulge their unwieldy joys, but to instruct, or improve, or amuse each other, by rational and cheerful conversation. For himself, when he left his study, leaving behind him, with the dust of his books, the anxious look, the wrinkled brow, the disturbed or absent thoughts, he also expected others to greet his arrival with the like freedom from cares of all sorts, and especially he disliked to have his hours of relaxation saddened with tales of misery, interesting to no one, unless, which is never the object of such narratives, there be a purpose of obtaining relief.

His conversation was cheerful, and it was varied. Vast information, copious anecdote, perfect appositeness of illustration,—narration or description wholly free from pedantry or stiffness, but as felicitous and as striking as might be expected from such a master—great liveliness, and often wit and often humour, with a full disposition to enjoy the merriment of the hour, but the most scrupulous absence of everything like coarseness of any description—these formed the staples of his talk. One thing he never tolerated any more than he did the least breach of decorum; it was among the few matters which seemed to try his temper—he could not bear evil speaking, or want of charity. No one was likely ever to wrangle with another before him; but he always put down at once any attempt to assail the absent. His own nature was singularly charitable and kindly; he always viewed the conduct of others in the least unfavourable light; and when he heard any objections urged, he would suggest something that at least left the blame mitigated when it could not be warded off or made doubtful. Of course, this remark applies to cases where the matter was ambiguous, and the general character and conduct were good. No man ever expressed a greater abhorrence of anything plainly bad, or a nobler scorn of anything mean; and his sentence went forth in such cases with an awful and an overpowering force.

His very decided opinions on all subjects of public interest, civil and religious, never interrupted his friendly and familiar intercourse with those who held different principles. With his colleague, Dr. Erskine, leader of his antagonists in the Church, he lived upon terms of uninterrupted friendship, as that great presbyter feelingly testified on preaching his funeral sermon. With Mr. Hume his intimacy is well known. His political principles were those of a moderate Whig, a Whig of 1688, as he used to express it; but no man held in greater contempt the petty manœuvres of party. Horace Walpole has thought fit to record a dialogue as having passed between them, in which he makes the Principal say, "You must know, sir, that I am a moderate Whig;" and himself answer, "Yes, Doctor, a very moderate Whig, I'll engage for it"—a sneer not likely to have been risked by such an amateur with such an artist. What the great historian intended by using the word "moderate" plainly was to guard himself against being supposed to enter into the squabbles of faction, and partake of its blind fury in a degree unsuited to his station. On religious matters he ever expressed himself with solemnity and warmth. While he was wishing well to liberty in France, before the excesses that profaned its name, and indeed before the revolution broke out, he was deploring the irreligious tone of French literature: "Really," said he, "one would think we were living under a new dispensation." Of American independence he was the warm friend; but Washington's character was far more to his mind than Franklin's, of whose violence and contempt of revealed religion he had formed a very unfavourable opinion.

His manner was not graceful in little matters, though his demeanour was dignified on the whole. In public

it was unimpassioned till some great burst came from
him ; then it partook of the fire of the moment, and
soon relapsed into dignified composure.   In private it
had some little awkwardnesses, not very perceptible
except to a near and minute observer.   His language
was correct and purely English, avoiding both learned
words and foreign phraseology and Scottish expressions, but his speech was strongly tinged with the
Scottish accent.   His voice I well remember, nor was
it easy to forget it ; nothing could be more pleasing.
It was full and it was calm, but it had a tone of
heartiness and sincerity which I hardly ever knew in
any other.   He was in person above the middle size—
his features were strongly marked—his forehead was
high and open—the expression of his mouth was that
of repose, of meditation, and of sweetness at the same
time.   The portrait, by Sir Joshua Reynolds, is a striking likeness, and it is the one which is engraved.   I
never knew an instance, I should say, of so strong a
resemblance as that which his eldest daughter, Mrs.
Brydone, bore him.   In her latter years, too, the sound
of her voice was nearly his own.   The only particulars
of his manners and person which I recollect are his
cocked hat, which he always wore, even in the country ;
his stately gait, particularly in a walk which he loved
to frequent in the woods at Brougham, where I attended him once while he visited there, and in which
he slowly recited sometimes Latin verses, sometimes
Greek ; a very slight guttural accent in his speech,
which gave it a peculiar fulness ; and his retaining
some old-fashioned modes of address, as using the word
" madam" at full length ; and, when he drank wine

with any woman, adding, " My humble service to you."
When in the country he liked to be left entirely to
himself in the morning, either to read or to walk or to
drive about; and he said that one of his great enjoyments at Lennel was Mr. Brydone and himself doing
precisely each as he chose, and being each as if the
other were not in the same house.

To give any notion of the anecdotes, simple, racy,
unpretending, which he would introduce when perfectly apposite to the subject matter, would not be
easy. Good nature and good humour prevailed through
his conversation, in which there was nothing ambitious
or forced, or any thing to show a desire of display.
It always seemed as if he merely wished to enjoy himself, and contribute his share to the enjoyment of
others. The late Lord Meadowbank, a kinsman of
his, and indeed his ward, when preparing his Lectures
on General History, of which he was Professor, asked
him if he had ever remarked how very superficial Mr.
Hume's Anglo-Saxon period is, more so than the
other parts, though the last written, of his ' History?'
" Why, yes, I have," said the Principal; " but the
truth is, David (so he always called him) had the
most unfortunate thing happen to him that can befall
an author—he was paid for it before he wrote it."

APPENDIX.

Address of Principal Robertson on laying the Foundation Stone of the Edinburgh College, 1791.—(Lord
Napier was the Grand Master of the Masons.)

" My Lord,

"From very humble beginnings the University of
Edinburgh has attained to such eminence as entitles it to be
ranked among the most celebrated seminaries of learning.
Indebted to the bounty of several of our sovereigns ; distinguished, particularly, by the gracious prince now seated on
the British throne, whom, with gratitude, we reckon amongst
the most munificent of our royal benefactors ; and cherished
by the continued attention and good offices of our honourable
patrons,* this University can now boast of the number and
variety of its institutions for the instruction of youth in all
the branches of literature and science.

" With what integrity and discernment persons have been
chosen to preside in each of these departments, the character
of my learned colleagues affords the most satisfying evidence.
From confidence in their abilities and assiduity in discharg-
ing the duties of their respective offices, the University of
Edinburgh has not only become a seat of education to youth
in every part of the British dominions, but, to the honour of
our country, students have been attracted to it from almost
every nation in Europe, and every state in America.

" One thing still was wanting. The apartments appropriated
for the accommodation of professors and students were so extremely unsuitable to the flourishing state of the University,
that it had long been the general wish to have buildings more
decent and convenient erected. What your Lordship has
now done gives a near prospect of having this wish accom-

---

* The magistrates of the city.

plished; and we consider it as a most auspicious circumstance that the foundation stone of this new mansion of science is laid by your Lordship, who, among your ancestors, reckon a man whose original and inventive genius places him high among the illustrious persons who have contributed most eminently to enlarge the boundaries of human knowledge.

" Permit me to add what I regard as my own peculiar felicity, that, by having remained in my present station much longer than any of my predecessors, I have lived to witness an event so beneficial to this University, the prosperity of which is near to my heart, and has ever been the object of my warmest wishes.

" May the Almighty God, without the invocation of whom no action of importance should be begun, bless this undertaking, and enable us to carry it on with success : may He continue to protect our University, the object of whose institutions is to instil into the minds of youth principles of sound knowledge, to inspire them with the love of religion and virtue, and to prepare them for filling the various stations in society with honour to themselves, and with benefit to their country. All this we ask in the name of Christ ; and unto the Father, the Son, and the Holy Spirit, we ascribe the kingdom, power, and glory.—Amen."

LETTER OF THE LATE PROFESSOR FERGUSON, THEN IN HIS NINETY-SECOND YEAR, TO THE LATE LORD ROBERTSON, ON THE SUBJECT OF HIS FATHER'S EPITAPH.

" MY DEAR LORD,   " St. Andrew's, Nov. 24th, 1814.

" I have received your letter, enclosing the two copies of the inscription on your father's monument, one for Mr. Dempster, which I have delivered, and know his sense of your kind remembrance, as well as my own of the honour you have done me. In these acknowledgments I am afraid you will think me all too slow ; but this is now the mode of my existence, and ill qualified to change it.

" It has enabled me to communicate with some of the learned here, who join me in applauding the elegance and the appropriate terms of that composition.

" The authority of Dr. Gregory has no need of such supports ; but I am fond to mention it.

" I thought your father's birth and mine had been more nearly dated; but I see that his preceded mine by two whole years, although I have survived so long to become my own monument—perishing you will say, but only more so, or less permanent, than some other grave-stones. I remember to have seen in Italy miles and leagues of ancient highways, strewed on right and left with continual vestiges of monuments, now destroyed or in ruins, with scarce a name to mark for whom they were intended; but your father's memory is independent of any such materials. More fortunate than Tacitus or Livy, his works entire remain for ages indefinite, to show that in his time the British style in able hands was fit to emulate or cope with theirs. It were too much vanity for me to think the opportunity will then exist of giving judgment how little I had profited by the example which he set me, of literary talents and intellectual eminence. My way is now directed to the trackless grave, and there my course should terminate, but for the happy thought that there is somewhat after death to which this nursery and school of human life is no more than a preparation or a prelude. Meantime, however, I remain, with just esteem and gratitude for kind attentions,

" Your most obliged and most humble servant,

"ADAM FERGUSON.

" The Right Honourable Lord Robertson,
        Edinburgh."

The translation, of which the following forms the first two pages of the Principal's MS., was made, as appears by the date January 21, 1742, when he was about twenty—he having been born 19th September, 1721. The whole is carefully and admirably executed, combining clearness with elegance.

The other translations which I have seen of the ' Meditations,' will bear no comparison with this; Gataker's (1692) in Latin seems the best, but it is not good. To give an example, take the first paragraph : το καλοηθες is rendered by the translation of 1692 " to be gentle and meek ;" by Mr. Graves's, of 1792, " virtuous disposition of mind." αοργητον, by the former " to refrain from all anger and passion ;" by the latter " habitual command of my temper." Robertson gives both together clearly and elegantly, " to be of a complaisant and dispassionate temper of mind." καλοηθες is a word only found in Antoninus. Stephanus renders it " qui pulcrâ indole—probus—honestus ;" the late editors of Passow, in their excellent work (Messrs. Liddell and Scott), have rendered it " well disposed :" Gataker (1692), " moris candidi." Robertson's version seems preferable, though not widely different. In the second paragraph we have αιδημον rendered, unhappily enough, by the edition of 1692, " shamefacedness," as αρφενικον is " manly behaviour ;" while Graves gives both prolixly " modesty and manly firmness on all occasions." In paragraph 16 we find ημερον και μενετικον ασαλευτως, the first word of which the edition of 1692 gives as " meekness ;" the edition of 1792, " mild condescension," which is a fanciful version ; the Oxford Greek-Latin edition of 1704, " mansuetudinem ;" and Robertson, " mild disposition."

BOOK I.

" Jan. 21, 1742.

" I. From my grandfather, Verus, I learned to be of a complaisant and dispassionate temper of mind.

" II. By the fame and reputation of my father I was taught to be modest, and yet at the same time to form steady and manly resolutions.

" III. By my mother I was taught to be of a religious turn of mind; and not only to abstain from all evil actions, but from every inclination towards them ; to study simplicity in my diet, and keep at a distance from all the vain pomp of riches.

"IV. By my great grandfather I was advised not to frequent the public schools of declaimers; but to hear the best masters in private, and to spare no expense in procuring such.

"V. By my governor I was taught to take no side in those factions which divide the Circus and Theatre; to be patient of labour, to be content with little, and to be able to work with my own hands; not to meddle in other men's matters, and to discourage all informers.

"VI. By Diognetus I was taught not to amuse myself with empty, trifling studies, not to give credit to the marvellous stories related of wizards, enchanters, and the exorcising of dæmons; not to spend my time in the breeding of quails and such like trifles; to endure it patiently when men speak freely of me, and to apply myself wholly to the study of philosophy. By his advice I heard Bacchius, Tyndarides, and Marcianus, and, when very young, employed myself in composing dialogues; used a mean bed, covered only with a skin; and in every other thing emulated the manners of the Grecian philosophers.

"VII. To Rupheus I am indebted for my resolution of reforming and watching over my own morals, and that I did not fall into an imitation of the pride of the Sophists; that I did not write upon merely speculative points, or compose quaint and finical exhortations to virtue; that my exercises were not calculated to strike the fancy, and to carry with them an air of importance and austerity; that I applied myself neither to rhetoric nor poetry, nor studied any affected elegance in my expressions; that I did not wear the stola while within doors, and shunned all extravagant pride in my dress. By him I was taught to write my letters in a simple style, after the model of those he sent from Sinuessa; to show myself of a placable disposition towards those who have injured and offended me, and ready to be reconciled to them whenever they desire to return to my favour; to read with accuracy, not to be content with a superficial consideration of things, and not rashly to give ear to great talkers. To him, likewise, I owe my acquaintance with the Commentaries of Epictetus, which he furnished me with.

"VIII. From Apollonius I learned to be at the same time free, and yet without any fluctuating uncertainty in my resolutions; to have a regard to nothing beside reason, even in things of the smallest moment; to preserve an equal mind under the most acute pain, upon the death of a child, and during the most lingering diseases; and by a living example in himself, he showed me that it was possible for the same person to be upon occasion rigid or humane; that we should instruct others with mildness and gentleness, and look upon our erudition and dexterity in delivering speculative truths as among the meanest of qualifications. By him also I was taught in what manner to receive presents from my friends, so as neither to appear too highly indebted to their favour, nor yet to dismiss them with cold indifference."

B L A C K.

THE physical sciences have few more illustrious names to boast than that of Joseph Black. With all the habits and the disciplined faculties of a true philosopher, with the temper as well as the capacity of a sage, he possessed that happy union of strong but disciplined imagination, powers of close undivided attention, and ample resources of reasoning, which forms original genius in scientific pursuits; and, as all these qualities may be combined in an individual without his happening to signalise his investigations of nature by any discovery, we must add that his life was crowned with the good fortune of opening to mankind new paths in which both himself and his followers successfully trod, enlarging to an incalculable extent the bounds of human knowledge. The modesty of his nature making him averse to publish his speculations, and the genuine devotion to the investigation of truth, for its own sake, rendering him most open in his communications with all who were engaged in the same pursuits, his incontestable claim to be regarded as the founder of modern chemistry has been oftentimes overlooked; and, while some have endeavoured more or less obscurely to mingle themselves with his discoveries, others have thought it becoming to post-date

the new system, that it might seem the produce of a somewhat later age. The interests of truth and justice therefore require that we should minutely examine the facts of the case ; and, happily, the evidence is so clear that it only requires an attentive consideration to remove all doubt from the subject. I feel it a duty imperatively cast upon me to undertake a task from which, did I not regard it as less difficult than sacred, I might shrink. But I had the great happiness of being taught by himself, having attended one of the last courses of lectures which he delivered ; and the knowledge thus gained cannot be turned to a better use than in recording the glory and in vindicating the fame of my illustrious master.

The story of a philosopher's life is soon told. Black was born, in 1721, at Bordeaux, where his father, a native of Belfast, was settled as a merchant : he was, however, a Scotchman, and his wife too was of a Scottish family, that of Gordon of Hillhead, in Aberdeenshire, settled like Mr. Black at Bordeaux. The latter was a person of extraordinary virtues, and a most amiable disposition. The celebrated Montesquieu honoured him with his especial regard ; and his son preserved, as titles of honour in his family, the many letters of the President to his parent. In one of them he laments the intended removal of the Black family as a thing he could not reconcile himself to, for his greatest pleasure was seeing them often, and living himself in their society. Though Mr. Black sent his son, at the age of twelve, for some years to a school in Ireland, he was removed to the College of Glasgow in the year 1746, and ever after lived in that which was, properly speaking, his native country. At that college he studied under the celebrated Cullen, then Professor of Anatomy and Lecturer on Chemistry; and, having removed in 1750 to Edinburgh for the benefit of that famous medical school, he took his degree there in 1754. In 1756 he was appointed to succeed Dr. Cullen in the chair of anatomy and chemistry at Glasgow, and he continued to teach there for ten years, when he was appointed to the chemistry professorship at Edinburgh. He then lectured for thirty years to numerous classes, and retiring in 1796 lived till 1799, and died on the 26th of November in that year. His health never was robust; it was indeed precarious at all times from a weakness in the bronchia and chest, but he prolonged life by a system of the strictest abstinence, frequently subsisting for days together on water gruel and diluted milk. He never was married; but he cherished with unvarying affection his near relatives, who well deserved his care. His favourite niece, Miss Burnet, a person of great sense and amiable temper, was married to his friend and second cousin, Professor Ferguson, the historian and moral philosopher. Dr. Black lived in a select circle of friends, the most illustrious men of the times in science and in letters, Watt, Hutton, Hume, Robertson, Smith, and afterwards with the succeeding generation of Scottish worthies, Robison, Playfair, Stewart. Delighting to commune, to speculate, and to investigate with them, he was careless of the fame which however he could not but be sensible his labours must achieve. He was extremely averse to publication, contemning the impatience with which so many men of science hurry to the press, often while their speculations are crude, and their inquiries not finished. Nor could the reason often urged in defence of this find much favour with one who seemed never to regard the being anticipated by his fellow-labourers as any very serious evil, so the progress of science was secured. Except two papers, one in the 'London Philosophical Transactions' for 1775 on the freezing of boiled water ; the other, in the second volume of the 'Edinburgh Transactions,' on the Iceland hot springs ; he never published any work after that of which we are now to speak, in 1755, and which, but for the accidental occasion that gave rise to it, would possibly, like his other original speculations, never have been given by himself to the press.

Upon taking his degree at Edinburgh College he wrote and published a Latin Thesis, after the manner of that as well as the foreign universities. The subject was 'Magnesia, and the Acid produced by Food in the Stomach' (*De Acido e Cibis orto ; et de Magnesia*), and it contained the outline of his discoveries already made. Having sent some copies of this Thesis to his father at Bordeaux, one was given to Montesquieu, who at once saw the vast importance of the truths which it unfolded. He called a few days after and said to Mr. Black, " I rejoice with you, my very good friend : your son will be the honour of your name and of your family." But though the discoveries were sketched distinctly enough in this writing, they were only given at large the following year in his celebrated work, 'Experiments on Magnesia, Quicklime, and other Alkaline Substances,' incontestably the most

beautiful example of strict inductive investigation since
the 'Optics' of Sir Isaac Newton.   His fervent admiration of that masterly work was indicated by his
giving it to Professor Robison, then a student, and
desiring him to "make it the model of all his studies,"
recommending him at the same time a careful study of
the mathematics.   It appears that this important
inquiry concerning the alkaline earths, the results
of which were destined to change the face of chemical
science, was suggested by the attempts then making to
find a solvent for the stone.   I distinctly recollect Dr.
Black, in his lectures, prefacing the admirable and
most interesting account which he gave of his discoveries, with the statement that the hopes of finding
a solvent which should not, like the caustic alkalies,
destroy the substance of the bladder in melting the
stone, first led him to this investigation.   Professor
Robison has given a note from his memorandum-book
indicating that he had at first fallen into the notion of
alkalies, when treated with quicklime, deriving from
it their caustic quality; the common belief (which
gave rise to the term caustic) being that lime obtained
from the fire the quality of growing extremely hot,
even to ignition when united with water.   But experiment soon corrected this idea; for, having exposed
the caustic or quicklime to the air till it became mild,
he says, "Nothing escapes (meaning no fire or heat);
the cup rises considerably by absorbing air."   Another
observation on the comparative loss of weight sustained
by chalk when calcined (in the fire), and when dis-
solved in an acid, is followed by the account of a
medical case, which the Professor knew to have

occurred in 1752. A third note follows, and proves him to have now become possessed of the true theory of causticity, namely, the expulsion of air, and of mildness, namely, its absorption. The discovery was therefore made as early as 1752—it was published generally in 1754—it was given in its fullest details in 1755. At this time M. Lavoisier was a boy at school—nine years old when the discovery was made—eleven when it was published—twelve when it was as fully given to the world as its author ever delivered it. No possibility therefore existed of that great man finding out when he composed his great work that it was a discovery of his own, as he did not scruple to describe oxygen, though Dr. Priestley had first communicated it to him in the year 1774 ; or that Black and he discovered it about the same time, as he was in the habit of stating with respect to other gases, with a convenient degree of ambiguity just sufficient for self-defence, should he be charged with unfair appropriation. Who that reflects on the noble part which this great philosopher acted, both in his life and in his death, can avoid lamenting that he did not rest satisfied with the fame really his due, of applying the discoveries of others, in which he had no kind of share, to the investigation of scientific truths, as entirely the result of his extraordinary faculty of generalization, and genius for philosophical research, as those discoveries, the materials of his induction, were the undivided property of others!

The capital discovery of Black, thus early made, and to any share in which no one has ever pretended, was that the causticity, as it was formerly termed upon a

false theory, of the alkalis and alkaline earths, was
owing to the loss of a substance with which they had
been combined, and that their reunion with this substance again rendered them mild.   But the nature of
this substance was likewise ascertained by him, and its
detection forms by far the most important part of the
discovery, for it laid the foundation of chemical science.
He found that it was a permanently elastic fluid, like
air in some of its mechanical qualities, those of being
transparent or invisible, and incondensable, but differing entirely from the air of our atmosphere in its
chemical properties.   It was separated from alkaline
substances by heat, and by the application of acids,
which, having a stronger elective affinity for them,
caused it to be precipitated, or to escape in the aëriform
state ; it was heavier than common air, and it gave a
slight acidulous flavour to water on being absorbed by it;
hence the inference that it was an acid itself.   A short
time afterwards (in 1757) he discovered that this peculiar
air is the same with that produced by the fermentation
of vegetable substances.   This he ascertained by the
simple experiment of partially emptying in a brewer's
vat, where the fermenting process was going on, the
contents of a phial filled with lime-water.   On shaking
the liquid that remained with the air that had entered,
he found it become turbid, from the lime having
entered into union with the air, and become chalk.
The same day he discovered by an experiment, equally
simple and equally decisive, that the air which comes
from burning charcoal is of the same kind.   He fixed a
piece of charcoal in the broad end of a bellows nozzle,
unscrewed ; and putting that in the fire, he inserted

the other end in a vessel filled with lime-water. The air that was driven through the liquid again precipitated the lime in the form of chalk. Finally, he ascertained by breathing through a syphon filled with lime-water, and finding the lime again precipitated, that animals, by breathing, evolve air of this description.

The great step was now made, therefore, that the air of the atmosphere is not the only permanently elastic body, but that others exist, having perfectly different qualities from the atmospheric air, and capable of losing their elasticity by entering into chemical union with solid or with liquid substances, from which being afterwards separated, they regain the elastic or aëriform state. He gave to this body the name of *fixed air,* to denote only that it was found fixed in bodies, as well as elastic and separate. He used the term "air" only to denote its mechanical resemblance to the atmospheric air, and not at all to imply that it was of the same nature. No one ever could confound the two substances together; and accordingly M. Morveau, in explaining some years afterwards the reluctance of chemists to adopt the new theory of causticity, gives as their excuse, that although this doctrine "admirably tallies with all the phenomena, yet it ascribes to fixed air properties which really make it a new body or existence" ("*forment réellement un nouvel être*").*

In order to estimate the importance of this discovery, and at the same time to show how entirely it

---

* Supplement to the 'Encyclopédie,' vol. ii. p. 274, published in 1777.

altered the whole face of chemical science, and how
completely the doctrine was original, we must now
examine the state of knowledge which philosophers
had previously attained upon the subject.

It has often been remarked that no great discovery was
ever made at once, except perhaps that of logarithms;
all have been preceded by steps which conducted the discoverer's predecessors nearly, though not quite, to the
same point. Some may possibly think that Black's discovery of fixed air affords no second exception to this
rule; for it is said that Van Helmont, who flourished
at the end of the sixteenth and beginning of the seventeenth century, had observed its evolution during fermentation, and given it the name of *gas silvestre*, spirit
from wood, remarking that it caused the phenomena
of the Grotto del Cane, near Naples. But though he
as well as others had observed an aëriform substance
to be evolved in fermentation and in effervescence,
there is no reason for affirming that they considered it
as differing from atmospheric air, except by having
absorbed, or become mixed with, certain impurities.
Accordingly, a century later than Van Helmont, Hales,
who made more experiments on air than any other of
the old chemists, adopts the commonly received opinion
that all elastic fluids were only different combinations
of the atmospheric air with various exhalations or
impurities;* and this was the universal belief upon
the subject, both of philosophers and of the vulgar.

---

* It may safely be affirmed that Van Helmont's observation,
which lay for a century and a half barren, threw no light of any
value upon the subject. No one questions Newton's title to the
discovery of the different refrangibility of light, and the true theory

It is now fit that we see in what manner the subject was treated by scientific men at the period immediately preceding Black's discoveries. The article ' Air' in the French ' Encyclopédie' was published in 1751, and written by D'Alembert himself. It is, as might be expected, able, clear, elaborate. He assumes the substance of the atmosphere to be alone entitled to the name of air, and to be the foundation of all other permanently elastic bodies: " L'air élémentaire, ou l'air proprement dit," he says. He describes it as " homogène," and terms it " l'ingrédient fondamental de tout l'air de l'atmosphère, et qui lui donne son nom." Other substances or exhalations mix with it, he says, but these he terms "passagères," passing vapours, and not permanent: the air alone (that is, the atmospheric air) he calls "permanent," or permanently elastic (vol. i. p. 225). So little attention had the observation of Van Helmont respecting the Grotto del

---

of the rainbow; yet at the beginning of the 17th century, Antonio de Dominis, Archbishop of Spalatro, had really made an ingenious and well-grounded experiment on the similarity of the rainbow colours with those formed by the sun's rays refracted twice and reflected once in a globe filled with water. The doctrine of universal gravitation was known to both Kepler and Galileo ; and Boulland (Astronomia Philolaica, lib. i., 1645) distinctly stated his belief or conjecture that it acted inversely as the squares of the distances. The famous proposition of equal areas in equal times was known to Kepler. The nearest approach to the Fluxional Calculus had been made by Harriott and Roberval and Fermat ; and to take but one other example, the electrical explosion of the Leyden jar, discovered in 1747, obtained the name of the *coup-foudroyant*, and was by Abbé Nollet conjectured to be identical with lightning, Franklin's celebrated experiment being only made in 1752.

Cane excited, that we find a conjecture hazarded in the
article ' Grotte' (vol. vii. p. 968), which appeared in
1756,—"peut-être respirent ils (les chiens), au lieu
d'air, des vapeurs minérales ;" but this was some time
after Black's discovery had taught us to distinguish such
permanently elastic vapours from atmospheric air.   In
the article ' Fermentation' (vol. vi. p. 523) we find
Van Helmont's doctrines of the connexion between
fermentation and digestion treated with ridicule, and
those who adopted them jocularly called the " fermen-
tateurs."

A few years later, however, the face of things
changed.   In the ' Supplement,' published in 1776, we
find an article on ' Fixed Air,' and a reference to Dr.
Black's discovery ; but nothing can be more indistinct
than the author, M. Morveau's, ideas respecting it;
for he leaves us in doubt whether it be the atmospheric
air or a separate substance, and yet he states that the
phenomena of fermentation and putrefaction are explained by the evolution or absorption of this air, and
that mineral waters derive from its presence their flavour.   An abstract of M. Venel's book had in 1765,
under the head of ' Mineral Waters,' given this explanation ; but instead of representing the air combined with
the water as a different substance, he calls it " véritable
air et même très pure."   We have, however, seen that,
in the following year (1777), M. Morveau's ideas were
perfectly distinct on the subject ; for he treats it as a
new substance, wholly different from atmospheric air.
The slowness with which Black's doctrine made its
way in France may be presumed from Morveau's remark on causticity, already cited, and also from this,

that the article on 'Magnesia,' published in 1765, dog-matically asserts Black to be in error when he de-scribes Epsom salts as yielding that earth, " because," says the author, " those salts are purely Seidlitian," "entièrement Seidlitiens" (vol. x. p. 858). In fact, Ep-som salts, magnesia, limestone, and sea-water are the great sources from which all magnesia is obtained. The first of these substances is in truth only a com-bination of magnesia with sulphuric acid.

The other discoveries to which Black's led were as slowly disseminated as his own. Oxygen gas had been discovered, in August, 1774, by Priestley, and soon after by Scheele without any knowledge of Priestley's previous discovery ; yet in 1777 Morveau, who wrote the chemical articles in the ' Supplement,' never mentions that discovery, nor the almost equally important dis-covery of Scheele, chlorine, made in 1774, nor that of azote, discovered by Rutherford in 1772, nor hydro-gen gas, the properties of which had been fully inves-tigated by Cavendish as early as 1766. Lavoisier's important doctrine, well entitled to be called a dis-covery, of the true nature of combustion, had likewise been published in 1774 in his ' Opuscules,' yet Mor-veau doggedly adheres to his own absurd theory of the air only being necessary to maintain those oscilla-tions in which he holds combustion to consist; and finding that the increase of weight is always the result of calcination as well as combustion, he satisfies him-self with making a gratuitous addition to the hypo-thesis of phlogiston, and supposes that this imaginary substance is endowed with positive levity ; nor does he allude to the experiments of Lavoisier on gases, on

combustion, and on oxidation, further than to say that
he had for a considerable time been engaged in these
inquiries. It was not indeed till 1787 that he became
a convert to the sound and rational doctrine, and
abandoned the fanciful hypothesis, simple and ingenious though it be, of Stahl. Berthollet, the earliest
convert, had come over to the truth two years before. Thus, discoveries had been made which laid the
foundation of a new science, and on which the attention of all philosophers was bent ; yet the greatest
scientific work of the age made no more mention
of them than if Black, Cavendish, Priestley, and
Scheele had not been. The conjecture may be allowed
to us, that if any of these great things had been done
in France, M. Morveau would not have been suffered
to preserve the same unbroken silence respecting them,
even if his invincible prejudices in favour of the doctrine of phlogiston had disposed him to a course so
unworthy of a philosopher.

The detail into which I have entered, sufficiently
proves that the discovery of fixed air laid at once the
foundation of the great events in the .chemical world
to which reference has just been made, because the
step was of incalculable importance by which we are
led to the fact that atmospheric air is only one of a
class of permanently elastic fluids. When D'Alembert wrote the article ' Air,' in 1751, he gave the doctrine then universally received, that all the other kinds
of air were only impure atmospheric air, and that this
fluid alone was permanently elastic, all other vapours
being only, like steam, temporarily aëriform. Once
the truth was made known that there are other gases

in nature, only careful observation was required to find them out. Inflammable air was the next which became the subject of examination, because, though it had long been known, before Black's discovery it had been supposed only to be common air mixed with unctuous particles. His discovery at once showed that it was, like fixed air, a separate aëriform fluid, wholly distinct from the air of the atmosphere. The other gases were discovered somewhat later. But it is a very great mistake to suppose that none of these were known to Black, or that he supposed fixed air to be the only gas different from the atmospheric. The nature of hydrogen gas was perfectly known to him, and both its qualities of being inflammable and of being so much lighter than atmospheric air; for as early as 1766 he invented the air balloon, showing a party of his friends the ascent of a bladder filled with inflammable air. Mr. Cavendish only more precisely ascertained its specific gravity, and showed what Black could not have been ignorant of, that it is the same, from whatever substance it is obtained.

But great as was the discovery of fixed air, and important as were its consequences, the world was indebted to its illustrious author for another scarcely less remarkable, both from being so unexpected, and from producing such lasting effects upon physical science. About the year 1763 he meditated closely upon the fact, that on the melting of ice more heat seems to disappear than the thermometer indicates, and also that on the condensation of steam an unexpected proportion of heat becomes perceptible. An observation of Fahrenheit, on the cooling of water below the tem-

perature of ice until it is disturbed, when it gives out
heat and freezes at once, appears also to have attracted
his careful consideration. He contrived a set of simple
but decisive experiments to investigate the cause of
these appearances, and was led to the discovery of
latent heat, or the absorption of heat upon bodies
passing from the solid to the fluid state, and from
the fluid to the aëriform, the heat having no effect on
surrounding bodies, and being therefore insensible to
the hand or to the thermometer, and only by its
absorption maintaining the body in the state which it
has assumed, and which it retains until, the absorbed
heat being given out, and becoming again sensible, the
state of the body is changed back again from fluid
to solid, from aëriform to fluid. He never published
any account of this discovery, but he explained it fully
in his Lectures, both at Glasgow and Edinburgh,
and he referred to it in the paper already mentioned,
which was printed in the ' Philosophical Transactions '
for 1775. Well, then, may we marvel that no mention
whatever of latent heat is made in the celebrated ' Encyclopédie,' which owed its chemical contributions to no
less a writer and experimentalist than Morveau.
The doctrine of latent heat, however, was immediately
applied by all philosophers to the production of the
different airs which were successively discovered. They
were found to owe their permanently elastic state to
the heat absorbed in their production from solid or
fluid substances, and to regain their fluid or solid state
by combining either together or with those substances, and in the act of union giving out in a
sensible form the heat which, while absorbed and

latent, had kept them in the state of elastic and invisible fluids.*

The third great discovery of Black was that which
has since been called the doctrine of *specific heat*, but
which he called the *capacity* of bodies for heat. Different bodies contain different quantities of heat in the
same bulk or weight; and different quantities of heat
are required to raise different bodies to the same sensible temperature. Thus, by Black's experiment, it
was found that a pound of gold being heated to 150°,
and added to a pound of water at 50°, the temperature
of both became not 100°, the mean between the two,
but 55°, the gold losing 95°, and the water gaining 5°,
because the capacity of water for heat is nineteen times
that of gold. So twice as much heat is required to
raise water to any given point of sensible heat as to
raise mercury, the volumes of the two fluids compared
being equal.

The true doctrine of combustion, calcination of
metals, and respiration of animals, which Lavoisier
deduced from the experiments of Priestley and Scheele
upon oxygen gas, and of Cavendish on hydrogen gas,
and which has changed the whole aspect of chemical
science, was founded mainly upon the doctrines of
latent and specific heat. It was thus the singular
felicity of Black to have furnished both the pillars
upon which modern chemistry reposes, and to have

---

* It is by no means impossible that one day we may be able to
reduce the phenomenon of light within the theory of latent heat. It
may be that this body when absorbed, that is, fixed in substances,
gives out heat; as, while passing through diaphanous substances and
remaining unfixed, its heat is not sensible.

furnished them so long before any one attempted to erect the superstructure, that no doubt could by any possibility arise respecting the source of our increased knowledge, the quarter to which our gratitude should be directed. Fixed air was discovered in 1752, and fully explained to the world in 1754 and 1755. Latent heat was yearly, from 1763, explained to numerous classes of students, before whom the experiments that prove it were performed by the author's own hands. Cavendish made his experiments on inflammable air in 1766 ; Priestley began his in 1768, first publishing in 1772 ; and he discovered oxygen in 1774, in which year the nature of combustion was first explained by Lavoisier, a boy at school when fixed air was discovered, and having made no experiments nor written any one line upon chemical subjects for seven years after latent heat was discovered.

But we shall form a more striking idea to ourselves of the revolution which Black thus effected in chemistry, if we attend a little to the state of that science in general before he began his labours. We have already seen the low condition of the knowledge then possessed respecting aëriform fluids ; the general condition of the science was in the same proportion humble.

The celebrated ' Preliminary Discourse' to the ' Encyclopédie' makes hardly any mention of chemistry among the sciences; and in the ' Arbre Encyclopédique,' on which the authors (D'Alembert and Diderot) plume themselves much, we find it not very distinctly represented, or in very good company. It is termed the science of interior and occult qualities of bodies, its objects being to imitate and rival nature, by decomposing, reviving, and transferring substances. It is represented as holding among the sciences the place which poetry occupies among other branches of literature. Its fruits are said to be alchemy, metallurgy, natural magic, and chemistry properly so called, which is stated to consist of pyrotechny and dyeing. Strange to tell, pharmacy is not given as one of its fruits, being referred wholly to the branch of medical science.

But the state of chemistry is better understood by the article itself in the ' Encyclopédie,' the elaborate work of M. Venel of Montpelier, well known for his researches concerning mineral springs, and author of most of the chemical articles in the original work, as M. Morveau was of those in the 'Supplement,' and whose mistakes on the subject of magnesia, arising from prejudice, have already been mentioned. This article begins with lamenting the low condition of his favourite science : " Elle est peu cultivée parmi nous. Cette science n'est que très médiocrement répandue, même parmi les savans, malgré la prétention à l'universalité des connaissances qui font aujourd'hui le goût dominant. Les chimistes forment un peuple distinct, très-peu nombreux, ayant sa langue, ses mystères, ses loix, et vivent presque isolés au milieu d'un grand peuple peu curieux de sa connaissance, n'entendant presque rien de son industrie." He then goes on to show that this " incuriosité, soit réelle, soit simulée," is yet extremely unphilosophical, inasmuch as it leads to a rash condemnation ; and that those who know any subject superficially may possibly be deceived in their own judgment upon it, "the consequence of which has been," he adds, "that owing to the prejudices entertained against the nature and reach of the science, it becomes a matter of no small difficulty or slight controversy to say clearly and precisely what chemistry is. Some make no distinction between the chemist and the quack who seeks after the philosopher's stone (*souffleur*); others think any one a chemist who has a still for preparing perfumes or colours. Many consider the compounding of drugs as containing the whole of the art. Even men of science know scarcely any thing about the chemists."—"What natural philosopher," he asks, "so much as ever names Becker or Stahl? Whereas those who, having other scientific illustrations, as John Bernouilli and Boerhaave, have written chemical works, or rather works on chemical subjects, are very differently thought of; so that the former's work on 'Fermentation,' and the latter's on 'Fire,' are known, cited, and praised, while the far greater views of Stahl on the same subjects only exist for a few chemists." He then goes on to cite other proofs of the low estimate formed of the science, and even the prevailing impression of chemists being mere workmen; and concludes, that "the revolution which should raise chemistry to the rank it merits, and place it on a level with natural philosophy, can only be accomplished by a great, an enthusiastic, and a bold genius." While waiting for the advent of this new Paracelsus, he says, it must be his task to present chemistry in a light which may show it worthy the notice of philosophers, and capable of becoming something in their hands.

If we go back to an earlier period, we shall find

that Lord Bacon, although he quite clearly perceived that chemistry might one day be advanced to the rank of a science (De Dig. et Aug. iii.), yet always treats the chemistry of his day as merely empirical (Nov. Org. s. lxiv. lxxiii.*). But I have preferred taking the account of chemical science from the ' Encyclopédie,' first, because it gives, if not the opinion or the testimony of the learned body at large who prepared that work, yet certainly an opinion and a testimony which had the sanction of its more eminent members ; and, secondly, because its date is at the eve of the great revolution in natural science of which we are speaking.

---

* " Itaque talis philosophia (in paucorum experimentorum argutiis et obscuritate fundata) illis qui in hujusmodi experimentis quotidie versantur atque ex ipsis phantasmatis contaminarunt, probabilis videtur, et quasi certa ; cæteris incredibilis et vana, cujus exemplar notabile est in chemicis eorumque dogmatibus."

It must be added that beside the injustice here done to Van Helmont, he goes on to rank Gilbert in the same empirical class, as he elsewhere does—a most incorrect view of Gilbert's induction, the most perfect by far of any before Lord Bacon's age, and, though mixed with some hypothetical reasoning, hardly in strictness excelled by any philosopher of after times. I cannot come so near the remarkable sixty-fifth section of the ' Novum Organum' without digressing so far from my subject as to cite the prophetic warning given to some zealots without knowledge of our own times against the "apotheosis errorum," the " pestis intellectus, si vanis accedat veneratio." " Huic autem vanitati (adds the pious and truly Christian sage) nonnulli ex modernis summâ levitate ita indulserunt ut in primo capitulo Geneseos et in libro Job et aliis scripturæ locis philosophiam naturalem fundari conati sunt ; inter mortua quærentes viva ;" a folly the more to be deprecated, he says, because " ex divinarum et humanarum malesana admistione non solum educitur philosophia phantastica, sed etiam religio hæretica." His practical conclusion, therefore, is to render unto faith the things alone which are faith's : " Admodum salutare, si mente sobriâ, fidei tantum dentur quæ fidei sunt."

The last passage which has been cited from that
work strikingly illustrates the low ebb at which
chemical science then was.—It is certain that after
the discoveries of Black had opened vast and new
views of nature, both as regards the operations of
heat, the most powerful and universal of all agents,
and as- regards the constitution of elastic fluids, the
most unknown of the four elements, no natural philosopher would have had the hardihood to doubt if chemistry was an important branch of his science, and
no chemist would have performed the superfluous task
of vindicating its claim to the title.

We have now gone through the whole of this interesting subject, rather occupied in contemplating the
foundations of a new science than in tracing the extension of the boundaries which confine an old one. The
universal operation of heat, and the agency which it
exerts by its absorption and its evolution on the structure of all bodies, renders the discovery of its nature
and action in these respects, next to that of gravitation,
the most important step which has been made in the
progress of physical science. The new field opened to
philosophical inquiry by the discovery of the gaseous
bodies is only second to the former step in the importance of its consequences. It is as objects of pure
science, the mere contemplation of scientific truth,
that we have been considering these great discoveries ;
yet they have amply contributed also to the advance-
ment of the arts. The illustrious improver of the steam
engine was too young to have joined in the experiments
on fixed air ; but in the course of those by which latent
heat was discovered, he had a constant and confidential

intercourse with Black, one of his earliest patrons; and although it is as certain that he did not owe to that philosopher's suggestions any of the steps by which his inventions were compassed, as it is that he had himself no share in Black's great discovery, it cannot be doubted that the knowledge thus acquired of the true nature of heat, of steam, of evaporation, and of condensation, contributed most essentially to his mighty improvements. As for the gases, it would be difficult to name the branch of art which has not in some manner and to some extent gained by their discovery. So that the great man whose history we are contemplating, had the satisfaction of seeing the triumphs of his youth bear fruit in every direction, exalting the power and increasing the comforts of mankind as well as extending the bounds of their knowledge and enlarging the range of their industry. He was but twenty-four years old when he made his first discovery, and thirty-four when his second was added. He lived to nearly fourscore.

It remains to consider him as a teacher; and certainly nothing could be more admirable than the manner in which for forty years he performed this useful and dignified office. His style of lecturing was as nearly perfect as can well be conceived; for it had all the simplicity which is so entirely suited to scientific discourse, while it partook largely of the elegance which characterized all he said or did. The publication of his lectures has conveyed an accurate idea of the purely analytical order in which he deemed it best to handle the subject with a view to instruction, considering this as most likely to draw and to fix the learner's

attention, to impress his memory, and to show him
both the connexion of the theory with the facts, and
the steps by which the principles were originally ascertained. The scheme of the lectures may thence be apprehended—the execution imperfectly ; for the diction
was evidently, in many instances, extemporaneous, the
notes before the teacher furnishing him with little
more than the substance, especially of those portions
which were connected with experiments. But still
less can the reader rise from the perusal to any conception of the manner.   Nothing could be more
suited to the occasion ; it was perfect philosophical
calmness ; there was no effort ; it was an easy and a
graceful conversation. The voice was low, but perfectly distinct and audible through the whole of a large
hall crowded in every part with mutely attentive listeners ; it was never forced at all any more than were the
motions of the hands, but it was anything rather than
monotonous. Perfect elegance as well as repose was the
phrase by which every hearer and spectator naturally,
and as if by common consent, described the whole delivery.   The accidental circumstance of the great
teacher's aspect, I hope I may be pardoned for stopping
to note, while endeavouring to convey the idea of a philosophic discoverer. His features were singularly graceful, full of intelligence, but calm as suited his manner
and his speech.   His high forehead and sharp temples
were slightly covered, when I knew him, with hair of a
snow-white hue, and his mouth gave a kindly as well
as most intelligent expression to his whole features. In
one department of his lecture he exceeded any I have
ever known, the neatness and unvarying success with

which all the manipulations of his experiments were
performed. His correct eye and steady hand contributed to the one; his admirable precautions, foreseeing
and providing for every emergency, secured the other.
I have seen him pour boiling water or boiling acid
from a vessel that had no spout into a tube, holding it
at such a distance as made the stream's diameter small,
and so vertical that not a drop was spilt. While he
poured he would mention this adaptation of the height
to the diameter as a necessary condition of success. I
have seen him mix two substances in a receiver into
which a gas, as chlorine, had been introduced, the effect
of the combustion being perhaps to produce a compound inflammable in its nascent state, and the mixture
being effected by drawing some string or wire working
through the receiver's sides in an air-tight socket. The
long table on which the different processes had been
carried on was as clean at the end of the lecture as it
had been before the apparatus was planted upon it.
Not a drop of liquid, not a grain of dust remained.

The reader who has known the pleasures of science
will forgive me if at the distance of half a century I
love to linger over these recollections, and to dwell
on the delight which I well remember thrilled me
as we heard this illustrious sage detail, after the
manner I have feebly attempted to pourtray, the steps
by which he made his discoveries, illustrating them
with anecdotes sometimes recalled to his mind by
the passages of the moment, and giving their demonstration by performing before us the many experiments which had revealed to him first the most
important secrets of nature. Next to the delight of

having actually stood by him when his victory was
gained, we found the exquisite gratification of hearing him simply, most gracefully, in the most calm
spirit of philosophy, with the most perfect modesty,
recount his difficulties, and how they were overcome;
open to us the steps by which he had successfully advanced from one part to another of his brilliant course;
go over the same ground, as it were, in our presence
which he had for the first time trod so many long years
before; hold up perhaps the very instruments he had
•then used, and act over again the same part before our
eyes which had laid the deep and broad foundations of
his imperishable renown.   Not a little of this extreme
interest certainly belonged to the accident that he had
so long survived the period of his success—that we
knew there sat in our presence the man now in his old
age reposing under the laurels won in his early youth.
But take it altogether, the effect was such as cannot
well be conceived.   I have heard the greatest under-
standings of the age giving forth their efforts in its
most eloquent tongues—have heard the commanding
periods of Pitt's majestic oratory—the vehemence of
Fox's burning declamation—have followed the close-
compacted chain of Grant's pure reasoning—been
carried away by the mingled fancy, epigram, and
argumentation of Plunket; but I should without
hesitation prefer, for mere intellectual gratification
(though aware how much of it is derived from association), to be once more allowed the privilege which
I in those days enjoyed of being present while the first
philosopher of his age was the historian of his own
discoveries, and be an eye-witness of those experiments

by which he had formerly made them, once more performed with his own hands.

The qualities which distinguished him as an inquirer
and as a teacher followed him into all the ordinary affairs
of life. He was a person whose opinions on every
subject were marked by calmness and sagacity, wholly
free from both passion and prejudice, while affectation
was only known to him from the comedies he might
have read. His temper in all the circumstances of life
was unruffled. This was perceived in his lectures when
he had occasion to mention any narrow prejudice or any
unworthy proceeding of other philosophers. One exception there certainly was, possibly the only one in his
life; he seemed to have felt hurt at the objections
urged by a German chemist called Meyer to his
doctrine of causticity, which that person explained by
supposing an acid, called by him *acidum pingue*, to
be the cause of alkaline mildness. The unsparing
severity of the lecture in which Black exposed the ignorance and dogmatism of this foolish reasoner cannot
well be forgotten by his hearers, who both wondered
that so ill-matched an antagonist should have succeeded
where so many crosses had failed in discomposing the
sage, and observed how well fitted he was, should
occasion be offered, for a kind of exertion exceedingly
different from all the efforts that at other times he was
wont to make.

The soundness of his judgment on all matters,
whether of literature or of a more ordinary description,
was described by Adam Smith, who said, he "had
less nonsense in his head than any man living." The
elegance of his taste, which has been observed upon as

shown in his lectures, was also seen in the efforts of
his pencil, which Professor Robison compares to that
of Woollett. The neatness of his manipulations was
not confined to his experiments when investigating or
when lecturing. I have heard one who happened to
see him at his toilette describe the operations as performed with exquisite neatness by a number of
contrivances happily adapted to the saving of trouble
and avoiding uneasiness. His perfect equanimity has
been adverted to, and it did not proceed from coldness
of disposition, for he was affectionately attached to his
friends. Having no family of his own, he may be said
to have fallen into those precise and regular habits
which sometimes raise in happier individuals a smile,
I stop not to inquire whether of envy or contempt, for
the single state. It was sometimes said, too, that his
habits were penurious. That the expenses of one who
had no love of pleasure and no fancy for ostentation
to gratify, must have been moderate, is certain ; but he
lived in the style and manner suited to one possessing
an ample income. The ground of the charge was, I
believe, that he was said to have a scale by him when
he received the fees of his students. I can answer for
the truth of this statement, for I well remember the
small brass instrument; but I also recollect that he
said it became necessary from the quantity of light
gold which he used at first to receive unsuspected from
one class, particularly, of his pupils. There was
certainly no reason why he should pay a sum of forty or
fifty pounds yearly out of his income on this account.
Both Professor Ferguson and Professor Robison have
positively denied the charge of avarice, and have given

ample testimony even to his generous nature. While he lived at Glasgow he lost three-fourths of his fortune by the failure of a house in which it was invested; and though he had foreseen the catastrophe for two years, he neither attempted to withdraw his funds, nor altered in any respect his kind demeanour towards the head of the firm, whom he knew. At Edinburgh he more than once incurred great risks to help friends in business.

The gradual decay of his strength brought about the extinction of life without pain and without any discomposure. Professor Robison told me that he was sure nothing could be more agreeable to his illustrious friend's wishes than this end, as nothing was more likely to vex and annoy him than the unavoidable accompaniments of a protracted illness and a sick-bed. He often indeed expressed a wish that he might be spared this suffering, and that wish was fully gratified. It seemed, said the Professor, as if he waited calmly until the last stroke of his pulse should be given. It is certain that he passed from this life so quietly as not to spill a cup of milk and water (a customary dinner with him) which he at the moment was holding in his hand, and which rested on his knee. His attendants saw him in this posture, and left the room supposing him still alive. On returning soon after they saw him exactly sitting as before, and found that he had expired.

W A T T.

THE intimacy of Mr. Watt with Dr. Black from his earliest years has been already mentioned. When the latter was a Professor at the University of Glasgow, Watt, then a young man, was employed as mathematical instrument maker to the Natural Philosophy class, and was in daily communication with the Professor while his experiments on heat, evaporation, and condensation were carried on. I well remember him afterwards, in his lectures at Edinburgh, mentioning that his young coadjutor employed himself at the same time in researches upon the nature of steam; and it is certain that his subsequent inventions were greatly aided by the discoveries of Black respecting heat. To the inquiries out of which these inventions arose, he appears to have been led by the accident of having a model of an engine to repair for the Professor of Natural Philosophy. But, before examining the foundations upon which his great and well-earned fame rests, it is fit that we should first consider the state in which he found the engine, which he almost created anew. This is following the same course which has been pursued with respect to the discoveries of Dr. Black.

The power of steam is far too generally perceived in the ordinary affairs of life to have wholly escaped the

as identure by Sir W.
[Seer tr...]

observations of men at any period. The ancients accordingly were so far acquainted with it as to have constructed an instrument, the æolipile, composed of a metallic ball, which, having some water in its bottom, was placed in the fire, and the steam, issuing through a small orifice or tube with great force, could, they conceived, blow a fire or even turn the vanes of a mill. No use, however, seems ever to have been made of this philosophical toy; nor does any attention appear to have been paid to steam, as an agent, until 1615, when Salomon de Caus, a French engineer, published a work on 'Moving Forces,' in which he describes a method of raising water by partially heating it, that is, converting a portion of it into steam, and, by its expansive force, driving the rest of the fluid through the tube connected with the reservoir or chamber.* In 1663 the Marquis of Worcester (known in our political history as Earl of Glamorgan, and as having been employed by Charles I. in 1646 to negotiate with the Irish Catholics) published his ' Century of the Names and Scantlings of Inventions,' of which Mr. Hume, in his ' History' (vol. vii., note o), has been pleased to say that it is "a ridiculous compound of lies, chimeras, and impossibilities, showing what might be expected from such a man." The better

---

* M. Arago is not entitled to complain of English writers for having "aimed at expunging every French name from this important chapter in the history of science." He says they at once gave up Lord Worcester's claims on discovering that Salomon de Caus had preceded him. Now both Mr. Farey and Mr. Stuart have done ample justice to Caus in their works on the steam engine. As for Lord Worcester, Mr. Stuart (whose history is far from accurate on this point) has both attacked and defended his claims in his several works.

opinion seems to be, that the historian had never read
the book he thus describes ; but being anxious to
relieve Charles I. from the blame of his Ambassador's
negotiation, which proved the source of much outcry
against the King, he states the low opinion which the
latter entertained of Worcester's judgment as a proof
that he never would authorise him to act in so delicate a
matter as religious concessions without the privity of the
Lord-Lieutenant, and he is very ready to strengthen
this view by showing that the opinion was well founded.
Be this, however, as it may, the ignorance and error
is all on Hume's side, for the work is highly creditable
to its author's learning and ingenuity, and it undoubtedly contains a proof that he had made one step
in advance of Caus towards the use of steam-power.
His Sixty-eighth Invention is entitled " an admirable
and most forcible way to drive up water by fire." He
describes his having made a " constant fountain stream
of water, raised in the proportion of forty times the
quantity of that which he converted into steam ;" and
he states that the height to which he raised it was forty
feet, clearly showing that it was not on the principle
of the sucking-pump, which can only raise water
thirty-three feet. He expressly says that, while the
atmospheric pressure by which the sucking-pump acts
is limited in its operation, the force of steam which he
employed " hath no other boundary than the strength
of the vessel which contains it." Finally, he seems
to have used a cannon as his boiler, which indicates his
having tried the experiment on a large scale. The
great doubt expressed by M. Arago whether or not
Lord Worcester ever executed the design more or less

clearly described in his book appears to me to have no foundation. The inference arising from the description seems to remove that doubt; but we have external evidence more precise and satisfactory still.* The travels in England of the Grand Duke of Tuscany, Cosmo de' Medicis, were written by his Secretary, Magalotti, a man of some scientific eminence; and a translation into English was published in 1821. The visit to London took place in the year 1669; and it appears that the Grand Duke "went to see, at Vauxhall, an engine or hydraulic machine invented by the Marquis of Worcester," and the account which he gives of it tallies with Lord Worcester's description of his " stupendous water-commanding engine."

The account of Lord Worcester is far from being clear and distinct, and nothing appears to have resulted from his suggestions. In 1690, Papin, an eminent and able French engineer, settled in London, and author of the digester which goes under his name, published a work in which he showed that he had made two most important steps in the use of steam. Caus and Worcester had applied the force directly to the body which it was intended to move; and it was evident that, while that was a condition of its use, very limited bounds must confine the operation. But Papin, observing the use of the piston in a common sucking-pump, applied this to the steam machine, making it work in the cylinder, and be the medium of

---

* See also the Marchioness of Worcester's correspondence with her Confessor, communicated by the Beaufort family to Mr. Partington for his edition of the ' Century.'

communicating motion to other apparatus. Next, he
applied steam directly as the agent, to raise the piston ;
and making a vacuum *by the condensation of the
steam*, he thus caused the atmosphere to press down
the piston. Guericke, the inventor of the air-pump,
had half a century earlier used the vacuum, made
by his machine in the same manner, as a mechanical
power, by the help of a piston and rod ;* and he
invented the valve, without which the vacuum could
not be produced. The application of the same
principle and of the same contrivance to steam was
Papin's ; and its importance, and his merit, are not
diminished by considering the source from which he
borrowed it.† Indeed the action of the air in the
sucking-pump is another form of the same experiment.
It must be added that to Papin also we owe the important invention of the safety-valve, although he did
not apply it to the steam engine. He introduced it as
a part of his digester, but suggesting that it was applicable to the steam engine.

It is, however, certain that the most rude and cumbrous part of the former invention was continued by
Papin. The fire was applied to the water, and when it
had filled the cylinder with steam, the condensation
was only effected by withdrawing or extinguishing the
fire. Savery about the year 1698 made considerable

---

* See the distinct figure in his plate xiv., p. 109, of ' Experi-
menta nova Magdeburgica de Vacuo Spatio.' Amstelodami, 1672.

† Acta Eruditorum, 1688. The paper has an excellent and
clear figure. Nothing can be more groundless than Mr. Stuart's
statement that Baptista Porta had anticipated Papin in this important step. The passage refers only to the rise of water in a vacuum.
See ' I tre Libri dei Spiritali,' 1606.

improvements on the apparatus; and though he did not use the vacuum as Papin had done, but only as it is used in the sucking-pump, he yet produced it by applying cold water to the outside of the cylinder. The machines made by him were so manageable that they were brought into use for raising water in many country houses. D'Alesme exhibited a machine before 1705 (as appears by the 'Histoire de l'Académie des Sciences' for that year, p. 137), in which water was made to spout to a great height by the force of steam alone.

It is extremely doubtful if Papin ever erected any steam engine, either upon his own or upon any other principle. It is certain that he did not adhere to the two great propositions which he had brought forward, the operating by a piston, and the operating by the pressure of the atmosphere; he recurred to the old plan of making the steam act directly upon the weight to be raised. In 1711 Newcomen, an iron-master of Dartmouth, and Calley, or Cawley, a glazier of the same town, constructed an engine upon Papin's principle of a piston and a condensing process, using, however, Savery's mode of creating a vacuum by cold affusion, for which they were led by an accident to substitute the method of throwing a jet or stream of cold water into the cylinder. This important improvement saved, in a considerable degree, the waste of heat occasioned by Savery's method of condensing. Their engine could be applied with advantage to raise water from mines, which Savery's was wholly incapable of effecting, its power being limited to that of the sucking-pump. Newcomen's engine, as it is generally called, made no use at all of the direct force of steam; it

worked entirely by means of the vacuum; and hence it
is sometimes and justly termed the atmospheric engine,
as its moving force is the pressure of the atmosphere.
Desaguliers, who has given the best description
of Newcomen and Cawley's engine, about the year
1717 or 1718 made several of those engines, in which
he executed Papin's suggestion of using the safety-
valve. In the same year Beighton perfected the mechanism whereby the engine itself shut and opened the
valves, by which the supply of steam to the cylinder
and of water to the boiler is regulated; and Smeaton
subsequently made some other mechanical improvements. With these exceptions the steam engine continued exactly in the same state from the time of Newcomen to that of Watt, above half a century later.

We have thus seen how very slowly this great
invention was brought to the state in which Mr. Watt
found it, and how considerable a number of persons contributed each a small share to its progress. Let us enu-
merate these steps: they are at least six in number. S.
de Caus made steam act to raise water; Worcester performed this operation in a more regular and mechanical
manner; Papin used the condensation of steam, and
through that the atmospheric pressure, as well as the
direct expansive force, and he worked the engine by a
piston; Savery condensed by refrigeration instead of the
mere absence of fire, but did not use the atmosphere;
Newcomen used the jet for condensing and the atmosphere for pressure, but did not use the direct force of
steam; Desaguliers introduced the safety-valve; Beighton and Smeaton improved the mechanism; D'Alesme
needs not be mentioned, as we are not informed what

plan he executed, but he certainly made no step himself. If the direct force of steam, as well as atmospheric pressure, had been both employed, with the jet of cold water, the safety-valve, and the contrivance for regulating the supply-valves, a far better engine than any ever known before the time of Watt would have been produced, and yet nothing whatever would have been added to the former inventions; they would only have been combined together. The result of the whole is, that one of the greatest theoretical steps was made by Papin, who was, during a long period, little commemorated; and that Savery and Newcomen, who have been by many called the inventors, were the first of all the ingenious and useful persons whose successive improvements we have now recorded, to apply the steam-engine to practical purposes. France has thus produced the man who, next to Watt, must be regarded as the author of the steam-engine: of all Watt's predecessors, Papin stands incontestably at the head; but it is almost certain that he never actually constructed an engine. Though the engine of Savery was of considerable use in pumping to a small height, and indeed has not entirely gone out of use even in our own times, and though Newcomen's was still more extensively useful from being applicable to mines, not only had no means ever been found of using the steam power for any other purpose than drawing up water, but even in that operation it was exceedingly imperfect and very expensive, insomuch that a water power was often preferred to it, and even a horse power in many cases afforded equal advantages. The great consumption of fuel which it required was its cardinal defect; the other imperfection was its loss of all direct benefit from the expansive force of the steam itself. That element was only used in creating a vacuum, and an air-pump might have done as much had it been worked by water or by horses. It was, in the strictest sense of the word, an air and not a steam engine.

When Mr. Watt was directed to repair the working model for the Professor at Glasgow, he of course examined it attentively. He was at that time, 1763, in his twenty-eighth year, having been born in 1736 at Greenock, where his father was a magistrate, and had learnt the business of a mathematical instrument maker. He had been prevented by delicate health from benefiting much by school instruction; but he had by himself studied both geometry and mechanics, having from his childhood shown a marked taste for those pursuits, in which his grandfather and uncle, teachers of the mathematics, had been engaged. It is related of him that a friend of his father's one day found the child stretched on the floor drawing with chalk numerous lines that intersected each other. He advised the sending the young idler, as he supposed him, to school, but the father said, "Perhaps you are mistaken; examine first what he is about." They found he was trying, at six years old, to solve a problem in geometry. So his natural turn for mechanics was not long in showing itself; and his father indulging it by putting tools in his hands, he soon constructed a small electrical machine, beside making many childish toys.

He occasionally visited his mother's relations at Glasgow, but never attended any lectures there, or elsewhere. The ardour of his active mind was superior to all the restraints which the weakness of his bodily frame could impose. He devoured every kind of learning. Not content with chemistry and natural philosophy, he studied anatomy, and was one day found carrying home for dissection the head of a child that had died of some hidden disorder. His conversation, too, was so rich, so animated, that we find, from the relation of Mrs. Campbell, a female cousin of his, the complaints made by a lady with whom he resided. She spoke of the sleepless nights which he made her pass by engaging her in some discussion or some detail of facts, or some description of phenomena, till the night was far advanced towards morning, and she found it impossible to tear herself away from his talk, or to sleep after he had thus excited her.

In 1755 he placed himself with Mr. Morgan, mathematical and nautical instrument maker, of Cornhill, and resided with him somewhat less than a year, during which he was chiefly employed in the preparation and adjustment of sextants, compasses, and other nautical instruments. But the same feeble health which had interrupted his studies at Glasgow again oppressed him; he was obliged to leave London, and return to Glasgow. On his arrival there he had the intention of setting up as an instrument maker, but the Glasgow Body of Arts and Trades, one of the sub-corporations in the municipal corporation of that city, opposed him as not free of their craft or guild, and therefore not entitled to exercise his calling within the limits of the charter. Attempts were made to obtain their leave for a very small workshop, on the humblest scale, but this was

peremptorily refused. The University therefore came
to his assistance, granted him a room in their
own building, and gave him the appointment of their
mathematical instrument maker. There remain small
instruments then made by him in this workshop, and
executed entirely with his own hands; they are of
exquisite workmanship. The earliest of his steam-
engine drawings are likewise preserved, and those
competent judges who have examined them, particularly
M. Arago, describe them as " truly remarkable for the
neatness, the strength, and the accuracy of their
outline." His manual dexterity and skill, therefore,
is clear, and he had good cause to plume himself as
he always did upon it, estimating the same quality in
others at its just value.

    In the course of a very few years, beside renewing his
intimacy with Mr. Robison, afterwards Professor there
and at Edinburgh, he became intimately acquainted with
the most eminent of the Glasgow Professors, Adam
Smith, Robert Simson, Robert Dick, and above all, Dr.
Black. Of these all but Mr. Dick have left the deep impress of their great names upon the scientific history of
their age; and he was always described by both Mr.
Watt and Professor Robison as a person of most admirable capacity and great attainments, treating natural
philosophy, too, with singular ability and success,
nor prevented from acquiring a more extensive and
lasting reputation by anything save his premature
death.

    While thus occupied and thus befriended by men of
great names, his own reputation increased daily as a
successful cultivator of natural science. His work-

shop became the resort of all zealous students and
enlightened inquirers into physical science, and was
particularly resorted to by the pupils of the University.
Professor Robison tells us that though regarding
himself as a proficient in the mixed mathematics and in
experimental philosophy, he was somewhat mortified
at finding Watt so greatly his superior in the same
favourite departments of study. In truth, it was the
ordinary practice to consult him as the oracle upon any
difficulty coming in the way of either students or inquirers. His fixed resolution to be deterred by
no difficulties was constantly apparent, and one
example is given by the Professor. The solution of a
problem which occupied Watt and his friends, seemed
to require the perusal of Leupold's Theatre of Machines,
and as it was written in German, he at once learnt that
language in order to consult the book. Another
instance of his indomitable perseverance against great
difficulties apparently irremovable, though not insuperable, may be added. He had no ear at all for music:
not only was he through life wholly insensible to its
charms, but he could never distinguish one note from
another; yet he undertook the construction of an organ;
and the instrument which he made not only had every
mechanical merit from the most ingenious contrivances
for conducting and regulating the blasts and the movements of the machine, but produced the most admirable
harmonic results, so as to delight the best performers.
He overcame the difficulties which lay in his way,
partly by the phenomenon of the beats of imperfect
consonances, a theory then little understood, and only
contained in a work at once very profound and very

obscure, Smith's 'Harmonics.' This treatise, of which only the first and less perfect edition was then published, must have been read and understood by the young engineer. While employed by Dr. Roebuck at his Works, he made a guitar for his daughter, afterwards Mrs. Stuart, which she still possesses, and relates the sum given for it to have been five guineas.

It only remains to add that all the reading and all the speculations of Watt were strictly confined to hours which did not interfere with his profession or his trade of an instrument maker. The whole of the day was devoted to his business, only subject to the interruption of the discussions raised by those who frequented his workshop in search of assistance and information. It was late in the evening, or rather in the night, that he prosecuted with zeal and close attention his philosophical studies; for his principle through life was steadily kept in view, and uniformly acted on, never to let anything whatever interfere with business, the transaction of which he regarded as a primary duty to be performed, and entitled, as such, to take precedence of all other pursuits.

There chanced to be among the apparatus of the Natural Philosophy class a model of Newcomen's steam-engine, which, from some defect in the construction, never could be got to work well; and Mr. Watt was desired to examine and report to the Professor, Mr. Anderson, successor of Dr. Dick, and better known afterwards as having founded by his will the class in which Dr. Birkbeck taught the working men, and thus gave rise to Mechanics' Institutes. The construction of this working model was found to be exceedingly imperfect, but Mr. Watt soon remedied all its defects. As far as the kind of engine could answer its purpose, the apparatus was found to perform its functions satisfactorily, being annually exhibited to the class with great success. He had, however, been taught by his examination of the model what were the defects of the machine itself, and which no care in repairing or adjusting that model could remove. He found first of all that the boiler was much too small in proportion to the column of water which the steam had to raise, and yet it was larger than the boiler used in practice. The cylinder was on the scale of two inches diameter, the height being half a foot. The vacuum being imperfect from the size of the boiler, he diminished the length of the piston rod. He found that the brass of which the cylinder was made carried off a great deal of heat, and that too large a surface was exposed to the steam. These observations set him upon making a variety of experiments upon steam, and upon the mode of applying it both directly and to produce a vacuum. He had, in the year 1759, while a fellow-student with Mr. Robison, received from that gentleman a suggestion of the application of steam to wheel-carriages, as he tells us in 1803, long before steam travelling was dreamt of.* They had together made experiments on Papin's digester, in order to ascertain the expansive force of steam ; but these speculations had for several years

---

* Mr. Murdock, in 1784, made a working model of a steam-carriage, which moved about the room. It was constructed upon the principle set forth in Mr. Watt's specification of 1769, Art. iv., and this is the very method used at the present day.

been given up. In 1760 and the two following years
Watt had been in familiar intercourse with Professor
Black, had witnessed his experiments on heat, and
had learnt from him the true cause of evaporation and
condensation. When, therefore, he began to experiment upon the mechanical application of steam, its
expansion, and its condensation, he enjoyed that inestimable advantage of thoroughly knowing the principles on which its changes and its action depended. His
own experiments now put him in possession of the
causes which determine the rapidity of evaporation,
the proportion which it bears to the surface exposed to
the fire, the effects of pressure upon the boiling-point,
and the quantity of fuel required to convert a given
quantity of water into steam—circumstances which
had hitherto been only vaguely and generally examined,
but which he now reduced to mathematical precision.

The first discovery which he made upon the atmospheric engine and its waste of fuel, was that the in-
jection of cold water which condenses the steam also
cools the cylinder to a degree which requires a great
expenditure of fuel again to give it the necessary heat
for keeping the steam expanded to fill it. He found
that three-fourths of the fuel employed were thus consumed ; in other words, that if the cylinder could be
kept at the temperature which it has before the jet is
thrown in, one-fourth of the fuel would suffice for the
operation.

The next defect of the process was scarcely less important. The water injected, coming in contact with
the steam, was itself heated ; the evolution of the
latent heat, which Black's discovery showed Watt

necessarily took place on its condensation, had the effect, together with the absorption of the steam's sensible heat, of converting a portion of the injected water itself into steam. Hence the vacuum was very far from perfect; and the resistance which the piston thus met with in its descent was found to be equal to one-fourth part of the atmospheric pressure, that is to say, the working power of the machine was diminished one-fourth.

From the distinct view thus obtained of the evil arose the suggestion of the remedy. The whole mischief proceeded from the condensation being performed in the cylinder, where the steam was thrown and the piston worked. It occurred to Watt, that if the condensation could be performed in a separate vessel, communicating with the cylinder, the latter could be kept hot while the former was cooled, and the vapour arising from the injected water could also be prevented from impairing the vacuum. The communication could easily be effected by a tube, and the water could be pumped out. This is the *first* and the grand invention by which he at once saved three-fourths of the fuel, and increased the power one-fourth, thus making every pound of coal consumed produce five times the force formerly obtained from it. But this was not all. He found it expedient to remove the air from the upper part of the cylinder, as it tended to diminish the heat. In effecting this he was, *secondly*, led to open a communication with the boiler, and introduce steam above the piston while it descended, thus making the upper chamber of the cylinder air-tight. The steam thus acted in aiding the descent of the piston, instead

of that descent being accomplished merely by the
atmospheric pressure. *Thirdly*—the counterpoise at
the pump-rod was done away, as a mere loss
of power, and the piston was now forced upwards by the steam entering to fill the cylinder.
These two great additional improvements only required
a communication to be opened by tubes with the con-
denser as well as the boiler, and they gave to the
machinery its right to be called a steam-engine; for it
now worked more by steam than by air. The upper
chamber was kept air-tight by making the piston-rod
work in a socket of tow saturated with grease, called
the stuffing-box, which also diminished greatly the
friction of the rod.

If Mr. Watt's invention had gone no further than
this, we may perceive that it not only increased the
power of the fuel fivefold directly, but obtained from
the steam as much additional force as could be derived,
the limit being only the strength of the materials,
within which limit the safety-valve of Papin always
enabled the engineer to keep his power. But the three
particulars which have been described were not the
whole of this great engineer's improvements upon the
mechanism of his predecessors. The smooth working
of the engine, especially if it be applied to other and
finer operations than those of the miner, depends
essentially on the accurate position of the piston rod,
with whatever velocity moving, and against whatever
weight contending. Its motion must be steadily
maintained in the same vertical straight line, or
in the same horizontal line, or in the same
straight line whatever be its direction, without

shaking or inclining so as to press at all against the
sides of the cylinder—any such lateral pressure occa-
sioning a loss of time, a jolting motion, a general de-
rangement of the machinery. The motion of the rod
and the piston must be perfectly equable, continuous,
and smooth : it must work, as the engineers sometimes
say, *sweetly*, at every instant, in order that the engine
may well perform its functions. The contrivance for
producing this motion of the rod so that it shall
be always in one line, parallel to some supposed line
whether vertical, as in a mine, or horizontal, or in any
other direction, is thence called the "*Parallel Motion*,"
and it is one of Mr. Watt's most exquisite discoveries,
and one to which scientific principle has the most con-
duced. If a circle or other curve has its curvature gradually changed, until from being concave to its axis it
becomes convex, it will pass through every possible
position or variation (whence the great refinement
upon fluxions, the *calculus of variations*, probably
derived its name, if not its origin), and at one point
it will be a straight line, or will coincide with a
straight line. So if a curve have two branches, one
concave to the axis, the other convex, as a cubic para-
bola for example, the point at which its concavity ends
and its convexity begins, is called for that reason a
point of contrary flexure. The contrivance of the
parallel motion consists in making the contrary circular motions of arms which bear on the rod always keep
to the point of contrary flexure and thus give a rectilinear motion to the rod, the tendencies to disturb it
correcting each other. It was long ago shown by Sir
Isaac Newton, in the 'Principia,' that if a circle moves

2 B

upon another of twice its diameter, each point describes
a straight line. This is precisely the principle of the
parallel motion. Three beams are made to revolve
round different centres, two of these being moveable in
the arm of the engine, and one fixed without it. These
three are connected together and with the piston-rods
of the cylinder and the pumps, which their revolutions cause to describe accurately straight lines.

A *fifth* invention is the *Float*, which, placed on the
surface of the water in the boiler, descends until the
water is so low as to require a supply; it then opens a
valve which lets in the quantity wanted; for, as soon as
it rises to a certain height, the valve is shut by the float.

The most refined contrivance of the whole may now
be mentioned, in the *sixth* and last place, the adaptation
of the *Governor*, previously used in wind and water
mills. It is evident that the velocity of the working
may be increased beyond what is required or convenient without the safety-valve giving any indication of the excess, and also that the warning
given by this valve does little more than point out the
risk without providing the remedy or preventive.
The governor is a far more subtle invention. Two
balls are fixed to the end of arms which are connected
with the engine by a moveable socket; this can play
up and down a vertical rod revolving by a band on the
axis or spindle of the fly-wheel, and it revolves, therefore, with the velocity of that spindle. The arms are
perfectly moveable on their centres, which are fixed in
the socket and on opposite sides of it. Their centrifugal force, therefore, makes them diverge, more or less,
in proportion as the rotatory motion of the spindle and

consequently the velocity of the engine increases; their divergence pushes the collar up the spindle, its axis, and as it rises, it closes, by means of cranks, a valve called the "throttle-valve," in the pipe which conveys the steam from the boiler to the cylinder, and this lessens the supply of steam: the motion of the engine is thus reduced, the centrifugal force is abated, the balls approach the spindle again, the collar descends, the throttle-valve is gradually opened, and the supply of steam again slowly increased, but never beyond the quantity required, because as soon as that is exceeded, the increase of centrifugal force causes the balls to diverge, the collars to rise, and the valve to close. Thus the engine itself provides for its continuing in the state of perfect adjustment required. As long as its motion continues uniform, the balls revolve at the mean distance from their axis without either receding or approaching, and the supply of steam continues the same. As soon as the motion becomes excessive, they diverge, and the supply of steam is diminished; as soon as the motion becomes defective, they converge, and the supply of steam is increased. But further, the balls themselves, by their increased motion, absorb part of the force, independent of their action on the throttle-valve, and so contribute to the adjustment.

The sagacious inventor soon satisfied himself that he had almost created a new engine of incalculable power, universal application, and inestimable value. But he had not the funds either to try his invention upon an adequate scale so as to bring it into use, or to secure his property in it by obtaining a patent. After some repulses, he happily met with Dr. Roebuck, a man of profound scientific knowledge, and of daring spirit as a speculator. He had just founded the Carron Iron Works, not far from Glasgow, and was lessee, under the Hamilton family, of the Kinneil Coal Works. He was the grandfather of the present Member for Bath, who, descended from him on the one side, and from the Tickells* on the other, may be said to unite in himself rare claims to hereditary distinction; but who is probably destined to exalt the name of his family still higher by his own virtues. Dr. Roebuck, like too many ingenious men, founded these Carron and Kinneil Works for the benefit of others; and though he agreed to Mr. Watt's terms of receiving two thirds of the profit, he was obliged by pecuniary embarrassments to retire from the partnership after a patent had been obtained in 1769, and an engine of an eighteen-inch cylinder had been erected at Kinneil. The success of this amply proved the solidity of the invention, but the inventor was obliged, for some years, to abandon the pursuit, and to labour in his profession of what is now termed a civil engineer; but the extensive operations of which Scotland soon became the scene, gave a much more ample scope to his talents. He was actively engaged in the surveys, and afterwards in the works, for connecting by a canal the Monkland coal-mines with Glasgow. He was afterwards employed in preparing the canal since completed by Mr. Rennie, across the Isthmus of

---

* His maternal grandfather was the author of 'Anticipation,' and grandson of Addison's friend, the poet.

Crinan; in the difficult and laborious investigations for the improvement of the harbours of Ayr, Greenock, and Glasgow; in improving the navigation of the Forth and the Clyde; in the Campbelton Canal, and in the surveys and plans preliminary to the Grand Caledonian Canal; beside several bridges of great importance, as those of Hamilton and Rutherglen. At Dr. Roebuck's Mr. Watt had early received much kindness, and many valuable lessons in chemical science. He was here, too, introduced to Dr. Black.

The various works which have been mentioned occupied his whole time from the disappointment experienced in 1769 respecting the steam engine, of which during that long interval he never despaired, to the year 1774, when he acceded to the proposal of Mr. Boulton, of Soho, near Birmingham, that he should be taken in Dr. Roebuck's place as partner in the patent, and in 1775 he settled there in this new business. An extension of the patent for twenty-five years from this time was obtained from Parliament, in consequence of the national importance which all men saw belonged to the invention; and the partners constructed many engines upon the terms of receiving one third of the fuel saved by the improvements. It is a convenient mode of illustrating the effect of the invention in saving fuel, to observe what were the gains of the partners under this stipulation. On one mine, that of Chasewater, in Cornwall, the proprietors compounded for 2400*l.* a year, instead of paying the third of the fuel saved. That saving then must very considerably have exceeded 7200*l.* a year. But there seemed some difficulty in carrying bargains of this kind into effect; and the genius of Watt, fertile in resources, immediately invented a small clock, called *the counter*, to be moved by the engine, and which accurately recorded every stroke it made.   Payment being in proportion to the number of strokes, the clock was enclosed in a box under a double lock, and thus the working could be easily and securely ascertained.*

The first consequence of this grand invention, and the great saving of fuel it occasioned, was the renewed working of mines which had become unprofitable under the old plan.   The next was the opening mines which Newcomen's engine could not drain at all. The steam-power, too, was no longer confined to draining mines.   Various contrivances, for which Watt took out no less than four patents between 1781 and 1785, enabled him to communicate a rotatory motion from the piston, so that the engine could now work any machinery whatever; could spin cotton, cut iron and brass, stamp cloth, grind corn, print books, coin money, in short, could perform on any scale any kind of work in which human labour was either inefficient or expensive; and while it was seen in one place pouring out rivers from the bowels of the earth with the arms of a giant, or cleaving rocks of granite formation, or clipping huge bars of stubborn iron into ribands, it was elsewhere to be found

---

* Such an engine could not be made and used secretly, and thus piracy was prevented.   It is far otherwise with small pieces of mechanism, and still more difficult would be the protection of patent rights in mere methods, though to these the protection of the law should be extended.

weaving or spinning like a quiet and industrious female, or turning a small lathe, or forming the fine
wheels of a watch, or drawing out a thread too fine
for sight; when the machine, instead of sawing the
air aloft, and making the ground tremble around it,
was placed quietly on a table like a candlestick or an
inkstand. The latest use of the power, and the most
important, is steam travelling by land and water.
Watt himself early perceived this application of his
engine; and in 1785 he took out a patent for moving
carriages by steam, but he does not appear to have
practically used his method. The attempts had been
numerous, and from very early times, to propel vessels
by steam. There seems reason to think that the
paddle-wheel, the only addition to the steam-engine
required for navigation, was known in ancient Egypt:
it certainly was known to the Romans. In the middle
of the sixteenth century a Spanish engineer exhibited
a steam-vessel to Charles V. The Marquis of Worcester appears to have turned his attention to the
subject from some parts of the work already cited, and
so superciliously condemned by Hume; and Jonathan
Hulls, in 1736, took out a patent for a kind of steam-
tug. Various similar attempts were afterwards made,
but with no success, and it was not until the steam-
engine had been improved and had become generally
used for all other purposes that it was applied to those
of locomotion.

It is truly painful to reflect, that among the rewards
which this great public benefactor was destined to
reap for his invaluable services, was the lot of having
to pass many years of his life in the unenviable situa-

tion of a party to suits at law and in equity, so numerous
as might well have worn out the patience of any one but
him, whose unwearied perseverance had already toiled
successfully against unnumbered difficulties of another
kind.   Such was, at that time, the patent law of this
country; such, in some degree, it still is, though much
improved.   Inventive genius is placed between two
dangers, and it can hardly escape the one without
falling into the other.—If the invention is such that
it requires some new demand to be created, or some
novel taste to be introduced, before it can be much
used, the period of the monopoly expires before any
gain can be reaped.   This is the more likely to
happen if it comes in competition with things already
made, and of which, at some expense, a considerable
stock has been prepared, because a formidable interest
is combined against the use of that new method which
must displace the old, and render valueless this collected stock.   I remember sitting on the trial of a
patent for a new and admirable pianoforte; the only
witness to its excellence being a sculptor of distinction
who had once made such instruments, but had no
longer any interest in crying down the invention:
none of the trade could be trusted to give their opinion
upon oath; all were, of course, in a combination
against that improvement, which, if adopted, would
render unsaleable their pianofortes already made.—If,
on the other hand, the superiority of the invention is
quite manifest, if the demand for it already exists, if no
combination can prevent its coming into general use—
for example, the making a new instrument for performing a known and necessary operation, or a new substance

for supplying a general want already existing—then
the inventor has to prepare himself for encountering
piracy in all its forms; capitalists, who would be
ashamed to violate the law in their own persons, encouraging men of no substance to infringe the patent,
and omitting to pay the patentee's costs when these
tools are defeated. My learned and ingenious kinsman, Dr. Forsyth, the inventor of the percussion
lock, passed the fourteen years of his patent right in
courts of justice, and in every instance prevailed ; but he
found the pirates pennyless, the costs were to be paid,
and he never gained one shilling by an invention
which is, I believe, more universally used all over
Europe than any other, except, perhaps, Argand's
lamp. That invention was defeated in court, in consequence of the imperfect state of the law in those
days, and of the absurd leaning of the Judges against
all patentees ; their Lordships displaying the utmost
ingenuity in discovering flaws, and calling into action
all the resources of legal astuteness in grinding, as
they went on, new law for the defeat of the inventor.
Of this, one instance only needs be given. If a specification contained ten good matters or processes, and
by oversight one was either not original, or did not
answer the description given in any other respect,*
the courts held the patent wholly void, and not merely
void for the erroneously described part, upon the
subtle and senseless ground that the Crown had been
deceived in the grant.

---

* Turner v. Winter, 6 T. R. ; Rex v. Fuller, 3 B. and A.
My Acts of 1835 and 1840 have in great part remedied these sad
defects in the law ; others still remain.

Mr. Watt had to struggle against this state of the law as well as against the shameless frauds, the conspiracies of dishonest, unprincipled men. During seven years and upwards he was condemned to lead the life of litigation; during seven years his genius was withdrawn from his own pursuits to become what he, no doubt, had, unfortunately for society, full time to make himself, an accomplished and learned lawyer; and it was not till five and thirty years after his invention had been made, that he was finally freed by a decision of the Court of King's Bench, in 1799, from a durance which lasted all the term of his patent, after all interest in the subject had expired by efflux of time. It was proved before a committee of the House of Commons in 1834, that had his statutory term in the patent only been secured to him, he would have been a great loser by the invention; and that for some years after the Act of Parliament had extended the time, he still was out of pocket: consequently it follows, that had he never taken a patent at all, but trusted entirely to the preference which his being the inventor would have given him in the market, as a maker of steam-apparatus, that is, had he taken only this indirect benefit instead of the direct gains of the monopoly, he would have been better off in a pecuniary point of view than he was by means of the grant of the patent and its Parliamentary extension. The Act which I introduced in 1835, grounded mainly upon that evidence, has removed some of the greatest defects in the law; and it has enabled, when coupled with the subsequent Act of last Session, an inventor to obtain, at a very inconsiderable cost, an extension for any additional period, not exceeding the duration of the original patent.* The expenses of obtaining patents, and especially the grievous burden of having to take out one for each of the three kingdoms, are the principal parts of the grievance which remain to be redressed.

Notwithstanding the serious drawbacks upon his gains which Watt thus experienced, he was, on the whole, successful in respect of profit, realizing an ample fortune, but which all men wished had been greater, and which, under a more just law, would have been thrice as great.

We have been contemplating the great achievement of Watt, but it would be a mistake to suppose that the steam-engine is the only monument of his scientific genius or his inventive skill. He was the author of the machine in general use for copying letters; of the method extensively used for heating buildings and hot-houses by steam; and of an ingenious mechanism for multiplying copies of busts and other sculptures; but he was also, without any doubt, the person who first discovered the composition of water. At this

---

* The course which a patentee ought to pursue if there be no opposition to his claim of extension, is to employ no solicitor and no counsel, but to appear in person before the Judicial Committee, as my gallant and truly ingenious friend Lord Dundonald (better known as Lord Cochrane) lately did. Their Lordships will always favour such a course, the rather as they thus obtain the advantage of hearing the explanations required from the person best able to give them. In opposed cases professional aid is requisite.

most important truth he arrived by a profound examination of all the experiments which had been made
by Warltire, by Macquer, and especially by Priestley, upon the combustion of hydrogen and oxygen
gases, then called inflammable, and vital or dephlogisticated airs. No former reasoner had come even
near the true theory of the phenomena observed in
those experiments. All had assumed that water was
a simple or elementary body ; that it was contained in
the airs burnt together, and was precipitated by their
explosion. He, on the contrary, showed that it was
formed by the union of the two gases, and their
parting with the latent heat which had held them in
the elastic or gaseous state, but which being withdrawn by their union, left them in a state of liquid or
aqueous fluidity.

As early as 1782, his attention had been closely
directed to the experiments in which air is produced
from water, and especially to those upon the combustion of inflammable air. In December of that year
he had matured his theory, for we find him then announcing to De Luc his discovery, that " one element
must be dismissed from the list ;" water being, according to his doctrine (stated more explicitly to Dr.
Black, April 1783,) " composed of dephlogisticated and
inflammable airs deprived of a portion of their latent
heat." To his whole correspondence with that great
philosopher, with Smeaton, with Priestley, De Luc, and
others, I have had access, and no trace is to be found
in it that either he or they had even entertained the
least suspicion of the same thing having before occurred

to any one else.* It is to be noted, too, that in 1784
Mr. Cavendish, after his celebrated experiment, had
not attained by any means so clear a notion of the
true doctrine as Mr. Watt explains in those previous
letters.† I examined minutely the whole of this
subject eight years ago, at the request of my distinguished colleague M. Arago, then engaged in
preparing his ' Eloge' of Mr. Watt, who had also been
our fellow-member of the Institute. The reader will
find my statement of the evidence annexed to this
account. But I cannot easily suppose that M. Arago
ever intended, and I know that I never myself intended,
to insinuate in the slightest degree a suspicion of Mr.
Cavendish's having borrowed from Mr. Watt. He had,
in all probability, been led to the same conclusion by his
own researches, ignorant of Mr. Watt's speculations,
a little earlier in point of time, just as Priestley when
claiming, and justly claiming, the important discovery
of oxygen (called by him, in accordance with the
doctrine of Stahl, " dephlogisticated air"), never denied
that Scheele also made the same discovery, calling it
" empyreal air," without being aware of another having
preceded him. Priestley, of course, treated the discreditable proceedings of Lavoisier in respect to this
gas very differently, and so must all impartial men.

It must on no account be supposed that Watt cannot
be considered as having discovered the composition of
water, merely because he made no new experiments of
particular moment, like Cavendish, to ascertain that

---

* Letters to Gilbert Hamilton of Glasgow, Fry of Bristol,
Smeaton, De Luc—all dated March and April, 1783.

† See Life of Cavendish for further particulars and explanations.

capital point. No one refuses to Newton the discovery of gravitation as the controlling and directing power of the solar system; and yet he made not one of those observations upon which his theory rests; nay, he threw it aside for sixteen years when the erroneous notion of a degree being only sixty miles appeared by its consequences to disprove his proposition, and instead of making any further experiments himself, waited until Picard's more accurate measurement became known to him accidentally in 1682, and enabled him to demonstrate his doctrine. In like manner, Lavoisier, who discovered no gas, and made no original experiments of the least value in pneumatic chemistry, is universally admitted to have discovered the true theory of combustion and calcination, by reasoning on the facts which others had ascertained. Watt's happy inference from the facts discovered by Warltire and Priestley was just as much entitled, and for the same reasons, to be regarded as the discovery of the composition of water.

The latter years of Mr. Watt's useful and honourable life were passed in the bosom of his family and the society of his friends, although he ever gave the due attention to the extensive concerns of the house in which he was the principal partner. He had been married as early as 1764 to Miss Miller, his cousin, and had by her a daughter who predeceased him, leaving children, and a son, James, who still survives, inheriting the scientific tastes, the extensive knowledge, the masculine understanding, and the scrupulous integrity of his father. With the late Mr. Robinson Boulton and Mr. Gregory Watt, he was admitted into the part-

nership, the concerns of which he extended, and, for
. the last quarter of a century, almost exclusively
conducted. By his second wife, Miss Macgregor,
whom he married in 1776, he had one son, Gregory,
who unfortunately died in October, 1804, at the age
of twenty-seven, after giving an earnest of brilliant talents and accomplishments. This loss was, no doubt, a
severe blow to his family, and the father shared fully
in their sorrow. But he bore it like a man: and I
feel great satisfaction in correcting an error into which
my illustrious friend and colleague M. Arago has fallen
through misinformation, when he represents Mr.
Watt's spirit as so entirely broken by the misfortune
that he "preserved an almost total silence during the
latter years of his life." The fact is, that he survived
his son's death between fourteen and fifteen years, and
never was more cheerful or enjoyed the pleasures of
society more heartily than during this period. ' I can
speak on the point with absolute certainty, for my own
acquaintance with him commenced after my friend
Gregory's decease. A few months after that event,
he calmly and with his wonted acuteness discussed
with me the composition of an epitaph to be inscribed
on his son's tomb. That autumn and winter he was a
constant attendant at our Friday club, and in all our
private circles, and was the life of them all. He has,
moreover, left under his hand an account of the effect
which the recent loss had produced upon his spirits,
and a flat contradiction to the notion that it had de-
pressed them. " I perhaps," he observes, "have said too
much to you and Mr. Campbell on the state of my
mind : I therefore think it necessary to say that I am

not low-spirited, and were you here you would find me as cheerful in the company of my friends as usual; my feelings for the loss of poor Gregory are not passion, but a deep regret that such was his and my lot." He then expresses his pious resignation to the will of "the Disposer of events." It is true, he adds that he had lost one stimulus to exertion, and with it his relish for his usual avocations, but he looks to time for a remedy, and adds, "meanwhile, I do not neglect the means of amusement which are within my power." This letter was written in January 1805, only a few weeks after the loss of his son. In another letter written in April to the same gentleman, his cousin, Mr. Muirhead, great uncle of the able and learned translator of M. Arago's 'Eloge,' after expressing his confident hopes that Gregory had changed this mortal state for a far happier existence, he says, as if anxious to avoid all suspicion of his giving way to excessive sorrow, "You are not to conceive that we give way to grief : on the contrary, you will find us as cheerful as we ought to be, and as much disposed to enjoy the friends we have left as ever. But we should approach to brutes if we had no regrets." In this letter he quotes the beautiful lines of Catullus, "Nunc it per iter tenebricosum," &c.

To this evidence at the period of his son's death let me add the testimony of Lord Jeffrey, who knew him well, and who brings down the account to the latest years of his life. "His health, which was deli-cate from his youth upwards, seemed to become firmer as he advanced in years ; and he possessed, up almost to the last moments of his existence, not only the full command of his extraordinary intellect, but all the alacrity of spirit and the social gaiety which had illumined his happiest days. His friends in this part of the country (Edinburgh) never saw him more full of intellectual vigour and colloquial animation, never more delightful or more instructive, than in his last visit in autumn 1817." It was after this period that he invented the machine for copying sculpture. He distributed among his friends some specimens of its performances, jocularly calling them " the productions of a young artist just entering into his eighty-third year."

In the summer of the following year, 1819, I saw him for the last time, and did not observe any change in his conversation or in his manner; but I understand that he suffered some inconvenience through the summer; though, until a few weeks before his death, he was not seriously indisposed. He soon became aware of the event which was approaching, and he seemed only anxious to impress upon his sorrowing family the circumstances calculated to minister consolation under the change which must soon take place. He expressed his sincere gratitude to Divine Providence for the blessings which he had been permitted to enjoy, for his length of days, his exemption from the infirmities of age, the calm and cheerful evening of his life passed after the useful labours of its day had closed. He died on the 25th of August, 1819, in his eighty-fourth year. His remains lie buried in Handsworth church, near his residence of Heathfield, and a statue, the work of Chantrey, is there erected to his memory by his son; and the same filial piety has presented a statue to the College of Glasgow, in grateful recollection of early patronage. But a truly noble monument is raised to him in West-

minster Abbey, by the genius of Chantrey, at the
expense of the Sovereign and of many Peers and
distinguished Commoners, who held a meeting in
honour of this illustrious man and great public benefactor. The Ministers of the Crown, and the chiefs
of the opposition in either House of Parliament, the
most eminent men of science, the most distinguished
cultivators of the arts, assembled with this view, and
the account of their proceedings was made public in an
authentic form. The Prime Minister, Lord Liver-
pool, presided; and it was none of the least remarkable
passages of that day, that his successor, the present
Premier, was anxious to declare the obligation under
which he lay to the genius of him they were comme-
morating, the fortunes of his family being reared by
manufacturing industry, founded upon the happy
inventions of Arkwright and Watt. It has ever
been reckoned by me one of the chief honours of my
life, that I was called upon to pen the inscription upon
the noble monument thus nobly reared.

The chisel of Chantrey, whose greatest work this
certainly is, has admirably presented the features of the
countenance at once deeply meditative and calmly
placid, but betokening power rather than delicacy and
refinement. The civilized world is filled with imperishable records of his genius, and the grateful
recollection of the whole species embalms his memory.
But for this, the author of the epitaph might well feel
how inadequately his feeble pen had performed its office
in attempting to pourtray such excellence : how much
more inadequately when its lines are traced in most
disadvantageous contrast with the signal success of the
sculptor ! He who has ever made the attempt to write

with a chisel in our language, little lapidary as it certainly is, will comprehend the extraordinary difficulties of the task, and will show mercy to the failure:—

NOT TO PERPETUATE A NAME
WHICH MUST ENDURE WHILE THE PEACEFUL ARTS FLOURISH
BUT TO SHEW
THAT MANKIND HAVE LEARNED TO HONOUR THOSE
WHO BEST DESERVE THEIR GRATITUDE
THE KING
HIS MINISTERS AND MANY OF THE NOBLES
AND COMMONERS OF THE REALM
RAISED THIS MONUMENT TO
JAMES WATT
WHO DIRECTING THE FORCE OF AN ORIGINAL GENIUS
EARLY EXERCISED IN PHILOSOPHIC RESEARCH
TO THE IMPROVEMENT OF
THE STEAM ENGINE
ENLARGED THE RESOURCES OF HIS COUNTRY
INCREASED THE POWER OF MAN
AND ROSE TO AN EMINENT PLACE
AMONG THE MOST ILLUSTRIOUS FOLLOWERS OF SCIENCE
AND THE REAL BENEFACTORS OF THE WORLD
BORN AT GREENOCK MDCCXXXVI
DIED AT HEATHFIELD IN STAFFORDSHIRE MDCCCXIX.

We have been considering this eminent person as yet only in his public capacity, as a benefactor of mankind by his fertile genius and indomitable perseverance; and the best portraiture of his intellectual character was to be found in the description of his attainments. It is, however, proper to survey him also in private life. He was unexceptionable in all its relations; and as his activity was unmeasured, and his taste anything rather than fastidious, he both was master of every variety of knowledge, and was tolerant of discussion on subjects of very subordinate importance compared with those on which he most excelled. Not

only all the sciences from the mathematics and astronomy, down to botany, received his diligent attention,
but he was tolerably read in the lighter kinds of
literature, delighting in poetry and other works of
fiction, full of the stores of ancient literature, and
readily giving himself up to the critical disquisitions
of commentators, and to discussions on the fancies of
etymology. His manners were most attractive from
their perfect nature and simplicity. His conversation
was rich in the measure which such stores and such
easy taste might lead us to expect, and it astonished all
listeners with its admirable precision, with the extraordinary memory it displayed, with the distinctness it
seemed to have, as if his mind had separate niches for
keeping each particular, and with its complete rejection
of all worthless and superfluous matter, as if the same
mind had some fine machine for acting like a fan,
casting off the chaff and the husk. But it had besides
a peculiar charm from the pleasure he took in conveying information where he was peculiarly able to give
it, and in joining with entire candour whatever
discussion happened to arise. Even upon matters on
which he was entitled to pronounce with absolute
authority, he never laid down the law, but spoke like
any other partaker of the conversation. You might observe him, however, with his pencil in his hand, ready to
prove what might require explanation, and he was an
adventurous disputant who would not rather see his intellect play in illustrations than descend with demon-
strative force. He was ever in pursuit of truth or the
gratification of a rational curiosity, and this attempered
as well as guided his talk. If he seemed occasionally to
be moved beyond the interest thus excited, it was when

he perceived any thing uncandid or unfair, or, above all, indirect and dishonest. The attempts of one man to appropriate another's inventive merit were the things that most roused his indignation; for, regarding discovery and invention as the most precious of all property, he could not bear the sight of its violation, and would stop minutely and curiously to ascertain the relative shares of different individuals, when any doubt was raised upon the distribution. His conversation was withal spirited and lively—it was easy and concise, and without the least of a lecturing formality. His voice was deep and low, and if somewhat monotonous, it yet seemed in harmony with the weight and the beauty of his discourse, through which however there also ran a current of a lighter kind; for he was mirthful, temperately jocular, nor could anything to more advantage set off the living anecdotes of men and things, with which the graver texture of his talk was interwoven, than his sly and quiet humour, both of mind and of look, in recounting them. No one who had the happiness of knowing him, no member, more especially, of the club in Edinburgh which he frequented as often as he visited that capital, can ever forget the zest which his society derived from the mixture of such various matters as those to which I have referred; and one of its most distinguished founders * has justly

---

* Lord Jeffrey. The club was called from the day, Friday, on which it met at supper, after the business of the week was over, and the half-holiday of Saturday only lightly hanging over the heads of the lawyers, who chiefly composed it. Mr. Watt was an honorary member. He had for his colleagues no less distinguished men than Professor Playfair, Sir Walter Scott, Lord Corehouse, Mr. Horner, Mr. Elmsley, Sir W. Drummond, and several who still survive and fill exalted places in the State.

said, that in no other person was there ever observed so "fine an expression of reposing strength and uninterrupted self-possession as marked his whole manner."

APPENDIX.

HISTORICAL NOTE ON THE DISCOVERY OF THE THEORY OF THE COMPOSITION OF WATER.

THERE can be no doubt whatever, that the experiment of Mr. Warltire, related in Dr. Priestley's fifth volume,* gave rise to this inquiry, at least in England; Mr. Cavendish expressly

---

* Mr. Warltire's letter is dated Birmingham, 18th April, 1781, and was published by Dr. Priestley in the Appendix to the seventh volume of his 'Experiments and Observations relating to various branches of Natural Philosophy; with a continuation of the Observations on Air,'—forming, in fact, the fifth volume of his 'Experiments and Observations on different kinds of Air;' printed at Birmingham in 1781.

Mr. Warltire's first experiments were made in a copper ball or flask, which held three wine pints, the weight 14 ounces; and his object was to determine " whether heat is heavy or not." After stating his mode of mixing the airs, and of adjusting the balance, he says, he " always accurately balanced the flask of common air, then found the difference of weight after the inflammable air was introduced, that he might be certain he had confined the proper proportion of each. The electric spark having passed through them, the flask became hot, and was cooled by exposing it to the common air of the room: it was then hung up again to the balance, and a loss of weight was always found, but not constantly the same; upon an average it was two grains."

He goes on to say, " I have fired air in glass vessels since I saw you (Dr. Priestley) venture to do it, and I have observed, *as you did*, that, though the glass was clean and dry before, yet, after firing the air, it became dewy, and was lined with a sooty substance."

It

refers to it, as having set him upon making his experiments.—
(Phil. Trans. 1784, p. 126.) The experiment of Mr. Warltire
consisted in firing, by electricity, a mixture of inflammable
and common air in a close vessel, and two things were said to
be observed: *first*, a sensible loss of weight; *second*, a dewy
deposit on the sides of the vessel.

Mr. Watt, in a note to p. 332 of his paper, Phil. Trans.
1784, inadvertently states, that the dewy deposit was first
observed by Mr. Cavendish; but Mr. Cavendish himself,
p. 127, expressly states Mr. Warltire to have observed it, and
cites Dr. Priestley's fifth volume.

Mr. Cavendish himself could find no loss of weight, and he
says that Dr. Priestley had also tried the experiment, and
found none.* But Mr. Cavendish found there was always a
dewy deposit, without any sooty matter. The result of many
trials was, that common air and inflammable air being burnt
together, in the proportion of 1000 measures of the former to
423 of the latter, "about one-fifth of the common air, and
nearly all the inflammable air, lose their elasticity, and *are
condensed into the dew* which lines the glass." He examined the
dew, and found it to be pure water. He therefore concludes,
that "almost all the inflammable air, and about one-sixth of
the common air, are turned into pure water."

Mr. Cavendish then burned, in the same way, dephlogisticated and inflammable airs (oxygen and hydrogen gases),
and the deposit was always more or less acidulous, accordingly as the air burnt with the inflammable air was more or
less phlogisticated. The acid was found to be nitrous. Mr.
Cavendish states, that "almost the whole of the inflammable
and dephlogisticated air *is converted into pure water;*" and,
again, that "if these airs could be obtained perfectly pure, the

---

It seems evident that neither Mr. Warltire nor Dr. Priestley
attributed the dew to anything else than a mechanical deposit of
the moisture suspended in common air.—[NOTE BY MR. JAMES
WATT.]

* Mr. Cavendish's note, p. 127, would seem to imply this; but I
have not found in any of Dr. Priestley's papers that he has said so.
—[NOTE BY MR. JAMES WATT.]

whole would be condensed." And he accounts for common
air and inflammable air, when burnt together, not producing
acid, by supposing that the heat produced is not sufficient.
He then says that these experiments, with the exception of
what relates to the acid, were made in the summer of 1781,
and mentioned to Dr. Priestley; and adds, that " a friend of
his (Mr. Cavendish's), last summer (that is, 1783), gave some
account of them to M. Lavoisier, as well as of the conclusion drawn from them, that dephlogisticated air is only water
deprived of its phlogiston; but, at that time, so far was M.
Lavoisier from thinking any such opinion warranted, that till
he was prevailed upon to repeat the experiment himself, he
found some difficulty in believing that nearly the whole of
the two airs could be converted into water." The friend is
known to have been Dr., afterwards Sir Charles Blagden;
and it is a remarkable circumstance, that this passage of Mr.
Cavendish's paper appears not to have been in it when originally presented to the Royal Society; for the paper is apparently in Mr. Cavendish's hand, and the paragraph, p. 134,
135, is not found in it, but is added to it, and directed to be
inserted in that place. It is, moreover, not in Mr. Cavendish's
hand, but in Sir Charles Blagden's; and, indeed, the latter
must have given him the information as to M. Lavoisier,
with whom it is not said that Mr. Cavendish had any correspondence. The paper itself was read 15th January, 1784.
The volume was published about six months afterwards.

M. Lavoisier's memoir (in the Mém. de l'Académie des
Sciences for 1781) had been read partly in November and
December 1783, and additions were afterwards made to it. It
was published in 1784. It contained M. Lavoisier's account
of his experiments in June 1783, at which, he says, Sir
Charles Blagden was present; and it states that he told M.
Lavoisier of Mr. Cavendish having " already burnt inflammable air in close vessels, and obtained a very sensible quantity
of water." But he, M. Lavoisier, says nothing of Sir Charles
Blagden having also mentioned Mr. Cavendish's conclusion
from the experiment. He expressly states, that the weight of
the water was equal to that of the two airs burnt, unless the
heat and light which escape are ponderable, which he hold

them not to be. His account, therefore, is not reconcilable with Sir Charles Blagden's, and the latter was most probably written as a contradiction of it, after Mr. Cavendish's paper had been read, and when the Mémoires of the Académie were received in this country. These Mémoires were published in 1784, and could not, certainly, have arrived when Mr. Cavendish's paper was written, nor when it was read to the Royal Society.

But it is further to be remarked, that this passage of Mr. Cavendish's paper in Sir Charles Blagden's handwriting, only mentions the experiments having been communicated to Dr. Priestley; they were made, says the passage, in 1781, and communicated to Dr. Priestley; it is not said when, nor is it said that " the conclusions drawn from them," and which Sir Charles Blagden says he communicated to M. Lavoisier in summer 1783, were ever communicated to Dr. Priestley; and Dr. Priestley, in his paper (referred to in Mr. Cavendish's), which was read June 1783, and written before April of that year, says nothing of Mr. Cavendish's theory, though he mentions his experiment.

Several propositions then are proved by this statement.

First, That Mr. Cavendish, in his paper, read 15th January, 1784, relates te capital experiment of burning oxygen and hydrogen gases in a close vessel, and finding pure water to be the produce of the combustion.

Secondly, That, in the same paper, he drew from this experiment the conclusion that the two gases were converted or turned into water.

Thirdly, That Sir Charles Blagden inserted in the same paper, with Mr. Cavendish's consent, a statement that the experiment had first been made by Mr. Cavendish in summer 1781, and mentioned to Dr. Priestley, though it is not said when, nor is it said that any conclusion was mentioned to Dr. Priestley, nor is it said at what time Mr. Cavendish first drew that conclusion. *A most material omission.*

Fourthly, That in that addition made to the paper by Sir Charles Blagden, he conclusion of Mr. Cavendish is stated to be, that oxygen gas is water deprived of phlogiston; this addition having been made after M. Lavoisier's memoir arrived in England.

It may further be observed, that in another addition to the paper, which is also in Sir C. Blagden's handwriting, and which was certainly made after M. Lavoisier's memoir had arrived, Mr. Cavendish for the first time distinctly states, as upon M. Lavoisier's hypothesis, that water consisted of hydrogen united to oxygen gas. There is no substantial difference, perhaps, between this and the conclusion stated to have been drawn by Mr. Cavendish himself, that oxygen gas is water deprived of phlogiston, supposing phlogiston to be synonymous with hydrogen; but the former proposition is certainly the more distinct and unequivocal of the two: and it is to be observed that Mr. Cavendish, in the original part of the paper, *i. e.* the part read January 1784, before the arrival of Lavoisier's, considers it more just to hold inflammable air to be phlogisticated water than pure phlogiston (p. 140).

We are now to see what Mr. Watt did; and the dates here become very material. It appears that he wrote a letter to Dr. Priestley on 26th April, 1783, in which he reasons on the experiment of burning the two gases in a close vessel, and draws the conclusion, " that water is composed of dephlogisticated air and phlogiston, deprived of part of their latent heat."* The letter was received by Dr. Priestley and delivered to Sir Joseph Banks, with a request that it might be read to the Royal Society; but Mr. Watt afterwards desired this to be delayed, in order that he might examine some new experiments of Dr. Priestley, so that it was not read until the 22d April, 1784. In the interval between the delivery of

---

* It may with certainty be concluded from Mr. Watt's private and unpublished letters, of which the copies taken by his copying-machine, then recently invented, are preserved, that his theory of the composition of water was already formed in December 1782, and probably much earlier. Dr. Priestley, in his paper of 21st April, 1783, p. 416, states, that Mr. Watt, prior to his (the Doctor's) experiments, had entertained the idea of the possibility of the conversion of water or steam into permanent air. And Mr. Watt himself, in his paper, Phil. Trans., p. 335, asserts, that for many years he had entertained the opinion that air was a modification of water, and he enters at some length into the facts and reasoning upon which that deduction was founded.—[Note by Mr. James Watt.]

this letter to Dr. Priestley, and the reading of it, Mr. Watt had addressed another letter to M. de Luc, dated 26th November, 1783,* with many further observations and reasonings, but almost the whole of the original letter is preserved in this, and is distinguished by inverted commas. One of the passages thus marked is that which has the important conclusion above mentioned; and that letter is stated, in the subsequent one, to have been communicated to several members of the Royal Society at the time of its reaching Dr. Priestley, viz. April, 1783.

In Mr. Cavendish's paper as at first read, no allusion is to be found to Mr. Watt's theory; but in an addition made in Sir C. Blagden's own hand, after Mr. Watt's paper had been

---

* The letter was addressed to M. J. A. de Luc, the well-known Genevese philosopher, then a Fellow of the Royal Society, and Reader to Queen Charlotte. He was the friend of Mr. Watt, who did not then belong to the Society. M. de Luc, following the motions of the Court, was not always in London, and seldom attended the meetings of the Royal Society. He was not present when Mr. Cavendish's paper of 15th January, 1784, was read; but, hearing of it from Dr. Blagden, he obtained a loan of it from Mr. Cavendish, and writes to Mr. Watt on the 1st March following, to apprise him of it, adding that he has perused it, and promising an analysis. In the postscript he states, " In short, they expound and prove your system, word for word, and say nothing of you." The promised analysis is given in another letter of the 4th of the same month. Mr. Watt replies on the 6th, with all the feelings which a conviction he had been ill-treated was calculated to inspire, and makes use of those vivid expressions which M. Arago has quoted; he states his intention of being in London in the ensuing week, and his opinion, that the reading of his letter to the Royal Society will be the proper step to be taken. He accordingly went there, waited upon the President of the Royal Society, Sir Joseph Banks, was received with all the courtesy and just feeling which distinguished that most honourable man; and it was settled that both the letter to Dr. Priestley of 26th April, 1783, and that to M. de Luc of 26th November, 1783, should be successively read. The former was done on the 22d, and the latter on the 29th April, 1784.—[NOTE BY MR. JAMES WATT.]

read, there is a reference to that theory (Phil. Trans. 1784, p. 140), and Mr. Cavendish's reasons are given for not encumbering his theory with that part of Mr. Watt's which regards the evolution of latent heat. It is thus left somewhat doubtful, whether Mr. Cavendish had ever seen the letter of April 1783, or whether he had seen only the paper (of 26th November, 1783) of which that letter formed a part, and which was read 29th April, 1784. That the first letter was for some time (two months, as appears from the papers of Mr. Watt) in the hands of Sir Joseph Banks and other members of the Society, during the preceding spring, is certain, from the statements in the note to p. 330; and that Sir Charles Blagden, the Secretary, should not have seen it, seems impossible; for Sir Joseph Banks must have delivered it to him at the time when it was intended to be read at one of the Society's meetings (Phil. Trans., p. 330, Note), and, as the letter itself remains among the Society's Records, in the same volume with the paper into which the greater part of it was introduced, it must have been in the custody of Sir C. Blagden. It is equally difficult to suppose, that the person who wrote the remarkable passage already referred to, respecting Mr. Cavendish's conclusions having been communicated to M. Lavoisier in the summer of 1783 (that is, in June), should not have mentioned to Mr. Cavendish that Mr. Watt had drawn the same conclusion in the spring of 1783 (that is, in April at the latest). For the conclusions are identical, with the single difference, that Mr. Cavendish calls dephlogisticated air, water deprived of its phlogiston, and Mr. Watt says that water is composed of dephlogisticated air and phlogiston.

We may remark, there is the same uncertainty or vagueness introduced into Mr. Watt's theory, which we before observed in Mr. Cavendish's, by the use of the term Phlogiston, without exactly defining it. Mr. Cavendish leaves it uncertain, whether or not he meant by phlogiston simply inflammable air, and he inclines rather to call inflammable air, water united to phlogiston. Mr. Watt says expressly, even in his later paper (of November 1783), and in a passage not to be found in the letter of April 1783, that he thinks that inflammable air contains a small quantity of water, and much elementary heat. It must be admitted that such expressions as these on the part of both of those great men, betoken a certain hesitation respecting the theory of the composition of water. If they had ever formed to themselves the idea, that water is a compound of the two gases deprived of their latent heat,—that is, of the two gases,—with the same distinctiveness which marks M. Lavoisier's statement of the theory, such obscurity and uncertainty would have been avoided.

Several further propositions may now be stated, as the result of the facts regarding Mr. Watt.

First, That there is no evidence of any person having reduced the theory of composition to writing, in a shape which now remains, so early as Mr. Watt.

Secondly, That he states the theory, both in April and November 1783, in language somewhat more distinctly referring to composition than Mr. Cavendish does in 1784, and that his reference to the evolution of latent heat renders it more distinct than Mr. Cavendish's.

Thirdly, That there is no proof, nor even any assertion, of Mr. Cavendish's theory (what Sir C. Blagden calls his conclusion) having been communicated to Dr. Priestley before Mr. Watt stated his theory in 1783, still less of Mr. Watt having heard of it, while his whole letter shows that he never had been aware of it, either from Dr. Priestley, or from any other quarter.

Fourthly, That Mr. Watt's theory was well known among the members of the Society, some months before Mr. Cavendish's statement appears to have been reduced into writing, and eight months before it was presented to the Society. We may, indeed, go further, and affirm, as another deduction from the facts and dates, that as far as the evidence goes, there is proof of Mr. Watt having first drawn the conclusion, at least that no proof exists of any one having drawn it so early as he is proved to have done.

Lastly, That a reluctance to give up the doctrine of phlogiston, a kind of timidity on the score of that long-established and deeply rooted opinion, prevented both Mr. Watt and Mr. Cavendish from doing full justice to their own theory; while

M. Lavoisier, who had entirely shaken off these trammels, first presented the new doctrine in its entire perfection and consistency.

All three may have made the important step nearly at the same time, and unknown to each other; the step, namely, of concluding from the experiment, that the two gases entered into combination, and that water was the result; for this, with more or less of distinctness, is the inference which all three drew.

But there is the statement of Sir Charles Blagden, to show that M. Lavoisier had heard of Mr. Cavendish's drawing this inference before his (M. Lavoisier's) capital experiment was made; and it appears that M. Lavoisier, after Sir C. Blagden's statement had been embodied in Mr. Cavendish's paper and made public, never gave any contradiction to it in any of his subsequent memoirs which are to be found in the Mémoires de l'Académie, though his own account of that experiment, and of what then passed, is inconsistent with Sir Charles Blagden's statement.

But there is not any assertion at all, even from Sir C. Blagden, zealous for Mr. Cavendish's priority as he was, that Mr. Watt had ever heard of Mr. Cavendish's theory before he formed his own.

Whether or not Mr. Cavendish had heard of Mr. Watt's theory previous to drawing his conclusions, appears more doubtful. The supposition that he had so heard, rests on the improbability of his (Sir Charles Blagden's) and many others knowing what Mr. Watt had done, and not communicating it to Mr. Cavendish, and on the omission of any assertion in Mr. Cavendish's paper, even in the part written by Sir C. Blagden with the view of claiming priority as against M. Lavoisier, that Mr. Cavendish had drawn his conclusion before April 1783, although in one of the additions to that paper reference is made to Mr. Watt's theory.

As great obscurity hangs over the material question at what time Mr. Cavendish first drew the conclusion from his experiment, it may be as well to examine what that great man's habit was in communicating his discoveries to the Royal Society.

A Committee of the Royal Society, with Mr. Gilpin the clerk, made a series of experiments on the formation of nitrous acid, under Mr. Cavendish's direction, and to satisfy those who had doubted his theory of its composition, first given accidentally in the paper of January 1784, and afterwards more fully in another paper, June 1785. Those experiments occupied from the 6th December, 1787, to 19th March, 1788, and Mr. Cavendish's paper upon them was read 17th April, 1788. It was, therefore, written and printed within a month of the experiments being concluded.

Mr. Kirwan answered Mr. Cavendish's paper (of 15th January, 1784) on water, in one which was read 5th February, 1784, and Mr. Cavendish replied in a paper read 4th March, 1784.

Mr. Cavendish's experiments on the density of the earth were made from the 5th August, 1797, to the 27th May, 1798. The paper upon that subject was read 27th June, 1798.

The account of the eudiometer was communicated at apparently a greater interval; at least the only time mentioned in the account of the experiments is the latter half of 1781, and the paper was read January 1783. It is, however, probable, from the nature of the subject, that he made further trials during the year 1782.

That Mr. Watt formed his theory during the few months or weeks immediately preceding April 1783, seems probable.* It is certain that he considered the theory as his own, and makes no reference to any previous communication from any one upon the subject, nor of having ever heard of Mr. Cavendish drawing the same conclusion.

The improbability must also be admitted to be extreme, of Sir Charles Blagden ever having heard of Mr. Cavendish's theory prior to the date of Mr. Watt's letter, and not mentioning that circumstance in the insertion which he made in Mr. Cavendish's paper.

---

* That the idea existed in his mind previously, is proved by his declarations to Dr. Priestley, cited by the latter; by his own assertions, p. 335 of his paper; and by the existing copies of his letters in December 1782.—[NOTE BY MR. JAMES WATT.]

It deserves to be farther mentioned, that Mr. Watt left the correction of the press, and every thing relating to the publishing of his paper, to Sir Charles Blagden. A letter remains from him to that effect, written to Sir Charles Blagden, and Mr. Watt never saw the paper until it was printed.

Since M. Arago's learned Eloge was published, with this paper as an Appendix, the Rev. W. Vernon Harcourt has entered into controversy with us both, or, I should rather say, with M. Arago, for he has kindly spared me ; and while I express my obligations for this courtesy of my reverend, learned, and valued friend, I must express my unqualified admiration of his boldness in singling out for his antagonist my illustrious colleague, rather than the far weaker combatant against whom he might so much more safely have done battle. Whatever might have been his fate had he taken the more prudent course, I must fairly say (even without waiting until my fellow champion seal our adversary's doom), that I have seldom seen any two parties more unequally matched, or any disputation in which the victory was so complete. The attack on M. Arago might have passed well enough at a popular meeting at Birmingham, before which it was spoken ; but as a scientific inquirer, it would be a flattery running the risk of seeming ironical to weigh the reverend author against the most eminent philosopher of the day, although upon a question of evidence (which this really is, as well as a scientific discussion) I might be content to succumb before him. As a strange notion, however, seems to pervade this paper, that everything depends on the character of Mr. Cavendish, it may be as well to repeat the disclaimer already very distinctly made of all intention to cast the slightest doubt upon that great man's perfect good faith in the whole affair ; I never having supposed that he borrowed from Mr. Watt, though M. Arago, Professor Robison,[*] and Sir H. Davy, as well as myself, have always

---

* Encyc. Brit., vol. xviii., p. 808. This able and learned article enters at length into the proofs of Mr. Watt's claims, and it was published in 1797, thirteen years before Mr. Cavendish's death.

been convinced that Mr. Watt had, unknown to him, anticipated his great discovery. It is also said by Mr. Harcourt that the late Dr. Henry having examined Mr. Watt's manuscripts decided against his priority. I have Dr. H.'s letter before me of June, 1820, stating most clearly, most fully, and most directly, the reverse, and deciding in Mr. Watt's favour. I must add, having read the full publication with fac-similes, Mr. Harcourt has now clearly proved one thing, and it is really of some importance. He has made it appear that in all Mr. Cavendish's diaries and notes of his experiments, not an intimation occurs of the composition of water having been inferred by him from those experiments earlier than Mr. Watt's paper of spring, 1783.

PRIESTLEY.

MENTION has already been more than once made of Dr. Priestley; and certainly history would imperfectly perform its office of recording the progress of natural knowledge should it pass over his important discoveries without the large share of attention and of praise which they are well entitled to claim. In turning, however, to recount the events of his life, we make a somewhat painful transition from contemplating in its perfection the philosophic character, to follow the course of one who united in his own person the part of the experimental inquirer after physical truth with that of the angry polemic and the fiery politician, leading sometimes the life of a sage, though never perhaps free from rooted and perverted prejudice—sometimes that of a zealot against received creeds and established institutions, and in consequence of his intemperance, alternately the exciter and the victim of persecution. Nevertheless, the services which he rendered in the former and better capacity, ought to be held in grateful remembrance by the cultivators of physical science. Nor are we to suppose that even in his polemical capacity he was not in pursuit of truth. He may have had a tendency to oppose established opinions; a disposition which led him, as he says himself, at the

age of twenty "to embrace what is generally called the heterodox side of every question,"* just as he had a disposition pertinaciously to keep by the received and erroneous chemical theory ; but if he thought for himself, and followed the bent of his convictions, we have no right to doubt his conscientious motives, the more especially as his heterodox dogmas, always manfully avowed, never brought him anything but vexation and positive injury in his temporal concerns. The pertinacity with which he defended to the end of his days the chemical doctrine of Phlogiston, and the equal zeal with which he attacked the theological tenets of original sin and the atonement, alike proceeded from sincere conviction, and no one has a right to blame him for either of these opinions, even if it be quite clear that he was wrong in both.

Joseph Priestley was the son of a cloth-dresser at Birstal-Fieldhead, near Leeds, and was born there 13th of March (old style), 1733. His family appear to have been in humble circumstances; and he was taken off their hands after the death of his mother by his paternal aunt, with whom he went to live when nine years old, and who sent him to a free school at Batley, in the neighbourhood. There he learnt something of Greek and Latin, and a dissenting minister taught him a little Hebrew in the vacation of the grammar-school. To this he added some knowledge of other Eastern languages connected with Biblical literature ; he made a considerable progress in Syriac and Chaldean, and began to learn Arabic ; he also had a little instruction in the mathematics from a teacher who had been

---

* Works.—Memoirs, vol. i. part i. p. 25.

educated under Maclaurin, at Edinburgh. But in this science he made very little proficiency.* Indeed his whole education was exceedingly imperfect, and excepting in Hebrew and in Greek he never afterwards improved it by any systematic course of study; but in both these languages he became well versed, and especially used always to read the Scriptures in the original tongues. Even in chemistry, which of the sciences he best knew and in which he made so important a figure, he was only half taught; and he himself acknowledged, after having failed to obtain a chemical lectureship, that he "never could have acquitted himself properly in it, never having given much attention to the common routine of the science, and knowing but little of the common processes."—"When I began my experiments," he says, "I knew very little of chemistry, and had in a manner no idea of the subject before I attended a course of lectures at an academy where I taught." So that he was not well-informed, and had never studied either the theoretical or the practical parts of it, but just got possession of such portions of the subject as occasionally came within the scope of the experiments he was making, and the doctrines he was discussing at the time. His whole writings, which are numberless, and without method, or system, or closeness, or indeed clearness, bear ample testimony to what we might expect would be the result of so very imperfect a found-

---

* This is manifest from several parts of his writings, although he in one passage of his correspondence speaks of having once been very fond of the study; for in the same paper he speaks of Baron Maseres' work ('Scriptores Logarithmici') as if he had been the author, instead of the collector.—Mem. i. part ii. p. 490.

ation as his scanty and rambling education had laid. That education, however, far from redounding to his discredit, very greatly enhances the merit of the man. He presents one of the memorable examples of knowledge pursued, science cultivated, and even its bounds extended, by those whose circumstances made their exertions a continued struggle against difficulties which only virtue and genius like theirs could have overcome.

He went to study for some years at the dissenting academy founded by Mr. Coward, at Daventry, and since transferred to London, where it is in a kind of union, mutually beneficial, with the University College. Mr. Ashworth had succeeded the learned and pious Dr. Doddridge as its principal teacher, and under him Priestley remained till 1755. During the three years that he studied here, he and his intimate friends used to make a point of reading, daily, ten pages of Greek, and every week one Greek play, a practice which they continued after they left the school, corresponding with each other on the subject of their studies. On quitting Daventry, having taken orders, he was appointed minister of a congregation at Needham Market, in Suffolk. He had been brought up by his father and aunt in the strictest Calvinistic principles, most of which he very soon from conviction abandoned; and so early did his spirit of free inquiry show itself, that having before he left his aunt's house desired to be admitted as a communicant at the chapel which she attended, he was rejected by the minister on his preparatory examination, in consequence of doubts expressed respecting original sin, and eternal damnation as its punishment. He describes the deep distress into which he was thrown by feeling that he was unable to experience due contrition and repentance for Adam's fault; and the rigid divine who tested the state of his mind on this point, withheld the sacred ordinances in consequence. At Needham his salary did not exceed thirty pounds, indeed it seldom amounted to so much, and he could only subsist by the aid which certain dissenting charities afforded to augment this poor stipend. His predecessor, Dr. Doddridge, had never received above thirty-five pounds a-year, and his board then (1723) only cost him ten pounds. Priestley's opinions proved distasteful to the congregation, who probably regarded the eternity of hell-torments as a peculiar privilege rudely invaded by him; and he removed in 1758 to Nantwich, in Cheshire, where he obtained some thirty pupils, beside a few young ladies and a private tutorship in an attorney's family. This increased his income, and enabled him, by means of the strictest frugality, to purchase a scanty apparatus; for he had now added a little natural philosophy to his favourite theological studies, the fruit of which had been already two works, one of them against the atonement. I say a little natural philosophy; for he confesses that when nine years later he began to write his 'History of Electricity,' he was but imperfectly acquainted with the subject. It is a careless and superficial work, hastily written, as is his 'History of Vision;' and the original experiments afforded no new information of any value. In 1761 he removed to Warrington Academy, in which he succeeded Dr. Aikin as tutor in the belles lettres. On settling at Warrington he married the daughter of Mr. Wilkinson, a respectable iron master in Wales.

She was an amiable woman, and endowed with great strength of mind, which was destined afterwards to be severely tried. By her he had several children, one of whom survived them both.

He appears to have chiefly devoted himself to theological studies, and hence the great disproportion which his Hebrew and Greek learning bears to his other acquirements. Metaphysical speculations, next to these, engaged his attention; and the influence produced in his mind, and even his conduct, by Dr. Hartley's celebrated work ('Observations on Man'), has been recorded by himself. " I hardly know," he says, " whether it more enlightens the understanding or improves the heart." He says he also had studied composition, and mainly by the help of writing poetry, of no merit, but according to him the best means of learning to write good prose. That his taste, however, was somewhat deficient in this respect we may fairly affirm, when we find him pronouncing, many years after, a decided opinion that Belsham's 'History' is written in a better style than Robertson's or Hume's.* The universality of his attempts may be judged from his delivering at Warrington a course of lectures on anatomy. He sought relaxation from music, and learnt to play on the flute. He strongly recommends this to students, especially, he says with some naïveté, such as have no fine ear, " for they will be the less annoyed by bad music."

As early as during his education at Daventry he had written a work which, however, was not published till twenty years later; it was the 'Institutes of

---

* Mem. and Cor. 1796, vol. i. part ii. p. 358.

Natural and Revealed Religion.' But having once
begun to publish in 1761, his appeals to the press were
incessant, and on almost every subject. A 'Theory
of Language,' books on 'Oratory and Criticism,' on
'History and General Policy,' on the 'Constitution and
Laws of England,' on 'Education,' a 'Chart of Biography,' a 'Chart of History;' these and others were
all written while he resided at Warrington, from 1761
to 1769. How well he was qualified to write on
oratory and on English law, we may easily conjecture,
from the circumstance that he could never have heard
any speaking save in the pulpits of meeting-houses, and
in all probability had never seen a cause tried; but even
if he had been present at debates and trials, it is difficult
to imagine anything more adventurous than the tutor
of an academy, afflicted with an incurable stutter, and
who devoted his time to teaching and to theology, pro-
mulgating rules of eloquence and of jurisprudence to
the senators and lawyers of his country. That we may
come without interruption to his really useful studies,
it may be well here to take notice of his other controversial writings. In consequence of a disagreement with
the Warrington trustees in 1767 he removed to Leeds,
where he became minister of the Mill-Hill chapel,
and wrote many controversial books and pamphlets
In after times he wrote 'Letters to a Philosophical
Institution;' 'An Answer to Gibbon;' 'Disquisitions
on Matter and Spirit;' 'Corruptions of Christianity;'
'Early Opinions on Christ;' 'Familiar Letters to the
Inhabitants of Birmingham;' 'Two Different Histories of the Christian Church;' 'On Education;' 'Comparison of Heathen and Christian Philosophy;' 'Doc-

trine of Necessity;' 'On the Roman Catholic Claims;' 'On the French Revolution;' 'On the American War;' beside twenty volumes of tracts in favour of the Dissenters and their rights. His general works fill twenty-five volumes,* of which only five or six are on scientific subjects: his publications being in all one hundred and forty-one (in one year ten), of which only seventeen are on scientific matters. He is one of the most voluminous writers of any age or country, and probably he is of all voluminous writers the one who has the fewest readers. This arises from the circumstance that, though his political opinions are shared by many, the bulk of his works are theological and metaphysical, but especially theological; and his religious opinions were confined to an extremely small class of persons. Indeed it may be questioned if he was not in several respects the only person who held his peculiar faith upon all points.

It happened, fortunately, that when he went to reside at Leeds in care of the Mill-Hill Chapel, his house immediately adjoined a common brewery, and this led him to make experiments upon the fixed air copiously produced during the process of fermentation. It must be observed, that long before this time the great step had been made by Black of ascertaining that there are other permanently elastic fluids than our atmosphere, and which have properties wholly different from it. Cavendish, too, had very recently subjected both fixed and inflammable airs (carbonic acid and

---

* Edited by the affectionate care of an able and worthy man, Mr. Towell Rutt.

hydrogen gases) to accurate experiments, showing
their relative specific gravities, and proving that they
were of the same nature from what bodies soever
they were obtained.   The probability was, that other
gaseous fluids existed in nature as well as those two
and common air.   The experimenter had, therefore,
thenceforth, his attention directed to meeting with
these: and an examination of all the products of
mixture and of heat, by precipitation or evaporation,
was now the natural course of experimental inquiry.
At first, Priestley only tried in what way fixed air
could be most easily combined with water; he published in 1772 a pamphlet upon the means of
effecting this union, and the condensing process which
he employed is used to this day.   He soon after gave
to the Royal Society his observations on different kinds
of air, which ascertained the important fact, that atmospheric air, after having been corrupted by the respiration of animals or by the burning of inflammable
bodies, is restored to salubrity by the vegetation of
plants; and that if the air is exposed to a mixture of
sulphur and iron filings, as in one of Hales's experiments, its bulk is diminished between a fourth and
a fifth, and the residue is both lighter than common
air and unfit to support life.   This residue he called
' Phlogistic air;' afterwards it was called ' Azotic ' or
' Nitrogen gas;' and Dr. Rutherford, of Edinburgh,
as well as Priestley, though unknown to each other,
discovered it about the same time.   For these experiments the Copley Medal was, in 1773, justly awarded
to him by the Royal Society.

The following year was destined to be the period

of a discovery most important for science, and truly glorious for its author. Having exposed red-lead, or minium, in a close vessel to the sun's rays concentrated by a burning-glass, he found that an aëriform body, permanently elastic, was evolved, and that this air had the peculiar property of increasing exceedingly the intensity of flame. This gas he called 'dephlogisticated air,' upon the principle that the matter of heat and light, the phlogiston of Stahl, being abstracted from it by the return of the calx to its metallic state, which phlogiston was supposed by that theory to effect, the air had great avidity for phlogiston, and seized it from the inflammable bodies it came in contact with. This most important discovery, which he thus connected with an erroneous theory, was made on the 1st of August, 1774. He afterwards discovered that its absorption by the lungs in the process of respiration gives its red colour to arterial blood, as it was proved to act through the substance of thin bladder; and he found that when plants grow in close vessels, and restore the purity of the air in which a candle has burnt or an animal breathed, they do so by evolving this pure air. The new nomenclature gave it the name of 'oxygen gas,' from the belief then generally entertained that it was the acidifying principle. Later experiments have proved that there is at least one great exception to this in chlorine, formerly called 'oxygenated muriatic acid;' but now found to be wholly without oxygen, and yet to have all the properties of an acid. But, indeed, water itself, and the atmospheric air, having neither of them the nature of acids, are both contrary to the theory; and the fixed alkalis are found to owe their alkaline state and lose their metallic, like other oxides, by uniting with oxygen.

Priestley is the undoubted discoverer of oxygen. He was the first who communicated a knowledge of it to Lavoisier, at Paris, soon after he had made the discovery; nor can anything be more disingenuous than that celebrated person's afterwards affirming that he, Priestley, and Scheele, had all discovered it "about the same time." He never discovered it until Priestley discovered it to him. Bergmann's suppressing in his book all knowledge of the experiments of Black and Cavendish, the former published twenty and the latter eight years before, was bad enough, but not equal to Lavoisier's positive assertion contrary to what must have been his positive knowledge.

This great discovery was far from being the last of its justly celebrated author. He discovered the gases of muriatic, of sulphuric, and of fluoric acids, ammonial gas, and nitrous oxide gas. He also discovered the combination which nitrous gas forms suddenly with oxygen; diminishing the volume of both in proportion to that combination; and he thus invented the method of eudiometry, or the ascertainment of the relative purity of different kinds of atmospheric air.

It must not be forgotten, in considering the great merits of Priestley as an experimentalist, that he had almost to create the apparatus by which his processes were to be performed. He, for the most part, had to construct his instruments with his own hands, or if he employed others, he had to make unskilful workmen form them under his own immediate direction.

His apparatus, however, and his contrivances for collecting, keeping, transferring gaseous bodies, and for exposing substances to their action, were simple and effectual, and they continue to be still used by chemical philosophers without any material improvement. It was fortunate in this respect that he began his pneumatic inquiries with seeking for the means of impregnating water with carbonic acid; this inquiry naturally turned his attention to the contrivance of apparatus and generally of manipulations, serviceable in the examination of bodies whose invisible form and elastic state renders inapplicable to them the machinery of the old laboratory, calculated only for solids and liquids.

The pertinacity with which Priestley clung to the phlogistic theory is marvellous. It might have been expected, that the fact of a combustion leaving the residue, whether of two gases, or of a gas and an inflammable body, exactly equal in weight to the sum of the weights of the bodies burnt and which had disappeared in the process, would have been accepted as a proof that these two bodies had entered into an union, giving out the latent heat which had previously held the gaseous body or bodies in a state of aëriform fluidity. It might, in like manner, have been expected, that when a metal, by absorbing oxygen gas, becomes calcined, and gains in weight precisely the weight of the gas which has disappeared, the calcination should be ascribed to the gas, and that the reproduction of the gas by heat, or by its abstraction by electric affinity for some other body, should be allowed to restore the metallic state by simply severing that

union of the gas and the metal which had changed
it. But nothing could overcome Priestley's repugnance
to give up phlogiston : he adhered to it while he lived ;
he never would believe that water was formed of the
two gaseous bodies whose combustion and disappear-
ance leaves a weight of liquid equal to their joint
weights ; he always imagined that water was held in
suspense by these gases and precipitated on their
disappearing. He never would believe that metals
owe their malleability and lustre to any cause other
than phlogiston, or lose their properties except by
combining with oxygen, which takes the phlogiston
from them. He never would believe that combustion
is anything but the phlogiston leaving the inflammable
body and joining the oxygen ; or that when an acid
is formed by the burning, that acid contains the
oxygen and the combustible base. That his obstinate
unbelief was perfectly disinterested no one can doubt.
The discoverer of oxygen, and of the true cause of respiration, had, of all men, the strongest interest in
assenting to a theory which was wholly founded upon
his own discovery, and which made him the immediate, as Black was the more remote, author of modern
chemical science—made him the philosopher who had
raised the superstructure upon the foundation which
his predecessor had laid.

The merit of Dr. Priestley, as a cultivator of science,
was the activity with which he made experiments—the
watchful attention with which he observed every
phenomenon, following the minutest circumstances of
each process—the versatility with which he prosecuted
each new idea that arose from his trials—his diligence

in recording all the particulars, as if well aware how
much depends in every branch of inductive philosophy
upon allowing no fact to escape, when we are con-
fessedly in search of light, and can never tell how any
given fact may bear on the unknown conclusion to
which our analytical process is leading us. As a
reasoner his powers were far less considerable. He
possessed not the sound judgment, the large circum-
spection, which enables men to weigh the relative value
of either reasons or facts. He was cautious enough and
drew little from his imagination in feigning hypotheses,
if it be not the reasons which he invented from time
to time for the purpose of sustaining the desperate
fortunes of the phlogistic theory, and making the
facts bend to it as they successively arose with a force
capable of shivering it in pieces. But he was also
deficient in the happy sagacity which pierces through
apparent dissimilarity, and ranges things apparently
unlike under the same class—he had not that chas-
tened imagination which can see beyond the fact present
to the senses—in a word, he was much greater as a
collector of new facts than a reasoner upon them—and
his inductive capacity was inferior to his power of ex-
perimenting and of contriving the means of observation.
Perhaps his want of general scientific acquirements,
and his confined knowledge of chemistry, itself contributed to the activity and the boldness with which he
performed novel experiments, while the same defect
impaired his capacity as an inductive philosopher. It
is extremely probable that the strict attention to principle, the methodical systematic spirit which prevailed
over the inquiries of Black and of Cavendish—the

scientific views which directed the contrivance of all
their processes, never leading them to make any trial
without some definite object in view, prevented them
from performing many experiments,—from stooping, as
it were, to try things which Priestley did not disdain
to try from his more empirical turn of mind—what
Mr. Watt, in a letter, calls "his random haphazarding."

In 1779, when Captain Cook was preparing to sail
upon his second voyage, Mr. Banks, who took a great
interest in it from having been engaged in the first,
invited Dr. Priestley to accompany the Captain as astronomer to the expedition. Advantageous terms were
proposed, including a provision for his family. He
entertained the proposal, and then agreed to it ; but
objections were taken by the clerical members of the
Board of Longitude, not to his ignorance of astronomy
and of natural history, but to his Socinian principles in
religion, which one might have supposed could exercise but a limited influence upon his observations of
the stars and of plants. I know not if the same
scientific authorities objected, on like grounds, in the
council of the Royal Society, to receiving papers upon
his chemical discoveries. It is certain that a like influence prevented Professor Playfair from afterwards
proceeding to India, where he had designed to prosecute
his inquiries into the science of the Hindoos. Such
passages stamp the history of a great nation with
indelible infamy in the eyes of the whole world.

In 1773, when his fame had been established by his
first discoveries, and the Royal Society had crowned his
paper with their medal, Priestley accepted an invitation from Lord Shelburne, afterwards first Marquis of

Lansdowne, to fill the place of librarian and philosophic companion, with a salary of 250*l*., reducible to
150*l*. for life should he quit the employment.   An
additional allowance of 40*l*. a-year was given by this
truly munificent patron for the expense of apparatus
and experiments ; homes were provided for his family
in the neighbourhood both of Lord Shelburne's town
and country residence ; nor can anything be easily
conceived more truly gratifying to a man of right
feelings, and of a noble ambition, than the reflection
must have been, that the discovery of oxygen was made
under his roof, and with the funds which his disinterested liberality had provided for his philosophic
guest.   With whatever difference of sentiments statesmen may at any time view Lansdowne House, the
lovers of science to the latest ages will gaze with
veneration on that magnificent pile, careless of its
architectural beauties, but grateful for the light which
its illustrious founder caused to beam from thence over
the whole range of natural knowledge ; and after the
structure shall have yielded to the fate of all human
works, the ground on which it once stood, consecrated
to far other recollections than those of conquest or of
power, will be visited by the pilgrim of philosophy with
a deeper fervour than any that fills the bosom near the
forum or the capitol of ancient Rome.

In 1780 Priestley settled at Birmingham, where he
was chosen minister of the principal Dissenting congregation.   He had left Lansdowne House without
any difference to interrupt the friendship of its inmates ;
and some years afterwards an offer to return, made on
the death of Lord Lansdowne's friends, Dunning and

2 E

Lee, was declined.* A subscription among his friends
furnished the means of prosecuting his experimental
researches; and he declined an offer to obtain for him
a pension from the Government. A shade is cast upon
this passage of his history by the circumstance of the
pecuniary aid which he thus received being only in a
small part rendered necessary for his experimental pursuits. Mr. Parker, the eminent optician, furnished him
for nothing all the instruments made by him, as did Mr.
Wedgwood all his earthenware utensils. Yet we find in
his correspondence a painful thankfulness expressed, in
any thing rather than the language of a philosopher, to
Mrs. Rayner and Mr. Lee, for " seasonable benefactions."
The "apology" which he evidently feels required for
this kind of dependence is not at all confined to the " expense of his philosophical and theological studies;" he
refers also to the education of his children, and to the
expenses of housekeeping occasioned by his reputation.†
It is not invidious to observe that, be a man's celebrity
ever so great, he is not bound to incur any expenses in
keeping hospitality, if these, " exceeding twice his own
income" (and that, with the pension of Lord Lansdowne, not an inconsiderable one), can only be met by
the large " benefactions" of his friends. He names
fifteen who gave him by subscription a yearly allowance, all the while he chose to decline an offer made to

---

* This offer, and Lord Lansdowne's frank declaration that he never
had any fault to find with his guest, entitles us to state that no
quarrel, nor anything like it, had occurred. Nevertheless Priestley's offer to visit his Lordship when he occasionally came to London
was politely declined. Political reasons apparently caused this
refusal.

† Memoirs, vol. i., part i., page 217.

procure a pension from the Government, "wishing to preserve himself independent of every thing connected with the Court." We must on this be content to remark, that different men entertain different notions of independence.

Settled at Birmingham, he continued, however, his controversial writings, and engaged eagerly in conflict with Gibbon upon his celebrated chapters respecting the Early History of Christianity, and with Bishop Horsley upon the Socinian doctrines. In the latter controversy the Episcopal and the Sectarian temperature, both high, were not very unequal; but in the former the minister of the Gospel had all the heat to himself—at least in the layman it was latent, if it existed at all. He was desirous of drawing his adversary into a controversy, and, failing in this, lost his temper, and had the vulgar recourse to calling names and imputing motives. Mr. Gibbon may have shown some superciliousness in his treatment of this angry polemic; but he certainly had a good right to marvel at the intolerance of one whose heterodoxy was so universal as to "condemn by circumscribing the inspiration of the Evangelists, and to condemn the religion of every Christian nation as a fable less innocent, not less absurd, than Mahomet's journey to the third heaven." How fortunate it was that Priestley lived in an age when the use of actual fire is withheld from theological disputants, as a mode of argumentation, must appear from the wonder he expresses at David Hume's monument having been so long suffered to offend the pious eyes of the Edinburgh people—an expression which might seem to convey a hint that he would have taken care to avoid, after he had himself felt the weight of the popular hand when called in to settle theological disputes.

Having taken, as was his wont, an active but not a very temperate part in the controversy to which the French Revolution gave rise, and having published a 'Reply' to Mr. Burke's famous pamphlet, he was early in 1791 made a citizen of the French Republic. An ironical and somewhat bitter pamphlet against the high church party still further excited the feelings of the people against him; and a dinner being given on the 14th of July to celebrate the anniversary of the attack upon the Bastille, the mob attacked the tavern where the party were assembled. Dr. Priestley was not present, but his chapel and house were immediately after assailed. His library, manuscripts, and apparatus were destroyed; his person and his family escaped. The compensation which he obtained, by an action against the hundred, fell short, according to his own account, by 2000*l.* of his loss. As, however, an ample subscription was made for him, and as his brother-in-law generously gave him 10,000*l.*, with an annuity of 200*l.* for life, he could not be other than a large gainer by the execrable violence of which he had been the victim; and as he never allowed any of his writings to remain unpublished for even the shortest time after they were finished, it is not likely that any loss of an irreparable kind was incurred by the burning of his papers. He found, however, that he could no longer reside with comfort in the scene of such outrageous proceedings, and among a community which had so shamefully countenanced

them. He removed to London, and succeeded his
friend, Dr. Price, as Principal of the Hackney
Academy. Late in the month of September, 1792,
he was elected by the department of the Orne a
member of the National Convention, about to assemble
after the subversion of the French monarchy. This
singular honour bestowed on him, as well for his
philosophical fame as for his political services and the
persecutions to which they had exposed him, he re-
spectfully declined, giving as his reason that he was
not familiar with the French language, and had not
devoted his time sufficiently to legislative duties. But
this moderation disarmed not his enemies—he was pursued by the intolerant spirit of the times. He found
himself shunned by his former associates in science.
Even the Royal Society did not afford an exception
to this persecuting loyalty, or a shelter from its effects;
and in the spring of 1794 he withdrew to America.
Here he again suffered considerable disappointment.
His religion was too much for those who had ceased to
care for sacred things, and far too scanty for those who
still were Christians, while his republican opinions
were exceedingly distasteful because they were tinged
with a decided admiration of France. He continued,
however, to inhabit the country, and to prosecute his
studies, chiefly theological. He received contributions
regularly from his benefactors in England, Mrs. Rayner
and the Duke of Grafton; but these, though acknowledged by him in the same unpleasant style as eleemo-
synary ("very acceptable benevolences"), were for the
most part on a different footing from the English

charities ; they appear generally to have been required for the propagation of their Unitarian opinions, to which the parties were all so zealously attached.

He settled at Northumberland, in an uncleared district, where he purchased three hundred acres of land ; and his youngest son, Henry, then a very fine young man of eighteen, devoted himself to the clearing and cultivating this woodland spot, working with his labourers and sharing their toils. The father himself partook of this labour for two or three hours daily. On Sundays he frequently preached, and when he visited Philadelphia he always did so. He devoted the rest of his time to his works, particularly his 'Church History ;' and he wrote answers to Paine and Volney. He was much obstructed in his philosophical pursuits by the want of proper accommodation for his apparatus, and he only wrote three tracts on chemical subjects during the ten years of his residence in America ; two of which were merely arguments on phlogiston, and the third alone had any experiments, written eight years before his death.

At the end of 1795 he suffered a heavy affliction in the death of his son Henry, after a few days' illness ; and in ten months more he also lost his wife. These blows, though he felt their weight, did not at all crush him ; his resignation was exemplary ; and his steady, enthusiastic faith in Revelation gave him a certain hope of meeting before many years should elapse with those whom he had lost. Indeed, his letters clearly show that he regarded the sundering of these ties far less attentively than their restoration. A few

days after his son's death he writes to his most intimate friend and constant correspondent, Theophilus
Lindsay, recounting the particulars of his loss, and he
adds that he is composing three discourses on Revela
tion against modern unbelievers. The letter next year
announcing his wife's death, begins with saying to the
same friend how much he stands in need of his sympathy, and goes on to add, " This day I bury my wife;
she died on Saturday after an illness of a fortnight."
He adds some remarks on his literary occupations, and
concludes with mentioning a plan he has of travelling
to distract his mind.* No one who reads his letters
and memoirs by himself can doubt that this stoical
firmness is not the result of a callous disposition, but
the signal triumph of a heartfelt belief in the promises
of Religion over the weakness of our nature.

It is, indeed, quite manifest that Religion was as
much an active principle in him as in any one who
ever lived. Not only is it always uppermost in his
thoughts, but he even regards temporal concerns of a
public nature always in connexion with the Divine
superintendence, and even with the prophecies of
Scripture. His letters are full of references to those
prophecies as bearing on passing events, and he
plainly says that since his removal to America he
should care little for European events but for their
connexion with the Old Testament. He also looked
for an actual and material second coming of Christ
upon earth.

It is not true to affirm that he was little of a poli-

---

* Mem., vol. i. part ii. p. 328, 354.

tician, though in declining the seat in the National
Convention he says* his studies had been little directed
towards legislation compared with theology and philosophy; and denies in a letter to William Smith that
he ever taught or even mentioned politics to his pupils,
as he had been charged with doing, among the innumerable falsehoods of which he was the subject.   Nor
is the circumstance of his not attending political meetings at all decisive of his being little of a political agi-
tator, because his incurable stutter prevented him from
taking a part in such proceedings.   But he wrote in
1774, at Franklin's request, an address to the people
on the American disputes, previous to the general
election.   He answered Mr. Burke's 'Reflections on
the French Revolution.'   He mixed in the question
of the Catholic claims; and he published in all no less
than eleven political works, almost every one upon the
topics of the day.   It is equally true, however, that
theological controversy occupied him far more constantly and engaged his mind far more deeply than
political matters; that he was regularly a theologian
and incidentally a partisan.

The cast of his political opinions was originally
little more tending to democracy than those of Whigs
usually are who have read and discussed more than
they have reflected and seen.   He used, indeed, to
say that in politics he was a Trinitarian, though a
Unitarian in religion.   It must, however, be confessed
that he went very much further in the same direction
after the French Revolution had set fire to the four

* Mem., vol. i. part ii. p. 190—198.

quarters of the political world, and his admiration of
republican principles might be measured by his zeal for
the innovators of France, with the success of whose
arms he deemed the safety of freedom to be bound up.
When we read his answer to the offer of a seat in 1792,
and reflect that it was penned about three weeks after
the horrible massacres of September, the worst of the
atrocities which disfigured the Revolution, it moves
our wonder to find a Christian minister accompanying
his acknowledgment of the honour proposed, that of
being enrolled among the authors of the tragedy so
recently enacted, with no protest against the bloody
course then pursuing, no exception to the unqualified admiration expressed of the youthful republic.

In America we find his leanings are all against the
Federal party, and his censures of the great Chief of
the Union little concealed. He felt for the demo-
cratic party, the French alliance, the enemies of English partialities, and he regarded Washington as ungrateful because he would not, from a recollection of
the services of France twenty years before to American
independence, consent to make America dependent
upon France. The indifferent reception which he met
with in society was probably owing to this party violence full as much as to the dislike of his Unitarian
opinions. But it must be added, that his temper was
so mild, and his manners so gentle, as to disarm his
most prejudiced adversaries whensoever they came into
his society. Many instances of this are given in his
correspondence, of which one may be cited. He happened to visit a friend whose wife received him in her
husband's absence, but feared to name him before a Cal-

vinistic divine present. By accident his name was mentioned, and the lady then introduced him. But he of
the Genevan school drew back, saying, "Dr. Joseph
Priestley?" and then added in the American tongue,
"I cannot be cordial." Whereupon the Doctor, with
his usual placid demeanour, said that he and the lady
might be allowed to converse until their host should
return. By degrees the conversation became general;
the *repudiator* was won over by curiosity first, then by
gratification; he remained till a late hour hanging
upon Priestley's lips; he took his departure at length,
and told the host as he quitted the house, that never
had he passed so delightful an evening, though he admitted that he had begun it "by behaving like a fool
and a brute." One such anecdote (and there are many
current) is of more force to describe its subject than a
hundred laboured panegyrics.

After the loss of his wife and his younger and
favourite son, he continued with unabated zeal to
pursue his theological studies, and published several
works, both controversial and historical, beside
leaving some which have been given to the world
since his decease. He endeavoured, too, as far as he
could, to propagate the tenets of Unitarianism, and to
collect and extend a congregation at Philadelphia
attached to that doctrine. At one time, in the summer of 1797, entertaining hopes of peace in Europe,
he had resolved to visit France, where he might
communicate personally with his English friends; and
he even thought of making a purchase in that country
on which he might reside during a part of each year.
So nearly did he contemplate this removal, that we

find him desiring the answers to letters he was
writing might be sent to the care of Messrs. Perregaux
at Paris. The revolution of Fructidor, however (4th
September, 1797), put an end to all prospects of peace,
and the war soon raged in every quarter with re-
doubled fury. He seems now to have derived his chief
comfort from tracing the fancied resemblance between
the events passing before him and the prophecies in
Scripture; though occasionally he felt much puzzled,
and the book of Daniel, especially, appears to have
given him trouble and perplexity. When the peace
came at last, his health was too much broken to
permit any plans to be executed such as he had four
years before contemplated.

In 1802 he became a confirmed invalid, suffering from internal, and apparently organic, derange-
ment. His illness was long and lingering, and he
suffered great pain with perfect patience for two
years. The prospect of death which he had before
him did not relax his application to literary labour,
his faculties remaining entire to the last. Neither did
that awful certainty, ever present to his mind, affect
him with sorrow or dismay. The same unshaken
belief in a future state, the same confident hope of
immortal life which had supported him under his
affliction for the death of others, cheered him while
contemplating the approach of his own. In this
happy frame of mind he gently expired on the 6th of
February, 1804, in the seventy-second year of his age.

His character is a matter of no doubt, and it is of a
high order. That he was a most able, most industrious, most successful student of nature, is clear; and

that his name will for ever be held in grateful remembrance by all who cultivate physical science, and placed among its most eminent masters, is unquestionable. That he was a perfectly conscientious man in all the opinions which he embraced, and sincere in all he published respecting other subjects, appears equally beyond dispute. He was, also, upright and honourable in all his dealings, and justly beloved by his family and friends as a man spotless in all the relations of life. That he was governed in his public conduct by a temper too hot and irritable to be consistent either with his own dignity, or with an amiable deportment, may be freely admitted; and his want of self-command, and want of judgment in the practical affairs of life, was manifest above all in his controversial history; for he can be charged with no want of prudence in the management of his private concerns. His violence and irritability, too, seems equally to have been confined to his public life, for in private all have allowed him the praise of a mild and attractive demeanour; and we have just seen its great power in disarming the prejudices of his adversaries.

CAVENDISH.

A GREATER contrast between two men of science, both eminent benefactors to the same branch of knowledge, can hardly be imagined than Cavendish offers to Priestley. He was thoroughly educated in all branches of the Mathematics and Natural Philosophy; he studied each systematically; he lived retired from the world among his books and his instruments, never meddling with the affairs of active life; he passed his whole time in storing his mind with the knowledge imparted by former inquirers and in extending its bounds. Cultivating science for its own sake, he was slow to appear before the world as an author; had reached the middle age of life before he gave any work to the press; and though he reached the term of fourscore, never published a hundred pages. His methods of investigation were nearly as opposite as this diversity might lead us to expect; and in all the accidental circumstances of rank and wealth the same contrast is to be remarked. He was a duke's grandson; he possessed a princely fortune; his whole expenditure was on philosophical pursuits; his whole existence was in his laboratory or his library. If such a life presents little variety and few incidents to the vulgar observer, it is a matter of most interesting contemplation to all who set its just value upon the cultivation of science, who reckon its successful pursuit as the greatest privilege, the brightest glory of our nature.

Henry Cavendish was born at Nice, whither his mother's health had carried her, the 10th of October, 1731. He was the son of Lord Charles Cavendish, the last Duke of Devonshire's great uncle, by the daughter of Henry Grey, Duke of Kent. His family, aware of the talents which he early showed, were anxious that he should take the part in public life which men of his rank are wont to do, and were much displeased with his steady refusal to quit the studies which he loved. An uncle, disapproving of the course pursued towards him, made him his heir; and so ample a fortune came into his possession that he left at his death a million and a quarter of money.* The Mathematics, and the various branches of Natural Philosophy, were the chief subjects of his study, and of all these sciences he was a consummate master.

The discoveries of Black on carbonic acid and latent heat, appear to have drawn his attention to the cultivation of pneumatic chemistry; and in 1766 he communicated to the Royal Society his experiments for ascertaining the properties of carbonic acid and hydrogen gas.† He carried his mathematical habits into the laboratory; and not satisfied with showing the other qualities which make it clear that these two

---

* M. Biot's article in the Biog. Univ. makes him the son of the Duke of Devonshire, and states his yearly income at 300,000l. sterling, and yet gives the property he left at only 1,200,000l.—so that he must have spent 300,000l. a year, and also dissipated five millions. Such errors seem incredible.

† Three papers containing experiments on factitious air. Phil. Trans., 1766, p. 141.

aëriform substances are each *sui generis,* and the same from whatever substances, by whatever processes, they are obtained ; nor satisfied with the mere fact that one of them is heavier, and the other much lighter, than atmospheric air,—he inquired into the precise numerical relation of their specific gravities with one another and with common air, and first showed an example of weighing permanently elastic fluids : unless, indeed, Torricelli may be said before him to have shown the relative weight of a column of air and a column of mercury: or the common pump to have long ago compared in this respect air with water. It is, however, sufficiently clear, that neither of these experiments gave the relative measure of one air with another : nor, indeed, could they be said to compare common air with either mercury or water, although they certainly showed the relative specific gravities of the two bodies, taking air for the middle term or common measure of their weights.

The common accounts in chemical and in biographical works are materially incorrect respecting the manner in which Mr. Cavendish was led to make his great experiment upon the composition of water in 1781 and the following years. It is said, that while making his experiments on air in 1765 and 1766, he had observed for the first time, that moisture is produced by the combustion of inflammable air, and that this led him, sixteen or seventeen years later, "to complete the synthetical formula of water, and to find that the moisture that he had before observed was simple water."* Nothing can be more erroneous than

---

* Penny Cyclopædia, vol. vi. p. 392. This and other similar

this whole statement. In Mr. Cavendish's paper, of 1766, upon fixed and inflammable airs, there is not one word said of the moisture formed by the combustion; and respecting inflammable air, the experiments are confined entirely to its burning or exploding, to its specific gravity, and to its production. The paper of 1784 is, in fact, entitled ' Experiments upon Air,' and it commences with stating, not that those experiments were undertaken with any view to the water formed by burning inflammable air, but that they were made " with a view to find out the cause of the diminution which common air is well known to suffer by all the various ways in which it is phlogisticated, and to discover what becomes of the air thus lost or consumed;" and the author adds, that besides " determining this fact, they also threw light on the constitution and means of production of dephlogisticated air." Instead of referring to any former observation of his own either in 1766, or subsequently, on the moisture left by burning inflammable air, he expressly refers to Mr. Warltire's observation of this moisture, as related by Dr. Priestley: and both Mr. Warltire's observation and Dr. Priestley's publication were made in 1781. Upon this observation Mr. Cavendish proceeded to further experiments, with the view of ascertaining " what becomes of the air lost by phlogistication."

---

accounts are plainly given by some persons who never read Mr. Cavendish's writings. But a still greater error occurs in them: they represent him as having first shown that fixed and inflammable airs are separate bodies from common air; whereas Dr. Black, in his Lectures from 1755 downwards, showed this distinctly by his experiments, proving clearly that these gases have nothing in common with the atmospheric air (vol. ii., p. 87, 88).

For this purpose, he introduced a portion of hydrogen gas into a globe or balloon of glass, sufficiently strong to resist the expansive force of the combustion which had often been observed in mines, and also in experiments upon a smaller scale, to produce an explosion. He adapted to the globe two wires of metal, fixing them in air-tight sockets, and bringing their points within a short distance of each other in the inside of the globe; so that, by an electrical machine, he could send the spark or the shock from the one point to the other, through the gases mixed together in the globe. He found that the whole of the hydrogen gas disappeared by the combustion thus occasioned, and a considerable portion also of the common air. Water was, as usual, found in small quantity, and an acid was also formed. He then weighed accurately the air of both kinds which he exposed to the stream of electricity, and he afterwards weighed the liquid formed by the combustion; he found that the two weights corresponded with great accuracy. It was difficult to resist the inference that the union of the two airs had taken place; and it might further have been inferred that the latent heat which held them in an elastic state had been given out, forming the flame which was produced; and that water was formed by the union of the two airs, having, of course, less latent heat than was required to keep them in a gaseous state; but Mr. Cavendish did not approve of this manner of stating the conclusion which Mr. Watt had adopted, because of doubts which he had respecting the nature of heat.* The residue of the com-

bustion, however, was two-fold: there was an aëriform
body left in the glass vessel, as well as liquid in the
bottom.   This was much smaller in volume than the
air which had filled the globe before the combustion,
because the hydrogen gas and part of the common
air had disappeared.   This aëriform residue was also
of a different nature from common air; it was found
to be the phlogistic air of Priestley ; the azotic air
of Rutherford : and the air consumed in burning
the hydrogen gas must, therefore, be the vital air
or oxygen gas of the atmosphere.   By another experiment he more fully ascertained this: for, burning
oxygen gas with hydrogen gas, nearly the whole
aëriform contents of the globe disappeared, and water,
equal in weight to the two gases taken together,
remained as the produce of the combustion ; but
still an acid was formed, unless in some cases, when
very pure oxygen gas was used.

   Thus was effected the important discovery of the composition of water, which Watt had inferred some time
before from a careful examination of the similar facts
collected by former experimentalists ; one of whom,
Warltire, had even burned the gases in a close vessel,
and by means of electricity.   The conclusion arrived at
by Mr. Cavendish from his capital experiment was, in
his own words, that " dephlogisticated air is in reality
nothing but dephlogisticated water, or water deprived of
its phlogiston, or in other words, that water consists of
dephlogisticated air united to phlogiston, and that
inflammable air is either pure phlogiston, or else water
united to phlogiston ;" and he then gives his reasons in
favour of the second inference, namely, that inflammable
air is water united to phlogiston ; but he repeatedly

dwells on the preference due to this inference over the conclusion that inflammable air is pure phlogiston.* This statement of the theory is somewhat less distinct than Mr. Watt's, who considered water to be dephlogisticated air united to inflammable air or pure phlogiston, and both deprived of their latent heat. But he, as well as Mr. Cavendish, expresses himself with some hesitation, and even, like him, in some passages entertains the idea of water as united in a small proportion with inflammable air. The theory, though nearly completed by those great chemists, was perhaps first stated with perfect certainty and distinctness by Lavoisier.†

In the combustion of hydrogen gas with common air, and even with impure oxygen gas, Cavendish had observed that the water was slightly tinged with acid, though not always when pure oxygen gas was used for the operation. He therefore devised an experiment which should ascertain the nature of this acid, and in what manner it was formed. He passed the electric spark through common air without any hydrogen gas being present; the air was in a receiver over mercury, and the operation was of long continuance, on account of the slowness with which the combination is formed of the two gases whereof the atmosphere is composed. He had not supposed that the hydrogen had any share in forming the acid: his theory being that water, and not acid, is the produce of that gas's combustion. He naturally

---

* Philosophical Transactions, 1784, p. 137, 140.
† See Appendix to the Life of Watt.

suspected the acid to be the produce of some union
between the azote and the oxygen of the atmosphere.
He left the process in the hands of a committee of his
scientific friends, fellow-members of the Royal Society;
and after some weeks of constantly passing the electric
fluid through a limited portion of air, a small quantity of liquid was formed, which readily combined
with a solution of potash in water sent up through
the mercury. This union was found to be common
nitre, having all the qualities of that well-known substance. It detonated with charcoal; it sparkled when
paper impregnated with it was burnt; it gave out
nitrous fumes when sulphuric acid was poured on it.
There could, therefore, no doubt whatever now exist
that nitrous acid is composed of the two airs deprived
of latent heat, which form our atmosphere; that it is
a true oxide of azote.

The undivided merit of this important discovery has
never been denied to Mr. Cavendish. Even Lavoisier
could not intrude; but his avidity to claim a share in
all discoveries had been exerted respecting the composition of water, which he asserts in his 'Elements of
Chemistry' to have been discovered by himself and Mr.
Cavendish about the same time. I have shown clearly
in the Appendix to the Life of Mr. Watt, that the discovery had been previously communicated to the French
philosopher; but it is worth while to consider the experiment upon which he grounded his claim; and
that experiment, when examined, is found wholly
insufficient to prove the position, even if it had been
contrived and performed before the communication of
Watt's and Cavendish's discovery. Of that discovery

it was plainly a corollary—by that discovery it was manifestly suggested.

The former experiments, both those of Cavendish and those on which Watt reasoned, were all synthetical and decisive—that of Lavoisier was analytical and radically defective. It proved nothing conclusively: it was well enough after the *experimentum crucis* had demonstrated the proposition ; to that proposition it was a corollary—it was nothing like a critical experiment. He placed water in a retort exposed to heat ; the vapour of the retort, when the water boiled, was passed through a tube (a gun barrel with the breech-pin knocked out was generally used) ; the tube, if made of earthenware, had iron filings placed in its course ; it was placed in a fire ; its further extremity was connected with a receiver, in which cold water or mercury rose to fill it entirely. As the water slowly boiled there came through the tube, and into the glass receiver, a current of gas, which, upon examination, was found to be hydrogen gas, while the iron filings were converted into calx or oxide. The weight of the gas produced, added to the weight acquired by the gun barrel or by the filings during the process, was found to be nearly equal to the weight lost by the water in the retort. Hence the inference was, that the lost portion of water had been decomposed into its two elements, the oxygen gas forming the calx of the iron and the hydrogen gas being received in the glass vessel. But the adversaries of the new doctrine had an answer to this inference far more formidable than any that they could urge against the conclusion drawn from the synthetical experiment. The analytical experiment was liable to all the uncertainty of the process called the destructive distillation. The substances found might have been the product, and not merely the educt of the process. It is known that if coal or oleaginous bodies be distilled in close vessels there are obtained gases and water and acids which never existed in the matters subjected to the action of the fire. The component parts of these matters enter into new combinations with one another under the action of heat, just as a tallow candle or an oil lamp gives lamp-black and water in burning, though no water, but only hydrogen, nor of course any lamp-black, exists in the tallow and the oil. So, in Lavoisier's experiment, the water might contain only oxygen and hydrogen, and the action of the hot iron might have separated them from each other. But it was also quite possible that the iron gave out hydrogen, and that the hot water was partly kept in solution by this gas, partly combined with the iron, for on that supposition the combined weight of the calcined iron and the hydrogen gas would be exactly equal to the united weight of the water evaporated, and of the iron before calcination. The previous discovery of Watt and Cavendish is liable to no such ambiguity; and it has the merit of also removing all ambiguity from the experiment of Lavoisier, which it manifestly suggested.

These great discoveries placed Cavendish in the highest rank of philosophers. No one doubted of nitrous acid; that he was the undisputed discoverer of the composition of water, before Mr. Watt's claim, is equally certain; nor, even now, is it necessary for the defenders of Watt's priority to deny that Cavendish made the great step without any previous knowledge of Watt's reasoning, while all admit that his *expe-rimentum crucis* was of the greatest value in com-pleting the foundation on which Watt's happy infer-ence had been built. Lavoisier's attempt to intrude himself was wholly unsuccessful; it had no effect whatever except to tarnish his reputation, already injured sufficiently by his similar attempt to share in the discovery of oxygen. All men held Cavendish's name as enrolled among the greatest discoverers of any age, and only lamented that he did not pursue his brilliant career with more activity, so as to augment still farther the debt of gratitude under which he had laid the scientific world.

The reader, especially the French reader, must not suppose that any prejudice respecting Lavoisier has dictated the remarks occasionally made in the course of this work upon his pretensions as a discoverer. It is scarcely possible to estimate too highly the services which he rendered to chemical science by his labours. The truly philosophic spirit which guided his researches had not been found to prevail much before his time in the speculations of chemists. He had a most happy facility in reducing the knowledge of scattered and isolated facts to a system. His talent for generalization has not often been surpassed; and it led him, together with his admirable freedom from preconceived preju-dice, and his resolute boldness of investigation in unfrequented paths, to make some of the most felicitous inductions, well deserving the title of discoveries, that have ever been made, although the materials of his inferences were obtained from the experiments and observations of his predecessors, and his own experi-

ments, except on the nature of the diamond, led to no
material extension of our chemical knowledge. Stript
of the plumes in which he sought to array himself, re-
pulsed from the avenues by which he would fain have
intruded himself among those whose experiments led
at once to great discoveries, he is now, on all hands,
allowed to have never made us acquainted with a single
new gas, or a new substance of any kind, or, except
as to carbon, with a single new combination of the
old. He did not, like Black, discover carbonic acid
or latent heat—he did not, like Priestley, discover
oxygen—he did not, like Scheele, discover chlorine
—he did not, like Davy, discover the alkaline metals—
or like Cavendish, by direct experiment, show how
water and nitrous acid are constituted—or, like Berthollet, explain of what ammonia consists. But it is
equally confessed that, by sound and happy reasoning
on the experiments of others, he showed how the
process of combustion and of calcination takes place,
and to him and his individual researches we owe the
important discovery that fixed air, however generated,
whether by respiration or by combustion or by fermentation (its three great sources, as proved by Black), is the
combination of oxygen and carbon. Nor is it any deroga-
tion from his claims to the title of a discoverer of physical
truths that his generalization pushed too far made him
regard oxygen as necessary to all combustion and all
acidification, whereas it has been found that heat and
light are abundantly evolved both by the combustion of
metals and sulphur in close vessels—by the combustion
of hydrogen and azotic gas—and by the combination of
metals with chlorine; and also that chlorine, an acid

of the strongest kind, contains no oxygen at all, while the alkalis themselves are oxides. The doctrine of latent heat was happily applied by him to the union of gases with bodies, and if he had only followed that doctrine more closely he would have avoided the error into which he fell, and perceived that other gases as well as oxygen may support flame, and that all, on becoming liquid or solid, must part with heat. Against his error respecting the constitution of acids may justly be set the great merit of his conjecture, that the fixed alkalis are oxides of metals; for this has been since proved, and the conjecture is a sufficient evidence that he did not doggedly adhere to his theory of the acidifying principle.

It does not appear that Mr. Cavendish ever after 1785, when he discovered the nature of nitrous acid, prosecuted his chemical inquiries so as to make new discoveries; but beside making numberless useful chemical experiments, about ten years later he engaged in some important experiments upon the force of attraction. It occurred to him that he could measure that force, and thereby ascertain the density of the earth by accurately observing the action of bodies suddenly exhibited in the neighbourhood of a horizontal lever nicely balanced, loaded with equal leaden balls of a small size at its two ends, and protected from all aërial currents by being inclosed in a box. In that box a telescope and lamp were placed, that the motions of the lever might be carefully observed. On approaching the external leaden balls made use of, whose diameter was eight inches, to the small ones inclosed, and near the lever, it was found that a horizontal oscillation took place. This was measured; and the oscillation caused by the earth on a pendulum being known, as well as the relative specific gravities of lead and water, it was found, upon the medium of his observations, that the earth's density is to that of water as eleven to two, or five-and-a-half times greater. Dr. Hutton, who repeated his calculations, made the result five three-tenths, or as fifty-three to ten. Maskelyne's experiments at Schehallion made the proportion as five to one. Zach's experiment on a smaller hill near Marseilles did not give a result materially different.

A paper on the civil year of the Hindûs, connected, like Newton's chronological works, with astronomical researches, an account of a new eudiometer, and some papers on electricity, form the rest of this great philosopher's works; and altogether they shrink into a very inconsiderable bulk compared with the voluminous works of inferior men. In this, as in other respects, we trace his resemblance to Black. Indeed the admirable contrivance of their experiments—their circumspect preparation of the ground by previous discussion of principles—the cautious following of facts, and yet the resolute adoption of legitimate consequences in their generalizations—the elegance of their processes, and the conciseness of their descriptions and remarks, with an unsparing rejection of everything superfluous—forms the characteristic of both those illustrious students of nature. While, as regards Cavendish's writings, it has been, and as regards Black's it might have been, justly said by one that every sentence will bear the microscope; another writer, the most eminent of his successors, has, with equal truth, described his processes as of so finished a nature,

so perfected by the hand of a master, as to require no
correction; and, though contrived in the infancy of the
science, yet to remain unsurpassed, perhaps unequalled,
for accuracy and beauty at the present day.

The world, even the scientific world, dazzled by the
brilliancy of those discoveries which we have described,
is wont to regard Cavendish as a chemist merely. But
it was not only in chemical science and in a few departments of natural philosophy that this great man had
thoroughly exercised himself; he was profoundly versed
in every branch of physics, and was a most complete and
accomplished mathematician. I have had access to the
manuscripts which he left behind him; and it would
be difficult to name any subject which had not engaged
his close attention: all had been made the subject not
only of his study, but of his original investigations.
The two papers on Electricity which he published in
the 'Philosophical Transactions' contain, the one of
1776, the first distinct statement of the difference between animal and common electricity; the other, in
1771, twenty-seven propositions upon the action of the
electric fluid, treated mathematically. They are
grounded upon the general hypothesis that the particles of the fluid repel one another, and attract those
of other matter with a force inversely as some lesser
power than the cube of the distance; and with this
theory the experiments which he examines are found
to tally perfectly. But his voluminous unpublished
papers show how constantly his life was devoted to
experimental inquiries, and analytical or geometrical
investigations. Beside ranging over the whole of chemical science, they relate to various branches of optics,

of physical and of practical astronomy—of the theory of mathematical and astronomical instruments—of mechanical and dynamical sciences, both theoretical and practical—of pure mathematics in all its branches, geometry, the integral and differential calculus, the doctrine of chances and annuities. He seems in his application of mathematics to physics to have disregarded elegance, and even simplicity, and to have chosen always the shortest and most certain path to his object. Accordingly this somewhat surprises the mathematical reader; as when we find him using $\dfrac{y\,d\,y}{d\,v}$ (or rather $\dfrac{y\,y'}{v'}$, for he always employs the Newtonian notation) for the subnormal, having taken x for some other quantity than the abscissa, and using three letters, as a, z, and x, to denote segments of the same line, when perhaps a is the whole line, and $a - x$ is equal to z. But that he had the most familiar and masterly knowledge of the calculus is plain throughout all his investigations, as it is that his trust in its powers induced him to throw himself willingly and habitually upon them. In this respect he stands not only at the head of chemical philosophers, but alone among them, with perhaps one or two exceptions in the French school.

In giving the history of his labours, and the character of his intellectual capacity, we have written the life of Cavendish. His personal history cannot be expected to have any striking interest; yet they who have been dwelling on his scientific eminence will not be displeased to know somewhat of his ordinary life. He was of a most reserved disposition, and peculiarly shy habits. This led to some singularity of manner, which was further increased by a hesitation or difficulty of speech, and a thin shrill voice. He entered diffidently into any conversation, and seemed to dislike being spoken to. He would often leave the place where he was addressed, and leave it abruptly, with a kind of cry or ejaculation, as if scared and disturbed. He lived in a house on Clapham Common, and his library, vast in extent, was at another place, because he made it accessible to all, and did not wish to be troubled by those who resorted to it. He allowed friends to take books from it, and he himself never took one without giving a receipt for it. On the death of his librarian he began the practice of himself attending one day in the week to give out and take in books. His large income was allowed to accumulate; and when his bankers, after finding that a very considerable balance was always left in their hands, mentioned the circumstance, suggesting that it might be invested to some profit, he answered with much simplicity, that if the balance was an inconvenience to them he could go to another banker. Himself a man of no expense, his habits never varied, nor did his style of living at all suffer a change on succeeding to his uncle's large fortune. His purse was ever accessible to the claims of charity, as well as to proposals for the promotion of scientific pursuits. Having formed a high opinion of Dr. (afterwards Sir Charles) Blagden's capacity for science, he settled a considerable annuity on him, upon condition that he should give up his profession and devote himself to philosophy; with the former portion of which condition the Doctor complied, devoting himself to the hopeless pursuit of a larger income in the person of Lavoisier's widow, who preferred marrying Count Rumford.* Mr. Cavendish received no one at his residence ; he ordered his dinner daily by a note which he left at a certain hour on the hall table, where the housekeeper was to take it, for he held no communication with his female domestics, from his morbid shyness. It followed, as a matter of course, that his servants thought him strange, and his neighbours deemed him out of his mind. He hardly ever went into society. The only exceptions I am aware of are an occasional christening at Devonshire or Burlington House, the meetings of the Royal Society, and Sir Joseph Banks' weekly conversaziones. At both the latter places I have met him, and recollect the shrill cry he uttered as he shuffled quickly from room to room, seeming to be annoyed if looked at, but sometimes approaching to hear what was passing among others. His face was intelligent and mild, though, from the nervous irritation which he seemed to feel, the expression could hardly be called calm. It is not likely that he ever should have been induced to sit for his picture ; the result therefore of any such experiment is wanting. His dress was of the oldest fashion, a greyish green coat and waistcoat, with flaps, a small cocked hat, and his hair dressed like a wig (which possibly it was) with a thick clubbed tail. His walk was quick and uneasy ; of course he never appeared in London unless lying back in the corner of his carriage. He probably uttered fewer words in the course of his life than any man who ever lived to fourscore years, not at all excepting the monks of La Trappe.

---

* He left Sir Charles a legacy of 15,000*l.* ; which was generally understood to have fallen much short of his ample expectations.

Mr. Cavendish died on the 10th of March, 1810, after a short illness, probably the first as well as the last under which he ever suffered. His habit of curious observation continued to the end. He was desirous of marking the progress of disease, and the gradual extinction of the vital powers. With this view, that he might not be disturbed he desired to be left alone. His servant returning sooner than he had wished was ordered again to leave the chamber of death, and when he came back a second time he found his master had expired.

D A V Y.

Sir Humphry Davy being now removed beyond the reach of such feelings, as he ought always to have been above their influence, that may be said without offence of which he so disliked the mention : he had the honour of raising himself to the highest place among the chemical philosophers of the age ; emerging by his merit alone from an obscure condition. His father was a carver in wood at Penzance, in Cornwall ; a man of some ingenuity in his craft. He possessed a small landed property in the village of Varfell, near Penzance, and Davy was born there in 1778. He received the rudiments of his education at a school in Truro, but was very early apprenticed to an apothecary at Penzance, where, disliking the profession to which he had been destined, he occupied himself with chemical experiments, ingeniously contriving to make the utensils of the shop and the kitchen serve for apparatus ; and it is remembered of him that he frequently alarmed the household by his explosions. The result of his dislike to the shop was a disagreement with his master, and he went to another in the same place ; but here he continued in the same course. Pursuing a plan of study which he had laid down for

himself, he became thoroughly acquainted with chemistry, and well versed in other branches of natural
philosophy, beside making some proficiency in geometry; but he never cultivated the mathematical
sciences, except that I recollect his telling me once,
late in life, of his intention to resume the study of
them, as he had begun to make progress in crystallo-
graphy. He does not appear to have given any early
indications of superior genius, or even of unusual
quickness; but he showed all along, in following the
bent of his intellectual taste, the perseverance, the
firm purpose, which is inseparable from a capacity of
the higher order, and is an indispensable condition, as
it is a sure pledge, of success in every pursuit.

It must be observed of the biographers both of Davy
and Scheele, that they seem to have made too much
of the difficulties interposed in the path of their early
studies by the want of apparatus, to which want, and
to their ingenious contrivances for finding substitutes,
a good deal of their experimental skill has been ascribed.
It should be recollected that an apothecary's shop is
not by any means so destitute of helps, especially for
the study of chemistry, as a workshop of almost any
other description. Crucibles, phials, mortars, galli-
pots, scales and weights, liquid measures, acids, alkalis, and neutral salts, are all to be found there, even
if a furnace and still be not a necessary appendage.
It may be allowed that nothing like an air-pump
might be there expected, unless cupping chanced to be
performed by the druggist. Accordingly Davy was
glad to obtain, in a case of surgical instruments from
a practitioner on board a French vessel wrecked on

the Cornish coast, to whom he had done some kind
service, the means of making some approximation to
an exhausting engine.

  It happened, fortunately for him, that Gregory
Watt, youngest son of the great engineer, and whom,
having had the happiness of knowing him, I have already
mentioned, came to reside in the house of Davy's
mother at Penzance, where he was ordered to pass
the winter for the benefit of his health. Being five
years older than the young chemist, and eminently
accomplished both in science and in letters, his conversation and advice was a great advantage, of which
Davy gladly availed himself. Another accident threw
him in the way of Mr. Davies Giddy, a cultivator of
natural as well as mathematical science, and he, finding that Davy had been devoting himself to chemistry,
gave him the use of an excellent library, and introduced him to Dr. Beddoes, who was then engaged in
forming an establishment called by him the Pneumatic
Institution, for the medical use of gases, as well as for
further investigating their properties. At the head of
this he placed his new friend, who was thus at once
enabled to pursue his scientific vocation as a profession,
and did not long delay giving to the world a proof
of his ingenuity, by the publication of a theory of
'Light and Heat,' fanciful no doubt, and ill-digested,
containing much groundless and imaginary, and even
absurd speculation, but disclosing great information
and no inconsiderable cleverness. It was published in
a periodical work edited by Dr. Beddoes, called 'Contributions to Medical and Physical Science;' and to the
same work he soon after gave a paper upon the 'Nitrous

Oxide,' on the respiration of which he had made some very curious experiments. The singular circumstances which he thus ascertained, gave him considerable reputation as an experimentalist, and he was soon after (1802) chosen first Assistant Lecturer in Chemistry, by the Royal Institution of London, and the year following, sole Chemical Professor. Nor must the boldness which he had shown in conducting his experiments be passed over. He had exposed himself to serious hazard in breathing some most deleterious gases, and both in his trials of gaseous mixtures, and in his galvanic processes, he had made many narrow escapes from the danger of violent explosions.

It is a singular fact that, although his attention had never been confined to his favourite science, for he had studied literature, and especially poetry to the extent of writing tolerable verses, yet he was of so uncouth an exterior and manners, notwithstanding an exceedingly handsome and expressive countenance, that Count Rumford, a leading director of the Institution, on seeing him for the first time, expressed no little disappointment, even regretting the part he had taken in promoting the engagement. But these feelings were of short duration. Davy was soon sufficiently humanized, and even refined, to appear before a London and a fashionable audience of both sexes with great advantage, and his first course of lectures had unbounded and unparalleled success. This he owed, certainly, to the more superficial accomplishments of good and lively language, an agreeable delivery, and, above all, an ingenuous enthusiasm for his subject which informed and quickened his whole discourse. But the

fame which he thus acquired would have been of
limited extent and of short duration, had his reliance
only been upon the fickle multitude whom such qualities can please. The first consequences of his success
in the line of mere exhibition were unfavourable, and
threatened to be fatal; for he was led away by the
plaudits of fashion, and must needs join in its frothy,
feeble current. For a while he is remarked to have
shown the incongruous combination of science and
fashion, which form a most imperfect union, and produce a compound of no valuable qualities, somewhat
resembling the nitrous gas on which he experimented
earlier in life, having an intoxicating effect on the
party tasting it, and a ludicrous one on all beholders.
They who have recorded this transformation, while
they lament the substitution of anything for "the
natural candour and warmth of feeling which had
singularly won upon the acquaintance of his early life,"
add most justly that the weakness which they describe
never "cooled his regard for his family and former
friends." I can vouch for the change, which was
merely superficial, being of very short duration; and
it is pleasing to add that, even while it lasted, there
was none of that most offensive of all the effects produced by such a transition state to be found in his conversation; he never for a moment appeared to be
ashamed of his great vocation, nor to shun the fullest
discussion of the subject on which he was at home,
in order to deal with topics to which he was of necessity a stranger. I am speaking, too, of his habits long
before his great discoveries; there would have been
little ground for praise, any more than for wonder,

that the discoverer of the alkaline metals should
be willing to have the conversation roll upon chemistry and galvanism ; but the time to which I
have been referring was when his fame rested chiefly
upon the success of his lectures to mixed companies in
Albemarle Street, and to lovers of agriculture in
Sackville Street, where the Board had chosen him
their Chemical Professor.

If his situation at the Royal Institution had exposed
him to the risk which we have seen he escaped, it had
put him in possession of invaluable helps to his pursuits. He had now an ample command of books; he
had assistants under him ; above all, he had an unlimited power of collecting and of making apparatus;
his income was secure; and his time was at his own
disposal. He failed not to avail himself diligently of
these great advantages ; and although he lived a good
deal in society, where he was always a welcome guest,
his principal relaxations during the rest of his life consisted in shooting, and especially in fishing, of which
he was from his earliest years passionately fond. The
intercourse he had held with Southey and with Cole-
ridge had given him not only his taste for poetry, but
an extraordinary love of rural walks, in the peaceful
solitude of which I have heard him say, answering the
ordinary and obvious objections of those who are not
smitten with the love of the " Angle," the gratifications of that propensity very mainly consist.

In 1801 he made his first important discovery, that
by which he ascertained the true nature of galvanic
action. That this was connected with electric or chemical affinity had been generally suspected, though de-

nied by Volta, the author of the pile, and indeed of the science which, like the continent of America, has borne the name of another than the discoverer. This had seemed probable from the presence being indispensable of a liquid capable of decomposing one or other of the metals, both supposed to be equally necessary to the production of the electric stream. Davy's experiments, which were numerous and admirably devised and most laboriously conducted, now showed that the presence of two metals was not required to provide the electricity. One metal, and one other substance separated from it, with a fluid acting upon either the metal or the substance; or a metal separating two fluids, one of which acts upon it; nay, one metal exposed to the same fluid, but acted upon differently on its different sides or surfaces by the fluid's strength differing on the different sides; or one and the same metal in different pieces plunged into the same fluid, at an interval of time—were all found to be combinations which gave the galvanic (or voltaic) shock, the same in kind, though varying in strength. In all these cases, and in every production of electricity by the voltaic process, the chemical action of a fluid upon the metallic substance was a necessary concomitant of the operation.*

During the five following years Davy continued his experiments; and in the autumn of 1806 he communicated to the Royal Society his discovery of the connexion between the different ends of the electric circle

---

* Subsequent experiments have shown that the effect may be produced by other than metallic, or even carbonaceous bodies.

and the different component parts of bodies submitted
to the action of the fluid. Nothing could be more
singular and unexpected than the laws which he now
found to regulate this operation, nor anything which
promised more clearly a rich harvest of new discoveries.
The effect of the current, whether of common or galvanic electricity, in decomposing substances through
which it passed, had been before known. Thus water
had been resolved into its two elements by the passing
of the fluid through wires whose points were opposite
to each other at a small distance. Nicholson had first
made this happy application of the voltaic pile; but
he and others had been much disturbed by finding
other substances produced as well as oxygen and hydrogen gases. This perplexing circumstance was carefully investigated by Davy; and he showed by a masterly course of experiments, that these substances owed
their origin entirely to impurities in the water.
When it was quite pure, they wholly disappeared.
But he now proceeded farther, and found that when
the electric current is thus passed, there is always a
separation operated differently at the negative and at
the positive part of the current. The oxygen of the
water, for example, was accumulated round the positive
wire; its hydrogen round the negative. So when a
neutral salt was subjected to the process, its acid was
evolved round the positive; its alkaline base round the
negative wire. The same thing happened when a metallic oxide was operated upon; its oxygen went to the
positive, its metallic base to the negative side. The
oxygen, or the acid with the oxygen, went to the former; the particles of the base were transferred to the

latter, along with the hydrogen of the water in which
the solution was made. But a still more extraordinary
phenomenon was observed. If there was a liquid interposed between the two poles and the body to be decomposed, the acid, or the oxygen, was found to pass
through that interposed liquid to the positive pole, the
hydrogen and the matter of the base to the negative
pole, and without acting upon the substance of the interposed liquid. Thus suppose a vegetable colour
tinging the water in an intermediate cup, acid will
pass through it without reddening it, and alkali without making it green. Nay, an acid will pass through
an alkaline solution, or an alkali through an acid,
without uniting in either case to form a neutral salt,
unless the neutral compound is insoluble, for in that
case it falls to the bottom. But muriatic acid will
pass through a solution of potash, having been carried
over from a solution of common sea salt by the electrical
current, or soda will pass through muriatic acid in the
same circumstances, without forming in the former
case nitrate of potash, or in the latter nitrate of soda.
It was also found that the exception in the case of insoluble compounds arises from the mechanical effect of
their insolubility, their falling to the bottom; for if
supported, as it were, on threads of any convenient
substance passing through the intermediate liquid in the
line of the electric current, the acid or alkali will pass
through that liquid. Thus films of asbestos conducting the electric stream, enabled magnesia or lime to
pass; and so were the particles of metal carried over
when separated by the operation from nitrate of
silver.

It thus appeared certain that an indissoluble connexion exists between chemical and electric action, if
indeed it was not even proved that chemical affinity
and electricity are identical.   The science of Electro-
Chemistry, at all events, now arose out of Davy's discoveries, and he is entitled to be regarded as its
founder.

It may easily be conceived that these important
truths excited generally the anxious attention of philosophers.   The French National Institute, greatly to
their honour, though the war between the two countries never raged more fiercely than now, and France
never reached a higher pitch of military glory, crowned
Davy with the first honour founded by Napoleon for
scientific desert.   But it was even more honourable to
the philosopher, that great as his discoveries had been,
expectation was high of the still more important results
which must soon come from the discovery of so new a
law of electrical and chemical action.   I can well remember that we used in discussing the subject to look
forward with perfect confidence to the analysis of the
bodies which had hitherto proved the most stubborn,
and expected soon to find the fixed alkalis, and even
the alkaline earths, shown to be oxides, as by some
very imperfect experiments they had at one time been
supposed to be proved, when it was ascertained that the
metallic buttons found at the bottom of the crucible in
which their reduction had been attempted by carbonaceous or phosphoric re-agents, had come from the
black lead in the pot.   Nor must we omit to mention
the truly candid and magnanimous proceeding of Davy,
so worthy of a philosopher, in making public, with the
fullest details, his proceedings, by which it was mani-

fest he intended still to persevere till he should make
other discoveries. Any one possessed of a strong bat-
tery, deeply reflecting on the paper of autumn 1806,
and perceiving that the positive wire had such a
strong attraction for oxygen as to take it from metallic
oxides, reducing them to their reguline state, might
well have bethought him of subjecting the alkalis to
his machine; and he would then have had the fame,
though, in truth, Davy would have had the merit, of
the grand discovery.

That discovery was not long delayed. About a year
after the former, that is in October 1807, after in vain
endeavouring to decompose the alkalis when mixed
with water, for he then only could decompose that
fluid, he exposed them in the dry state; that is, made
liquid by fusion, without any other substance but heat
to dissolve them—and, to his great delight, he found,
as he had a right to expect, that the process of deoxi-
dation proceeded by the positive wire attracting the
oxygen, while globules of a metallic substance were
found at the negative wire. The great attraction of this
metal for oxygen made it impossible to keep it either
in the air or in water. It burnt spontaneously in the
air and became alkali—it decomposed water in like
manner, and formed an alkaline solution. The two
fixed alkalis both yielded in this process metallic bases;
but that of potash had alone the quality of combustion
at the temperature of 150°, and it was, though a metal,
lighter than water in the proportion of 97 to 100.
When thrown into water in the air, it detonates and
burns with violence, forming a solution of potash.
The metal from soda is still lighter, being to water as
86 to 100; but it does not so easily unite with oxygen,

though it decomposes water with a hissing noise, and
makes with it a solution of soda. To these metals the
discoverer gave the name of *potassium* and *sodium*. The
glory of having now made the greatest discovery of the
age was plainly Davy's; and it was not the result of
happy accident, but of laborious investigation, conducted
with a skill and a patience equally admirable, and
according to the strict rules of the soundest philosophy. He had indeed begun by discovering the laws
of electrical action, and had thus formed the means of
his new discovery, which was the fruit of the science
he had founded, as Newton's theory of dynamics and
of astronomy was the fruit of the calculus which he
had so marvellously discovered when hardly arrived at
man's estate.

The wonder excited by the strange bodies with
which philosophers were thus brought acquainted, was
of course in part owing to their novel and singular
properties, which formed no part of the discoverer's
merits, yet might be reckoned as the perquisites of his
genius. His praise would have been the same if instead of at once discovering the alkalis to be oxides,
and the metal forming the base to be one lighter than
water, or bees'-wax or box-wood, and the other to burn
unheated in the open air, he had only shown those
salts to be oxides of well-known metals. Yet, as his
investigation had been crowned with the discovery of
strange substances, metallic, and yet like no other
metals, we justly admire the more, and the more
thank him for his double service rendered to science.

The long labour thus ending in so mighty a result,
and the excitement naturally enough produced in an
irritable habit, threw him into an illness of a most

serious complexion. For many days he lay between
life and death in a low nervous fever, and it was not till
the following March that he could resume his inquiries
into the composition of the alkaline earths. It is to
the credit of chemists that no one deemed himself at
liberty to interfere with him, as any one might now
by only following his footsteps have done, and thus
analysed these earthy bodies. He himself, early in
the summer following his illness, had reduced lime,
magnesia, strontites, and barytes. In these experiments
he was greatly assisted by the ingenious contrivances
which Gay-Lussac and Thenard had recently used
for the reduction of the alkaline oxides. The metals
thus discovered were not any wise light or fusible like
potassium and sodium ; but they burnt with a bright
light on being exposed to considerable degrees of heat,
and they decomposed water ; and either by their combustion, or their exhibition to water, they reproduced
the alkaline earths.

A number of other experimental researches led
Davy to new and curious observations on the constitution and habits of different substances. But we need
only mention the most important of these, for it was a
discovery very unexpected both by himself and the
chemical world at large. The acid hitherto called oxygenated muriatic, or oxymuriatic, on account of its
powerful acid qualities, had been always from thence
supposed to contain an excess of oxygen, believed to be
the acidifying principle. At last Gay-Lussac and
Thenard, in 1809, concluded from some experimental
researches, or rather they suspected, that it might be a
simple and elementary substance ; but they on the whole
still inclined to think it contained oxygen according to

the old and received opinion. Davy now found, by a course of satisfactory experiments which have fixed the opinions of all philosophers on the subject, that the suspicion of those eminent men was well founded; that the oxymuriatic acid is a simple substance, containing no oxygen; that it unites with oxygen to form an acid, which forms with alkalis the detonating salts hitherto called oxymuriates, as being supposed to contain oxymuriatic acid combined with alkaline bases; and finally, that with hydrogen it forms the acid long and well known as the muriatic or marine. To the oxymuriatic acid he gave the name of *chlorine* from its green colour, and to common muriatic acid that of *hydrochlorine*. The union of chlorine and oxygen he calls *chlorine* acid, and its compounds, of course, *chlorates*. This is justly reckoned one of the most important of Davy's many brilliant discoveries.

It remains to make mention of the valuable present which this great philosopher offered to humanity—his safety-lamp. The dreadful ravages made on human life by the fire-damp explosions—that is, the burning of hydrogen gas in mines—had often attracted the notice of both the mine-owner and the philanthropist. Various inventions had been fallen upon to give light in those recesses of the earth with so low a degree of heat as should be insufficient to explode the gas. One of them was a series of flints playing by machinery against each other so as to give a dim light; but this had very little success; it was clumsy, and it was not effectual so as to cause its use by miners. The ventilation of the galleries by furnaces and even by air-pumps was chiefly relied on as a preventive; but gas would collect

in spite of all preventives, and the destruction of a
hundred or more lives was not an unusual calamity.
Davy about the year 1815 turned his attention to the
subject, and after fully ascertaining that carburetted
hydrogen is the cause of the fire-damp, and finding in
what proportions it must be mixed with air in order to
explode (between six and fourteen times its bulk), he
was surprised to observe, in the course of his experiments made for the purpose of ascertaining how the
inflammation takes place, that the flames will not pass
through tubes of a certain length or smallness of bore.
He then found that if the length be diminished, and the
bore also reduced, the flames will not pass; and he further found that by multiplying the number of the tubes,
their length may safely be diminished to hardly anything, provided their bore be proportionably lessened.
Hence it appeared that gauze of wire, whose meshes were
only one twenty-second of an inch diameter, stopped
the flame, and prevented the explosion. The candle
or lamp being wrapt in such gauze, and all access to
the external air prevented except through the meshes,
it is found that the lamp may be safely introduced into
a gallery filled with fire-damp; a feeble blue flame will
take place inside the gauze, but no explosion, even if
the wire be heated nearly red.

The theory is, but it seems very questionable, that the
conducting power of the wire carrying off the heat prevents a sufficient quantity reaching the explosive compound. Subsequent inquiries seem to prove that
although in a still atmosphere of explosive gas the lamp
is a perfect protection, yet it does not prevent a current of gas from penetrating to the flame and exploding.

It is attempted to guard against this by interposing a tin shield or screen ; but a current very often in mining operations arises before any notice can be given. Had Davy's life and health been prolonged, he might have further improved his invention so as to meet this objection. He certainly never was fully convinced of its force, as I know from having discussed the subject with him ; and no doubt the testimony of so great an engineer as the late Mr. Buddle, given before a Parliamentary Committee to whom the examination of this important subject was referred, deserves great attention. He positively affirmed that " having seen 1000, and sometimes 1500 safety-lamps in daily use, and in all possible varieties of explosive mixtures, he had never known one solitary instance of an explosion." As for the lamentable accidents which continue to happen, we can scarcely doubt that they originate in the dreadful carelessness of their own and of other men's lives, which seems to be engendered in those who are habitually exposed to great danger. That they themselves are the first to suffer for it, can only suppress the outward expression of the feelings which recklessness like this is fitted to produce. ·

It redounds to the credit of the north country mineowners that in 1817 they invited the inventor of the Lamp to a public entertainment, and presented him with a service of plate of two thousand pounds value. It must be remembered that he had generously given to the public the whole benefit of his invention, and thus sacrificed the ample profit which a patent must have enabled him to acquire for himself.

Davy had as early as 1806 been chosen a foreign associate of the French Institute. In 1812 he received

from the Regent the honour of knighthood. About
the same time he married Mrs. Apreece, a lady whose
ample fortune was by far the least valuable part of her
accomplishments—a person of great virtue, admirable
talents, and extensive information. Of this marriage
there has been no issue. In October, 1813, he published
his 'Elements of Chemical Philosophy,'—a hasty and
even somewhat crude work, but abounding, as whatever he wrote was sure to abound, in important and
ingenious observations. The following year appeared
his 'Elements of Agricultural Chemistry,' of which
the same general character may be given. In 1816
he was created a baronet.

Napoleon had, during the war, given him permission to visit the extinguished volcanoes in Dauvergne,
and to pass through France towards Naples, Vesuvius
being then in a state of eruption. His reception at
Paris was very warm, but unfortunately he failed to
retain the affection of his colleagues in the Institute.
Their complaint against him for having interfered, as
they termed it, with their recent discovery of iodine,
on which, having obtained a specimen, he chose,
naturally enough, to make experiments, appears incomparably absurd. He had never complained of their interference, during his illness in 1807, with the process
of deoxygenation by means of galvanic action; on the
contrary, he had availed himself thankfully of the
lights shed by their ingenuity on his process, and had
immediately after made new discoveries, at which they
had failed to arrive. It may be more true that his
manners were unpleasing; and, as ever happens when
a great man is also a shy one, he was charged with
being supercilious and cold. They who knew him

will at once acquit him of any such charge; but he was painfully timid by nature when mixing with society; and hence the mistake of our neighbours, who, though great critics in manner, are far from being infallible, and are exceedingly susceptible—fully as susceptible as he was shy. Possibly they looked down upon him in consequence of a peculiarity which he no doubt had. He was fond of poetry, and an ardent admirer of beauty in natural scenery. But of beauty in the arts he was nearly insensible. They used to say in Paris that on seeing the Louvre, he exclaimed that one of its statues was "a beautiful stalactite;" and it is possible that this callousness, or this jest, whichever it might be, excited the scorn or the humour of men not more sincere lovers of sculpture than himself, or more able judges of its merits, but better disposed to conceal their want of taste or want of skill.

When Sir Joseph Banks terminated his long and respectable course in 1820, Davy was unanimously chosen to succeed him as President of the Royal Society, and continued to fill that distinguished office until, his health having failed, he resigned it in 1827, and was succeeded by his early patron Davies Giddy. Towards the end of 1825 he had an apoplectic seizure, which, though slight (if any such attack can be so called), left a paralytic weakness behind, and he was ordered to go abroad in search of a milder and dryer climate. He returned home in the following autumn, not very ill, but not much restored in strength, and unable to continue his scientific labours. The work on fly-fishing called 'Salmonia' was the amusement of those hours in which, comparatively feeble, his mind yet exerted what energy remained to it, on the favourite pursuit of his leisure. It contains both curious information on natural history, and many passages of lively and even poetical description. The same may be said of many things in his latest work, ' Last Days of a Philosopher,' which he wrote in the year after, when he again went to the continent in search of health. He wintered at Rome, and in May 1829, on his arrival at Geneva, after passing the day in excellent spirits, and dining heartily on fish, he had a fatal apoplectic attack in the night, and died early in the next morning, 29th May, without a struggle.

There needs no further remark, no general character, to present a portrait of this eminent individual. Whoever has perused the history of his great exploits in science, with a due knowledge of the subject, has already discerned his place, highest among all the great discoverers of his time. Even he who has little acquaintance with the subjects of his labours may easily perceive how brilliant a reputation he must have enjoyed, and how justly; while he who can draw no such inference from the facts would fail to obtain any knowledge of Davy's excellence from all the panegyrics with which general description could encircle his name.*

---

* It may not be impertinent to relate here a singular proof of the admiration in which his name was held by his countrymen, and how well it became known even among the common people. Retiring home one evening he observed an ordinary man showing the moon and a planet through a telescope placed upon the pavement. He went up and paid his pence for a look. But no such thing would they permit. "That's Sir Humphry," ran among the people; and the exhibitor, returning his money, said, with an important air which exceedingly delighted him, that he could not think of taking anything from a brother philosopher.

S I M S O N.

THE wonderful progress that has been made in the
pure mathematics since the application of algebra to
geometry, begun by Vieta in the sixteenth, completed
by Des Cartes in the seventeenth century, and especially the still more marvellous extension of analytical
science by Newton and his followers, since the invention of the Calculus, has, for the last hundred years and
more, cast into the shade the methods of investigation which preceded those now in such general use,
and so well adapted to afford facilities unknown while
mathematicians only possessed a less perfect instrument
of investigation. It is nevertheless to be observed
that the older method possessed qualities of extraordinary value. It enabled us to investigate some
kinds of propositions to which algebraic reasoning is
little applicable; it always had an elegance peculiarly
its own; it exhibited at each step the course which
the reasoning followed, instead of concealing that
course till the result came out ; it exercised the faculties more severely, because it was less mechanical than
the operations of the analyst. That it afforded evidence of a higher character, more rigorous in its nature than that on which algebraic reasoning rests,

cannot with any correctness be affirmed; both are
equally strict; indeed if each be mathematical in its
nature, and consist of a series of identical propositions
arising one out of another, neither can be less perfect
than the other, for of certainty there can be no degrees.   Nevertheless it must be a matter of regret—
and here the great master and author of modern mathematics has joined in expressing it—that so much less
attention is now paid to the Ancient Geometry than its
beauty and clearness deserve; and if he could justly
make this complaint a century and a half ago,
when the old method had but recently, and only in
part, fallen into neglect and disuse, how much more
are such regrets natural in our day, when the very
name of the Ancient Analysis has almost ceased to be
known, and the beauties of the Greek Geometry are
entirely veiled from the mathematician's eyes!   It becomes, for this reason, necessary that the life of Simson, the great restorer of that geometry, should be
prefaced by some remarks upon the nature of the science, in order that, in giving an account of his works,
we may say his discoveries, it may not appear that we
are recording the services of a great man to some science different from the mathematical.

The analysis of the Greek geometers was a method
of investigation of peculiar elegance, and of no inconsiderable power.   It consisted in supposing the thing
as already done, the problem solved, or the truth of
the theorem established ; and from thence it reasoned
until something was found, some point reached, by
pursuing steps each one of which led to the next, and
by only assuming things which were already known

being ascertained by former discoveries. The thing
thus found, the point reached, was the discovery of
something which could by known methods be performed, or of something which, if not self-evident, was
already by former discovery proved to be true; and in
the one case a construction was thus found by which
the problem was solved, in the other a proof was obtained that the theorem was true, because in both cases
the ultimate point had been reached by strictly legitimate reasoning, from the assumption that the problem
had been solved, or the assumption that the theorem
was true. Thus, if it were required from a given point
in a straight line given by position, to draw a straight
line which should be cut by a given circle in segments,
whose rectangle was equal to that of the segments of
the diameter perpendicular to the given line—the thing
is supposed to be done; and the equality of the rectangles gives a proportion between the segments of the
two lines, such that, joining the point supposed to be
found, but not found, with the extremity of the diameter, the angle of that line with the line sought but
not found, is shown by similar triangles to be a right
angle, *i. e.*, the angle in a semicircle. Therefore the
point through which the line must be drawn is the
point at which the perpendicular cuts the given circle.
Then, suppose the point given through which the line
is to be drawn, if we find that the curve in which the
other points are situate is a circle, we have a local
theorem, affirming that, if lines be drawn through any
point to a line perpendicular to the diameter, the rectangle made by the segments of all the lines cutting the
perpendicular is constant; and this theorem would be

demonstrated by supposing the thing true, and thus
reasoning till we find that the angle in a semicircle is
a right angle, a known truth.   Lastly, suppose we
change the hypothesis, and leave out the position of
the point as given, and inquire after the point in the
given straight line from which a line being drawn
through a point to be found in the circle, the segments will contain a rectangle equal to the rectangle under the perpendicular segments—we find that
one point answers this condition, but also that the
problem becomes indeterminate ; for every line drawn
through that point to every point in the given straight
line has segments, whose rectangle is equal to that
under the segments of the perpendicular.   The enunciation of this truth, of this possibility of finding such
a point in the circle, is a *Porism*.   The Greek geometers of the more modern school, or lower age, defined
a Porism to be a proposition differing from a local
theorem by a defect or defalcation in the hypothesis ; and
accordingly we find that this porism is derived from the
local theorem formerly given, by leaving out part of
the hypothesis.   But we shall afterwards have occasion to observe that this is an illogical and imperfect
definition, not coextensive with the thing defined ; the
above proposition, however, answers every definition of
a Porism.

The demonstration of the theorem or of the construction obtained by investigation in this manner of proceeding, is called *synthesis*, or *composition*, in opposition to the *analysis*, or the process of investigation ;
and it is frequently said that Plato imported the whole
system in the visits which he made, like Thales of
Miletus and Pythagoras, to study under the Egyptian

geometers, and afterwards to converse with Theodorus
at Cyrene, and the Pythagorean School in Italy. But
it can hardly be supposed that all the preceding geometers had worked their problems and theorems at
random; that Thales and Pythagoras with their disciples, a century and a half before Plato, and Hip-
pocrates, half a century before his time, had no
knowledge of the analytical method, and pursued no
systematic plan in their researches, devoted as their
age was to geometrical studies. Plato may have improved and further systematized the method, as he was
no doubt deeply impressed with the paramount importance of geometry, and even inscribed upon the gates
of the Lyceum a prohibition against any one entering
who was ignorant of it. The same spirit of exaggeration which ascribes to him the analytical method, has
also given rise to the notion that he was the discoverer
of the Conic Sections; a notion which is without any
truth and without the least probability.

Of the works written by the Greek geometers some
have come down to us; some of the most valuable, as
the 'Elements' and 'Data' of Euclid, and the 'Conics'
of Apollonius. Others are lost; but, happily, Pappus,
a mathematician of some merit, who flourished in the
Alexandrian school about the end of the fourth century, has left a valuable account of the geometrical
writings of the elder Greeks. His work is of a mis-
cellaneous nature, as its name, 'Mathematical Collections,' implies; and excepting a few passages, it has
never been published in the original Greek. Commandini, of Urbino, made a translation of the whole
six books then discovered: the first has never been

found, but half the second being in the Savilian library
at Oxford, was translated by Wallis a century later.
Commandini's translation, with his learned commentary, was not printed before his death, but the Duke of
Urbino (Francesco Maria) caused it to be published
in 1588, at Pisa, and a second edition was published
at Venice the next year : a fact most honourable to
that learned and accomplished age, when we recollect
how many years Newton's immortal work was published before it reached a second edition, and that in
the seventeenth and eighteenth centuries.

The two first books of Pappus appear to have been
purely arithmetical, so that their loss is little to be
lamented.   The eighth is on mechanics, and the other
five are geometrical.   The most interesting portion is
the seventh ; the introduction of which, addressed to
his son as a guide of his geometrical studies, contains
a full enumeration of the works written by the Greek
geometers, and an account of the particular subjects
which each treated, in some instances giving a summary
of the propositions themselves with more or less obscurity, but always with great brevity.   Among them
was a work which excited great interest, and for a
long time baffled the conjectures of mathematicians,
Euclid's three books of 'Porisms:' of these we shall
afterwards have occasion to speak more fully.   His
'Loci ad Superficiem,' apparently treating of curves
of double curvature, is another, the loss of which was
greatly lamented, the more because Pappus has given
no account of its contents.   This he had done in the
case of the 'Loci Plani' of Apollonius.   Euclid's four
books on conic sections are also lost: but of Apol-

lonius's eight books on the same subject, the most important of the whole series, the 'Elements' excepted, four were preserved, and three more were discovered in the seventeenth century. His Inclinations, his Tactions or Tangencies, his sections of Space and of Ratio, and his Determinate section, however curious, are of less importance ; all of them are lost.

For many years Commandini's publication of the 'Collections' and his commentary did not lead to any attempt at restoring the lost works from the general account given by Pappus. Albert Girard, in 1634, informs us in a note to an edition of Stevinus, that he had restored Euclid's 'Porisms,' a thing eminently unlikely, as he never published any part of his restoration, and it was not found after his decease. In 1637, Fermat restored the 'Loci Plani' of Apollonius, but in a manner so little according to the ancient analysis, that we cannot be said to approach by means of his labours the lost book on this subject. In 1615, De la Hire, a lover and a successful cultivator of the ancient method, published his Conic Sections, but synthetically treated ; he added afterwards other works on epicycloids and conchoids, treated on the analytical plan. L'Hôpital, at the end of the seventeenth century, published an excellent treatise on Conics, but purely algebraical. At the beginning of the eighteenth century, Viviani and Grandi applied themselves to the ancient geometry ; and the former gave a conjectural restoration (Divinatio) of Aristæus's 'Loci Solidi,' the curves of the second or Conic order. But all these attempts were exceedingly unsuccessful, and the world was left in the dark, for the most part, on the

highly interesting subject of the Greek geometry. We
shall presently see that both Fermat and Halley, its
most successful students, had made but an inconsiderable progress in the most difficult branches.

How entirely the academicians of France were
either careless of those matters, or ignorant, or both,
appears by the 'Encyclopédie;' the mathematical
department of which was under no less a geometrician
than d'Alembert. The definition there given of analysis makes it synonymous with algebra: and yet
mention is made of the ancient writers on analysis,
and of the introduction to the seventh book of Pappus,
with only this remark, that those authors differ
much from the modern analysts. But the article
'Arithmetic' (vol. i., p. 677) demonstrates this
ignorance completely; and that Pappus's celebrated
introduction had been referred to by one who never
read it. We there find it said, that Plato is supposed to have invented the ancient analysis; that
Euclid, Apollonius, and others, including Pappus
himself, studied it, but that we are quite ignorant
of what it was: only that it is by some conceived to
have resembled our algebra, as else Archimedes could
never have made his great geometrical discoveries. It
is, certainly, quite incredible that such a name as
d'Alembert's should be found affixed to this statement,
which the mere reading of any one page of Pappus's
books must have shown to be wholly erroneous; and
our wonder is the greater, inasmuch as Simson's admirable restoration of Apollonius's 'Loci Plani' had
been published five years before the 'Encyclopédie'
appeared.

Again, in the 'Encyclopédie,' the word Analysis, as meaning the Greek method, and not algebra, is not even to be found. Nor do the words synthesis, or composition, inclinations, tactions or tangencies occur at all ; and though Porisms are mentioned, it is only to show the same ignorance of the subject: for that word is said to be synonymous with 'lemma,' because it is sometimes used by Pappus in the sense of subsidiary proposition. When Clairault wrote his inestimable work on curves of double curvature, he made no reference whatever to Euclid's ' Loci ad Superficiem,' much less did he handle the subject after the same manner ; he deals, indeed, with matters beyond the reach of the Greek geometry.

Such was the state of this science when Robert Simson first applied to it his genius, equally vigorous and undaunted, with the taste which he had early imbibed for the beauty, the simplicity, and the closeness of the ancient analysis.

ROBERT SIMSON was born on the 14th October (O.S.), 1687, at Kirton Hill, in the parish of Wester Kilbride, in Ayrshire. His father, John Simson, was a merchant in Glasgow : his grandfather, Patrick, was minister of Renfrew, and Dean of the Faculties in the University of Glasgow. Having been deprived at the Restoration, on being reinstated at the Revolution, he accompanied Principal Carstairs and a deputation as one of the Commissioners from the Kirk of Scotland to address the Sovereigns. Being a man of fine presence, it is related that the Queen and her maids of honour mistook him for the Principal, till the King set them

right by presenting Carstairs to them. The grandson,
Robert, is said to have been the eldest of seventeen
children; and the estate of Kirton Hill, which had
been in the family for several generations, being inconsiderable, it was necessary for him, as well as his
brothers, to be placed in some profession. The assertion is made in one account, written by a son of
Professor Millar, and is likely to be correct, that
he was intended for the medical profession, and
being sent to Leyden studied under Boerhaave. He
appears to have been at first intended for the Church,
and to have changed his plan. Dr. Traill, however,
says, that he was always intended for the Church, and
that when the University of St. Andrew's in 1746
wished to confer on him a degree, they made him a
Doctor of Medicine, because he had studied botany in
his youth. Nothing can be more improbable than
this story; for to give him a degree they had only to
make him Doctor of Laws, instead of taking a step
which for ever threw discredit upon their medical
honours. Mr. Millar must have heard the truth from
his father and the other professors, who had the
honour of knowing Dr. Simson personally, and never
could have imagined or invented the circumstance of
his studying under Boerhaave.*

Of his early years we know little; but that he was
always extremely fond of reading is certain; and he

* The account which I have seen was in the late Earl of Buchan's
possession, and was extended by matters collected when he himself
studied at Glasgow. It seems by the mathematical appearance of it
to have come from James Millar, himself one of the Professors.

must have had a considerable turn for mechanical pursuits if the tradition in the neighbourhood of Kirton
Hill be well founded, which ascribes to him the making, or at least designing and placing a dial of a curious
form (which I have seen) on a neatly ornamented pe-
destal in the garden of his father's house. At the usual
early age of matriculation in Scotland, he was sent to
the University of Glasgow, and he had there made considerable progress in his studies before the love of mathematical pursuits appeared to possess him. His attention was directed to theology, to logic, to Oriental
learning; and in the latter he had made such progress,
that a relation who taught the class having fallen ill,
Simson easily supplied his place for part of a session,
the Scottish academical year. It was while engaged
in theological studies that the mathematics first seized
hold of his mind. He used in after life to relate how,
wearied with the controversies to which his clerical
studies led him, he would refresh himself with philosophical reading; and not seldom finding himself
there also tossed about by conflicting dogmas, he
retired for peace and shelter to the certain science of
necessary truth; "and then," said he, " I always
found myself refreshed with rest."

It happened that no lecture or teaching of any kind
was given by the professor who filled the mathematical
chair, receiving its emoluments, and neglecting its
duties, when Simson went to the University. But
curiosity, a propensity ever strong in his nature through
his whole life, made him wish to see what the science
was, and he borrowed from a friend a copy of Euclid,
the work which he was destined afterwards to give

forth in a perfection that has made all other editions
of that great classic be forgotten.   Over the elements
of the science he pored assiduously and alone, with
only the aid of suggestions occasionally given by a
student some years older than himself; and the study
falling in with his genius and his taste, he soon made
himself master of the first six books, comprising plain
geometry, and the eleventh and twelfth, treating of
solids, those at least which are bounded by planes or
by circular arches.   But he did not neglect the other
branches of science taught at the College; and he
also gave his attention to the literary parts of education, so well mastering the Latin and Greek languages
as to become a learned and accurate scholar.   It was
in the mathematics, however, that he chiefly excelled;
and his accomplishments in that science becoming
known to the professorial body (the Senatus Academicus), in whom is vested the patronage of the mathematical chair, and an early vacancy being foreseen,
they offered him the succession in that event.   Being
then in his twenty-second year, he modestly declined
to undertake so important a charge, but requested a
year's delay, during which he might repair to London,
and become more familiar with the science and its cultivators. We may hence perceive that there could then
have been no one at all versed in the mathematics at
Glasgow; and the allowing so important a branch of
science to remain for so many years untaught because
the teacher who received the ample emoluments of the
chair either could not or would not perform its duties,
affords a sufficient commentary upon the great abuse
likely to flow from vesting the patronage of a profes-

sorship in the colleagues of the teacher. I have known a professor's son appointed to the same chair, with few or no mathematical acquirements, because his father was much and justly respected among the members of the academical body. The same thing could not happen in Edinburgh, where the Crown or the magistrates have the patronage of all the professorships excepting one, and that is in the representative of the founder.*

Simson repaired accordingly to London, where he became intimately acquainted, among others, with Jones the optician, with Henry Ditton of Christ's Hospital, under whose tuition he placed himself, with Carswell, above all, with Edmund Halley, then a captain in the Navy, afterwards so celebrated as Dr. Halley; of whom he used to assert that "he had never known any other man of so acute and penetrating an understanding, and of so pure a taste." From him he received much personal kindness, and what he had reason to value still more, the advice to prosecute his study of the Ancient Geometry, and attempt restoring its lost books. Halley made him a present of his copy of Pappus, with notes in his own hand. But though these accidental circumstances tended to direct his attention towards the scrupulous rigour as well as surpassing elegance of the Greek methods, it is a great mistake to suppose that he objected to the strictness of the modern analysis as inadequate. That he deemed its beauty inferior, and that he was right in so deeming, is certain; but that he questioned the solidity of

---

* Agriculture, in the Pulteney Family.

its foundations is wholly untrue. Not only did he always explain its principles to his pupils, though in a manner peculiar to himself, but he has left behind him a treatise demonstrating the fundamental laws of the calculus, and we now possess it in a printed form. Equally groundless is the notion that he questioned the soundness of the Newtonian Philosophy. He was not enabled to make Sir Isaac's acquaintance during his residence in London; but among those he lived with he constantly had seen him viewed with a peculiar observance, and Halley in particular regarded him as hardly human, and his attainments in science as exalting our species, while they ennobled himself, its rarest individual. Simson's copy of the 'Principia' is fully noted in the margin with illustrations, showing that he entirely assented to the results of the investigations in the several propositions, and only wished to substitute certain steps in the demonstrations. Professor Robison has also related (Art. Simson, Encyc. Brit. xvii. 505) his constant remark, that the celebrated proposition in the 'Principia' on inverse centripetal forces "was the most important ever delivered to mankind in the mixed mathematics."

While he remained in London the expected vacancy occurred in the chair at Glasgow, and he returned thither. The professors appear to have thought it right that their former neglect of duty should be compensated by a very superfluous show of more than needful attention to it on this occasion; for they required Mr. Simson to give proof of his fitness to succeed the sinecure incumbent, by solving a geometrical problem, of which it is all but absolutely certain that they could have no knowledge, unless the question was so simple as to afford no test of the candidate's capacity. He produced, however, what they might better understand, testimonials from known mathematicians in London, a farther proof of there being no cultivators of the science then resident in the metropolis of Scottish manufactures.

He was thus appointed professor in 1711, and immediately began the regular course of instruction, which he continued for half a century. He taught two classes five days a week for seven months every year. Though geometry was his own favourite study, he was a thorough algebraist also, and so well versed in mathematical science at large, that he gave lectures on its general history. With astronomy, and the other branches of the mixed mathematics, he was no less conversant; and in various departments of physics he had made great progress. In botany he was particularly expert; it formed his chosen amusement during the walks in which he relaxed from his severer studies. His curiosity led him into other paths of science. To logic, that of the schools, he had given so much attention, that of a tract, composed by him upon its principles, some portion remains among his papers; it is said to possess great merit; and doubtless this study was congenial to the one which he mainly pursued, nor could it fail to aid his strict and luminous method of both defining, demonstrating, and explaining the truths of geometry.

Among his colleagues, after he had been professor a few years, were some of the most eminent men of that, or indeed of any age. Moore, professor of Greek, and author of the admirable and elegant 'Grammar;'

Hutcheson, and Adam Smith, successively teachers of moral philosophy; Cullen, the celebrated physician; Black, the great founder of modern chemistry—all taught while Simson flourished; Millar only became professor of law at the close of the brilliant period now referred to, and Robison succeeded Black in 1761, soon after Simson's resignation.

But a teacher's influence is nothing in surrounding himself with illustrious colleagues: of great pupils he may more easily obtain a following. Of these, Dr. Simson had some whose names are still honoured among mathematicians. Williamson, afterwards his assistant in the class, a man of great promise, whose early death at the Factory of Lisbon, to which he was chaplain, alone prevented him from following with distinction his master's footsteps; Scott, preceptor to George III. when Prince of Wales, afterwards a Commissioner of Excise in London, perhaps the most accomplished of all amateur mathematicians who never gave their works to the world; Traill, author of the excellent elementary treatise of algebra, of a very learned and exceedingly ill-written, indeed, hardly readable, life of his friend and teacher, but a man of great capacity for science, entirely extinguished, together with his taste for its pursuits (as Professor Playfair used to lament), by the sinecure emoluments of the Irish Church; but above all, Matthew Stewart, Simson's favourite pupil, and whose suggestions, and indeed contributions, he records in his works with appropriate eulogy, as he does on one occasion an ingenious theorem of Traill—these were among his scholars, and were, with Robison, the most distinguished of their number. His method of lecturing is, by both of the pupils who have written his history, Professor Robison and Dr. Traill, described as singularly attractive. His explanations were perfectly clear, and were delivered with great spirit, as well as with the pure taste which presided over all his mathematical processes. His elocution was distinct and natural, his whole manner at once easy and impressive. He did not confine his tuition to the chair, but encouraged his pupils to propound their difficulties in private, and was always accessible to their demands of assistance and advice. Hence the affectionate zeal with which they followed his teaching and ever cherished his memory.

Successful, however, as he proved in the chair, his genius was bent to the diligent investigation of truth in the science of which he was so great a master. The ancient geometry, that of the Greeks of which I have spoken, early fixed his attention and occupied his mind by its extraordinary elegance, by the lucid clearness with which its investigations are conducted, by the exercise which it affords to the reasoning faculties, and above all, by the absolute rigour of its demonstrations. He never undervalued modern analysis; it is a great mistake to represent him as either disliking its process, or insensible to its vast importance for the solution of questions which the Greek analysis is wholly incapable of reaching. But he considered it as only to be used in its proper sphere: and that sphere he held to exclude whatever of geometrical investigation can be, with convenience and elegance, carried on by purely geometrical methods. The application of algebra to geometry, it would be ridiculous to suppose that either he or his celebrated pupil Stewart disliked or undervalued. That application forms the most valuable service which modern analysis has rendered to science. But they did object, and most reasonably and consistently, to the introduction of algebraic reasoning wherever the investigation could, though less easily, yet far more satisfactorily, be performed geometrically. They saw, too, that in many instances the algebraic solution leads to constructions of the most complex, clumsy, unmanageable kind, and therefore must be, in all these instances, reckoned more difficult, and even more prolix than the geometrical, from the former being confined to the expression of all the relations of space and position, by magnitudes, by quantity and number, (even after the arithmetic of sines had been introduced,) while the latter could avail itself of circles and angles directly. They would have equally objected to carrying geometrical reasoning into the fields peculiarly appropriate to modern analysis; and if one of them, Stewart, did endeavour to investigate by the ancient geometry physical problems supposed to be placed beyond its reach—as the sun's distance, in which he failed, and Kepler's problem, in which he marvellously succeeded, that of dividing the elliptical area in a given ratio by a straight line drawn from one focus— this is to be taken only as an homage to the undervalued potency of the Greek analysis, or at most, as a feat of geometrical force, and by no means as an indication of any wish to substitute so imperfect, however beautiful, an instrument, for the more powerful, though more ordinary one of the calculus which " alone can work great marvels." At the same time, and with all the necessary confession of the merits of the modern method, it is certain that those geometricians would have regarded the course taken by some of its votaries in more recent times as exceptionable, whether with a view to clearness or to good taste: a course to the full as objectionable as would be the banishing of alge-braical and substituting of geometrical symbols in the investigations of the higher geometry. La Place's great work, the ' Mécanique Céleste,' and La Grange's 'Méca-nique Analytique,' have treated of the whole science of dynamics and of physical astronomy, comprehending all the doctrine of trajectories, dealing with geome-trical ideas throughout, and ideas so purely geometrical that the algebraic symbols, as far as their works are concerned, have no possible meaning apart from lines, angles, surfaces ; and yet in their whole compass they have not one single diagram of any kind. Surely,

we may ask if $\dfrac{y}{dy}\sqrt{dx^2+dy^2}$, $\dfrac{ds^3}{dx^2 d\left(\dfrac{dy}{dx}\right)}$ * can pos-

sibly bear any other meaning than the tangent and the radius of curvature of a curve line : that is, a straight line touching a curve, and a circle whose curvature is that of another curve where they meet; any meaning, at least, which can make it material that they should ever be seen on the page of the analyst. These expressions are utterly without sense, except in reference to geometrical con-

---

* Or $\dfrac{(dx^2+dy^2)^{\frac{3}{2}}}{dx^2 d\left(\dfrac{dy}{dx}\right)}$

siderations; for although x and y are so general that they express any numbers, any lines, nay, any ideas, any rewards or punishments, any thoughts of the mind, it is manifest that the square of the differential of a thought, or the differential of the differential of a reward or punishment, has no meaning; and so of every thing else but of the very tangent or osculating circle's radius : consequently the generality of the symbols is wholly useless; the particular case of two lines being the only thing to which the expressions can possibly be meant to apply. Why, then, all geometrical symbols should be so carefully avoided when we are really treating of geometrical examples and geometrical ideas, and of these alone, seems hard to understand.

As the exclusive lovers of modern analysis have frequently and very erroneously suspected the ancients of possessing some such instrument, and concealing the use of it by giving their demonstrations synthetically after reaching their conclusions analytically, so some lovers of ancient analysis have supposed that Sir Isaac Newton obtained his solutions by algebraic investigations, and then covered them with a synthetic dress : among others, Dr. Simson leant to this opinion respecting the ' Principia.' He used to say that he knew this from Halley, by whose urgent advice Sir Isaac was induced to adopt the synthetic form of demonstration, after having discovered the truths analytically. Machin is known to have held the same language ; he said that the ' Principia' was algebra in disguise. Assuredly, the probability of this is far greater than that of the ancients having possessed and kept secret the analytical process of modern times. In the preface to his ' Loci Plani,' Dr. Simson fully refutes this notion respecting the ancients: a notion which, among others, no less a writer than Wallis had strongly maintained.*

Dr. Simson is by some supposed to have had at one time the intention of discussing at large the proper limits of the ancient and the modern analysis in the investigation of mathematical truths. This no doubt appears to be the meaning of a passage in his preface to the Conic Sections: " In quantum autem differat analysis geometrica ab eâ quæ calculo instituitur algebraico, atque *ubi hæc aut illa sit usurpanda, alias disserendum.*" Professor Robison thought he had seen a portion of the work; but he must have been mistaken; for in answer to Mr. Scott's letter urging him to publish this, and referring to the preface in the words just cited, he expressly says, that though this passage might well mislead, he never meant, except by " blundering in the expression, anything of the kind, had no paper, and never wrote anything about the matter:" and this was written in 1764, four years before his death, and eleven or twelve years after Professor Robison attended his class. Nothing can be more clear than that between 1764 and his death, in 1768, he never attempted any work of moment; much more any work such as the one in

---

* Algebra Præf. " Hanc Græcos olim habuisse non est quod dubitemus; sed studio celatam, nec temere propalandam. Ejus effectus (utut clam celatæ) satis conspicui apud Archimedem, Apollonium, aliosque." It is strange that any one of ordinary reflection should have overlooked the utter impossibility of all the geometricians in ancient times keeping the secret of an art which must, if it existed, have been universally known in the mathematical schools, and at a time when every man of the least learning or even of the most ordinary education was taught geometry.

question, which we thus have his own authority for saying he never had previously entertained any intention of
composing. It is much to be lamented that he never
did give such a work to the world. His thoughts had
often been very profoundly directed to the subject;
and no one was so well fitted to handle it with the
learning and with the judgment which its execution
required.

That he did not undervalue algebra and the calculus
to which it has given rise, appears from many circumstances—among others, from what has already been
stated; it appears also from this, that in many of his
manuscripts there are found algebraical formulas for
propositions which he had investigated geometrically.
Maclaurin consulted him on the preparation of his
admirable work, the ' Fluxions,' and received from him
copious suggestions and assistance. Indeed, he adopted
from him the celebrated demonstration of the fluxion (or
differential) of a rectangle.* But Simson's whole mind,
when left to its natural bent, was given to the beauties
of the Greek geometry; and he had not been many
months settled in his academical situation when he
began to follow the advice which Halley had given
him, as both calculated, he said, to promote his
own reputation, and to confer a lasting benefit upon
the science cultivated by them both with an equal devotion. It is even certain that the obscure and most
difficult subject of Porisms very early occupied his
thoughts, and was the field of his researches, though to
the end of his life he never had made such progress in

---

* Book i. ch. ii. prop. 3.

the investigation as satisfied himself. Before 1715, three years after he began his course of teaching, he was deeply engaged in this inquiry; but he only regarded it as one branch of the great and dark subject which Halley had recommended to his care. After he had completely examined, corrected, and published, with most important additions, the Conics of Apollonius, which happily remain entire, but which, as we have seen, had been most inelegantly and indeed algebraically given by De la Hire, L'Hôpital, and others, to restore the lost books was his great desire, and formed the grand achievement which he set before his eyes.

We have already shown how scanty the light was by which his steps in this path must be guided. The introduction to the seventh book of Pappus contained the whole that had reached our times to let us know the contents of the lost works. Some of the summaries which that valuable discourse contains are sufficiently explicit, as those of the Loci Plani and the Determinate Section. Accordingly, former geometricians had succeeded in restoring the Loci Plani, or those propositions which treat of loci to the circle and rectilinear figures. They had, indeed, proceeded in a very unsatisfactory manner; Schooten, a Dutch mathematician of great industry and no taste, had given purely algebraic solutions and demonstrations. Fermat, one of the greatest mathematicians of the seventeenth century, had proceeded more according to the geometrical rules of the ancients; but he had kept to general solutions, and neither he nor Schooten had given the different cases, according as the data in each proposition were varied, so that their works were nearly

useless in the solution of problems, the great purpose
of Apollonius, as of all the authors of the τοπος
αναλυομενου—the thirty-three ancient books. As for
the analysis, it was given by neither, unless, indeed,
Schooten's algebra is to be so termed: Fermat's demonstrations were all synthetical. His treatise, though
written as early as 1629, was only published among
his collected works in 1670. Schooten's was published
among his 'Exercitationes Mathematicæ' in 1657. Of
the field thus left open Dr. Simson took possession,
and he most successfully cultivated every corner
of it. Nothing is left without the most full discussion ; all the cases of each proposition are thoroughly
investigated. Many new truths of great importance
are added to those which had been unfolded by the
Greek philosopher. The whole is given with the perfect precision and the pure elegance of the ancient
analysis; and the universal assent of the scientific
world has even confessed that there is every reason to
consider the restored work as greatly superior to the
lost original.

The history of this excellent treatise shows in a
striking manner the cautious and modest nature of its
author. He had completed it in 1738 ; but, unsatisfied
with it, he kept it by him for eight years. He could
not bring himself to think that he had given the
" ipsissimæ propositiones of Apollonius in the very
order and spirit of the original work." He was then
persuaded to let the book appear, and it was published
in 1746. His former scruples and alarms recurred ;
he stopped the publication ; he bought up the copies
that had been sold ; he kept them three years longer

by him; and it was only in 1749 that the work really appeared. Thus had a geometrician complied with the rule prescribed by Horace for those whose writings have no standard by which to estimate their merits with exactness.

In the meantime he had extended his researches into other parts of the subject. Among the rest he had restored and greatly extended the work on Determinate Section, or the various propositions respecting the properties of the squares and rectangles of segments of lines passing through given points. There is no doubt that the prolixity, however elegant, with which the ancients treated this subject, is somewhat out of proportion to its importance; and as it is peculiarly adapted to the algebraical method, presenting, indeed, little difficulty to the analyst, the loss of the Pergæan treatise is the less to be deplored, and its restoration was the less to be desired. Apollonius had even thought it expedient to give a double set of solutions; one by straight lines, the other by semicircles. Dr. Simson's restoration is most full, certainly, and contains many and large additions of his own. It fills above three hundred quarto pages. His predecessors had been Snellius, whose attempt, published in 1608, was universally allowed to be a failure; and Anderson, a professor of Aberdeen, whose work, in 1612, was much better, but confined to a small part only of the subject.

About the time that Dr. Simson finally published the Loci Plani, he began his great labour of giving a correct and full edition of the Elements. The manner in which this has been accomplished by him is well

known. The utmost care was bestowed on the revision of the text; no pains were spared in collating
editions; all commentaries were consulted; and the
elegance and perfect method of the original has been
so admirably preserved, that no rival has ever yet risen
up to dispute with Simson's Euclid the possession of
the schools. The time bestowed on this useful work
was no less than nine years. It only was published in
1758. To the second edition, in 1762, he added a
similarly correct edition of the Data, comprising
several very valuable original propositions of his own,
of Mr. Stewart, and of Lord Stanhope, together with
two excellent problems to illustrate the use of the
Data in solutions.

. We thus find Dr. Simson employed in these various
works which he successively gave to the world, elaborated
with infinite care, and of which the fame and the use
will remain as long as the mathematics are cultivated,
some of them delighting students who pursue the
science for the mere speculative love of contemplating
abstract truths, and the gratification of following the
rigorous proofs peculiar to that science ; some for the
instruction of men in the elements, which are to
form the foundation of their practical applications of
geometry. But all the while his mind never could be
wholly severed from the speculation which had in his
earliest days riveted his attention by its curious and
singular nature, and fired his youthful ambition by
its difficulty, and vanquished all his predecessors in
their efforts to master it. We have seen that as early
as 1715 at the latest, probably much earlier, the obscure
subject of Porisms had engaged his thoughts ; and soon

after, his mind was so entirely absorbed by it that he could apply to no other investigation. The extreme imperfection of the text of Pappus, the dubious nature of his description, his rejection of the definition which appeared intelligible, his substituting nothing in its place except an account so general that it really conveyed no precise information, the hiatus in the account he subjoins of Euclid's three books, so that even with the help of the lemmas related to these propositions of the lost work, no clear or steady light could be descried to guide the inquirer—for the first porism of the first book alone remained entire, the general porism being given wholly truncated (mancum et imperfectum)—all seemed to present obstacles wholly insurmountable, and after various attempts for years he was fain to conclude with Halley that the mystery belonged to the number of those which can never be penetrated. He lost his rest in the anxiety of this inquiry; sleep forsook his couch; his appetite was gone; his health was wholly shaken; he was compelled to give over the pursuit; he was " obliged," he says, " to resolve steadily that he never more should touch the subject, and as often as it came upon him he drove it away from his thoughts."*

It happened, however, about the month of April, 1722, that while walking on the banks of the Clyde with some friends, he had fallen behind the company; and musing alone, the rejected topic found access to

* " Firmiter animum induxi hæc nunquam in posterum investigare. Unde quoties menti occurrebant, toties eas arcebam."—(Op. Rel. 320. Præf. ad Porismata.)

his thoughts. After some time a sudden light broke in upon him; it seemed at length as if he could descry something of a path, slippery, tangled, interrupted, but still practicable, and leading at least in the direction towards the object of his research. He eagerly drew a figure on the stump of a neighbouring tree with a piece of chalk; he felt assured that he had now the means of solving the great problem; and although he afterwards tells us that he then had not a sufficiently clear notion of the subject (eo tempore Porismatum naturam non satis compertam habebam),* yet he accomplished enough to make him communicate a paper upon the discovery to the Royal Society, the first work he ever published (Phil. Trans. for 1723). He was wont in after life to show the spot on which the tree, long since decayed, had stood. If peradventure it had been preserved, the frequent lover of Greek geometry would have been seen making his pilgrimage to a spot consecrated by such touching recollections. The graphic pen of Montucla, which gave such interest to the story of the first observation of the transit of Venus by Horrox in Lancashire, and to the Torricellian experiment,† is alone wanting to clothe this passage in colours as vivid and as unfading.

This great geometrician continued at all the intervals of his other labours intently to investigate the subject on which he thus first threw a steady light.

His first care upon having made this discovery was to extend the particular propositions until he had obtained

---

* Op. Rel. 320.   † Hist. de Math. vol. i.

the general one. A note among his memoranda appears to have been made, as was his custom, of the date at which he succeeded in any of his investigations.*—"Hodie hæc de porismatis inveni, R. S., 23 April 1722." Another note, 27th April, 1722, shows that he had then obtained the general proposition; he afterwards communicated this to Maclaurin when he passed through Glasgow on his way to France; and on his return he communicated to Dr. Simson without demonstration a proposition concerning conics derived from it, which led his friend to insert some important investigations in his Conic Sections. In 1723 the publication of his paper took place in the Philosophical Transactions; it is extremely short, and does not appear to contain all that the author had communicated; for we find this sentence inserted before the last portion of the paper:—" His adjecit clarissimus professor propositiones duas sequentes libri primi Porismatum Euclidis, a se quoque restitutas." The paper contains the first general proposition and its ten cases, and then the second with its cases. No general description or definition is given of Porisms; and it is plain that his mind was not then finally made up on this obscure subject, although he had obtained a clear view of it generally.

---

* In one there is this note upon the solution of a problem of tactions,—" Feb. 9, 1734 :—Post horam primam ante meridiem ;" and much later in life we find the same particularity in marking the time of discovery. His birthday was October 14, and having solved a problem on that day, 1764, he says—

Deo Opt. Max. benignissimo Servatori
      Laus et gloria.

14 Octobr. 1764.
14 Octobr. 1687.

77 (scil. Anno Ætatis.)

At what time his knowledge of the whole became matured we are not informed; but we know that his own nature was nice and difficult on the subject of his own works; that he never was satisfied with what he had accomplished; and he probably went on making constant additions and improvements to his work. Often urged to publish, he as constantly refused; indeed he would say that he had done nothing, or next to nothing, which was in a state to appear before the world; and moreover, he very early began to apprehend a decay of his faculties, from observing his recollection of recent things to fail, as is very usual with all men; for as early as 1751, we find him giving this as a reason for declining to undertake a work on Lord Stanhope's recommendation, when he was only in his sixty-fifth year. Thus, though he at first used to say he had nothing ready for publication, he afterwards added, that he was too old to complete his work satisfactorily. In his earlier days he used occasionally to affect a kind of odd mystery on the subject, and when one of his pupils (Dr. Traill) submitted to him some propositions, which he regarded as porisms, Dr. Simson would neither admit nor deny that they were such, but said with some pleasantry, " They are propositions." One of them, however, he has given in his work as a porism, and with a complimentary reference to its ingenious and learned author.

Thus his life wore away without completing this great work, at least without putting it in such a condition as satisfied himself. It was left among his MSS., and by the judicious munificence of a noble geometrician, the liberal friend of scientific men, as well as the successful cultivator of science, Earl Stanhope,* it was, after his death, published, with his restoration of Apollonius' treatise De Sectione determinatâ, a short paper on Logarithms, and another on the Method of Limits geometrically demonstrated, the whole forming a very handsome quarto volume; of which the Porisms occupies nearly one-half, or 277 pages.

This work is certainly the master-piece of its distinguished author. The extreme difficulty of the subject was increased by the corruptions of the text that remains in the only passage of the Greek geometers which has reached us, the only few sentences in which any mention whatever is made of porisms. This passage is contained in the preface or introduction to the seventh book of Pappus, which we have already had occasion to cite. But this was by far the least of the difficulties which met the inquirer after the hidden treasure, the restorer of lost science, though Albert Girard thought or said, in 1635, that he had restored the Porisms of Euclid. As we have seen, no trace of his labours is left; and it seems extremely unlikely that he should have really performed such a feat and given no proofs of it. Halley, the most learned and able of Dr. Simson's predecessors, had tried the subject, and tried it in vain. He thus records his failure:—"Hactenus Porismatum descriptio nec mihi intellecta nec lectori profutura." These are his words, in a preface to a translation which he published of Pappus's seventh book, much superior in execution to that of Commandini. But this eminent geometrician was

---

* Grandfather of the present Earl.

2 K

much more honest than some, and much more safe
and free from mistake than others who touched upon
the subject which occupied all students of the ancient
analysis. He was far from pretending, like Girardus,
to have discovered that of which all were in quest. But
neither did he blunder like Pemberton, whom we find,
the very year of Simson's first publication, actually
saying in his paper on the Rainbow — "For the
greater brevity I shall deliver them (his propositions)
in the form of porisms, as, in my opinion, the ancients
called all propositions treated by analysis only" (Philosophical Transactions, 1723, p. 148); and, truth to
say, his investigation is not very like ancient analysis
either. The notion of D'Alembert, somewhat later,
has been alluded to already ; he imagined porisms to be
synonymous with lemma, misled by an equivocal use
of the word in some passages of ancient authors, if
indeed he had ever studied any of the writers on the
Greek geometry, which, from what I have stated before, seems exceedingly doubtful. But the most extraordinary, and indeed inexcusable ignorance of the subject is to be seen in some who, long after Simson's
paper had been published, were still in the dark ; and
though that paper did not fully explain the matter, it
yet ought to have prevented such errors as these fell
into. Thus Castillon, in 1761, showed that he conceived porisms to be merely the constructions of Euclid's Data. If this were so, there might have been
some truth in his boast of having solved all the Porisms
of Euclid; and he might have been able to perform
his promise of soon publishing a restoration of those lost
books.

It is remarkable enough that before Halley's attempts and their failure, candidly acknowledged by himself, Fermat had made a far nearer approach to a solution of the difficulty than any other of Simson's predecessors. That great geometrician, after fully admitting the difficulty of the subject, and asserting* that, in modern times, porisms were known hardly even by name, announces somewhat too confidently, if not somewhat vaingloriously, that the light had at length dawned upon him,† and that he should soon give a full restoration of the whole three lost books of Euclid. Now the light had but broke in by a small chink, as a mere faint glimmering, and this restoration was quite impossible, inasmuch as there remained no account of what those books contained, excepting a very small portion obscurely mentioned in the preface of Pappus, and the lemmas given in the course of the seventh book, and given as subservient to the resolution of porismatic questions. Nevertheless Fermat gave a demonstration of five propositions, " in order," he says, " to show what a porism is, and to what purposes it is subservient." These propositions are, indeed, porisms, though their several enumerations are not given in the true porismatic form. Thus, in the most remarkable of them, the fifth, he gives the construction as part of the enuncia-

---

* " Intentata ac velut disperata Porismatum Euclidæa doctrina.—Geometrici (ævi recentioris) nec vel de nomine cognoverunt, aut quod esset solummodo sunt suspicati."—(Var. Opera, p. 166.)

† "Nobis in tenebris dudum cæcutientibus, tandem se (Natura Porismatum) clara ad videndum obtulit, et purà per noctem luce refulsit."—(Epist. ib.)

tion. So far, however, a considerable step was made ;
but when he comes to show in what manner he discovered the nature of his porisms, and how he defines
them, it is plain that he is entirely misled by the
erroneous definition justly censured in the passage of
Pappus already referred to. He tells us that his propositions answer the definition ; he adds that it reveals
the whole nature of porisms ; he says that by no other
account but the one contained in the definition, could
we ever have arrived at a knowledge of the hidden
value ;* and he shows how, in his fifth proposition,
the porism flows from a locus, or rather he confounds
porisms with loci, saying porisms generally are loci,
and so he treats his own fifth proposition as a locus, and
yet the locus to a circle which he states as that from
which his proposition flows has no connexion with it,
according to Dr. Simson's just remark ('Opera Reliqua,'
p. 345). That the definition on which he relies is
truly imperfect, appears from this : there could be
no algebraical porism, were every porism connected
with a local theorem. But an abundant variety of
geometrical porisms can be referred to, which have no
possible connexion with loci. Thus, it has never been
denied that most of the Propositions in the Higher
Geometry, which I investigated in 1797, were porisms,
yet many of them were wholly unconnected with loci ;
as that affirming the possibility of describing an hyperbola which should cut in a given ratio all the areas
of the parabolas lying between given straight lines.†

---

* Var. Op., p. 118.
Phil. Trans., 1798, p. 111.

Here the locus has nothing to do with the solution, as if the proposition were a kind of a local theorem : it is only the line dividing the curvilineal areas, and it divides innumerable such areas. Professor Playfair, who had thoroughly investigated the whole subject, never in considering this proposition doubted for a moment its being most strictly a porism.

Therefore, although Fermat must be allowed to have made a considerable step, he was unacquainted with the true nature of the porism ; and instead of making good his boast that he could restore the lost books, he never even attempted to restore the investigation of the first proposition, the only one that remains entire. A better proof can hardly be given of the difficulty of the whole subject.*

Indeed it must be confessed that Pappus's account of it, our only source of knowledge, is exceedingly obscure, all but the panegyrics which, in a somewhat tantalizing manner, he pronounces upon it. "Collectio," says he, "curiosissima multarum rerum spectantium ad resolutionem difficiliorum et generaliorum problematum" (lib. vii., Proem). His definition already cited is, as he himself admits, very inaccurate ; because the

* The respect due to the great name of Fermat, a venerable magistrate and most able geometrician, is not to be questioned. He was, indeed, one of the first mathematicians of the age in which he flourished, along with the Robervals, the Harriots, the Descartes. How near he approached the differential calculus is well known. His correspondence with Roberval, Gassendi, Pascal, and others, occupies ninety folio pages of his posthumous works, and contains many most ingenious, original, and profound observations on various branches of science.

connexion with a locus is not necessary to the porismatic nature, although it will very often exist, inasmuch as each point in the curve having the same relation to certain lines, its description will, in most
cases, furnish the solution of a problem, whence a
porism may be deduced. Nor does Pappus, while admitting the inaccuracy of the definition, give us one of
his own. Perhaps we may accurately enough define
a porism to be the enunciation of the possibility of
finding that case in which a determinate problem becomes indeterminate, and admits of an infinity of
solutions, all of which are given by the statement of
the case.

For it appears essential to the nature of a porism
that it should have some connexion with an indeterminate problem and its solution. I apprehend that the
poristic case is always one in which the data become
such that a transition is made from the determinate to
the indeterminate, from the problem being capable of
one or two solutions, to its being capable of an infinite
number. Thus it would be no porism to affirm that
an ellipse being given, two lines may be found at right
angles to each other, cutting the curve, and being in a
proportion to each other which may be found : the two
lines are the perpendiculars at the centre, and are of
course the two axes of the ellipse; and though this
enunciation is in the outward form of a porism, the
proposition is no more a porism than any ordinary problem ; as that a circle being given a point may be found
from whence all the lines drawn to the circumference
are equal, which is merely the finding of the centre.
But suppose there be given the problem to inflect two

lines from two given points to the circumference of an ellipse, the sum of which lines shall be equal to a given line, the solution will give four lines, two on each side of the transverse axis. But in one case there will be innumerable lines which answer the conditions, namely, when the two points are in the axis, and so situated that the distance of each of them from the farthest extremity of the axis is equal to the given line, the points being the foci of the ellipse. It is, then, a porism to affirm that an ellipse being given, two points may be found such that if from them be inflected lines to any point whatever of the curve, their sum shall be equal to a straight line which may be found; and so of the Cassinian curve, in which the rectangle under the inflected lines is given. In like manner if it be sought in the cubic hyperbola ($y\,x^2 = x - a$) to inflect from two given points in a given straight line, two lines to a point in the curve, so that the tangent to that point shall, with the two points and the ordinate, cut the given line in harmonical ratio ; this, which is only capable of one solution in ordinary cases, becomes capable of an infinite number when the two points are in the axis, one of them the curve's apex, and the other at the distance equal to the given line a from the apex ; for in that case every tangent that can be drawn, and every ordinate, cut the given line harmonically with the curve itself and the given point.[*]

---

[*] This curve has many curious and elegant properties : for example—All the lines which can be drawn in every direction from any point out of the curve are cut harmonically by the tangent, the ordinate, and the lines joining the two given points. This

Dr. Simson's definition is such that it connects itself with an indeterminate case of some problem solved, but it is defective, in appearance rather than in reality, from seeming to confine itself to one class of porisms. This appearance arises from using the word "*given*" (*data* or *datum*) in two different senses, both as describing the hypothesis and as affirming the possibility of finding the construction so as to answer the conditions. This double use of the word, indeed, runs through the book, and though purely classical, is yet very inconvenient; for it would be much more distinct to make one class of things those which are assuredly data, and the other, things which may be found. Nevertheless, as his definition makes all the innumerable things not given have the same relation to those which are given, this should seem to be a limitation of the definition not necessary to the poristic nature. Pappus's definition, or rather that which he says the ancients gave, and which is not exposed to the objection taken by him to the modern one, is really no definition at all; it is only that a porism is something between a theorem and a problem, and in which, instead of anything being proposed to be done, or to be proved, something is proposed to be investigated.

---

might be called the *Harmonical Curve*, did not another of the 12th order rather merit that name, which has its axis divided harmonically by the tangent, the normal, the ordinate, and a given point in the axis. Its differential equation is $2 \, d \, y^2 + d \, x^2 = \dfrac{y \, d \, y \, d \, x}{x}$, which is reducible, and its integral is an equation of the 12th order. There is another Harmonical Curve, also, a transcendental one, in which chords vibrate isochronously.

This is erroneous, and contrary to the rules of logic from its generality; it is, as the lawyers say, void for uncertainty. The modern one objected to by Pappus is not uncertain; it is quite accurate as far as it goes; but it is too confined, and errs against the rules of logic by not being coextensive with the thing proposed to be defined.

The difficulty of the subject has been sufficiently shown from the extreme conciseness and the many omissions, the almost studied obscurity, of the only account of it which remains, and to this must certainly be added the corruption of the Greek text. The success which attended Dr. Simson's labours in restoring the lost work, as far as that was possible, and, at any rate, in giving a full elucidation of the nature of porisms, now, for the first time, disclosed to mathematicians, is, on account of those great difficulties by which his predecessors had been baffled, the more to be admired. But there is one thing yet more justly a matter of wonder, when we contrast his proceedings with theirs. The greater part of his life, a life exclusively devoted to mathematical study, had been passed in these researches. He had very early become possessed of the whole mystery, from other eyes so long concealed. He had obtained a number of the most curious solutions of problems connected with porisms, and was constantly adding to his store of porisms and of lemmas subservient to their investigation. For many years before his death, his work had attained, certainly the form, if not the size, in which we now possess it. Yet he never could so far satisfy himself with what has abundantly satisfied every one else, as to make it public, and he left it un-

published among his papers when he died. Nothing
can be more unlike those who freely boasted of having
discovered the secret, and promised to restore the
whole of Euclid's lost books. It is as certain that
the secret was never revealed to them as it is that
neither they nor any man could restore the books.
But how speedily would the Castillons, the Alberts,
even the Fermats, have given their works to the
world had they become possessed of such a treasure as
Dr. Simson had found! Yet though ready for the
press, and with its preface composed, and its title
given in minute particularity, he never could think
that he had so far elaborated and finished it as to
warrant him in finally resolving on its publication.

There needs no panegyric of this most admirable
performance. Its great merit is best estimated by the
view which has been taken of the extraordinary
difficulties overcome by it. The difficulty of some
investigations—the singular beauty of the propositions,
a beauty peculiar to the porism from the wonderfully
general relations which it discloses—the simplicity of
the combinations—the perfect elegance of the demonstrations—render this a treatise in which the lovers of
geometrical science must ever find the purest delight.

Beside the general discussions in the preface, and
in a long and valuable scholium after the sixth proposition, and an example of algebraical porisms, Dr. Simson has given in all ninety-one propositions. Of
these four are problems, ten are loci, forty-three are
theorems, and the remaining thirty-four are porisms,
including four suggested by Matthew Stewart, and
the five of Fermat improved and generalized ; there
are, besides, four lemmas and one porism suggested

by Dr. Traill, when studying under the Professor.
There may thus be said to be in all ninety-eight propositions. The four lemmas are propositions ancillary
to the author's own investigations ; for many of his
theorems are the lemmas preserved by Pappus as ancillary to the porisms of Euclid.

In all these investigations the strictness of the
Greek geometry is preserved almost to an excess ; and
there cannot well be given a more remarkable illustration of its extreme rigour than the very outset of
this great work presents. The porism is, that a point
may be found in any given circle through which all
the lines drawn cutting its circumference and meeting
a given straight line shall have their segments within
and without the circle in the same ratio. This,
though a beautiful proposition, is one very easily
demonstrated, and is, indeed, a corollary to some of
those in the 'Elements.' But Dr. Simson prefixes a
lemma : that the line drawn to the right angle of a
triangle from the middle point of the hypotenuse, is
equal to half that hypotenuse. Now this follows,
if the segment containing the right angle be a semicircle, and it might be thought that this should be
assumed only as a manifest corollary from the proposition, or as the plain converse of the proposition,
that the angle in a semicircle is a right angle, but
rather as identical with that proposition ; for if we
say the semicircle is a right-angled segment, we also
say that the right-angled segment is a semicircle.
But then it might be supposed that two semicircles
could stand on one base : or, which is the same thing,
that two perpendiculars could be drawn from one

point to the same line; and as these propositions had
not been in the elements, (though the one follows
from the definition of the circle, and the other from
the theorem that the three angles of a triangle are
equal to two right angles,) and as it might be supposed
that two or more circles, like two or more ellipses,
might be drawn on the same axis, therefore the lemma is demonstrated by a construction into which the
centre does not enter. Again, in applying this lemma
to the porism (the proportion of the segments given
by similar triangles), a right angle is drawn at the
point of the circumference, to which a line is drawn
from the extremity of a perpendicular to the given
line; and this, though it proves that perpendicular to
pass through the centre, unless two semicircles could
stand on the same diameter, is not held sufficient; but
the analysis is continued by help of the lemma to show
that the perpendicular to the given line passes through
the centre of the given circle, and that therefore the
point is found. It is probable that the author began
his work with a simple case and gave it a peculiarly
rigorous investigation in order to explain, as he immediately after does clearly in the scholium already
referred to, the nature of the porism, and to illustrate
the erroneous definitions of later times (νεοτερικοί) of
which Pappus complains as illogical.

Of porisms, examples have been now given both in
plain geometry, in solid, and in the higher: that is,
in their connexion both with straight lines and
circles, with conic sections, and with curves of the
third and higher orders. Of an algebraical porism it
is easy to give examples from problems becoming inde-

terminate; but these propositions may likewise arise from a change in the conditions of determinate problems. Thus, if we seek for a number, such that its multiple by the sum of two quantities shall be equal to its multiple by the difference of these quantities, together with twice its multiple by a third given quantity, we have the equation $(a+b) x = (a - b) x + 2cx$ and $2bx = 2cx$; in which it is evident, that if $c=b$, any number whatever will answer the conditions, and thus we have this porism : Two numbers being given a third may be found, such that the multiple of any number whatever by the sum of the given numbers, shall be equal to its multiple by their differences, together with half its multiple by the number to be found. That number is in the ratio of 4 : 3 to the lesser given number.

There are many porisms also in dynamics. One relates to the centre of gravity which is the porismatic case of a problem. The porism may be thus enunciated ;—Any number of points being given, a point may be found such, that if any straight line whatever be drawn through it, the sum of the perpendiculars to it from the points on one side will be equal to the sum of the perpendiculars from the points on the other side. That point is consequently the centre of gravity : for the system is in equilibrium by the proposition. Another is famous in the history of the mixed mathematics. Sir Isaac Newton, by a train of most profound and ingenious investigation, reduced the problem of finding a comet's place from three observations (a problem of such difficulty, that he says of it, " hocce problema longe difficilimum omnimodo aggressus,"*) to the drawing a straight line through four lines given by position, and which shall be cut by them in three segments having given ratios to each other. Now his solution of this problem, the corollary to the twenty-seventh lemma of the first book, has a porismatic case, that is, a case in which any line that can be drawn through the given lines will be cut by them in the same proportions, like the lines drawn through three harmonicals in the porism already given of the harmonical curve. To this Newton had not adverted, nor to the unfortunate circumstance that the case of comets is actually the case in which the problem thus becomes capable of an infinite number of solutions. The error was only discovered after 1739, when it was found that the comet of that year was thrown on the wrong side of the sun by the Newtonian method. This enormous discrepancy of the theory with observation, led to a full consideration of the subject, and to a discovery of the porismatic case.

When the studies of a philosopher, and especially of a mathematician, have been described, his discoveries recorded, and his writings considered, his history has been written. His private life is generally un-varied, filled with speculative inquiry, amused by scien-tific reading, variegated only by philosophic conversa-tion, unless when its repose is broken by controversy, an incident scarcely possible in the story of mathe-maticians. Dr. Simson loved to amuse his leisure hours, and unbend his mind in the relaxation of so-ciety; and from the simplicity of his manners and the

---

* Principia, lib. iii. prop. xli.

kindliness of his disposition, as well as from his very universal information, he was ever a most welcome member of the circles which he frequented. He lived in his college chambers to the last, but received his friends occasionally at a neighbouring tavern, where a room was always kept at his disposal. He attended a club near the college, and in good weather its members dined every Saturday at Anderston, a suburb of Glasgow. In these meetings his chair was always reserved for him, being left vacant when he happened to be absent. It is also said to have been his habit to sit covered. He was fond of playing for an hour or two in the evening at whist, and of calculating chances, at which he generally failed; but he was on the whole a good player, though he was not very patient of his partner's blunders, nor always bore a bad hand of such partner with philosophic meekness. He was fond of music, and sometimes would sing a Greek ode to a modern air. Professor Robison says he twice heard him sing in this manner " a Latin hymn to the Divine Geometer," and adds, that the tears stood in his eyes as he gave it with devotional rapture. His voice was fine, says the Professor, and his ear most accurate. That he did not always interrupt his geometrical meditations in the hours of relaxation is very plain, not only from the singular anecdote already related of his discovery of porisms, but from the date of " Anderston " attached to some of his solutions, indicating that they had occurred to him while attending the Saturday meetings of the club in that suburb. In all his habits he was punctual and regular, even measuring the exercise which he took by the number of paces he

walked. Anecdotes are related of him when interrupted by some one on his accustomed walk, and after
hearing what was said, continuing at the number he
had just before marked, and surprising his acquaintance by speaking the next number aloud. He was
exceedingly absent; and the younger part of the university pupils were wont to play upon this peculiarity.
It is related that one of the college porters being
dressed up for the purpose, came to ask charity, and in
answer to the Professor's questions, gave an account
of himself closely resembling his own history. When
he found so great a resemblance, adds the story, he
cried out, " What's your name?" and on the answer
being given, " Robert Simson," he exclaimed with great
animation, " Why, it must be myself!"—when he awoke
from his trance. Notwithstanding his absent habits,
he was an exceedingly good man of business; he filled
the office of Clerk of the Faculty in the University for
thirty years, and managed its financial and other
concerns with great regularity and success. Like all
minds of a higher order, his not only had no contempt
for details, but a love of them; and while clerk he
made a transcript with his own hand of the University
records, for which he received a vote of thanks from
the Senatus Academicus.

In 1758, being turned of threescore and ten, he
found it necessary to employ an assistant; when one of
his favourite pupils, Dr. Williamson, was appointed his
helper and successor. The University passed a resolution stating his merits fully, recording in detail his
services to the college and to science at large, and pronouncing a warm but just panegyric upon him. He

continued for ten years in the pursuit of his favourite studies, and the enjoyment of the same social intercourse as before. His health, which through his long life had been unbroken, remained entire till within a few weeks of its close, and he died on the 1st of October, 1768, having almost completed his eighty-first year.

He is represented to have been of a calm and pleasing presence, of a portly figure, of easy and not ungraceful manners. A portrait of him in the college library remains, and is said to do him justice. His pupil, Dr. Moore, the Greek professor, and author of the celebrated Grammar, also an excellent mathematician and great admirer of the ancient geometry, wrote the inscription which appears under it, marking its author's own taste in more ways than one:—

"Geometriam sub tyranno barbaro, sævâ servitute, diu languentem, vindicavit unus."

His character was lofty and pure : nothing could exceed his love of justice, and dislike of anything sordid or low; nor could he ever bear to hear men reviling one another, and, least of all, speaking evil of the absent or the dead. In this he closely resembled his celebrated pupil Mr. Watt. His religious as well as moral feelings were strong, and they were habitual. No one in his presence ever ventured on the least irreverent or indecorous allusion ; and we find the periods of his geometrical discoveries mentioned with the date and the place, and generally an addition of " Deo" or " Christo laus," an example of which we have above presented.

He never was married. Of his brothers, one, Thomas, was Professor of Medicine at St. Andrew's, and author of an ingenious and original work on the Brain ; his son succeeded him as professor. Another brother was a dissenting minister at Coventry; and a third, also settled there, had a son, Robert, first in the army, afterwards in the English Church—Mr. Pitt, probably from his love of the mathematics, having presented him to a living in the north of England. He was Dr. Simson's heir-at-law, and to him the estates were left. He sold them in 1789, as well Kirton Hill as Knock Ewart, which had been purchased by the Professor's father in 1713. A niece of Dr. Simson was married to Dr. Moore, the well-known novelist, and was mother of the General. That illustrious warrior was therefore great nephew of the mathematician. Mrs. Moore survived to a recent period, and died in extreme old age.

He bequeathed his mathematical library and manuscripts to the University of Glasgow, with special directions touching their disposition, custody, and use. They form, it is believed, the most complete collection of books and papers in that department of science anywhere to be seen.

The extraordinary genius of Dr. Simson for mathematical pursuits has been fully described in recording his achievements in that difficult branch of science. That he greatly furthered the progress of mathematical knowledge by his excellent publications of the elementary works of Euclid and Apollonius cannot be denied; nor can it be doubted that to him we owe a revival of the taste for the ancient analysis, the pure geometry, and the means now afforded of gratifying it. At the same time there is some room for lamenting that his great powers of mind and his patient industry of research were not devoted to the pursuit of more useful objects; and there is good reason to agree in the opinion expressed by one of his most eminent pupils, Professor Robison, that he might have better succeeded in his favourite object of recovering the purely geometrical methods of investigation, had he relaxed a little more from their rigour in applying them to the present state of science, and shown the ancient analytical investigation dismembered of its prolixity, relieved from its extreme scrupulousness, and subservient to the investigations of the problems now become the main subjects of mathematical inquiry. This has in a great measure been performed by the most celebrated of his school, Matthew Stewart, who actually has solved Kepler's problem, and treated almost the whole doctrine of central forces by means of the ancient method.[*] At the same time we have only to cast our eye upon his diagrams to be convinced that though he has solved the problems and demonstrated the theorems with a most wonderful skill, by means purely geometrical, yet he never could have obtained either the solutions or the demonstrations had not Newton preceded him, "his own analysis carrying the torch before."[†] The most celebrated proposition in all the ' Principia,' the general solution of the inverse problem of central forces[‡], (lib. i. prop. xli.) is closely followed by Stewart, and the diagrams are nearly the same.

---

[*] His paper on the sun's distance, in which he also employs the ancient analysis, has been long since proved erroneous by my friend Mr. Dawson of Sedbergh, who wrote anonymously a demonstration of the error in 1772.

[†] " Suâ mathesi facem præferente."—HALLEY.

[‡] I am aware of Professor Robison's statement, already cited, of Dr. Simson's opinion that the thirty-ninth proposition is the greatest of all, but I cannot help suspecting the forty-first to be intended.

This, however, is not the only ground of regret; for had it been so, the teacher's defect has been thus supplied by the scholar. But good cause remains to lament that both of those great masters did not abate somewhat of their devotion to the Greek Geometry, and instead of being captivated only with the view of its incomparable beauty, did not help forward by their discoveries those branches of the science which, though they may have far less grace, have yet a far wider range and far greater usefulness. Surely it is deeply to be lamented that such extraordinary powers of original investigation as both these great men possessed should, especially in the case of Stewart, have been wasted upon what Professor Robison's learned wit terms "a superstitious palæology," and in the overcoming of difficulties raised by themselves—of reaching the point in view by a devious and hard ascent, when a short and an easy path lay open before them—of doing, and not very well doing, by an imperfect though elegant tool, and with no help from machinery, the same work which might with far better success and greater facility have been performed by the most perfect instrument that ever man invented; like the laborious, patient, and ignorant Hindû, who with a knife will carve the most beautiful ivory trinket, on which he spends a lifetime that might have been employed in the most important works by the aid of fit implements—nay, who might have turned by a simple lathe myriads of the same kind of toy.

THE END.

London: Printed by WILLIAM CLOWES & SONS, Stamford Street.

Lightning Source UK Ltd.
Milton Keynes UK
UKHW011959060219
336834UK00010B/453/P